joint ventures involving tax-exempt organizations

2022 Cumulative Supplement

Subscriber Update Service

BECOME A SUBSCRIBER!

Did you purchase this product from a bookstore?

BECOME A SUBSCRIBER!

Did you purchase this product from a bookstore?

If you did, it's important for you to become a subscriber. John Wiley & Sons, Inc. may publish, on a periodic basis, supplements and new editions to reflect the latest changes in the subject matter that you **need to know** in order to stay competitive in this ever-changing industry. By contacting the Wiley office nearest you, you'll receive any current update at no additional charge. In addition, you'll receive future updates and revised or related volumes on a 30-day examination review.

If you purchased this product directly from John Wiley & Sons, Inc., we have already recorded your subscription for this update service.

To become a subscriber, please call **1-877-762-2974** or send your name, company name (if applicable), address, and the title of the product to:

mailing address:

**Supplement Department
John Wiley & Sons, Inc.
10475 Crosspoint Blvd.
Indianapolis, IN 46256**

e-mail: **subscriber@wiley.com**
fax: **1-800-605-2665**
online: **www.wiley.com**

For customers outside the United States, please contact the Wiley office nearest you:

Professional & Reference Division
John Wiley & Sons Canada, Ltd.
90 Eglinton Ave. E. Suite 300
Toronto, Ontario M4P 2Y3
Canada
Phone: 416-236-4433
Phone: 1-800-567-4797
Fax: 416-236-8743
Email: canada@wiley.com

John Wiley & Sons Australia, Ltd.
42 McDougall Street
Milton, Queensland 4064
AUSTRALIA
Phone: 61-7-3859-9755
Fax: 61-7-3859-9715
Email: aus-custservice@wiley.com

John Wiley & Sons, Ltd.
European Distribution Centre
New Era Estate
Oldlands Way
Bognor Regis, West Sussex
PO22 9NQ, UK
Phone: (0)1243 779777
Fax: (0)1243 843 123
Email: customer@wiley.co.uk

John Wiley & Sons (Asia) Pte., Ltd.
1 Fusionopolis Walk
#07-01 Solaris South Tower
SINGAPORE 138628
Phone: 65-6302-9838
Fax: 65-6265-1782
Customer Service: 65-6302-9800
Email: asiacart@wiley.com

joint ventures involving tax-exempt organizations

2022 Cumulative Supplement

Fourth Edition

Michael I. Sanders

WILEY

Published by John Wiley & Sons, Inc., Hoboken, New Jersey.
Published simultaneously in Canada.

For general information on our other products and services or for technical support, please contact our Customer Care Department within the United States at (800) 762-2974, outside the United States at (317) 572-3993 or fax (317) 572-4002.

Wiley also publishes its books in a variety of electronic formats. Some content that appears in print may not be available in electronic formats. For more information about Wiley products, visit our web site at www.wiley.com.

Library of Congress Cataloging-in-Publication Data is Available:

ISBN 9781118317112 (main edition)
ISBN 9781119985204 (supplement)
ISBN 9781119985389 (ePDF)
ISBN 9781119985372 (ePub)

Cover Design: Wiley
Cover Image: © Felix MAckel/iStockphoto
SKY10038203_111022

To my wife of 50+ wonderful years,
Judy, whose love, devotion, and patience
have made this book possible;
and to David, Patty, Hayley, and Jacob;
Noah, Brooke, Emme, and Ryder Aaron;
Adam, Randi, Gabby, and Eva;
and Sammy, Rebecca, Benjamin, and Jonah.

Special dedication: This supplement is dedicated to the memory of two giants in the exempt organization field: Tom Troyer and Bruce Hopkins. Tom paved the way for me as a mentor, having followed him to Treasury, teaching Tax Treatment of Charities at Georgetown University Law School, and becoming active in the ABA Tax Section EO Committee. Most importantly, following the passage of the 1969 Tax Reform Act, he, along with Leonard Silverstein, among others, formed the Washington Lawyers Group, at which former Treasury officials met to analyze the legislation and make recommendations to the IRS and Treasury with regard to resolving open issues in the regulations. Much of the language that remains in the foundation language today was drafted during these sessions.

Bruce Hopkins was a lion in the EO field; he authored countless books and journals, and was a true literary giant in the EO tax world. In fact, it was Bruce who recommended me to John Wiley & Sons, the publisher of this text, suggesting that I author a book on joint ventures involving tax-exempts. Bruce was a contemporary for more 50 years—brilliant, a good friend, and recognized as the dean of the tax-exempt bar.

Contents

CONTENTS

CONTENTS

Preface

As the new year began I was hopeful that the application of effective vaccines would control the COVID-19 pandemic and, as a result, we would have a resurging economy that would relieve the financial pressures on the nonprofit sector. Although the pandemic has been somewhat ameliorated, other crises, including inflationary pressures; the Russian attack on Ukraine and its impact worldwide; hurricanes; gun violence; mass shootings in Uvalde, Buffalo, and so forth; and the need the resettle the Afghan refugees and those in the southwest border, all continue to pressure the EO sector. As the demands on the charitable sector have continued—and, indeed, grown—it has responded to the needs of society, including diversity, equity, and inclusion, by developing new workplace strategies and business practices to sustain their missions.

As I have said over the years, charities are being faced with the need to balance their own financial demands and the loss of funding, compounded by inflationary pressures, in the face of growing needs in the communities; accordingly, the sector has been using joint venture structures, impact-investing, mission-creating investments, among other techniques to accomplish their charitable goals. The concern is even greater as prominent economists are predicting a downturn in the economy as it moves into full inflation-fighting mode. As an aside, there is concern within the sector that many successful entrepreneurs are using the LLC for-profit structures rather than organizing and funding charitable organizations in order to migrate into the philanthropy arena . . . which muddies the distinction between commerce and charity; its purpose is to work around compliance with the IRS regulatory framework. In this regard, the Chan Zuckerberg Initiative ("CZI") and donor-advised funds sponsored by major investment companies such as Fidelity Charitable are examples of the application of for-profit philanthropy, which appears to be expanding. Many commentators suggest that this approach threatens the public's trust, which has been central to charity law.

The nondistribution constraints of the existing charity law ensure that entrepreneurs may not enrich themselves at a charity's expense. However, elites have been criticized for setting aside philanthropy laws, including the private foundation rules created by the 1969 Tax Reform Act, which has been one of the cornerstones of the American tax system for decades. The concern is that many entrepreneurs using this LLC structure offer little public benefit as assets accumulate and donors and staff benefit in an unduly manner. Nevertheless, notwithstanding the above, the use of joint ventures continues to maintain a critical role to the sustainability in the charitable sector.

In Chapter 2, as to "charitable organizations," there is a discussion about whether minority-owned businesses and individuals connected with primary beneficiaries who are impoverished, underprivileged, or similarly distressed constitute a charitable class. There is also a review regarding the conflict between federal and state and local laws pertaining to cannabis or marijuana distribution. Finally, there is a discussion related to the contributions of cryptocurrencies (which are being used as fundraising vehicles by charities) as capital gain property.

In Chapter 3, there is a detailed analysis (including comments from the American Bar Association and attorneys general) of the recent IRS Notice 2021-56, which sets forth the first formal guidance on the standards that multiple-member LLCs must satisfy to be recognized as exempt under Section 501(c)(3).

In Chapter 5, under intermediate sanctions and compensation, there is a discussion of the propriety of college coaching contracts that appear to provide lucrative compensation, and as to whether the structure contributes to the overall educational mission of the university.

In Chapter 6, there is an expanded discussion of benefit and flexible purpose corporations, including conversions, with a checklist and key considerations for the practitioners.

In Chapter 9, under the § 5.14(c)(9) exception, there is a discussion of the recent Sixth Circuit decision in the Mayo Clinic case in regard to the lack of formal instruction as interpreted by the Treasury Regulations.

In Chapter 13, there is an update on opportunity zone (OZ) funds, including an analysis of the legislative proposal (April, 2022), along with a discussion of various "open" OZ issues relative to certification versus noncertification of a qualified opportunity fund; a proposal to stimulate investment in operating businesses to promote job growth; the use of intangible property and the working capital safe harbor and 70 percent tangible property test; valuation of contributed property; and the need to increase investment in affordable housing. Finally, there is a discussion of the 2021 corrective amendments resolving the ambiguity in the application of the 2020 amendments to the start-up business working capital safe harbor.

In Chapter 14, relative to modes of participation by universities in joint ventures, there is a new subchapter on UBIT implications for universities as a result of the emergence of NIL (name, image, and likeness) deals for college athletes.

In Chapter 16, regarding the area of syndicated conservation easements, there is a discussion of the overvaluation issue; and, further, an update of a number of recent decisions that affect various aspects of the contribution deduction.

The bottom line, once again, is that there is no one paradigm for joint ventures, especially in view of the recent COVID-19 pandemic and other societal crises including inflationary pressures, the Russian attack on Ukraine, hurricanes, gun violence, mass shootings, and so on, all of which have continued to pressure the charitable organization's budget and impacted fund raising. Accordingly, exempt organizations need to be even more creative and forge new paths to create and solve many issues affecting their future, society, and so on. This text is intended to suggest mechanisms to accomplish the worthy goal of the charitable communities. We also believe that the opportunity zone fund law, which was enacted in 2017, will be modified with new legislation in 2022, requiring additional reporting and disclosure requirements, modifying census tracts, as well as increasing the tax incentives for investors. The legislation should further the application of funds being redirected to low-income communities and expand start-up businesses and development opportunities.

Acknowledgments

I want to call attention to the work of DyTiesha Dunson, a graduate tax student at Georgetown University Law School, who has taken the class Special Topics in Exempt Organizations, and has written an excellent paper on NILs that serves to provide substantive materials included in this text. Also, Tyler Buchholz provided research and included materials updating the conservation organization chapter; and Cynthia Paine updated the LIHTC materials. I also want to thank Ronald Schultz at Alliant Group for his outstanding contributions over the years in co-teaching classes at Georgetown Law Center and editing sections of this text. Ron has recently retired from the practice to devote time to his wonderful family.

I especially acknowledge Linda Schrader, whose extraordinary kindness and sensitivity have been invaluable in the preparation of the manuscript as well as her coordination with the staff at John Wiley & Sons; Linda has been critical to the entire process since the beginning of this treatise.

CHAPTER 1

Introduction: Joint Ventures Involving Exempt Organizations

§ 1.4 UNIVERSITY JOINT VENTURES

p. 11. *Add the following new paragraph at the end of this section:*

There is continued congressional focus on university endowments in light of the soaring cost of tuition and the perceived relatively low rate of financial assistance provided by colleges and universities with substantial endowments. See Chapter 14 for a discussion on policy changes that are being proposed, including imposing an annual payout requirement on endowment funds, among others.

§ 1.5 LOW-INCOME HOUSING AND NEW MARKETS TAX CREDIT JOINT VENTURES

pp. 13–14. *Delete the last paragraph on p. 13 and replace with the following:*

The CDFI Fund has made 1,254 allocation awards totaling $61 billion in allocation authority since the NMTC Program's inception. Since inception through FY 2019, CDEs have disbursed a total of $52.5 billion in QEI proceeds to low-income community businesses (QALICBs).

§ 1.6 CONSERVATION JOINT VENTURES

p. 15. *Add the following to the last paragraph of this section:*
In January 2014, Treasury and the IRS issued Revenue Procedure 2014-12, 2014-3 I.R.B. 414, which established a safe harbor for federal historic tax credit investments made within a single tier through a master lease pass-through structure. The guidance was issued in response to the *Historic Boardwalk* decision referenced earlier.

§ 1.8 REV. RUL. 98-15 AND JOINT VENTURE STRUCTURE

p. 18. *Add the following to the end of footnote 65:*
PLR 201744019 (revocation of exemption of a § 501(c)(3) exempt hospital that was not operated exclusively for § 501(c)(3) purposes because it lacked the ability to require a for-profit manager to operate for charitable purposes).

§ 1.10 ANCILLARY JOINT VENTURES: REV. RUL. 2004-51

p. 21. *Add the following new paragraph to the end of this section:*
In Section 4.10, there is an analysis of a virtual joint venture hypothetical, as to which a similar rationale should apply in a case in which the IRS proposes the revocation of an existing 501(c)(3) organization, alleging impermissible private benefit following an examination of its relationship with a for-profit entity. This commentator believes that the rationale should apply, notwithstanding the fact that no formal joint venture arrangement exists between the parties.

§ 1.14 THE EXEMPT ORGANIZATION AS A LENDER OR GROUND LESSOR

p. 28. *Insert the following at the end of this section:*
The Internal Revenue Service recently issued final guidance for private foundations that updates examples that relate to program-related investments that pass muster under § 4944(c). The rules (T.D. 9762) provide changes and examples that were first provided in the 2012 Proposed Regulations. See subsection 6.5(b) for a detailed discussion of the new examples.

In April 2016 the IRS issued final guidance for private foundations that updates a number of examples of program-related investments that won't trigger excise taxes. Final Rules (T.D. 9762) illustrate changes to the examples provided in the 2012 Proposed Rules. In one change involving Example 11, a private foundation that invested in a drug company subsidiary developing a vaccine for disease predominantly affecting poor people in developing countries recognizes that, in addition to distributing the vaccine at affordable prices, the subsidiary is allowed to sell the vaccine to those who can afford it at fair market value prices. In Chapter 6, each of the examples and its revised Treasury guidelines are set forth.

§ 1.15 PARTNERSHIP TAXATION

(a) Overview

p. 30. *Add the following new paragraph to the end of this subsection:*
In the Bipartisan Budget Act of 2015, the partnership audit rules have been revised, the effect of which is that adjustments of income, gain, loss, deduction, or credit are to be determined at the partnership level and the taxes attributable thereto will be assessed and collected at the partnership level. The new rules are effective beginning taxable years after December 31, 2018, although small partnerships may opt out before then. See Chapter 3 for a discussion of the application of the new rules.

(b)   Bargain Sale Including "Like Kind" Exchange

p. 30. *Add the following to the end of footnote 101:*
See discussions regarding contribution of LLC/partnership interests to charity in subsection 2.11(f), *infra*, and Section 3.11, Sale or Other Disposition of Assets or Interests.

§ 1.17   USE OF A SUBSIDIARY AS A PARTICIPANT IN A JOINT VENTURE

p. 34. *Add the following paragraph after the first full paragraph on this page:*
In September 2015, National Geographic Society formed a joint venture with 21st Century Fox, called the National Geographic Partners, a for-profit media joint venture. In this new venture, Fox contributed a substantial amount of cash to National Geographic, which increased its endowment to nearly $1 billion, in exchange for the contribution of significant assets, including its television channels and related digital and social media platforms. See subsection 6.3(b)(iv) for an analysis of the structure.

§ 1.22 LIMITATION ON PRIVATE FOUNDATION'S ACTIVITIES THAT LIMIT EXCESS BUSINESS HOLDINGS

p. 45. *Add the following footnote to the end of this section:*

[163.1] See discussion regarding the contribution of LLC/partnership interests to charity in subsection 2.11(f).

§ 1.24 OTHER DEVELOPMENTS

p. 47. *Add the following as footnote 175 to the last sentence of this section:*

[175] In *Burwell v. Hobby Lobby Stores, Inc.*, the Supreme Court cited p. 555 in this book, which described Google.org advancing its charitable goals while operating as a for-profit corporation. See footnote 24 of the *Hobby Lobby decision*, 134 S.Ct. 2751 (2014). The court recognized that while operating as a for-profit corporation, it is able to invest in for-profit endeavors, do lobbying, and tap Google's innovative technology and workforce. It acknowledged that states have increasingly adopted laws formally recognizing hybrid corporate forms.

p. 47. *Add the following at the end of the subsection:*

With the growing impact of COVID-19, many business owners are interested in providing financial assistance to their furloughed or terminated employees, even though they cannot afford to keep them on their payroll. An attractive option is the creation of an employer-sponsored charity to raise tax-deductible contributions to be distributed to former employees who demonstrate need. In addition, a supplemental unemployment benefit trust under §501(c)(17) can be formed as part of a plan to pay supplemental unemployment compensation benefits. Under section 139, employers can provide assistance directly to an employee free of income tax, provided the funds are used to pay or reimburse amounts that are reasonably expected to be incurred for incremental personal, family, or living expenses as a result of the COVID-19 crisis.

Under section 139, payments may cover the following expenses: (1) unreimbursed medical expenses and health-related expenses; (2) home expenses due to telecommuting; (3) housing costs for additional family members; (4) increased childcare and tutoring costs due to school closings; (5) additional commuting expenses; and (6) increased costs of home office supplies.

An employer-sponsored charity may cover not only those employees who are suffering under the impact of COVID-19 but may cover future hardships as well. However, charities benefiting individuals are permissible if the class of eligible beneficiaries is broad enough to be considered "indeterminable." For example, a charity designed to benefit past, current, and future employees of an entire restaurant group due to the pandemic and future disasters is broad enough and the beneficiaries are not immediately identifiable because unknown future employees and current employees who are victims of future disasters are eligible beneficiaries. Secondly, the individuals who are invested with the authority to make the grants—the board of directors or a committee appointed by the board—must consist of a majority of individuals who do not exert "substantial influence" over the business with rank-and-file employees and should be included among the decision makers. Finally, individuals who demonstrate a financial need are eligible to receive assistance, but the charity should avoid giving a "one size fits all" grant to every employee. Acceptable purposes for such grants include payment of necessary healthcare expenses; providing cost of childcare or educational expenses for children of employees; or short-term grants meant to cover basic living expenses.

CAVEAT

The charity should retain documentation regarding the employee's eligibility for a grant and verification that the employee used the funds for eligible purposes.[176]

CAVEAT

Businesses that contemplate severance payments to workers should consider structuring such payments so that they qualify under section 139. If so, the payments would appear to be exempt from income tax and most payroll taxes. However, any payments pursuant to a legal or contractual obligation to pay severance would be difficult to categorize as section 139 payments. Secondly, section 139 contemplates payments commensurate with expenses they intend to offset, while severance payments are often computed based upon years of service and salary levels.

In Notice 2020-46, the IRS provided guidance to employers for how to exchange employee elections to forgo vacation, sick, or personal leave for cash payments that the employer makes to charitable organizations for COVID-19 relief. An employee who elects to relinquish aid leave will not be taxed on the value of the leave, if the payments in exchange for the leave are made by the individual's employer prior to January, 1, 2021, to a § 170(c) organization that provides "relief to victims of the COVID-19 pandemic."

---

[176]It is important to note that as an alternative, employers may be able to assist their employees by making qualified disaster relief payments on a tax-free basis under section 139 of the Code, previously discussed.

> **CAVEAT**
>
> Although not explicit in the IRS notice, the use of the phrase "victims of the COVID-19 pandemic" can be read to mean that the permissible use of the donations extends not only to assist people who contract the disease, but also to people who lose their jobs or are otherwise financially harmed by the pandemic.[177]

The CARES Act expanded the definition of educational assistance for purposes of section 127 of the Internal Revenue Code of 1986, as amended, to include certain employer payments made after March 27, 2020 under an "educational assistance program"[178] for repayment of employee student loans. As a result, through the end of the 2025 taxable year, an employer can make tax-free payments to its employees for student loan assistance of up to $5,250 per year. Payments in excess of $5,250 per year (and payments that are not made pursuant to an educational assistance program (as described below)) would be included in the employee's gross income. Additional rules and requirements related to qualified payments and educational assistance programs are described below.

- The payments can be made to the employee or directly to the lender, for repayment of either principal or interest, so long as the payments are made with respect to a "qualified education loan" and certain requirements under section 127 of the Code are met. A qualified education loan would generally include any student loan that is part of a federal postsecondary education loan program that is incurred for "qualified education expenses" of the employee's education, such as tuition and fees, room and board, books, certain supplies and equipment, and certain other necessary expenses for the employee's education. The qualified education expenses must generally be paid or

---

[177]Employers will have the choice of deducting these contributions either under the rules of Code § 170, as a charitable contribution deduction, or under section 162, which relates to the deduction for ordinary and necessary business expenses. The benefit of taking a deduction under Code § 162 as opposed to Code § 170 is that the employer will not be subject to certain limitations that section 170 imposes on the amount of the payment that is deductible in the year of the payment.

[178]The term "educational assistance" means (a) the payment, by an employer, of expenses incurred by or on behalf of an employee for education of that employee (including, but not limited to, tuition, fees, and similar payments, books, supplies, and equipment); (b) in the case of payments made before January 1, 2021, the payment by an employer, whether paid to the employee or to a lender, of principal or interest on any qualified education loan (as defined in § 221(d)(1)) incurred by the employee for education of the employee; and (c) the provision, by an employer, of courses of instruction for such employee (including books, supplies, and equipment), but does not include payment for, or the provision of, tools or supplies that may be retained by the employee after completion of a course of instruction, or meals, lodging, or transportation. The term "educational assistance" also does not include any payment for, or the provision of, any benefits with respect to any course or other education involving sports, games, or hobbies. (See § 127(c)(1).)

incurred with student loan proceeds within a reasonable period of time before or after the employee takes out the loan.

- In order for the payments to employees to qualify for the gross income exclusion, the payments must be made pursuant to a separate written educational assistance program established for the exclusive benefit of the employer's employees so as to provide them with educational assistance.

- The employer can establish certain restrictions (subject to the nondiscrimination rules under section 127 of the Code, discussed below) on an employee's eligibility under the program such as job relationship requirements, limitation on when and where the courses can be taken, preapproval by the program manager or the employee's supervisor, proof of completion of the course, minimum course grades, and completion of a certain period of employment after completion of the course.

- The following are additional requirements of the educational assistance program under section 127 of the Code:

  - The program benefits employees who qualify under rules set up by the employer (such as those described above in the immediately preceding bullet point) that do not discriminate in favor of highly compensated employees (i.e., an employee who (i) during the current or preceding tax year is or was a more than 5 percent owner with respect to the employer, or (ii) earned compensation in excess of $130,000 (for the 2021 tax year) unless such employee was not also in the top 20 percent of employees by pay for the preceding year and the employer chooses not to treat such individual as a highly compensated employee);

  - The program does not provide for more than 5 percent of its total benefits during the year to its more than 5 percent shareholders or owners (or their spouses or dependents);

  - The program does not allow the employees to receive cash or other benefits that must be included in gross income instead of educational assistance; and

  - The employer must give reasonable notice of the program to its eligible employees.

- An employer can choose to treat the following individuals as employees for purposes of the income exclusion rules: a current employee; a former employee who retired, left on disability, or was laid off; a leased employee who provided services under the employer's primary direction or control on a substantially full-time basis for at least a year; and self-employed individuals (such as an owner of a business if the employer is a sole proprietorship, or a partner who performs services for a partnership if the employer is a partnership).

- The program does not need to be funded to qualify.
- The employer may, but is not required to, obtain a determination letter from the IRS that the program is a qualified educational assistance program.

CHAPTER 2

Taxation of Charitable Organizations

§ 2.1 INTRODUCTION

p. 50. *Insert quotation marks around* **IRC** *on line 8 and add a comma after* **contributions and churches** *in footnote 2.*

p. 52. *Insert the following after the last paragraph of this section:*
In the 2017 Tax Act (Pub. L. No. 115-97) (the "Tax Act"), the following changes affect tax-exempt organizations:

1. New 2017 Legislation

A. Charitable contributions are likely to decline as a result of the lowering of the individual income tax brackets (a maximum rate of 37 percent) while doubling the standard deduction. These rates and the standard deduction sunset after December 31, 2025. It is projected that only 5 percent of taxpayers will have sufficient itemized deductions that exceed the standard deduction that will enable them to continue to claim a charitable contribution deduction, which may curtail charitable giving. Moreover, the estate tax exemption was doubled so that individuals now have $11 million of exemption and married couples are able to exclude $22.4 million from their estate tax. This provision also sunsets after December 31, 2025. Finally, there is a reduction in the C Corporation rates to 21 percent, which is a permanent change. It is important to note that C Corps have been the largest investor in joint ventures, including the low-income house tax credit and new market tax credits. (See Chapter 13.)

B. The AGI annual limitation has been increased to 60 percent for cash contributions; the provision also sunsets after December 31, 2025. There is obvious concern that major donors are likely to be the only taxpayers in a position to give away up to 60 percent of their AGI in a given year. In addition, the rule that requires contemporary written acknowledgment (§ 170(f)(8)(D)) no longer applies if the donee organization files a return that includes similar content. See subsection 2.11(f). The charitable sector benefits because they have been pressured by donors to fill forms out in lieu of providing a standard acknowledgment. The proposed regulations required the reporting of the donors' tax ID numbers/ FNS, and charities were concerned that it could lead to theft.

C. Code § 4960 proposes a new 21 percent excise tax on tax-exempt organizations (modeled on § 162(m)) for (i) any "remuneration" paid to a covered employee that exceeds $1 million (whether or not such amounts are reasonable) and (ii) on "excess parachute payments" paid to a covered person under a separation agreement (i.e., severance payments that exceed 3 times the person's annual compensation averaged over the past five years). In this regard "covered employees" include the top five most highly compensated employees (or former employees) from the tax year or anyone who was a covered employee from any preceding taxable year beginning in 2017. "Remuneration" is defined as "all wages" under § 3401(a), excluding Roth contributions, paid by a tax-exempt organization or related party with respect to employment of the covered person. See subsection 5.4(b).[5.1]

	CAVEAT

The intermediate sanctions and excess benefit rules of Code § 4958 still apply.

[5.1]For a more detailed discussion of the scope of Code § 4960 and the 2019 Interim Guidance, see Section 5.4.

CAVEAT

The Act extends these new executive compensation limitations to tax-exempts not limited to 501(c)(3)s or 501(c)(4)s, but including businesses, federal and state and local entities under § 115(1), and political organizations. Unlike the intermediate sanctions excise tax, § 4960 tax applies to the organization itself, not a covered employee or organizational manager.

The excess tax applies to deferred compensation remuneration, which is viewed as paid where it is no longer subject to a substantial risk of forfeiture under § 457(f)(3)(B). Thus, amounts that are "vested" but not yet received by a covered employee will be subject to tax.[5.2]

D. There is a new, unrelated business income tax (UBIT) on transportation, parking, and gym fringe benefits unless the amounts are deductible under Code § 274 because they are treated as part of the employee's taxable compensation. Note that this has been repealed under the Taxpayers Certainty and Disclosure Act of 2019.

E. The unrelated business income tax rate is now 21 percent, which will provide relief to many exempt organizations that have been paying as much as 35 percent on unrelated taxable income. However, this rate reduction may be offset by the new rule that net operating losses from one activity may no longer offset income from another activity. Tax-exempt organizations will need to calculate tax on each unrelated business separately.

QUERY

May all "investment" activities be treated as one activity for offsetting purposes? Will each of the gains and losses have to be separately stated? Treasury will need to publish regulations to resolve this issue.

F. There is now a new 1.4 percent tax on net investment income of certain colleges and universities defined as "applicable educational institutions" (i) that have at least 500 tuition-paying students, (ii) that have more than 50 percent of tuition-paying students located in the United States, and (iii) whose assets aggregated at fair market value are at least $500,000 per student at the end of the preceding taxable year. See Section 14.1. Related organizations to colleges

---

[5.2]There is a special carve-out to payments made to licensed medical professionals, such as physicians and veterinarians, so that the compensation related to performance to medical services will not count toward the $1 million threshold. Accordingly, healthcare organizations will need to track time allocated between medical services and administrative services.

and universities are required to have their assets and net income considered when determining whether the institution meets the asset-per-student threshold and for purposes for determining net investment income.

CAVEAT

This new legislation is targeted at highly compensated college and university athletic coaches and presidents, some of whom have million-dollar salaries.

CAVEAT

The new Bipartisan Budget Act of 2018 clarifies the Tax Act to provide that the "at least 500" and "more than 50 percent" of students tests both refer only to <u>tuition-paying</u> students.

CAVEAT

This new excise tax is estimated to raise approximately $1.8 billion in revenue over ten years and affect only about 35 institutions.

G. A related organization will include one in which the educational institution (a) controls or is controlled by (b) one or more persons who control the institution or (c) are supported organizations or supporting organizations with respect to the institution. The foregoing rules will require Treasury Regulations to clarify the scope of the new provision.

H. Section 170(l) is amended to eliminate the special rule and now denies deductions for college booster seats including season tickets.

2. Provisions That Did Not Survive the Tax Act

It is important to examine a number of provisions that were considered by the House and Senate but that did not survive the Conference Committee. The following provisions may well be reconsidered the next time extensive tax legislation is considered by Congress. Beware of the potential that some, if not all, of these provisions will be in play in the near future.

A. In the application of the initial tax on a disqualified person pursuant to the intermediate sanctions rules, the rebuttable presumption of reasonableness would have been eliminated. (See subsection 5.4(c)(ii).) Procedures would be promulgated by the IRS to establish that an organization has performed minimum standards of due diligence (essentially the same as those that pertain in connection with the previously described presumption) with respect to a transaction or other arrangement involving a disqualified person (proposed IRC § 4958(d)(3)). The existing rule by which an organization manager's participation in a transaction ordinarily is not "knowing" participation for purposes of the intermediate sanctions rules if the manager relied on professional advice would be eliminated (proposed IRC § 4958(g)). The definition of a disqualified person, for purposes of the intermediate sanctions rules, would be expanded to include investment advisors and athletic coaches at private educational institutions (see proposed IRC § 4958(f)(1)(G), proposed revision of IRC § 4958(f)(8)(B)).[5.3]

B. The private foundation's excise tax would be reduced to a single rate of 1.4 percent (revised IRC § 4940(a), proposed repeal of IRC § 4940(e)). Also a rule would be enacted stating that an entity cannot be a private operating foundation as an art museum unless the museum is open during normal business hours to the public for at least 1,000 hours annually (proposed IRC § 4942(j(6))).

C. A sale or licensing by an exempt organization of the entity's name or logo (including any related trademark or copyright) would be treated as an unrelated business regularly carried on (proposed IRC §§ 512(b)(20), 513(k)). Income derived from such licensing would be included in the organization's gross unrelated business income, notwithstanding the exclusion for certain types of passive income (including other forms of royalties). See subsection 8.5(d). The unrelated business income tax would not apply to research limited to publicly available research (see IRC § 512(b)(9)). The application of UBIT to state and local retirement plans (proposed IRC § 511(d)) would be clarified.

D. Charitable organizations would be allowed to make statements relating to political campaigns in the ordinary course of program activities, where the expenses are de minimis (proposed IRC § 501(s)), a very controversial proposal opposed by both the Independent Sector and the Council on Foundations.

E. The tax exemption for professional sports leagues (IRC § 501(c)(6)) would be repealed.

[5.3]The intermediate sanctions rules would become applicable to labor organizations (IRC § 501(c)(5) entities) and business leagues (IRC § 501(c)(6) entities) (proposed revision of IRC § 4958(e)(1)).

F. The standard mileage rate for the use of an automobile for charitable purposes would be adjusted to take into account the variable costs of operating the vehicle rather than the existing law's 14-cents-per-mile deduction.

G. Additional reporting requirements for sponsoring organizations of donor-advised funds would be enacted, consisting of the average amount of grants expressed as a percentage of asset value and a statement as to whether the organization has a policy as to the frequency and minimum level of distributions (proposed IRC § 6033(k)(4)).

At the end of its spring term, the Supreme Court issued a decision that some have speculated could lead to governmental outsourcing of more activities to nonprofits. The case, *Manhattan Community Access Corp. v. Halleck et al.*, 587 U.S. ___ (2019), involved the question of whether a nonprofit was a "state actor" when New York City delegated the operation of public access channels to it. A cable operator typically operates public access channels itself unless the local government elects to operate them or selects a private entity to do so. If found to be a state actor, the organization would be subject to the First Amendment. In this case, New York City designated a nonprofit to operate the public access channels of a New York cable system. The nonprofit, MNN, aired a film that was critical of it, but later barred the film's producers from future access to the channels. The producers brought suit on grounds that this action violated their First Amendment free-speech rights. The five–four split focused on whether operating public access channels is a traditional, exclusive public function, with the majority ruling that very few functions are exclusive public functions. Consistent with this ruling, if the government delegates an activity to a private organization, such as a nonprofit, and does not direct its operations or act in partnership with it, the nonprofit's speech-related activities will not be subject to First Amendment limits.

3. CARES Act

The newly enacted Coronavirus Aid, Relief, and Economic Security Act (commonly known as the "CARES Act") includes a number of provisions designed to encourage charitable contributions of cash to both individuals and corporations. Individual donors making gifts to qualified charities may deduct up to 100 percent of their 2020 adjusted gross income over and above the usual cap of 60 percent (or 50 percent if charitable contributions are made through a combination of cash and other assets). Corporate taxpayers that make qualified contributions can deduct such contributions up to 25 percent of adjusted taxable income, rather than the 10 percent limitation from the 2017 Tax Cuts and Jobs Act. Excess contributions may be carried forward for the next five taxable years; however, various deduction limitations should be restored in 2021 and thereafter. Qualified contributions do not include contributions for the establishment of new or maintenance of an existing donor-advised fund, or for gifts to private foundations (other than pass-through foundations and private operating foundations).

For tax years beginning in 2020, individual taxpayers who claim the standard deduction on their federal tax return as opposed to itemizing deductions are permitted to make qualifying contributions up to $300 annually and to use such contributions as an above-the-line deduction in computing their adjusted income.

§ 2.2   CATEGORIES OF EXEMPT ORGANIZATIONS (REVISED)

p. 52. *Delete the last two sentences in footnote 9 and replace with the following:*

According to the National Center for Charitable Statistics, there were 1,202,719 § 501(c)(3) organizations as of April 2016. http://nccs.urban.org/statistics/quickfacts.cfm.

p. 54. *Delete the last sentence in this subsection and insert the following:*
See Section 2.3 and subsequent sections for analysis and discussion of these rules. The following presents a brief comparison of § 501(c)(3) and § 501(c)(4) organizations, social welfare organizations that are being formed with increasing frequency.

(a)   § 501(c)(4) Organizations: A Brief Overview

Section 501(c)(4) organizations have greater organizational and operational flexibility than § 501(c)(3) organizations. Their numbers have substantially increased since the Supreme Court *Citizens United* case,[22.1] with further growth anticipated as a result of the 2017 increase in the standard deduction. See subsection 2.6(c). In light of changes in the Tax Act reducing the numbers of taxpayers eligible to claim a deduction for contributions to § 501(c)(3) organizations, there is an expectation of increased donations to § 501(c)(4) organizations that can, as described later, engage in unlimited lobbying and a certain amount of political activity on behalf of candidates and issues they support.

[22.1]See subsection 2.3(c)(4).

Section 501(c)(4) provides tax exemption for civic organizations and local associations of employees that are not organized and operated for profit and are operated exclusively for the promotion of social welfare.[22.2] Like § 501(c)(3) organizations, the earnings of § 501(c)(4) entities cannot inure to the benefit of any private shareholder or individual,[22.3] and the § 4958 excise tax is imposed on excess benefit transactions between a disqualified person and § 501(c)(4) organization.[22.4] See Section 5.4.

Contributions to § 501(c)(4) organizations are not deductible as charitable contributions under § 170(c),[22.5] although dues or contributions to § 501(c)(4) organizations may be deductible as business expenses under § 162.[22.6]

A § 501(c)(4) organization must be operated exclusively for the promotion of social welfare.[22.7] However, regulations under § 501(c)(4) have defined "exclusively" to mean "primarily" engaged in the promotion of social welfare.[22.8] Accordingly, unlike the absolute prohibition on political activity by § 501(c)(3) organizations, a § 501(c)(4) organization may engage in political activity provided that the organization's political activity does not constitute its primary activity. If a § 501(c)(4) organization's political activities exceed this restriction, the organization may be subject to a tax on expenditures made for political activities under § 527(f).[22.9]

Neither the IRC nor the regulations contain a numerical definition of "primarily." Some practitioners advise § 501(c)(4) organizations that "primarily" may be interpreted as 51 percent of their total expenditures, in effect allowing § 501(c)(4)s to allocate up to 49 percent of total expenditures to political activity.[22.10] Other practitioners take a more conservative approach to minimize risk of a challenge to tax exemption or imposition of excise taxes and advise limiting political activity to less than 40 percent of total expenditures to political activity.

[22.2]§ 501(c)(4); Reg. § 1.501(c)(4)-1(a)(1).

[22.3]§ 501(c)(4); Reg. § 1.501(c)(4)-1.

[22.4]§ 4958; Reg. § 53.4958-1; Reg. § 53.4958-4.

[22.5]§ 501(c)(4) organizations do not fall under the enumerated categories of organizations allowed a deduction for contributions under §170. A § 501(c)(4) organization may be required to disclose that contributions are not deductible when it solicits contributions, but donations to volunteer fire companies and certain war veterans organizations may be deductible. See § 170; Reg. § 1.170A-1; § 6113; Rev. Rul. 74-361, 1974-2 C.B. 159.

[22.6]Amounts paid to a § 501(c) organization that are specifically for political campaign activities or lobbying are not deductible under § 162. See § 170(f)(9); § 162(e).

[22.7]§ 501(c)(4); Reg. § 1.501(c)(4)-1.

[22.8]Reg. § 1.501(c)(4)-1(a)(2)(i).

[22.9]§ 527(f).

[22.10]Alliance for Justice, Alliance for Justice Action Campaign, *Primer on Social Welfare Organizations Using 501(c)(4) Organizations for Good* (2016), available at https://www.bolderadvocacy.org/wp-content/uploads/2016/09/AFJ_c4-Primer.pdf.

Section 501(c)(4) organizations may also engage in an unlimited amount of lobbying, provided that the lobbying is related to the organization's exempt purpose to promote social welfare.[22.11] Consequently, an organization whose substantial lobbying activities would cause it to be characterized as an action organization under § 501(c)(3), and therefore disqualified as a § 501(c)(3), may nonetheless qualify for exemption under § 501(c)(4).[22.12]

Political advocacy has become an essential way for policy to be shaped in the United States in order to better represent communities across the country. In view of the limitations that charitable organizations face in order to participate in this political process, organizations formed under § 501(c)(4) may fill the gaps left by public charity spending as well as respond to corporations with incentives to advocate for policy that is counteractive to a charitable purpose, even if inadvertent. Section 501(c)(4) organizations provide essentially the same services as a § 501(c)(3) charity without the benefit of tax deductibility of donations. With regard to this growing requirement to participate in some form of policymaking influence, the § 501(c)(4) organization stands as a critical element to serve those in need by maximizing the activities that will help benefit the underprivileged.

Furthermore, in the wake of COVID-19, billions of lives have been impacted all over the world, many adjusting to a new reality when it comes to social norms of each society as well as the potential economic hardships that lie ahead. The need for representation is essential with regard to the enactment of stimulus packages that benefit large corporations to a greater extent than the average American taxpayer.[22.13] This is one of the challenges that organizations that engage in charitable activities must face as the political class is dividing up the slices of pie and the traditional § 501(c)(3) public charities cannot compete with the level of lobbying and political participation permitted. The § 501(c)(4) organization stands ready as a David to many Goliaths that appear to pillage and enjoy the spoils of legislative victories at the expense of many needy Americans. While the highly politicized Supreme Court decision *Citizens United* has plagued § 501(c)(4) organizations as a veil to hide corporate and super PAC influence, social welfare organizations are an important part of serving communities at large. COVID-19 has brought a new understanding of what it means to be a community, and hopefully the next tax-exempt organizations that

---

[22.11]However, § 18 of the Lobbying Disclosure Act prohibits a § 501(c)(4) that chooses to engage in any lobbying from receiving federal grants, loans, awards, contracts, etc. Therefore, a § 501(c)(4) in need of government support must evaluate the costs and benefits of choosing between lobbying or accepting federal money. LDA § 18.

[22.12]Reg. § 1.501(c)(4)-1(a)(2).

[22.13]These comments are adapted from Chase McBeath's graduate tax paper at Georgetown University Law Center, Special Topics in Exempt Organizations.

"rise out of the flames" of COVID-19 will help illuminate the community good provided by § 501(c)(4) organizations as well as the need to be politically involved.

The IRS has issued final regulations, effective July 19, 2019, addressing the requirement of § 501(c)(4) organizations to submit Form 8976, "Notice of Intent to Operate Under Section 501(c)(4)." The final regulations are consistent with the temporary regulations in requiring that the form be filed within 60 days of the date the organization is formed (T.D. 9873). In addition, if an entity seeks a determination letter from the IRS recognizing its exempt status, it can *elect* to file Form 1024-A.[22.14] Section 501(c)(4) organizations are also subject to annual filing requirements using Form 990 or 990EZ.[22.15] See subsection 2.6(c) and Section 2.8. See Rev. Proc. 2000-8 regarding electronic filing of Forms 1024. The IRS revised and updated Form 1024 and provided for it to be electronically submitted at www.pay.gov. Organizations seeking determination under § 501(a) (other than those described in § 501(c)(3) or § 501(c)(4) and those seeking group rulings), including those organizations that have been required to submit letter requests to seek determination, are generally required to electronically submit the Form 1024 effective date of January 3, 2022. There is a 90-day transition period for late filings provided as well.

As a general rule, § 501(c)(3) organizations could qualify under § 501(c)(4), whereas not all § 501(c)(4) organizations would qualify as a § 501(c)(3) under the more stringent rules placed on § 501(c)(3) organizations.[22.16]

In a bow to pressure from conservative groups in Congress, the IRS changed longstanding policy in regard to disclosure of donor names by § 501(c)(4) organizations, which traditionally has been done on Form 990 for transparency. Following the 2010 *Citizens United* decision, there has been a substantial uptick in the formation and political activity of § 501(c)(4) organizations, which would no longer have to disclose their donors on Form 990. The names of donors disclosed on Schedule B of Form 990 were not made available to the public, only to the IRS; nevertheless, many commentators were critical of the new rules as facilitating "dark money" in politics. According to a former director of the IRS's exempt organizations division, donor information "is of material importance for determining whether organizations are operating appropriately and within the boundaries of the rules" (Rev. Proc. 2018-38, 2018-31 I.R.B., July 17, 2018).[22.17] However, on July 30, 2019, a federal judge overturned the IRS ruling. The state of

---

[22.14]Rev. Proc. 2018-10.

[22.15]Section 6033 requires nonprofits under § 501(a) to file information returns. See § 6033; Reg. § 1.6033-2(a).

[22.16]See Reg. § 1.501(c)(4)-1(a)(2).

[22.17]https://www.nytimes.com/2018/07/17/us/politics/irs-will-no-longer-force-kochs-and-other-groups-to-disclose-donors.html.

Montana, joined by the state of New Jersey, brought a lawsuit alleging that the IRS could not simply waive the donor disclosure requirements, which were established by IRS regulation, without providing an opportunity for public comment in accordance with the Administrative Procedure Act.

In May 2020, the IRS issued final regulations on donor disclosure, providing that social welfare organizations as well as § 501(c)(6) trade associations are no longer required to report large donors ($5,000 or more) on Schedule B on Form 990. Section 501(c)(3) organizations and section 527 political organizations remain subject to statutory requirements for donor disclosure.[22.18]

Gifts to a 501(c)(4) organization, whether in cash or appreciated securities, are not subject to gift tax; however, such amounts are not deductible from the donor's taxable income regardless of whether the gifts are in the form of cash, securities, or other assets. If the gift is in the form of appreciated securities, the subsequent sale of the securities does not cause the § 501(c)(4) organization to be liable for tax on the appreciation. See subsection 2.11(e) regarding charitable contributions to SMLLCs.

§ 2.3 § 501(C)(3) ORGANIZATIONS: STATUTORY REQUIREMENTS

(a) Organizational Test

(iii) Dedication of Assets. p. 57. *In footnote 36, change brackets to parentheses.*

(b) Operational Test

p. 57. *In footnote 38, change note 40 to note 37.*

p. 58. *Add the following to the end of footnote 42:*
The IRS will revoke the exempt status of an organization that conducts no activities at all. See PLR 201623011.

(i) Operating Exclusively for Exempt Purposes. p. 59. *The second paragraph under this section is a continuation of the first paragraph and should not be indented.*

[22.18]See Treas. Reg. § 1.47-7. In the preamble to the regulations, the IRS states that each such state is free to require reporting of information to the state and to maintain its information at its own expense. Many states are likely to adopt their own reporting requirements including submitting a copy of the EO's most recent Form 990 with a completed Schedule B. Both New Jersey and New York have requested such donor information. It is important to note that states may provide different rules (from state to state) that may require nonprofits active in more than one state to prepare different versions of their Form 990, some of which identify donors and in some cases do not.

p. 60. *The first full paragraph on this page is a continuation of the previous paragraph and should not be indented.*

p. 61. *Delete the citation in footnote 65 and replace with the following:*
Kentucky Bar Foundation, 78 T.C. at 930.

(ii) Prohibition against Inurement. **p. 62.** *Delete the citation in footnote 72 and replace with the following:*
American Campaign Academy, 92 T.C. at 1068.

p. 63. *Combine footnotes 74 and 75 into one footnote 74.*

(iii) The Commensurate Test. **p. 69.** *Add the following at the end of the subsection (following Note) and renumber current (iv) to (v):*
In view of the recent COVID-19 pandemic and the budgetary pressures that followed, charities are pursuing more diverse means of generating revenues, including impact investing (Section 6.8), tax credit structures (Chapter 13), and opportunity zone funds (Section 13.11), some of which may run afoul of the commerciality doctrine.[107.1]

(iv) The Commerciality Doctrine. The commerciality doctrine is a court-created outgrowth of the operational test. The concern is that nonprofits will be competing with for-profits that otherwise shoulder a tax burden that nonprofits can avoid. As discussed above, the operational test generally requires a nonprofit to be (both organized and) operated exclusively to accomplish its exempt purposes. It also requires that no more than an insubstantial part of its activities further a nonexempt purpose. An organization can operate a business as a substantial part of its activities provided that the business furthers the organization's exempt purpose. (See Section 2.3(i).) The commerciality doctrine can be traced to a 1924 Supreme Court case, *Trinidad v. Sagrada Orden de Predicadores*, 263 US 578 (1924). Since then courts have continued to develop the commerciality doctrine in the process of expanding the operational test, ruling that organizations are operated for nonexempt commercial purposes based on the "business-like/commercial" manner by which they conduct their activities. In other words, the organization's activities are arguably substantially the same as those of commercial activities. When the commerciality doctrine has been evoked in recent private letter rulings denying exempt status, it is often accompanied by citing two cases: *Living Faith* and *Airlie Foundation*. In *Living Faith Inc.*,[107.2] an integral question in the analysis of commerciality was whether the primary activity of the organization is a business with a commercial character. It was held that Living Faith, a restaurant, was

---

[107.1]This subsection is based upon a paper submitted by Philip Harris from in his graduate tax class at Georgetown University Law Center, Special Topics in Exempt Organizations (Spring 2021).
[107.2]*Living Faith Inc v. Commissioner*, 950 2nd 365 (2nd Cir. 1991).

in direct competition with other restaurants, because "competition with commercial firms is strong evidence of the predominance of a nonexempt purpose."[107.3] It was held that Living Faith was in direct competition with other restaurants operating in a shopping center near other restaurants and food stores and it priced its foods competitively with the business area, using formulas common to retail food businesses. In *Airlie Foundation*,[107.4] it was held that the operator of a conference center was not entitled to exempt status because it engaged substantially in a commercial enterprise in violation of the commercialism doctrine. It operated its conference center, which was in competition with for-profit entities. The court also focused on the extent and degree of below-cost services, pricing policies and reasonableness of financial reserves, its promotional methods (e.g., advertising), and the extent to which the organization received charitable contributions or grants.[107.5]

CAVEAT

In a review of 254 private letter rulings from 2004 to 2017, the commerciality doctrine was applied as a reason to deny tax-exempt status. Of the explanations provided, 63.4 percent of the letters (170) stated the organization promoted or distributed its goods the same way as for-profit companies, 48.5 percent (130) of organizations charged market rates for goods or services, 43.7 percent (117) of organizations either received little or no donations or public support, instead relying on sales, and 28 percent (75) of organizations sold goods or services at or above the cost of production, which indicates a profit motive. These numbers add up to more than 100 percent of the total letters because more than one reason can be given for failing the commerciality doctrine test. See Terri L. Kelge, *Rejecting Charity. Why the IRS Denies Tax Exemption to 501(c)(3) Applicants*, 14 Pitt. Tax Rev. 40-42 (2016).

It is the author's view that the current list of factors used to determine the commerciality of an organization are antiquated as a result of the growth of various alternative means to generate revenues for nonprofit organizations. Since the penalty for violating the commerciality doctrine is full revocation of the organization's exempt status rather than an intermediate remedy, it is argued that a more reasonable approach would be the application of the unrelated business income tax regime (which would allow the preservation of the tax-exempt status). This is so especially

---

[107.3]*BSW Group, Inc. v. Commissioner of the Internal Revenue*, 70 TC 352 (1978); also *Fides Publishers Association v. US*, 263 Fed. Sup. 924 (ND Ind. 1967) (the publisher of religious materials was denied tax exemption because they were engaged in publishing, which is not an exempt purpose).
[107.4]283 Fed. Sup. 2nd 58, 66 (DDC, 2003).
[107.5]See also PLR 202053020 (Dec. 31, 2020).

because the commerciality doctrine is ambiguous for numerous reasons. It is difficult to evaluate the ratio of donations relative to income generated from business activities, which does not consider the societal changes impact on household donations and other circumstances, such as COVID-19. As previously stated, there is pressure on the boards of nonprofits to generate income in order to sustain their operations. Accordingly, more exempt organizations are venturing into the commercial space in order to preserve their existence and carry out their charitable purposes.[107.6]

CAVEAT

Perhaps the best solution is to take a completely different approach by disregarding the financial returns available for unrelated business activities and expanding UBIT to cover *all* commercial revenues. Many commentators have suggested a commercially-based test for taxation as opposed to a relatedness test to address the unfair competition issue. The latter approach may well address the major policy concerns of tax-based erosion, managerial diversion, and economic sufficiency as well as simplify the existing law with respect to the commerciality doctrine.[107.7]

---

§ 2.4 CHARITABLE ORGANIZATIONS: GENERAL REQUIREMENTS

(a) Organization Must Benefit a Charitable Class

p. 98. *Insert the following at the end of the subsection:*

Panera Bread Foundation, related to Panera Bread, the for-profit restaurant chain, has filed a Tax Court petition for reversal of the IRS revocation of its tax exemption.[280.1] The Panera Foundation asserts that it provides grants and assistance by giving away free food through its Panera Cares Café program, which operates cafes in the location of former Panera restaurants; payment for food is voluntary in the cafes. It also provides job training to high-risk youth and persons with developmental disabilities. Panera Bread, the for-profit, is Panera Cares' primary source of funds besides the voluntary payments from customers. The relationship between the for-profit and nonprofit was described in the Foundation's Form 1023. The IRS revoked the Foundation's exemption, explaining that most customers have the ability to pay for its products:

[107.6]For an excellent analysis of the commerciality doctrine see John D. Columbo, *Commerciality Activity in Charitable Tax Exemption*, 44 Wm. & Mary L. Rev. 47 (2002).

[107.7]See *id.*, 557.

[280.1]*Panera Bread Foundation, Inc. v. CIR*, Tax Court petition filed March 15, 2019.

Providing food and drink to members of the general public absent a showing of need is not a charitable purpose under section 501(c)(3). In addition, operating a restaurant open to the general public during commercial business hours and accepting retail cost or greater in payments from individuals receiving the food items indicate a substantial non-exempt purpose. Also, this activity was funded primarily through support by a related for-profit entity and through the operation of cafes similar in appearance and operation to the related for-profit, rather than through donations or other support indicating community oversight from the general public, further showing that the operations of the cafes were for substantial non-exempt private rather than public purposes.

CAVEAT

Practitioners have predicted that the IRS will settle the case. The IRS's rationale, that primary funding from a related for-profit rather than donations or other community support demonstrate substantial nonexempt private purposes, seems to be a stretch.

---

§ 2.5 CATEGORIES OF CHARITABLE ORGANIZATIONS (NEW)

(a) Charitable

p. 101. *Add the following new paragraph after the first paragraph on this page:*

The IRS continues to rely on existing federal law to supersede state and local laws pertaining to cannabis or marijuana distribution relying on their illegality to justify its position.

CAVEAT

The possession, distribution and cultivation of cannabis is presently illegal under federal law. This is so despite a relaxation of enforcement at Department of Justice under the last two Democratic administrations. In addition, the District of Columbia and 37 states have decriminalized the substance. Yet cannabis is classified as a Schedule I substance pursuant to the federal controlled Substances Act of 1970 ("CSA"). 21 U.S.C. § 801, *et seq* which states that as a Schedule I drug, cannabis has "a high potential for abuse," "no currently accepted medical use in treatment," and "a lack of accepted safety for use . . . under medical supervision."[296.1]

[296.1]21 U.S.C. § 812(b)(1).

The classification of cannabis as a Schedule I substance would cause those who illegally manufacture, distribute or possess with intent to distribute the drug or related substances to face criminal prosecution. See, for example, 21 U.S.C. § 846 (conspiracy); 21 U.S.C. §§ 960, 963 (importation and conspiracy to import); 18 U.S.C. § 2 (aiding and abetting); 21 U.S.C. § 844 (simple possession); 21 U.S.C. § 841(a)(1) and (b)(1) (substantive violation). Accordingly, transactions that promote or disguise the drug activity, or launder proceeds from drug trafficking, would violate the federal money laundering statues. See 18 U.S.C. §§ 1956, 1957, 1960.

This is so notwithstanding the fact that there is a conflict with many state laws relative to the federal law. A recent denial letter, 202014109, confirms the IRS position. In denial 201224036, an organization formed pursuant to and in compliance with California state law that allows for the cultivation and use of cannabis by seriously ill individuals upon a physician's recommendation was held illegal under federal law, and those in the organization are not entitled to exemption under §501(c)(3). The IRS stated that "the fact that State (presumably California) legalized distribution of cannabis to a limited extent is not determinative because under Federal law distribution of cannabis is illegal." However, see in this regard the Statement in the 1993 EO CPE Textbook at page 165:

> It is theoretically possible that a State or local law could contravene fundamental Federal policy. In that case service revocation of exempt status on the basis of a violation of that statute would be arguably inappropriate. To date, no such case has arisen.[296.2]

p. 102. *Add the following after the last paragraph of this subsection:*

The term "charitable purpose" includes aid or assistance to individuals, representatives, or groups that have been impacted by structural or institutional racisms, regardless of whether such individuals are themselves impoverished, underprivileged, or similarly distressed.

Treas. Reg. § 1.501(c)(3)-1 defines "charitable purpose" to include "(i) to lessen neighborhood tensions; (ii) to eliminate prejudice and discrimination; (iii) to defend human and civil rights secured by law; or (iv) to combat community deterioration and juvenile delinquency." Some IRS guidance, however, suggests that assistance to ameliorate invidious discrimination is not charitable unless the beneficiaries also suffer financial distress. See, for example, Gen. Couns. Mem. 38,841.

[296.2]See *Tan Truck Rentals, Inc. v. Comm'r*, 356 U.S. 30 (1958); Rev. Rul. 71-447, 1971-2 C.B. 230 (racially discriminatory private schools); GCM 34631 (Oct. 4, 1971); Rev. Rul. 75-384, 1975-2 C.B. 204 (antiwar protest organization); GCM 36153 (Jan. 31, 1975); *Bob Jones University v. U.S.* 461 U.S. 574 (1983); "Activities That Are Illegal or Contrary to Public Policy," 1985 EO CPE Textbook 109; "Illegality and Public Policy Considerations," 1993 (for FY 1994) EO CPE Textbook 155.

> **CAVEAT**
>
> There is no indication that all minority-owned businesses and individuals connected with them, who are the primary beneficiaries of the purchasing councils' activities, are impoverished, underprivileged or similarly distressed. On the contrary, these business owners' status would tend to refute such a classification. Under these circumstances, it does not appear that the business owners who are the direct beneficiaries constitute a charitable class. Thus, as aid to minority business owners in general is not itself a charitable purpose under § 501(c)(3), exemption will be dependent upon the charitable results achieved through a program which provides assistance to these primary beneficiaries.

(d) Educational Organizations

(i) Schools p. 113. *Insert as footnote 356.1 at the end of the last sentence of this subsection:*

[356.1] See *Mayo Clinic vs. United States* (8th Cir. 2021), Section 9.3, footnote 43.

(ii) Other Educational Organizations. p. 115. *Add the following new paragraph at the end of this subsection:*

In August 2021, the IRS issued PLR 202144028 relative to the Aegis for Dreams Foundation, which planned to produce a movie about the relationship between Alexander Hamilton and George Washington and its importance to the American struggle for independence. The IRS determined that the Foundation did not qualify for exemption under § 501(c)(3) with its attempt to raise $30 million to produce the film, based on the screenplay by Matthew W. Ryan. Any profits from the film were to be donated to charities dedicated to children or soldiers. The IRS cited Rev. Rul. 77-4 and Rev. Rul. 60-351, claiming that the Foundation was not engaged in exempt activity; rather, just as organizations that produce a magazine or newspaper, the activity was similar in manner to a for-profit commercial company. The organization filed a declaratory judgment action in Tax Court under Section 7428, challenging the denial of § 501(c)(3) exemption for an organization making a film about the Revolutionary War.

§ 2.6 APPLICATION FOR EXEMPTION

(a) Individual Organizations (Revised)

p. 118. *Before the first paragraph of (a) Individual Organizations, insert the following:*

(i) General Procedure

(A) INDIVIDUAL ORGANIZATIONS

p. 118. *Delete the citation in footnote 396 and replace with the following:*
Rev. Proc. 2019-5, 2019-1 I.R.B. 230 (12/28/2018). Note that the information contained in Rev. Proc. 2019-5 is updated annually in January.

pp. 118–119. *Delete the second and third sentences of the first paragraph under (a) and substitute with the following:*
Beginning in early 2020, the IRS converted the Form 1023 application for recognition of exemption from a paper to online format. In effect, organizations must electronically file the form in order to apply for recognition of exemption under §501(c)(3). To submit a Form 1023, the organization must register for an account on pay.gov, enter "1023" in the search box, and select Form 1023 and complete the form. The user fee structure has been simplified and is now $600 for recognition of exemption under § 501 using Form 1023 and Forms 1024 and 1024-A (see subsection 2.6(c)). Smaller organizations are eligible to file Form 1023-EZ electronically at www.pay.gov along with a $275 user fee.

p. 119. *Insert the following before the first full paragraph on this page:*

NOTE

As of January 2018, IRS has issued revised Form 1023, Form 2848 (Power of Attorney), Form 1023-EZ (which includes a short summary of an organization's exempt purposes), as well as Form 1024-A to be used only by organizations seeking exemption under § 501(c)(4). (See subsection 2.6(c).) It is important to use the newest version of these forms because the IRS has indicated that it will return applications on the old forms and ask that the applicant resubmit using the current version. Specifically, the current version of Form 1023 is dated December 2017 and Form 1024 is dated January 2018. Form 8718, User Fee for Exempt Organization Determination Letter Request, should be submitted with exemption applications *other than those using Forms 1023 and 1023-EZ.*

---

p. 121. *Insert the following after the first full sentence on this page:*
Although the IRS has improved its turnaround time for reviewing exemption applications, it has concurrently shortened the amount of time given to respond to a request for additional information, which underscores the importance of timely response to IRS information document requests (IDRs). In addition, in the past, when an applicant did not respond to one or more IDRs, EO would *close* the case as "failure to establish." Going forward, where there is a failure to respond to an IDR, or a follow-up IDR, the IRS will issue a proposed denial, which will trigger a new process. Rather than supplementing the application, the applicant will now have to file a

protest with Appeals, which actually provides a right it did not have under the former procedures of "failure to establish." From the IRS's viewpoint, a denial letter will take agents more time to prepare than "failure to establish," but when a denial becomes final, it will serve to instruct the public as to the issues it "is denying."[407.1]

p. 121. *Add the following to the end of the first full paragraph on this page:*

The streamlined application for small organizations, Form 1023-EZ, can only be filed electronically at https://irs.gov/form1023. (See 2.6(a)(ii), Special Procedure for Small Organizations.)

p. 122. *Insert the following new subsection before (b):*

(ii) Special Procedure for "Small" Organizations On July 1, 2014, the IRS released a short-form application for recognition of § 501(c)(3) tax-exempt status, the Form 1023-EZ, Streamlined Application for Recognition of Exemption Under § 501(c)(3) of the Internal Revenue Code.[418.1] According to IRS Commissioner John Koskinen, the short form was introduced in part to "reduce lengthy processing delays" for organizations seeking exemption from tax. In January 2018, IRS introduced a new version of Form 1023-EZ that seeks some additional information, such as a brief statement of purpose, but remains much simpler to complete and file than Form 1023, with an application fee of $275. The revised Form 1023-EZ adds two "disqualifiers"—that is, criteria that render an organization ineligible to file for exemption using the simplified form. Organizations that are or were exempt under a different subsection of § 501(c) cannot use Form 1023-EZ, which is consistent with the IRS's policy, announced in 2017, that an organization cannot alter the § 501(c) provision under which it was exempt in settlement of an audit that proposes revocation. The other new disqualifier is that organizations with a pending Form 1023 cannot submit Form 1023-EZ, which had been a strategic maneuver by organizations frustrated by slow review times.

Before an organization can complete and file the Form 1023-EZ, it must review the 30 questions on the eligibility worksheet. If the answer to any of the questions is "yes," then the organization is ineligible to use the Form 1023-EZ. Organizations seeking exemption under § 501(c)(3) that are ineligible to use the Form 1023-EZ may still file the Form 1023.

The questions include the following:

1.   Do you project that your annual gross receipts will exceed $50,000 in any of the next three years?

[407.1]Transcript of February 24, 2017, remarks by Sunita Lough, Commissioner, TE/GE, as reported in *EO Tax Journal* 2017-50, March 13, 2017.
[418.1]IR 2014-77.

2. Have your annual gross receipts exceeded $50,000 in any of the past three years?

3. Do you have total assets the fair market value of which is in excess of $250,000?

4. Were you formed under the laws of a foreign country (United States territories and possessions are not considered foreign countries)?

5. Is your mailing address in a foreign country (United States territories and possessions are not considered foreign countries)?

6. Are you a successor to, or controlled by, an entity suspended under § 501(p) (suspension of tax-exempt status of terrorist organizations)?

7. Are you organized as an entity other than a corporation, unincorporated association, or trust?

8. Are you formed as a for-profit entity, or are you a successor to a for-profit entity?

9. Were you previously revoked, or are you a successor to a previously revoked organization (other than an organization the tax-exempt status of which was automatically revoked for failure to file a Form 990-series return for three consecutive years)?

10. Are you a church or convention or association of churches described in § 170(b)(1)(A)(i)?

11. Are you currently recognized as tax exempt under another section of IRC § 501(a), or were you previously exempt under another section of IRC § 501(a)?

12. Are you a school, college, or university described in § 170(b)(1)(A)(ii)?

13. Are you a hospital or medical research organization described in § 170(b)(1)(A)(iii) or a hospital organization described in § 501(r)(2)(A)(i)?

14. Are you applying for exemption as a cooperative hospital service organization under § 501(e)?

15. Are you applying for exemption as a cooperative service organization of operating educational organizations under § 501(f)?

16. Are you applying for exemption as a qualified charitable risk pool under § 501(n)?

17. Are you requesting classification as a supporting organization under § 509(a)(3)?

18. Is a substantial purpose of your activities to provide assistance to individuals through credit counseling activities such as budgeting,

personal finance, financial literacy, mortgage foreclosure assistance, or other consumer credit areas?

19. Do you or will you invest 5 percent or more of your total assets in securities or funds that are not publicly traded?

20. Do you participate, or intend to participate, in partnerships (including entities or arrangements treated as partnerships for federal tax purposes) in which you share losses with partners other than § 501(c)(3) organizations?

21. Do you sell, or intend to sell, carbon credits or carbon offsets?

22. Are you a health maintenance organization (HMO)?

23. Are you an accountable care organization (ACO) or an organization that engages in, or intends to engage in, ACO activities (such as participation in the Medicare Shared Savings Program [MSSP] or in activities unrelated to the MSSP described in Notice 2011-20, 2011-16 IRB 652)?

24. Do you maintain or intend to maintain one or more donor-advised funds?

25. Are you organized and operated exclusively for testing for public safety and requesting a foundation classification under § 509(a)(4)?

26. Are you requesting classification as a private foundation?

27. Are you applying for retroactive reinstatement of exemption under § 5 or 6 of Rev. Proc. 2014-11, after being automatically revoked?

As a result of the worksheet, Form 1023-EZ is primarily designed for smaller, U.S.-based, public charities (e.g., public charities with gross receipts of $50,000 or less and assets of $250,000 or less). The IRS estimates that "as many as 70 percent of all applicants qualify to use the [Form 1023-EZ]."[418.2]

There are several key differences between the long-form Form 1023 and the short-form Form 1023-EZ. First, whereas Form 1023 is 26 pages long, Form 1023-EZ is only 2½ pages long. Second, Form 1023-EZ can only be filed electronically.[418.3] Third, applicants filing Form 1023-EZ are asked to provide a description of their activities not to exceed 255 characters, which is substantially less information than required on Form 1023. Finally, Form 1023-EZ does not require applicants to provide copies of their governing documents; instead, applicants are required to attest that (1) the governing documents limit the organization's purpose to one or more exempt purposes within § 501(c)(3);[418.4] (2) the governing documents do not expressly empower the applicant to engage, other than as an insubstantial part of its

---

[418.2]IR 2014-77.
[418.3]See generally § 2.6(a)(1) for Form 1023 filing procedure.
[418.4]Form 1023-EZ, Part II, Line 5.

activities, in activities that in themselves are not in furtherance of one or more exempt purposes;[418.5] (3) the governing documents contain the dissolution provision required under § 501(c)(3) or the applicant does not need an express dissolution provision in its governing documents because it relies on the operation of state law in the state in which it was formed for its dissolution provision.[418.6]

According to the IRS, as of March 2015, the IRS is able to process a Form 1023-EZ in less than 30 days. During the previous six months, the IRS approved more than 90 percent of the Form 1023-EZ applications that it received. Additionally, the backlog of applications that were more than 270 days old was reduced by 91 percent. Those Form 1023-EZ applications that were not approved were denied because an organization used the form when it was not eligible to do so.

CAVEAT

Some practitioners have been critical of Form 1023-EZ. George Yin, current University of Virginia Law professor and former chief of staff on the Joint Committee on Taxation, in particular has argued that Form 1023-EZ is a misuse of IRS compliance resources because the IRS has "created a self-certification process to obtain (c)(3) status"[418.7] by "obtaining no information from the applicant upfront."[418.8] According to the National Taxpayer Advocate Nina Olsen, the IRS has approved some exemption applications that it should not have.[418.9] Additionally, Form 1023-EZ has solved the backlog of exemption applications, but instead of determining whether an organization should be granted exemption from tax, Form 1023-EZ shifts enforcement to the back end and forces the IRS to perform an audit or compliance check to determine whether the organization should have been granted exemption from tax in the first place.[418.10]

Form 1023-EZ submissions comprised 65 percent of total applications filed for exemption under § 501(c)(3), a percentage the IRS stated was higher than anticipated.[418.11]

During its 2017 fiscal year, the IRS continued its "post determination compliance examinations" of 565 organizations from a randomly selected pool of entities that were granted exempt status via Form 1023-EZ. A total of 49 percent of the examinations were closed with no change; 51 percent

---

[418.5]Form 1023-EZ, Part II, Line 6.

[418.6]Form 1023-EZ, Part II, Line 7.

[418.7]George K. Yin, *The IRS's Misuse of Scarce EO Compliance Resources*, 75 The Exempt Org. Tax Rev. 127, 127 (2015).

[418.8]*Id.* at 130.

[418.9]David van den Berg, *Olson: Exemption Applicants Are Being Wrongly Approved*, 75 The Exempt Org. Tax Rev. 662, 662 (2015).

[418.10]*Id.*

[418.11]"Tax Exempt and Government Entities FY 2017 Accomplishments," March 19, 2018.

closed with amendments to organizing documents or other "written advisories," and five (less than 1 percent) resulted in terminations or revocations.[418.12] By comparison, the same report disclosed that examinations of 1,400 organizations that filed Form 1023 or Form 1024 resulted in 57 percent being closed with no change; 43 percent resulted in changes to organizational documents or failure to file returns, with 1 percent being revoked or terminated. Based on this information from the IRS, the results of post-determination compliance exams do not appear to reflect major statistical differences for those organizations filing Form 1023-EZ versus Form 1023.

(b)   Group Exemption

p. 122. *Insert at the end of the first paragraph:*

The IRS has published a proposed revenue procedure, notice 2020-36, after 40 years, to update conditions for obtaining, maintaining, and qualifying as a subordinate for a group exemption letter. The proposed revenue procedure updates Revenue Procedure 80-27, the IRS primary authority on group exemptions, which has been in effect since January 1980.

CAVEAT

The IRS states in the proposed revenue procedure that it oversees more than 4,000 group exemptions, which includes more than 440,000 subordinates and imposes a significant administrative burden. It proposes among other things to increase its efficiency and improve the integrity of data collected, and increase transparency and compliance.

The proposed revenue procedure would add two requirements that a "central" organization needs to meet to obtain or maintain its exemption:

1. To have at least five subordinate organizations to obtain a group exemption, at least one subordinate organization thereafter; and
2. Maintain only one group exemption.

The details are provided in the proposed revenue procedure regarding a central organization's relationship with a subordinate organization along with the additional requirements for a subordinate organization. Contrary to Rev. Proc. 80-27, the new rules will permit a subordinate organization to operate in a foreign country if it is organized in the United States. Among other rules, if an organization described as a 501(c)(3) is classified as a type 3 supporting organization it may not be a subordinate organization for this purpose.

[418.12] *Id.*

Moreover, when an organization whose exemption was automatically revoked and has not yet been reinstated, it could not be a subordinate organization in a group exemption.

The revenue procedure also provides a list of information that the central organization must submit in its annual supplemental group ruling information (SGRI) that describes changes in subordinates' identities, purposes, or activities. The procedure also provides for a transitional period and a grandfather rule in order to make a group exemption process more streamlined and uniform and reduce the administrative burden on the IRS. For a substantial number of organizations the new ruling will have minimum impact due to the extensive grandfathering rule. But the revenue procedure will create additional administrative burdens on many other organizations and limit the type of organizations that will qualify as new subordinate organizations.

CAVEAT

In reviewing Notice 2020-36 a number of issues remain; for example, are the control factors too rigid? Do they ignore how many church denominations are structured? Does the number of existing "mixed" groups show how common and necessary the structure is? In effect will the IRS be overrun with a large number of organizations having to obtain their own exemption because arguably the requirements are too stringent?

It is important to note that the group exemption holders represent a large portion of the exempt organization community. The proposed rules will make significant changes to those that have been in place since the 1960s and impact group structures that have been in place since the 1940s, so the proposed rules have a significant impact on the basic structure of many religious organizations. To conclude, couldn't the IRS achieve its goals through a less intrusive and draconian set of requirements?

p. 123. *Insert the following new subsection at the end of Section 2.6:*

(c) Social Welfare Group Exemptions

Until recently, a § 501(c)(4) social welfare organization could elect to apply for recognition of exempt status from the IRS by filing an application for recognition of exemption or it could "self-declare" and not file an application. Notification to the IRS is now mandatory pursuant to new § 506, added to the Code by the 2015 Path Act,[420.1] which *requires* that organizations formed

---

[420.1]Protecting Americans from Tax Hikes Act of 2015 (Pub. L. No. 114-113, div. Q).

to operate under § 501(c)(4) file Form 8976 with the IRS within 60 days of formation.

Although filing a notice may appear simple, the process is not without complexity. First, filing the form serves as a declaration of intent to operate as a § 501(c)(4) organization—it does not trigger issuance of an IRS determination letter that the IRS recognizes the entity as a § 501(c)(4) organization. An entity would still need to submit an application for recognition of tax exemption, Form 1024-A, to obtain a determination letter.[420.2] Moreover, *filing Form 1024-A, even within 60 days of formation, does not obviate the need for filing Form 8976 in a timely fashion.*[420.3]

Form 8976 may only be submitted online within 60 days of organization with the requisite user fee. Failure to timely file triggers a two-tier penalty system: $20 per day with a maximum of $5,000 imposed on the organization and $20 per day on a person or persons responsible for failure to file after receipt of an IRS written demand requesting submission by a date determined by the IRS to be reasonable. The maximum to be paid by all such persons is $5,000. There is a mechanism to request relief from imposition of the penalty upon demonstration of reasonable cause.[420.4] The IRS reports that it has rejected approximately 15 percent of the Forms 8976 submitted, either because the applicant is excepted from filing under transitional rules or had not paid the fee; to the extent failure to pay is attributable to the complexity of its website directions, the IRS is focusing on editing and clarifying those instructions.[420.5]

CAVEAT

A new organization formed under Code § 501(c)(4) must file Form 8976 within 60 days of formation to "self-declare" *and* must file Form 1024-A if it wants to receive an IRS determination letter that it is recognized as a §501(c)(4) organization. Filing Form 1024-A within 60 days of formation *does not* obviate the need to timely file Form 8976.

[420.2]In January 2018, the IRS released Form 1024-A to be used to apply for recognition of exemption for § 501(c)(4) entities only. The revised form basically simplifies the application process by deleting portions seeking information applicable to other non–§ 501(c)(3) organizations.

[420.3]Rev. Proc. 2016-41, 2016-30 I.R.B. 165, § 7.05.

[420.4]Rev. Proc. 2016-41, section 8.

[420.5]Transcript of February 24, 2017, remarks by Sunita Lough, Commissioner TE/GE, as reported in *EO Tax Journal*, March 13, 2017.

§ 2.7 GOVERNANCE

p. 124. *Insert the following after the first paragraph of this section:*

<div align="right">**Caveat**</div>
The IRS is more receptive in its review of an exemption application when the organization has a "first-class" board. Nevertheless, a leading commentator has challenged the IRS, claiming it has no statutory basis for its good governance policy. He traced through its beginnings in PLRs and the Service's ultimately relying on the private benefit doctrine, which he believes is based on common law and not based on the statute as is private inurement. He believes that the IRS policy encouraging large boards, community-based representatives, and independent directors is based on the private benefit doctrine, as to which he disagrees with the cases and rulings that uphold the principles of good governance.[420.6]

p. 126. *Insert the following after the first full paragraph on this page:*

As of the writing of the 2018 Supplement, Congress had not codified good governance reporting requirements, which had led to the publication of a book by Bruce Hopkins, a leading expert in the nonprofit area. In Mr. Hopkins's book, *Ultra Vires: Why the IRS Lacks the Jurisdiction and Authority to Regulate Nonprofit Governance* (Talbot Publishing, 2017), he argues that in the absence of statutory authority, the IRS relies on the private benefit doctrine and one Tax Court case, *Bubbling Well Church* (49 F.2d 104, 9th Cir., 1981), to support its application of the good governance concept. Mr. Hopkins argues that there is "no meaningful data to back up its rationale" and "the IRS's policy is arbitrary and capricious under the Administrative Procedure Act's standards." (Book summary provided by Mr. Hopkins to the author, June 2017.) Mr. Hopkins is critical of the IRS's assertion that independent board members help nonprofits operate in furtherance of their exempt goals and that there are only a couple of rulings that reflect that "related boards do not automatically lead to denial or loss of exemption but require a closer scrutiny of the underlying facts." (*Id.*)

It is interesting to note that the theoretical framework of both Rev. Rul. 98-15 and Rev. Rul. 2004-51 is based on the principles of control, in regard to the board of a joint venture vehicle and regarding control of major joint venture decisions to ensure furtherance of the nonprofit partner's exempt purposes.

[420.6]See Bruce Hopkins's outline at *Georgetown Law Continuing Legal Education: Representing and Managing Tax Exempt Organizations*, April 28, 2016.

§ 2.8   FORM 990: REPORTING AND DISCLOSURE REQUIREMENTS (REVISED)

(a)   Who Must File

p. 132. *Delete* **of the Internal Revenue Code** *in the first sentence of this section.*

p. 133. *Insert quotation marks around* **PPA** *on the first line on this page.*

p. 134. *Insert the following after the first full paragraph on this page:*

Since the automatic revocation policy was implemented in 2010, approximately 9,000 out of 550,000 organizations were automatically revoked in error.[478.1] Rev. Proc. 2014-11[478.2] provides the procedures for reinstating the tax-exempt status of organizations that had their exempt status automatically revoked for failure to file a Form 990 for three consecutive years.

An organization that was eligible to file a Form 990-EZ, Short Form Return of Organization Exempt from Income Tax, or Form 990-N, e-Postcard, for each of the three consecutive years that it failed to file, and that has not previously had its tax-exempt status automatically revoked, may use the streamlined retroactive reinstatement process. An organization eligible to use the streamlined process is required to (1) complete and submit a new Form 1023 or Form 1024 and (2) include the appropriate user fee with the application. The new Form 1023 or Form 1024 should clearly state "Revenue Procedure 2014-11, Streamlined Retroactive Reinstatement" at the top of the application to ensure it is handled appropriately.

An organization that is not eligible to use the streamlined process may, within 15 months after the later of the date of the organization's revocation letter or the date on which the IRS posted its name on the Revocation List, (1) complete and submit a new Form 1023 or Form 1024; (2) include the appropriate user fee; (3) include a statement establishing reasonable cause for its failure to file the required annual return for at least one of the three consecutive years in which it failed to file; (4) file properly completed and executed annual returns for all taxable years in the consecutive three-year period for which the organization was required, and failed, to file, and mail the annual returns to the Department of the Treasury at the Internal Revenue Service Center, Ogden, UT 84201-0027; and (5) include a statement with its application confirming that it has filed its annual returns. An organization seeking retroactive reinstatement more than 15 months after the later of the date of the organization's revocation letter or the date

---

[478.1]Fred Stokeld, *IRS Must Act to Stop Erroneous Revocations, Olson Says*, 73 The Exempt Org. Tax Rev. 123 (2014).

[478.2]Rev. Proc. 2014-11, 2014-3 I.R.B. 411.

on which the IRS posted its name on the Revocation List must complete the same requirements; however, the statement establishing reasonable cause must establish reasonable cause for the organization's failure to file the required annual return for all three years that it failed to file its annual returns.

p. 134. *Add the following to the end of footnote 479:*

The Advisory Committee on Tax Exempt and Government Entities has recommended that the IRS adopt a new Form 990-T; however, the IRS has no immediate plans to revise the form.

p. 135. *Insert the following after the word "Id." in footnote 481:*

Effective FYE 2020, a Form 990 has to be filed electronically.

p. 135. *Insert the following after the first full paragraph on this page:*

The Taxpayer First Act (H.R. 3151), signed into law on July 1, 2019, extends mandatory electronic filing of annual information returns, for example, Form 990, Form 990-PF, Form 990-EZ, Form 990-T, and Form 887 (Political Organization Report of Contributions and Expenditures). Previously, organizations with more than 250 returns and assets greater than $10 million and small exempt organizations, that is, those that filed Form 990-N, had to file electronically. The electronic filing provisions apply to tax years beginning after the bill's enactment, but the IRS can provide a two-year delay to some organizations. In addition, the law requires the IRS to give notice to organizations that are in jeopardy of losing their exempt status due to nonfiling for two years (revocation occurs for failure to file for three years) and to publicly release data from the Forms 990 as soon as possible, in machine-readable format.[483.1]

The U.S. Supreme Court, in *Americans for Prosperity Foundation v. Bonta*,[483.2] issued its decision holding unconstitutional under the First Amendment the requirement of the California Attorney General that charities soliciting in the state file Form 990, Schedule B, listing names, addresses, and amounts of donations from large donors.

(b) Disclosure of Returns

p. 135. *Insert the following after* hours *on the third line:*

or by providing a copy of their Forms 990 and 1023

p. 135. *Insert the following to the end of the first sentence of this subsection:*

other than a reasonable fee for any reproduction and mailing costs.

p. 135. *Insert a period after* 30 days *on line 5 and delete remainder of the sentence found on p. 136 (keep the footnote).*

[483.1]"BGOV Bill Summary: H.R. 3151, IRS Services and Enforcement," *Daily Tax Report,* June 10, 2019.
[483.2]594 U.S. ____ (2021).

p. 136. *Add the following to the end of footnote 486:*

In May 2020, the IRS issued final regulations on donor disclosure that did not provide an exception for § 501(c)(3) organizations or section 527 political organizations, both of which are subject to statutory requirements for disclosure, which includes Schedule B of Form 990.

p. 137. *Insert the following before the Caveat on this page:*

CAVEAT
Although the IRS now makes data on electronically filed Forms 990 accessible in machine-readable format through Amazon Web Services, organizations must still make their Forms 990 available for public inspection upon request.

p. 137. *Insert the following after* **public** *on the third line of the Caveat:*

or the IRS. IRS Examinations is currently planning on conducting computerized scans of Forms 990 to spot inconsistencies and missing information

§ 2.9   REDESIGNED FORM 990 (NEW)

(h)   Compensation of Officers, Directors, Trustees, Key Employees, and Five Highest-Compensated Employees

(i) Overview of Compensation Reporting.   p. 156. *Add the following new paragraph after the first paragraph of this subsection:*

The IRS revoked Announcement 2001-33, which had allowed tax-exempt organizations to report the name of a management company that they had hired, rather than the person who directly provided the services, in the compensation section of Form 990. The result would be that the amount was paid to the management company rather than as the compensation of each person employed through the management company. Announcement 2021-18 now requires filing organizations to follow the Form 990 instructions and abolishes the reasonable cause exception from penalties from the prior reporting procedure.

§ 2.10   THE IRS AUDIT (REVISED)

(b)   Surviving an Audit

p. 182. *After the last bullet point on this page, add the following new paragraphs:*

Further, with regard to surviving an audit, there are some additional points that should be considered:

1. It is important that the organization not let its exemption be automatically revoked.

2. If the organization was exempt under a section _other_ than §501(c)(3), the chances of getting the IRS to approve §501(c)(3) status is relatively low.

3. In the alternative, it would be best to organize a completely new entity and not apply as a "successor" organization. It is always important to fully respond expeditiously to any IRS request for additional information after filing the Form 1023.

4. If the organization is a combination of educational purposes and activities as compared to providing member industry benefits in the context of §501(c)(6) (or potentially limited lobbying or political intervention activities), it is critical to stress the "educational" side of the organization and expand those activities if practicable.

5. If the IRS denies the request, it is important to file a timely protest and be prepared to argue the facts and circumstances, and perhaps "negotiate" an acceptable resolution in order for the organization to receive exemption.

p. 183. _Insert the following after the last paragraph at the top of the page:_
The IRS initiated certain new audit policies and procedures in early 2017 that underscore the importance of transparent annual reporting and good record keeping practices. First, the IRS is using statistical information from annual returns to select organizations for audit and the type of exam to be conducted (e.g., compliance check, correspondence audit, or field exam). TE/GE has initiated some exams based on returns that appear to have an indicator of private benefit or inurement.[590.1] Transparent reporting of operations that are consistent with exempt organization guidelines is essential to avoid triggering an examination.

In addition, the importance of organized record keeping is underscored by the announcement that IRS examiners are being instructed to clarify the focus of an exam (i.e., identify whether there is one particular salient issue).[590.2] The agent will generally give a 30-day window for responses to information document requests (IDRs) made in connection with audits, although there is flexibility and opportunity for reasonably based extensions. At the same time, the agent will provide a date by which

---

[590.1] Transcript of February 24, 2017, remarks by Sunita Lough, Commissioner, TE/GE, as reported in _EO Tax Journal_ 2017-50, March 13, 2017.
[590.2] _Id._

the supplied documents will be reviewed. Where appropriate, the IRS is going to follow up unanswered requests with summonses. Maintaining organized records will obviously facilitate timely responses, whereas disorganized record keeping can cause undue delay and perhaps even failure to comply.

In another significant development, the IRS has announced what practitioners view as a significant change in position regarding organizations that seek to convert exempt status from one section of § 501(c) to another. This scenario can arise in the context of an audit that results in the proposed revocation of exemption of a § 501(c)(3) organization. In this situation, a stop gap position for the organization typically has been a conversion to § 501(c)(4) status. The IRS is now taking the position that such conversions cannot take place, a policy EO officials maintain has been in the Internal Revenue Manual in regard to audits for more than a decade.[590.3]

Although EO officials brought attention to the policy in public forums during winter/spring 2017, it was announced in Rev. Proc. 2017-5, which states that circumstances under which determination letters are not "ordinarily" issued include:

> an organization currently recognized as exempt under § 501(c)(3) seeks a determination letter recognizing the organization as described in a different subsection of § 501(c). An organization currently recognized as described in § 501(c)(3) may seek a determination letter under a different subsection of § 501(c) *once it has dissolved and re-formed as a new entity.*[590.4] [Emphasis added]

For example, if an examiner determines that an organization is not operating consistent with § 501(c)(3) requirements and issues a proposed revocation of its § 501(c)(3) status, the entity will not be able to convert to a § 501(c)(4) or other §501(c) subsection as a compromise position incident to closing the audit.[590.5] Rather, the organization will have to go through the formality of dissolving and reapplying under another code section. TE/EO representatives explain the position on the two grounds: (1) that examiners

---

[590.3] Transcript of February 24, 2017, remarks by Janine Cook, TE/GE Deputy Associate Chief Counsel, as reported in *EO Tax Journal* 2017-68, April 6, 2017.

[590.4] 2017-1 I.R.B. 230 (12/29/2016), § 3.02(8). In 2017, EO combined what used to be several revenue procedures describing processes for various EO issues into one procedure, 2017-5. Transcript of February 24, 2017, annual meeting of the Joint TE/GE councils as reported in *EO Tax Journal* 2017-52, March 15, 2017. After passage of the PATH Act, the IRS issued an Internal Guidance Memo, IGM TEGE 04-0216-003, a ruling for examiners that set forth the rule of no modification in the exam context. As the IGM explains, § 406 of the PATH Act extended declaratory judgment rights under Code § 7428 to all Code § 501(c) and (d) organizations in regard to initial or continuing qualification. Because Code § 7428 rights were expanded to all organizations, modifications of tax-exempt status from one subsection to another "are no longer applicable."

[590.5] See IGM TEGE 04-0216-003, issued February 22, 2016, wherein agents are instructed that because modifications from one subsection to another will not be allowed, "[d]o not use 'the modification of exempt status' option" on Form 6018, Consent to Proposed Adverse Action.

are not determination agents and therefore cannot make determination decisions; and (2) that assets of incorporation of § 501(c)(3) organizations must be dedicated to charitable purposes or be distributed to other § 501(c)(3) organizations, which would not be met under a conversion scenario, absent special arrangements such as charitable assets being placed in a segregated fund. The IRS has noted the concerns voiced by practitioners and has requested that practitioners submit comments on the issue.

Although some practitioners have noted that the use of the word "ordinarily" in the Revenue Procedure and in the oral presentations of EO representatives may reflect some flexibility, your author believes that practitioners cannot rely on this when advising clients or engaging in strategic planning.

p. 183. *Insert the following new subsections (c) and (d):*

(c) Strategies in the Event of a Proposed Revocation of § 501(c)(3) Status

Audits can result in proposed revocations. In a much discussed revenue procedure issued in early 2017, the IRS announced what many in the EO community perceived as a policy change: that, ordinarily, § 501(c) organizations under audit cannot request approval of a conversion to a different § 501(c) status as part of the examination process.[590.6] Pursuant to the revenue procedure, an organization can seek a determination as to its status under a different § 501(c) section "after it has dissolved and re-formed as a new entity."[590.7]

Although the EO bar reacted with surprise to the announcement, IRS EO officials took the position that this has been a long-standing policy. According to a February 22, 2016, Internal Guidance Memo (TEGE-04-0216-0003) issued to EO examinations managers and revenue agents, the policy is based on § 406 of the PATH Act, which expanded the declaratory judgment rights of § 7428 to all § 501(c) and (d) organizations whose exemption is revoked. The rationale is that because declaratory judgment rights are now given to all exempt organizations facing revocation of their exemption, all revoked organizations will have to dissolve and reapply under a different section of § 501.

In EO tax conferences, EO officials explained that these changes make sense as examiners perform different functions than those who review exemption applications and make determinations as to qualifications for exemption, "almost like a tax planning component."[590.8] In effect, EO

[590.6]Rev. Proc. 2017-5, 2017-1 I.R.B. 230, § 3.02(8).
[590.7]*Id.*
[590.8]Remarks of Janine Cook, Deputy Associate Chief Counsel (TEGE), presented at Washington Nonprofit Legal and Tax Conference, March 24, 2017, as reported in *EO Tax Journal* 2017-60, March 27, 2017.

officials consider the policy to be based on both legal (the PATH Act) and administrative reasons.[590.9]

In regard to § 501(c)(3) organizations specifically, the IRS maintains that the prohibition on conversion from § 501(c)(3) to § 501(c)(4) has been in the Internal Revenue Manual for more than a decade. Moreover, both federal and state laws require charitable assets remain dedicated to charitable purposes, so a conversion to non–§ 501(c)(3) status, where assets could be used for non–§ 501(c)(3) purposes, does present challenges. In response to feedback that dissolution with distribution of charitable assets to charitable organizations may be impractical for organizations with substantial assets or particular assets such as bonds, EO officials have indicated a willingness to consider other alternatives, such as a segregated fund for the charitable assets in the surviving entity.

One more noteworthy procedural change is in Rev. Proc. 2017-1[590.10] addressing private letter ruling requests. Rev. Proc. 2017-1 addresses presubmission conferences, whereby an organization can discuss the issues with IRS representatives before paying the appropriate fee ($28,000 for larger organizations). The conferences are usually by telephone, and the IRS now requires submission of a written submission outlining the proposed requests before scheduling the presubmission conference.

(d)   IRS Compliance Strategy Examinations (New)

The IRS Tax-Exempt & Government Entities (TE/GE) division has initiated several examinations to address noncompliance including: hospital organizations with unrelated business income as to which the IRS focused on the UBIT reported on Form 990-T where expenses materially exceed gross income; audits of organizations that were previously for-profit entities prior to the conversion to § 501(c)(3) organizations; organizations that show indicators of potential private benefit or inurement to individuals or private entities by way of private foundation loans to disqualified persons; with regard to social clubs (§ 501(c)(7)), there is a focus on investment income and nonmember income by the social club. The IRS has also initiated a data-driven compliance examination that relates to filing requirements, employee classification, UBIT, and operational and organizational requirements, as well as unreported or excess compensation.

The exempt organization branch closed 95,864 determination applications in fiscal year 2020, including 85,509 approvals, 79,730 of which were approvals for § 501(c)(3) status. Furthermore, based on the information released by the TE/GE commissioners, the exempt organization branch

---

[590.9]*Id.*
[590.10]2017-1 I.R.B. 1 (12/29/2016).

completed examinations of 3,240 returns in fiscal year 2020 including the Form 990 series and their associated employment and excise tax returns. In addition, approximately two-thirds of the applications filed used Form 1023-EZ, which provides limited information to the IRS.

The Treasury and IRS released their 2020–2021 priority guidance and plan, which included, among others, 14 projects in the tax-exempt and charitable giving context, *inter alia*:

1. Guidance regarding a private foundation's investment in a partnership in which disqualified persons are also partners in the context of section 4941.

2. Final regulations concerning supporting organizations (section 509(a)(3)).

3. Final regulations concerning IRS disclosure of tax exempt information to state officials (section 6104(c)).

4. Final regulations designating the appropriate high-level Treasury official under the church audit rules (section 7611).

5. Guidance for revising the group exemption rules (Rev. Proc. 80-27).

6. Guidance for circumstances under which a limited liability company can qualify for recognition for exemption as a charitable entity.

7. Guidance updating the electronic filing requirements for exempt organizations reflecting changes made by the Taxpayer First Act.

8. Final regulations concerning the fractions rule (IRC § 514(c)(9)(E)) (see Sections 9.6(a) and 9.6(c)).

9. Guidance regarding charitable contributions of inventory (section 170(e)(3)).

10. Regulations regarding charitable contributions in determining the limitation on allowing partnership loss (section 704(d)) (see Section 3.8).

§ 2.11 CHARITABLE CONTRIBUTIONS (REVISED)

p. 183. *Delete the citation in footnote 591 and replace it with the following:*
   Sanders, *Traps for the Unwary Concerning Gifts of Appreciated Property to Charity: New § 170(e)*, 24 U. of So. Cal. Law Ctr. Rev. 719 (1972).

p. 183. *Insert as footnote 595.1 at the end of the last sentence of the third paragraph:*
   [595.1] In March 2019, the U.S. Department of Justice charged a college advisory consultant, along with 33 parents and several college coaches and college entrance exam administrators, with crimes involving admission improprieties. The charges followed an undercover operation (named "Varsity Blues") tracking the college advisor, William Singer. Singer had set up a Code § 501(c)(3) charity to which his clients made contributions in exchange for their children being accepted into a variety of colleges and universities. Singer in turn used a

portion of the contributions to make payments to coaches to pave the way for admission of students who otherwise likely would not have been admitted as athletes in the respective sports or for payments to persons who assisted in improving students' test results. Senators Grassley and Widen have asked the IRS Commissioner to investigate Singer's foundation, and others have discussed introducing legislation to deny charitable deductions to donors whose children attended colleges and universities that received the contributions.

NOTE

While the circumstances of the Varsity Blues investigation appear to be particularly outrageous, it is a commonly known practice for colleges and universities to receive contributions around the time a family member might be submitting an admission application. Contributions in such scenarios are arguably made in exchange for a quid pro quo and not with detached and disinterested generosity, as required for a gift eligible for a tax deduction. It remains to be seen whether the Varsity Blues scandal will lead to a reexamination of this practice by colleges and universities as well as in Congress and the IRS. It has been reported that one of the colleges has retained a prominent law firm "to review how its athletes are recruited and how athletics-related gifts are accepted." https://urldefense.proofpoint.com/v2/url?u=https-3A__www.nytimes.com_2019_07_17_sports_stanford-2Drowing-2Dcollege-2Dadmissions-2Dscandal.html-3Fsmid-3Dnytcore-2Dios-2Dshare&d=DwIFaQ&c=qmgb7o64HbcJ-G-pnw2rSw&r=PUDFR_4BqNy7eB1p9R1XAYu RgNhGahnTGgr3uG8k7es&m=oJG2KUlIS_wFN0kbx0NagRwklSO9owDMBT4htGtQT_g &s=k4QajhncdEfCsen5rx3VVzeMGMjUH1Qfr_-0nozpaYw&e.

(a) Contributions of Cash, Ordinary Income Property, and Short-Term Capital Gain Property (Revised)

p. 184. *Add the following to the end of footnote 597:*

Under the CARES Act, for tax years beginning 2020, individuals who claim the standard deduction on their federal income tax return, as opposed to itemizing deductions, are permitted to make qualifying contributions of up to $300 and to use such contribution as an above-the-line deduction in computing their adjusted gross income. Individual taxpayers who itemize their deductions can make qualifying contributions and deduct such contributions up to 100 percent of adjusted gross income instead of the 50 percent limitation. Corporate taxpayers that make qualifying contributions may deduct such contributions up to 25 percent of the adjusted taxable income, rather than the 10 percent limitation from the 2017 Tax Cut and Jobs Act. Excess contributions may be carried forward for the next five taxable years. See Section 2.1. The CARES Act provided significant temporary tax relief and charitable giving benefits. The Consolidated Appropriations Act of 2021 enacted on December 27, 2020, extends these benefits for one additional year. See also Adine S. Momoh, "A Permanent Fix to a Temporary Solution: Making Permanent a Universal Charitable Giving Deduction to Encourage and Preserve Charitable Giving and Capture Wealth Transfer," a paper submitted in her graduate tax class at Georgetown University Law Center.

The CARES Act made a new charitable deduction available to individual taxpayers who do not itemize their deductions. This benefit, also referred to as a universal deduction, allows for a charitable deduction for cash contributions to qualifying public charities of up to $300 per individual. The Consolidated Appropriations Act of 2021 further extends this benefit, permitting a charitable deduction of up to $600 on their 2021 federal income tax return for couples filing jointly. This is an above-the-line contribution that is deducted from the individual taxpayer's income prior to the calculation of their adjusted gross income.

In addition to the universal deduction, the CARES Act provides incentives for both individuals and corporations by temporarily increasing the available deductions on qualified charitable contributions. The Consolidated Appropriations Act of 2021 extends these increased limits through 2021:

- Individual taxpayers who itemize their deductions can deduct 100 percent of their adjusted gross income on their 2021 federal income tax return.

- Corporations can deduct 25 percent of taxable income in 2021, increased from the 10 percent limit. A qualified contribution does not include a charitable contribution to a private nonoperating foundation, supporting organization, or donor-advised fund, but contributions to such organizations remain deductible up to the general 10 percent limit.

Corporations (and individuals, in some instances) are also allowed special deductions for contributions of inventory. (See §170(e)(3).) Normally, charitable inventory contributions are limited to the lesser of basis (cost) or fair market value, with inventory reduced by the contributions (as a result of this limitation, any inventory cost that is in excess of fair market value can still be deducted in calculating taxable income as the cost of goods sold).

For C corporations contributing inventory to 501(c)(3) organizations for the care of the ill, the needy, or infants, special rules provide an enhanced deduction equal to the basis plus half the difference between the fair market value and basis, not to exceed twice the basis. A similar enhanced deduction exists for businesses (both corporate and noncorporate) for food inventory contributions for the care of the ill, needy, and infants.

Cash basis taxpayers who do not keep inventories (including many farmers and some other small businesses) are allowed to deduct half their fair market value under the enhanced food inventory deduction, even though they already deduct these costs as a business expense. This enhanced deduction for food inventory is limited to 15 percent of taxable income from the business for both individuals and corporations.

Unused charitable deductions that exceed the income limits can be carried forward and deducted in the following five years.

To conclude, the CARES Act repealed the limit on cash gifts of individuals to public charities (but not to donor-advised funds, supporting organizations, or private foundations). It increased the limit on charitable contributions from corporations to 25 percent of taxable income, including donations of qualified food inventory. The deduction for contributions of qualified food inventory for individuals was also increased to 25 percent. This provision was extended through December 31, 2021, by the Taxpayer Certainty and Disaster Tax Relief Act of 2020, enacted as Division EE of the Consolidated Appropriations Act, 2021 (P.L. 116-260).

p. 184. *Delete the citation in footnote 599 and replace it with the following:*

See also Sanders, footnote 591.

(b) Contributions of Capital Gain Property (New)

p. 186. *Add the following as new paragraph (i) at the end of the subsection:*

(i) Cryptocurrencies.

Tax-exempt organizations are increasingly intersecting with cryptocurrency and related technologies to help facilitate fund raising, which is gaining significant attention around the world.[604.1]

Cryptocurrency ("crypto") may be generally defined as a medium of exchange, a security, an asset pegged to fiat currency (stable coins), that is, a tokenization of assets, or a combination of the above.[604.2] It is a decentralized digital asset, without legal tender status as fiat currency in any jurisdiction.

NOTE
Parties transact directly without an intermediary using blockchain technology, a shared distribution ledger that verifies, records, and settles transactions on a secured, encrypted

---

[604.1] See Andrea S. Kramer, *Financial Products: Taxation, Regulation and Design* (2022).
[604.2] The tokens are actually referred to as smart contracts, which have empedded in their metadata information about what they provide, what their rights are, what their obligations are, and so on.

network. It is an intangible asset without a physical location. Each non-fungible token ("NFT") is a unique digitized certificate, often referred to as a token; it is a digital unit of data stored on a blockchain. NFTs are typically purchased and sold using the type of cryptocurrency or digital token used or accepted on that particular blockchain. Once an NFT is created and stored on a blockchain, all of its subsequent sales are tracked and recorded.

Tax-exempt entities are accepting more and more crypto as gifts; in fact, approximately $450,000,000 of crypto were donated in 2021.[604.3] Accordingly, American taxpayers have been deducting crypto donations.[604.4]

Since crypto is generally treated as property, donors may avoid capital gains and receive charitable deductions according to the IRS[604.5] if the holding period is long term, that is, more than a year, the deduction is the fair market value of the virtual currency at the time of donation. If not held long term, the deduction is limited to the lessor of tax basis or fair market value.[604.6]

U.S. convertible virtual currency is property for tax purposes. Accordingly, the general tax rule that applies to donations of non-cash property would be applicable. Record keeping and documentation is more detailed as the donation increases in value. Donations of more than $5,000 require a Form 8283 to be filed and retention of a qualified appraiser with at least two years of experience in valuing the type of property involved. The appraiser needs to determine the fair market value of the donation.

NOTE

There are various methods of making crypto donations, such as donating to a donor-advised fund, using a processor,[604.7] or using an embeddable checkout experience, so donors can contribute crypto to a donor-advised fund (DAF) and the third-party DAF platform converts

---

[604.3] Charities are using crypto and blockchain for diverse purposes . . . from membership voting to humanitarian supply chain management to carbon sequestration. SEVA.LOVE was created by Deepak Chopra to assist charities in using the blockchain. City Kids Foundation is an example of a project using crypto and blockchain to organize children around art projects online. They are selling NFTs to raise money, but the project itself is being organized on blockchain using tokens and Discord servers; they have different levels of membership, each represented by a different token with different rights and privileges.

[604.4] Crypto currency is now included on Form 1040.

[604.5] IRS FAQs question 34, donation of convertible virtual currency is not a sale of the capital asset.

[604.6] The contribution of the capital asset held by a donor for more than 12 months to a public charity is generally deductible at the fair market value of the asset, up to 30 percent of the donor's adjusted gross income. See Code § 170(b)(1)(C); see Section 2.11.

[604.7] Purpose-built platforms, such as The Giving Block, are companies that work with hundreds of nonprofit clients and are knowledgeable in crypto, its operations, and marketing. They enable the nonprofit to focus on fundraising and impact and allow the nonprofit exposure to a new donor community. In addition to The Giving Block, other processors, including Bitpay or Coinbase Commerce, are suitable to receive passive donations.

the crypto to U.S. dollars or another fiat currency. The nonprofit would not need to set up a virtual currency wallet and would not assume the risk and expenses of converting the fiat currency. Accordingly, the nonprofit may insulate itself from undesirable donors who could impact its mission or impose a reputational risk.

In a situation where a taxpayer has substantial appreciation, they may be concerned about contributing to a donor-advised fund because the decision as to when to liquidate will be in the hands of a third party. Accordingly, it may be advisable for the donor to create an LLC and donate the crypto through the newly created entity so that the donor-advised manager will receive an interest in the LLC rather than the property, as such.

It is also important for the nonprofit to establish a gift acceptance policy that would cover which crypto to accept, liquidation, valuation, and reporting, as well as rules regarding prearranged sales. The policy would also determine whether anonymous donations would be acceptable. It is recommended that the policy also contain a procedure to protect the nonprofit from security breaches, such as hacking.

CAVEAT

The nonprofit should consider engaging a blockchain analytic firm to analyze transactions and determine whether there is money laundering, sanctioned country, terrorist financing, or potential impact on reputation risk.

CAVEAT

Blockchain is public and includes the public addresses of each party to the transfer; however, it does not contain information about the individual or the donor. See, in this regard, the *Americans for Prosperity Foundation v. Bonta* discussion in Section 2.8.

To summarize, since cryptocurrency is considered a capital asset for income tax purposes, a donor can avoid capital gains tax on appreciated cryptocurrency by donating it to a charity, and receive a charitable contribution deduction. If the gift is over $5,000, the nonprofit must also sign the Noncash Charitable Contributions form (Form 8283) acknowledging the receipt of property, as well as have the cryptocurrency donation appraised by a "qualified appraiser."[604.8] See subsection 2.11(f).

[604.8] If the charity sells the donated cryptocurrency within three years of donation, the charity must provide the Donee Information Return form, also known as Form 8282, to the IRS (and a copy to the donor) within 125 days of sale. Also, as with any other donation, if the value of the cryptocurrency donation was over $250, the organization must provide a donor acknowledgment letter.

Under generally accepted accounting principles (GAAP), cryptocurrency is treated as an intangible asset, rather than cash, investments, or inventory. The gift of the cryptocurrency donation is to be recorded at fair value at the time of donation, but if the cryptocurrency is held for a longer period, the organization would not need to adjust the value of the cryptocurrency for market fluctuations. It would, however, need to test for impairment each year.[604.9]

(c) Contributions of Conservation Easements

p. 185. *Delete* **Internal Revenue** *from the second sentence.*

p. 185. *In footnote 605, replace* **Section 170(f)(3)(B)(iii); see Joe Stephens, with the following:**
§ 170(f)(3)(B)(iii); see Stephens,

p. 185. *Delete* **Because** *and capitalize* **The** *to begin the fourth sentence of this paragraph.*

(e) Charitable Contributions to SMLLCs (Revised)

p. 186. *Delete the citation in footnote 609 and replace with the following:*
Reg. § 301.7701-2(c)(2)(i).

p. 186. *Delete the citation in footnote 610 and replace with the following:*
Reg. § 301.7701-2(a).

p. 186. *Delete the citation in footnote 613 and replace with the following:*
§§ 170(f) and 6115.

p. 186. *Insert at the end of the subsection:*

CAVEAT

The federal tax aspects of an LLC formed to conduct charitable activities will depend on who the members of the LLC are, and whether it elects to be treated as a corporation. A single-member LLC with a 501(c)(3) as the member is disregarded for federal tax purposes, so gifts to it are deemed to be tax-deductible gifts to the member-charity. The IRS takes the position that an LLC with an organizing document that meets the organizational and operational tests for 501(c)(3) status can qualify for tax exemption as a charity. See also Section 2.2.

---

p. 186. *Insert the following new subsection (f) after subsection (e), and re-letter existing subsections (f) and (g) accordingly:*

[604.9] See memorandum by Snyder-Cohn CPA, Cryptocurrencies Issues for Exempt Organizations (March, 2022). See also Bloomberg newsletter, *Cryptocurrency as Compensation: A Tax Primer*, written by Dan Morgan (June, 2022).

(f) Contribution of LLC/Partnership Interests to Charity

(i) In General.[614.1] In view of the pressure on boards of charities to raise funds, there often are opportunities to receive contributions of LLC or partnership interests. Although there may be substantial value and benefit, there are a number of potential traps for the unwary that need to be understood, including the subsequent obligations that may accompany the receipt of the interest, the bargain sales rules, and the additional sanctions that may apply to private foundations as recipients of the gifts.

A charitable transfer can create an attractive tax-planning opportunity for an individual holding an interest in a business or an investment taxed as a partnership, such as an LLC interest. However, both the donor and the donee charity need to understand the consequences of a contribution of such interest, which may be more complex than it appears. Private foundations must also be aware of the additional tax implications of the contribution of a limited partnership or LLC interest.

From a nontax standpoint, the operating agreement of the LLC or limited partnership agreement may contain a capital contribution requirement (including cram-down provisions for failure to fund). There also could be a requirement under the agreement to return prior distributions (referred to as a "claw back" obligation).

If the donee organization intends to hold the LP or LLC interest for a period of time, the governing documents should be reviewed carefully to confirm the charity's rights and obligations. For example, if the company is being sold to a third party, the charitable organization may become a party to the third-party deal. Before proceeding, the charity should engage attorneys to review the sales documents and provide any required legal opinions.

CAVEAT

There are potential risks: Although LPs and LLCs generally provide liability protection for their owners, creditors of the company may attempt to "pierce the corporate veil" and look to the owners to pay the company's liabilities if the business is not operated correctly. Consider the type of interest being donated—general partner interest versus limited partner interest. In any event, a charitable organization should consider holding the donated interest through a wholly owned LLC.

[614.1]For a detailed analysis of the issue, see Strafford Webinar, October 27, 2016, presented by Amanda Nussbaum (Proskauer Rose LLP, New York, NY), Richard Riley (Foley and Lardner LLP, Washington, DC), and Michael Sanders (Blank Rome LLP, Washington, DC).

There are tax advantages to a donor to contribute LP or LLC interests to a public charity (including a donor-advised fund) as compared to a private foundation, especially if the underlying property is likely to be sold in the near future. Any capital gains tax may be minimized or eliminated (that would have been incurred on the sale of the donated interests). There is also an opportunity to take an income tax deduction equal to the fair market value (FMV) of the interests (as determined by a qualified appraisal) on the date of the contribution (vs. tax basis for private foundations).[614.2] A similar result would apply if the contribution is made to an LLC that is wholly owned by the charitable organization and is treated as a disregarded entity for income tax purposes.[614.3] Further, public charities are not subject to a mandatory annual grant distribution requirement or an excise tax on net investment income, and the excess business holding rules do not apply to public charities (except for donor-advised funds and certain supporting organizations).

(ii) Application of Bargain Sales Rules. When a partner receives consideration and the total amount realized is less than the FMV of the interest, the transfer is classified as a "bargain sale"; that is, FMV is greater than amount realized. In such case, the transaction is separated into a gift and a sale. The total amount realized is subtracted from the FMV of the interest.[614.4] The difference is treated as a charitable contribution.

CAVEAT
However, a trap for the unwary exists relative to the basis adjustment. Under § 1011(b), the partnership's adjusted basis for determining the gain on the transfer is that portion of the adjusted basis that bears the same ratio as the amount realized by the transferor to the property's fair market value. The remaining charitable contribution deduction flows through to the partners, subject to any limits on the contributions contained in § 170(b).

The amount of the allowable deduction for the charitable contribution of a partnership interest is determined based on whether the underlying property is ordinary income property or capital gain property. If the property is ordinary income property, the amount that can be deducted as a contribution is its FMV, less the amount that would be recognized as ordinary income. This generally limits the contribution deduction to the basis in the

---

[614.2]Contributions of appreciated property are generally deductible up to 30 percent of a donor's adjusted gross income (vs. 20 percent for private foundations). See IRC § 170(b). See also Section 2.11.
[614.3]See Notice 2012-52. See also subsection 2.11(e).
[614.4]See subsection 3.11(e).

property.[614.5] However, if the property is capital gain property, the amount that can be deducted as a charitable contribution deduction is its FMV.

CAVEAT

If the interest is transferred to a charity subject to indebtedness, the amount of indebtedness is treated as an amount realized on the transfer, regardless of whether the charity agrees to assume or pay the indebtedness. To the extent the donor's share of liabilities is in excess of the donor's basis in the contributed partnership interest, the contribution may result in a deemed distribution of cash to the donor even if no cash is paid. This can cause the contribution to be treated as a bargain sale and the realization of "phantom income," especially if the partner has unrealized receivables, appreciated inventory, or income tax credit (ITC) subject to recapture.

(iii) "Burned Out" Shelters[614.6] Partners may also be faced with annual allocations of phantom income without any cash flow distribution from investments in "burned out" shelters, which often occurs in a subsidized low-income housing partnership. In these circumstances, it is often a good strategy for the partnership to transfer the property to a charitable organization in consideration for some cash, with the charity taking subject to a HUD-insured mortgage. If the property can be appraised at an amount substantially in excess of the purchase price, the individual limited partner may be entitled to a current charitable contribution deduction in a bargain sale transaction.

(iv) Bargain Sales and Private Foundation: Act of Self-Dealing. A sale, including a bargain sale, between a private foundation and a disqualified person is a prohibited act of self-dealing subject to unwinding and excise taxes on parties to the transaction. A disqualified person may include a participating "foundation manager" as defined in IRC § 4946(a) (e.g., an officer, trustee, or substantial contributor).[614.7]

Under IRC § 4943, a private foundation is permitted to hold limited interests in unrelated business enterprises (i.e., the excess business holdings rule). With regard to an incorporated business enterprise, the general rule is that a private foundation and all disqualified persons together may not own more than 20 percent of voting stock. This restriction increases to

---

[614.5]Ordinary income property is also known as § 751 "hot assets" and includes unrealized receivables, appreciated inventory, and depreciation recapture. See IRC § 751.
[614.6] See subsection 3.11(f).
[614.7]Treas. Reg. § 53.4941(d)-2(a)(1) provides that a sale of stock or other securities by a disqualified person to a private foundation in a bargain sale is treated as an act of self-dealing regardless of the amount paid. But not so if an individual becomes a disqualified person as a result of a bargain sale.

35 percent if not in control. Nonvoting stock is permitted, but only if all disqualified persons together do not own more than 20 percent of the voting stock. Holdings are determined with reference to the foundation's own holdings and holdings of all "disqualified persons." See Section 10.2.

Similar rules exist for partnerships, joint ventures, and LLCs. No holdings are permissible in the case of a business enterprise operated in proprietorship form.

Excess business holding rules apply only to entities that are "business enterprises." Business enterprises do not include:

i.   A trade or business that is not an unrelated trade or business (as defined in IRC § 513); and

ii. Any trade or business at least 95 percent of the gross income of which is derived from "passive sources."

These rules are consistent with Congress's intent to prevent tax-exempt organizations from competing unfairly with taxable businesses, but to permit tax-exempt organizations to engage in passive investment activities.[614.8]

As previously stated, IRC § 4943 precludes a private foundation from long-term ownership of more than 20 percent of the voting stock of a corporation or other business enterprise in combination with a disqualified person. However, if a § 501(c)(4) organization is not disqualified, it could own a business enterprise with one or more private foundations in a way that would avoid violating the prohibition against excess business holdings. An owner of interests in a closely held business could transfer its interests to both a private foundation and a § 501(c)(4) organization at the same time so that only 20 percent of the voting stock is held by the private foundation and 80 percent is held by the § 501(c)(4) organization, thus avoiding excess business holdings.

If a § 501(c)(4) organization is controlled by one or more disqualified persons, it would be permissible for a private foundation and the § 501(c)(4) organization to enter into transactions that ordinarily would be treated as self-dealing. For example, a § 501(c)(4) organization could:

i.   Purchase or borrow assets from a related private foundation.

ii. Lease real estate to a related private foundation.

iii. Co-own and co-invest with a related private foundation.

[614.8]A 10 percent excise tax is imposed on excess business holdings on the last day of the foundation's taxable year. It is calculated for each enterprise and based on the amount of excess holdings on the day when excess holdings were largest. It does not apply if the foundation disposes of the excess holdings within 90 days after it knew or should have known of the holdings. An addition to tax of 200 percent of the value of excess holdings will also be imposed if excess holdings are not disposed of by the close of the taxable period. No addition is assessed if excess holdings are reduced to zero within the correction period (90 days after a deficiency notice). See Sections 10.2 and 10.3.

(v) Contribution of Partial Interest. As a general rule, a taxpayer who contributes an LLC or partnership interest to a charitable organization may take a charitable deduction for that contribution equal to the FMV of the interest. But a deduction is not permitted when the partner contributes only a portion of his or her LLC or partnership interest (contribution of partial interest) rather than the entire LLC or partnership interest.[614.9] A deduction is also disallowed where a property was subdivided for the purposes of circumventing this rule.

QUERY

If a partner has both a general and a limited partnership interest in a partnership and contributes only one of these interests (i.e., less than his or her entire ownership), is this a contribution of a partial interest? Can a donor transfer only a carried interest without his or her limited partnership interest? Does it make a difference if the structure/ownership is old and cold?

(vi) Application of Like Kind Exchange Rules: § 1031. The "like kind" exchange rules of IRC § 1031 may apply to minimize the tax liability involved in the sale portion of a bargain sale while still preserving the charitable deduction on the gift portion.[614.10] No gain or loss is recognized when property held for productive use in a trade or business or for investment is exchanged solely for property of a like kind and held for similar use. The exchange must meet a 180-day time limit for the exchange and a 45-day time limit for identification of the property being received. See § 1031(a)(3).

[614.9]See IRC § 170(f)(3)(A).
[614.10]See subsection 3.11(f).

C H A P T E R 3

Taxation of Partnerships and Joint Ventures

§ 3.1 SCOPE OF CHAPTER

p. 195. Insert the following at the end of this subsection:

(a) Treatment of Business Income to Noncorporate Taxpayers

For tax years beginning after 2017 (subject to a sunset at the end of 2025), the 2017 Tax Act (Pub. L. No. 115-97) (the "Tax Act") will allow an individual taxpayer (including a trust or estate) who participates in a joint venture with a nonprofit a deduction of 20 percent of the individual's domestic qualified business income of a partnership, S Corp, or sole proprietorship.

An individual's qualified business income is the net amount of domestic qualified items of income, gain, loss, and deduction with respect to a taxpayer's "qualified business." Qualified business generally is defined to include any trade or business <u>other</u> than a "specified service trade or business," which includes any trade or business activity involving the performance of services in the field of health, law, accounting, actuarial signs, performing arts, consulting, athletics, financial services, brokerage services, and any trade or business the principal asset of which is "reputation or skill" of one or more of its owners or employees. Engineering and architecture are excluded from the limitation.

> **CAVEAT**
>
> However, the deductions may apply to income from a specified service, trade, or business if the taxpayer's taxable income does not exceed $315,000 (for married individuals filing jointly, or $157,500 for other individuals). There is a phase-out regarding the income limitation.

There is an important limitation, however: the deduction is subject to a limit based either on wages paid or wages paid plus a capital element. Specifically, the limitation is the greater of (i) 50 percent of wages paid with respect to a qualified trade or business or (ii) the sum of 25 percent of the W-2 wages with respect to a qualified business plus 2.5 of the unadjusted basis (determined immediately after the acquisition) not including land of all qualified property. The latter additional modification apparently has been added as a result of the real estate industry, although it presents significant accounting issues, including a determination of the remaining useful life of property.

> **CAVEAT**
>
> Treasury is required to provide regulations applying the provisions to tiered entities as well as short tax years during which the taxpayer acquires a major portion of the property. Further guidance is needed to assist taxpayers in applying the rules in the event a like kind exchange (§ 1031) transaction is involved.

> **CAVEAT**
>
> It is important to note that the 20 percent deduction expires after eight years, whereas the corporate tax reduction appears to be permanent. This distinction needs to be evaluated by taxpayers considering whether to operate their businesses in the pass-through forms compared with converting to C corporation status.

EXAMPLE: EO and taxpayer (T) enter into an equal joint venture in an LLC to be taxed as a partnership, organized to train unemployed handicapped high school graduates. T's allocable share of the net operating income from the LLC is $150,000 for 2018. T also earns $600,000 of taxable income from sources unrelated to the handicap business, which subjects him to the maximum tax bracket. The LLC pays its employees $50,000 in wages during 2018 and has $300,000 in unadjusted basis in its equipment used in the business for which the recovery period for depreciation purposes is under § 168.

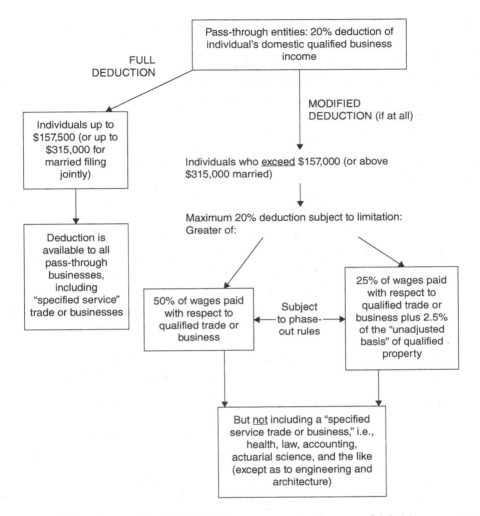

T's deduction under § 199(A) is equal to the lesser of (1) 20 percent of T's allocable share of qualified income from the trade or business (which is not a "specified service" business otherwise excluded) or (2) the greater of (a) 50 percent of T's allocable share of W-2 wages paid by the LLC or (b) 25 percent of T's allocable share of W-2 wages paid by the LLC, plus 2.5 percent of the unadjusted basis of qualified property used in the LLC's trade or business. Based on T's 50 percent ownership, the initial computation under § 199(A) would allow a deduction equal to 20 percent of $75,000, or $15,000 as an initial deduction. However, pursuant to the restriction that provides a limitation equal to the greater of the following: 50 percent of T's $25,000 share of W-2 wages paid by the LLC ($12,500) or 25 percent of T's $25,000 share of W-2 wages paid by the LLC ($6,250) plus 2.5 percent of T's $150,000 share of the unadjusted basis of the qualified property held by the LLC ($3,750), as a result, T's deduction under § 199(A) is capped at $10,000, which is less than $15,000 under the general rule.

§ 3.3 CLASSIFICATION AS A PARTNERSHIP (REVISED)

(b) Overview of the Check-the-Box Regulations

(iv) Consequences of Electing to Change Classification. p. 203. Add quotation marks around the first sentence under paragraph (D).

(c) Classification of Exempt Organizations (New)

p. 205. *Insert the following before the last paragraph that began on the page 204:*

i. Revised Standards for § 501(c)(3) Status of Limited Liability Companies. For a number of years, the IRS has recognized LLCs as tax exempt under § 501(c)(3) of the Code. In 2012, Notice 2012-52 provided that disregarded LLCs with single 501(c)(3) members may receive charitable contributions, and the Form 1023 instructions have long indicated that these entities enjoy the § 501(c)(3) status of their sole members without a separate exemption application. However, Treasury regulations and IRS guidance have largely remained silent on the use of a multiple-member LLC as a § 501(c)(3). Notice 2021-56 sets forth the first formal guidance on the standards that multiple-member LLCs must satisfy to be recognized under § 501(c)(3).[49.1]

CAVEAT

The Notice does not affect the status of LLCs that are currently recognized as described in § 501(c)(3), nor does it affect LLCs that are treated as a disregarded entity of a 501(c)(3) organization. Announcement 99-102 (cited below) permits an exempt organization to establish a disregarded LLC and report the LLC's finances and activities on the exempt organizations Form 990.

The Notice points out that § 1.501(c)(3)-1(3), which sets forth the organizational test, was issued in 1959, prior to the enactment of the first LLC statute in the United States. Accordingly, the Treasury regulations under § 501(c)(3) do not specifically address LLCs and nothing formally has been issued addressing the requirements that LLCs as organizations described in § 501(c)(3). Historically, the standards the IRS has applied for purposes of issuing determination letters have generally included a requirement that all members of an LLC must themselves be § 501(c)(3) organizations, government units,

---

[49.1] The Notice also requests public comment on the standards related to the tax-exempt status for LLCs to assist Treasury and the IRS in determining whether additional guidance is needed.

or wholly-owned instrumentalities of the state political subdivision thereof. The Notice states that in order to assure that an LLC is organized and operates exclusively for exempt purposes, including that its assets are dedicated to its exempt purposes and do not inure to private interests, the LLC's articles of organization and operating agreement must include each of the following:

° Provisions requiring that each member of the LLC be either (i) an organization described in § 501(c)(3) and exempt from taxation under § 501(a) or (ii) a governmental unit described in § 170(c)(1) (or wholly-owned instrumentality of such a governmental unit).

° Express charitable purposes and charitable dissolution provisions in compliance with §§ 1.501(c)(3)-1(b)(1) and (4).

° The express Chapter 42 compliance provisions described in § 508(e)(1), if the LLC is a private foundation.

° An acceptable contingency plan (such as suspension of its membership rights until a member regains recognition of its § 501(c)(3) status) in the event that one or more members cease to be §501(c)(3) organizations or governmental units (or wholly-owned instrumentalities thereof).

CAVEAT

In an informal guidance issued in 2000 and updated in 2001, the IRS stated that LLCs had to satisfy 12 different conditions in order to qualify for § 501(c)(3) exempt status. These revised standards simplify the approach by reducing the number of conditions from 12 to four. Of course the Notice carries more weight than the less formal Internal Revenue Manual.

The Notice acknowledges that in some states, LLC law may not allow an LLC to be organized and operated exclusively for charitable purposes. (See section 4.01(3) of the Notice.) In addition, most states' LLC statutes include default provisions whereby the members' economic rights in net assets upon dissolution would be inconsistent with the §501(c)(3) requirements if the members were private shareholders or individuals within the meaning of § 1.501(a)-1(c) (section 4.01(o) of the Notice). Finally, some states do not permit a statement of LLC purposes in the articles of organization and it may only be included in the operating agreement, which is not filed with the state (section 4.01(6)).

The Notice then requests comments that would support recognition of § 501(c)(3) status for organizations whose memberships include individuals and/or organizations other than § 501(c)(3) organizations, governmental units, or instrumentalities of the state or political subdivision thereof. More specific guidance is needed to ensure that the LLC would be able to satisfy the existing federal statutory and regulatory requirements, including the requirement that assets remain dedicated to an exempt purpose and the prohibition against private inurement.[49.2]

In particular, the Treasury Department and the IRS request comments with respect to the following:

A. What are the potential advantages and disadvantages of forming an entity for exclusively charitable purposes under a state LLC law rather than under a state not-for-profit (or nonstock) corporation or charitable trust law?

B. Do state laws regulating charitable assets apply to assets held by charitable LLCs to the same degree as such laws apply to assets held by trusts or state-law corporations formed for charitable purposes?

C. Most state LLC statutes specify that an LLC may be formed for any lawful purpose. In a few states, however, the LLC statute appears to require that an LLC be a profit-seeking enterprise. In those states, is it permissible as a matter of state law for an LLC to be formed exclusively for § 501(c)(3) purposes?

D. Most state LLC statutes appear to provide that, upon dissolution and after payment of creditors, an LLC may dispose of its remaining assets among its members or otherwise in whatever manner specified in its articles of organization (also referred to as a certificate of organization or certificate of formation) or operating agreement (also referred to as a limited liability company agreement). In those states, the state LLC statute merely provides default rules that apply in the absence of any provision in the articles or operating agreement. Other state LLC statutes, however, appear to require distributions of net assets only to members upon dissolution as immutable rules.

    i. In a state in which the LLC statute appears to require distributions of net assets only to LLC members on dissolution, could LLC members at the time of creation of an LLC effectively "disclaim" their financial interests in the LLC or assign

---

[49.2] Additionally, comments are requested from state attorneys general and charity officials as well as the general public with regard to the interpretation of LLC laws' reference to other pertinent laws and the applicability of state charity laws to an LLC formed for charitable purposes.

or transfer their financial interests to the LLC or to another § 501(c)(3) charity as a means of satisfying the dissolution clause requirement under § 1.501(c)(3)-1(b)(4), notwithstanding the state dissolution requirements?

    ii. Would such a disclaimer be enforceable against the LLC members?

    iii. Would such a disclaimer be enforceable against creditors of the members?

E. Are there state laws that satisfy the dissolution requirements and § 508(e) requirements for charitable LLCs?

CAVEAT

The organizational test regulations under § 1.501(c)(3)-1(b) generally require certain language (in particular, stated charitable purposes and charitable distribution of assets upon dissolution) to appear in the articles of organization, defined as the written instrument by which the organization is created. Private foundations also must include certain language in their articles of organization to be in compliance with § 508(e). See § 1.508-3.

In many cases, state law satisfies the dissolution requirements and § 508(e) requirements for charitable trusts and corporations if there is no contrary provision in the articles of organization. State LLC statutes generally provide that an LLC is created upon filing its articles of organization with the state. In addition to the articles of organization, an operating agreement governs the affairs and activities of an LLC. However, unlike the articles of organization, the operating agreement is not filed with the state. State laws differ as to which document is controlling. In some states, the articles control; in other states, the articles control the extent to which outside parties reasonably rely on the public record, but the operating agreement governs relations among the LLC's members and between the members and the LLC.

F. Is there any reason why an LLC should not be required to include appropriate charitable purpose and dissolution language (and § 508(e) language, if applicable) in both its articles of organization and its operating agreement? (See subsection 4.01(b).)

G. Most state LLC statutes do not restrict the ability of an LLC to include the language required under § 1.501(c)(3)-1(b) (and § 508(e), if applicable) in its articles of organization. However, a few states appear to strictly limit what provisions may be included in an LLC's articles of organization. Should the regulations under the § 501(c)(3) organizational test and § 508(e) requirements be revised to accommodate LLCs organized in states that limit what provisions may be included in an LLC's articles of organization and in the LLC's operating agreement?

CAVEAT
Should it matter that the operating agreement (unlike the articles of organization) is not filed with the state, and therefore may not be readily available to the IRS and the public?

H. Several states have enacted special statutory provisions for non-profit LLCs (beyond a mere provision in the statute that allows an LLC to be formed for a nonprofit purpose), subjecting them to regulation as nonprofit organizations and, in some cases, limiting membership. In such states, must a charitable LLC form under the state's nonprofit LLC law, or are charitable LLCs permitted to form under the state's general LLC law?

NOTE
Some commenters have raised concerns that LLC statutes do not provide the same degree of notification to the state attorney general for "life-cycle" transactions as would be for nonprofit corporations.

I. State laws generally provide an LLC's members with management authority unless the articles of organization (or, in some states, the operating agreement) delegate management authority to one or more managers. With respect to qualification for § 501(c)(3) status, should LLCs managed by "managers" be treated the same as LLCs managed by "members"? Should LLC managers be treated as officers for federal exempt organization tax purposes generally, including, for example, the compliance provisions of Chapter 42? Are there any other provisions of the LLC law in one or more states that may affect the ability of an LLC to qualify under § 501(c)(3)?

J. Are there any specific provisions that should be included in an LLC's articles of organization and operating agreement in addition to, or in lieu of, those discussed above (3.02 of the Notice), to address particular provisions of state LLC law?

K. Are there circumstances in which an LLC seeking recognition under § 501(c)(3) should be permitted to have members that are not themselves § 501(c)(3) organizations, governmental units, or wholly-owned instrumentalities of governmental units?[49.3]

NOTE

Commenters also raised the issue of how fiduciary duties would apply to an exempt LLC, particularly if an exempt LLC were to have nonexempt members. In general, fiduciary duties of loyalty and care are owed to both the LLC and to the members, but state LLC law may permit modifications to each. Several commenters also suggested permitting exempt LLCs with non-501(c)(3) members in certain limited situations. These commenters proposed recognizing an LLC with private members where the private members don't have an economic interest in the LLC, where the fiduciary duties are modified in such a way as to permit the LLC to comply with the requirements of § 501(c)(3), where the LLC otherwise meets the requirements for exemption, and where the LLC represents that all provisions in its articles of organization and operating agreement are consistent with state law and legally enforceable. See the following subsection summarizing detailed comments made by NASCO, ABA, and so forth.

It is noteworthy that the IRS does not appear to establish a position as to whether and under what circumstances that LLC may qualify for exemption under <u>other</u> § 501(c)(3) categories. It also refrains from referencing "pass-through" entities, such as partnerships that are involved in joint ventures or for-profit social enterprises such as "B-corporations" or title closing companies, trade associations, or other types of noncharitable exempt organizations.

ii. Summary of Comments in Response to Notice 2021-56. A number of organizations, which include state charity divisions, have provided comments to Notice 2021-56. Rather than provide a detailed summary of the comments, the next section highlights some of the salient points that were made by the National Association of State Charity Officials (NASCO), American Bar Association, Tax Section, among others. The comments generally commend Treasury and the IRS for providing the guidance set forth in the Notice that is intended to provide clarity to § 501(c)(3) sector as tax-exempt entities for alternative organizational funds. An executive summary of the ABA comments may be summarized as follows:

[49.3] The Treasury Department and the IRS also request comments as to whether there should be special requirements or considerations for recognition of tax-exempt status for LLCs under paragraphs of § 501(c) <u>other</u> than § 501(c)(3).

A. The fundamental standards for exemption should apply equally, regardless of entity form or organizing jurisdiction, with minimal accommodations made for the LLC as a unique organizational form. The following limited accommodations for LLCs seeking § 501(c)(3) tax exemption apply:

   i. An LLC formed under a state LLC law that prohibits the addition of provisions to articles of organization should be deemed to satisfy the organizational test if the LLC's operating agreement includes the four provisions of the Notice provided that the articles of organization and operating agreement do not include any inconsistent provisions.

   ii. An LLC with members that are not § 501(c)(3) organizations ("non-501(c)(3) members") should qualify for § 501(c)(3) status only in limited circumstances, when each of the following conditions are met to the Service's satisfaction:

   a. The laws of the state under which the LLC was formed allow it to have members that are not entitled to a financial interest and its articles of organization or operating agreement (for LLCs formed under state law that prohibits the addition of provisions to articles of organization) prohibit any non-501(c)(3) member from having an equity interest;

   b. The laws of the state under which the entity was formed allow modification of any default statutory fiduciary duties that would be owed by LLC members and managers to non-501(c)(3) members;

   c. The modification of fiduciary duties permits the entity to comply with the operational requirements of § 501(c)(3) status in a legally enforceable manner;

   d. The applicant is otherwise able to satisfy the organizational and operational requirements; and

   e. As required by the Notice (Section 3.03), the applicant represents to the Service in its exemption application under penalty of perjury that all provisions in its articles of organization and operating agreement are consistent with applicable state LLC law and are legally enforceable.

B. With respect to the qualifications for § 501(c)(3) status, LLCs managed by "managers" should generally be treated the same as LLCs managed by "members."

C. In a case where the federal tax law imposes specific requirements with respect to the "governing body" of an organization for purposes of qualifying as an exempt organization described in § 501(c)(3):

    i. For manager-managed LLCs, the manager(s) would comprise the governing body;

    ii. For member-managed LLCs with a single member that is an organization, the governing body of the sole member would be considered the governing body of the LLC; and

    iii. For member-managed LLCs with two or more members that are organizations, the governing body of the LLC would be deemed to meet such requirements only if the governing body of each member of the LLC meets such requirements, and otherwise, the governing body of the LLC would be considered to be the group of members.

D. LLC managers would be presumed to be directors, rather than officers, for federal exempt organization purposes, including for purposes of the compliance provisions of Chapter 42, unless the facts and circumstances clearly indicate that managers instead have the authority or responsibility equivalent to officers, or equivalent to neither officers nor directors.

E. Treasury and the IRS should issue guidance permitting an LLC to seek recognition as, or self-attest to, tax-exempt status under a paragraph of § 501(c) other than § 501(c)(3), so long as the LLC can otherwise satisfy all the existing federal tax law requirements applicable to that status.

iii. **Comments were filed by the Massachusetts Attorney General that may be summarized as follows:**

A. In Massachusetts, most charitable entities that have a corporate (as opposed to a trust) form have been organized pursuant to its nonprofit corporations statute. While there is no prohibition on using the LLC statute to create a charitable entity in Massachusetts, there is no separate statute that governs the creation of nonprofit LLCs.[49.4]

B. The corporate form of a public charity—or the lack thereof—is not determinative of the authority of the Massachusetts Charities Division over that charity's assets and activities. Under Massachusetts

---

[49.4] This can be contrasted with states that have a separate nonprofit LLC statute, like Minnesota; see, for example, Minn. Stat. 322C.1101.

law, a public charity may be a nonprofit corporation, an entity formed under an instrument of trust, and even an unincorporated association. The definition, therefore, includes both "public charities" and "private foundations," as those terms are used by the IRS. It would also include any LLC that has declared charitable purposes, or whose activities are charitable in nature.

C.   Certain provisions that are contained in the Massachusetts nonprofit corporations statute place affirmative obligations on charitable entities formed under that chapter—which is the vast majority of charitable entities operating in Massachusetts—and establish additional, more formal, reporting requirements to the Charities Divisions. The two areas in which this is most notable are:

   i.   With regard to the conveyance (through sale, transfer, or otherwise) of "all or substantially all" of a public charity's assets,[49.5] and

   ii.   With regard to dissolutions of public charities.[49.6]

These provisions are not replicated in the Massachusetts LLC statute. Because of that distinction, the Charities Division could reasonably expect to receive fewer of these formal "life-cycle" types of notices from charitable entities that elect to form under the LLC statute—because they simply are not required by that statute. Those diminished regulatory reporting requirements—without more—may be an incentive for charitable entities to elect to form as an LLC, and gives the Charities Division reason for concern.

CAVEAT

Both classes of formal reporting, conveyance of assets and dissolutions, have significant value to the oversight of charitable assets in Massachusetts. The required reporting of these events helps to buttress the informal communications that the Charities Division receives with regard to even broader categories of fundamental transactions that public charities may be planning to undertake. Through these communications, it can better fulfill its role in seeing to the due application of charitable assets in the Commonwealth.

[49.5] See Massachusetts General Laws ch. 180, §8A. Section 8A(c) addresses the conveyance of all or substantially all of a charitable corporation's assets, coupled with a material change in the nature of its activities; section 8A(d) addresses the conveyance of the assets of an acute-care hospital or HMO to a for-profit entity, and provides the AGO with additional authority in conducting a review of the proposed transaction.

[49.6] See Massachusetts General Laws ch. 180, §11A, which provides for a voluntary dissolution process for charitable corporations.

D. On the issue of dissolution of charitable entities, there are additional layers of concern.

Under the Massachusetts nonprofit corporations statute, there is a very specific process in the statute to accomplish dissolution of a charitable corporation—one that involves judicial review and approval when there are remaining assets in a dissolving charity, and that always includes the Charities Division as a party.[49.7] Under the charities law in Massachusetts, the court will oversee and authorize the transfer of remaining assets to another public charity, under principles of *cy pres* that ensure that charitable assets remain committed to their charitable purposes.

The dissolution provisions of the Massachusetts LLC statute, however, are much more flexible[49.8] and permit a significant degree of autonomy in the members of the LLC to effect a dissolution. There is also no requirement of reporting, because the LLC statute does not specifically address charitable assets. In addition, when considering the even more essential question of where assets are to be distributed upon dissolution, and for what purpose, the LLC statute's provision about distributions to members does not, by itself, go far enough to protect the charitable nature of assets that might be held by an LLC. This is an issue that is of paramount importance to Massachusetts, and likely the IRS, when reviewing determination requests.

E. Under the statutory section on allowable distributions,[49.9] distributions may be made to any members of the LLC, which may include natural persons, "in the manner provided for in the operating agreement" of the LLC.[49.10] This raises two separate issues, one involving potential inurement, and the second involving decreased transparency in charitable oversight.

F. In Massachusetts, under case law, grounded in general principles of charities law, a transfer by a charitable entity of a large part of its assets, without receiving fair market value for those assets, must be presented to the court for review and approval.[49.11] This case law applies without regard to the form of the charity.

[49.7] There is also an administrative dissolution process for charitable corporations with no remaining assets, in which the Charities Division has been granted authority under statute to effect such dissolutions. See Massachusetts General Laws ch. 180, §11A(c).

[49.8] See Massachusetts General Laws ch. 156C, §§ 43, 44, and 70.

[49.9] See Massachusetts General Laws ch. 156C, § 30.

[49.10] The Charities Division requires charitable LLCs to submit their certificate of organization and operating agreement upon registration and any amendments thereto. See Massachusetts General Laws ch. 12, §§ 8E and 8F.

[49.11] See *Massachusetts Charitable Mechanics Association v. Beede*, 320 Mass. 601 (1947).

> **NOTE**
>
> The Charities Division has published guidelines on the requirements established in the *Beede* case,[49.12] including recommendations on when public charities should provide notice of such proposed transfers to the Charities Division.[49.13] Those guidelines indicate that public charities should inform the Charities Division of such transfers. And while *Beede* guidelines do not address directly the issue of dissolution, it is clear that the dissolution of a charitable LLC should require the same informal notice that is contemplated for other transfers of charitable assets, and that transfer of assets upon LLC dissolution will, without question, require notice pursuant to the *Beede* guidelines. But the state LLC statute, because it does not address the operations of charitable entities, does not address any such notice to the Charities Division.

G. In conclusion, the Massachusetts Attorney General recommends that:

    i. The IRS continue to require that any member of a tax-exempt LLC be a § 501(c)(3) organization, governmental unit, or wholly-owned instrumentality of a governmental unit; and

    ii. The IRS notify tax-exempt LLCs that they should consult state law to determine, among other things, whether they (a) have obligations to file operating agreements and other information with state officials and (b) have obligations to notify state officials of any member distribution or intent to dissolve.

iv. **Comments filed by the Deputy Chief of the Charities Bureau, Karen Kunstler Goldman, on behalf of the Office of New York Attorney General, may be summarized as follows:**

A. Responsible management of charitable assets and entities by their fiduciaries is crucial to a strong charitable sector, which, in New York State, constitutes 18 percent of the state's private workforce. New York law grants the Attorney General board responsibility for oversight of organizations that hold charitable assets and/or engage in charitable activities in the state. Charitable LLCs domiciled in other jurisdictions are subject to some of that oversight, including pursuant to the Estates, Powers and Trusts Law ("IPTL"), but are likely not statutorily subject to the same oversight or fiduciary responsibilities as are charitable trusts and charitable corporations formed pursuant to the not-for-profit

---

[49.12] *Massachusetts Charitable Mechanic Association v. Beede*, 320 Mass. 601 (1947).

[49.13] These guidelines can be found at https://www.mass.gov/files/documents/2016/08/pm/beede-memo-.pdf.

corporation law, or foreign corporations and their fiduciaries under section 1319 of the not-for-corporation law.[49.14]

New York limited liability companies are permitted to be organized only for and to engage in "lawful business purposes" under section 201 of the New York Limited Liability Company Law. As set forth in section 102(e) of that law, business "means every trade, occupation, profession or commercial activity" and so would not include an LLC organized for exclusively charitable purposes. As such, the IRS should not recognize § 501(c)(3) status for LLCs domiciled in New York.[49.15]

B. The New York Charities Bureau suggests that the IRS consider requirements that where charitable LLCs are authorized by their domicile jurisdiction, they be required to include in their articles of organization and operating agreements the following provisions:

1. A prohibition on merging with a for-profit entity;

2. A prohibition on transferring any of their assets to a for-profit entity; and

3. A requirement that the charitable LLC give notice to the attorney general of the state of formation of any transaction, litigation, or other circumstance to the extent that such notice is required by the state's laws governing nonprofit organizations.

C. As recognized in the Notice, laws governing charitable LLCs vary from state to state and some states may not regulate them at all. Therefore, the New York Attorney General says that any guidance prepared by the IRS should refer the public and counsel to the need to review applicable state laws when forming and/or applying for tax exemption on behalf of a charitable LLC. Where state law, as in New York, does not authorize creation of an LLC for charitable purposes, the IRS should refuse to authorize § 501(c)(3) eligibility for LLCs domiciled in that jurisdiction.

v. Response by Texas Attorney General may be summarized as follows: Texas law does not have a specific charitable LLC category,

---

[49.14] As referenced by IRS note in 2001 EO CPE text, "Some states (California, Indiana, Iowa, Maryland, Minnesota, New York, North Dakota, Rhode Island, Texas, Utah, and Virginia) and the District of Columbia appear to require that an LLC be formed for a business purpose."
[49.15] *Id.*

and assets held by an LLC are not maintained to the same degree of accountability as assets held by nonprofit charitable corporations.[49.16]

A. A Texas LLC statute is generally written to assume, though not require, that an LLC will be formed for for-profit purposes. The statute contains none of the provisions regarding director liability, prohibition on loans to directors or dividends to members, access to records by the public, disclosure of interested director transactions, or distribution to charitable purposes on dissolution as contained in state statutes governing charitable nonprofit corporations and unincorporated charitable nonprofit associations.

B. Texas is like most states in that it provides that an LLC may be formed for "any lawful purpose." Section 2.001, Texas Business Organizations Code provides that a "domestic entity has any lawful purpose or purposes, unless otherwise provided by this code." No other provision of the code expressly prohibits a Texas LLC from being formed for strictly charitable purposes. Texas law requires distribution of net assets only to LLC members on dissolution (Tex. Bus. Orgs. Code §§ 11.053 and 101.054). It is unclear whether a disclaimer of interests considering these statutory requirements would be effective in satisfying federal law requirements.

The Attorney General of Texas, Financial Litigation Division, also had the following comments:

C. As to transparency/accountability:

   ° A charitable Texas LLC may be less transparent and accountable to the public than either a Texas nonprofit charitable corporation or a Texas unincorporated charitable association, both of which must make basic records available to the public.

   ° A Texas LLC managed by a manager, rather than the members, does not have to identify its members on the certificate of formation filed with the secretary of state. In addition, a Texas LLC is not required to file the company agreement with the secretary of state.

[49.16] Under Texas law, a "[c]haritable entity" means a corporation, trust, community chest, fund, foundation *or other entity* organized for scientific, educational, philanthropic, or environmental purposes, social welfare, the arts and humanities, or another civic or public purpose described by § 501(c)(3) of the Code (Tex. Prop. Code § 123.001(1) (emphasis added). Further, the Texas Uniform Prudent Management of Institutional Funds Act includes a solely charitable LLC in its definition of "institution" for purposes of the requirements for managing charitable funds. Tex. Prop. Code § 163.003.

- A Texas LLC is also not required to make their company agreement or other books and records available to the public. But Texas nonprofit corporations and unincorporated nonprofit organizations are.

- Finally, a Texas LLC is not required to make charitable distributions or file an IRS Form 990 with its tax return. There are also no restrictions for investing in for-profit enterprises as well as charitable or noncharitable causes they support.

D. As to governance/director liability:

- A Texas LLC may be managed by one person, whereas a Texas nonprofit corporation requires a minimum of three directors.

- Loans to a director of a charitable nonprofit corporation are statutorily prohibited, but this rule does not apply to a Texas LLC.

- The fiduciary duties and related liabilities of members, managers, officers, or other persons may be expanded or restricted without limitation, under the company agreement (Tex. Bus. Org. Code, §§ 7.011 and 101.401). In contrast, officers and directors of Texas nonprofit corporations are expected, pursuant to the statute, to act in good faith, with ordinary care in the best interest of the corporation.

E. As to merger/dissolution/fundamental change:

- The Texas Nonprofit Corporation Act, including Chapter 22 of the Business Organizations Code (nonprofit corporations), governs nonprofit corporations and includes specific requirements regarding a decision to wind up, a mandatory distribution plan, limits to distributions on winding up, and other related topics.

- A Texas nonprofit corporation or nonprofit association is also prohibited from merging into another entity if such a merger would cause it to lose or impair its charitable status (Tex. Bus. Orgs. Code, § 10.010).

- However, no such provisions exist for a charitable Texas LLC.

(f) IRS Analysis: The Double-Prong Test and Rev. Rul. 98-15

(vi) United Cancer Council. p. 214. *The citation in footnote 76 should be deleted and replaced with the following:*
109 T.C. 326 (Dec. 2, 1997).

§ 3.4 ALTERNATIVES TO PARTNERSHIPS

(b) Title-Holding Companies

p. 218. *Add the following to the end of footnote 91:*
See subsection 13.6(w)(v) regarding the use of a title-holding company as a QALICB.

§ 3.7 FORMATION OF PARTNERSHIP

(b) Partnership Interest in Exchange for Services

p. 233. *Insert the following at the end of this subsection:*
New § 1061 provides a special rule for taxpayers holding an applicable partnership interest, which generally is a partnership interest transferred to or held by a taxpayer in connection with the performance of substantial services by the taxpayer in any "applicable trade or business," the latter of which encompasses any activity conducted on a regular, continuous, and substantial basis, which consist of (a) raising or returning capital and (b) investing in or developing a range of specified assets consisting of a broad range of financial investments, including securities, commodities, option, derivatives, and cash equivalents as well as real estate held for rent or investment. See § 1061(c)(2), (3). Section 1061 lengthens the holding period for determining long-term capital gain in this context, by imposing a three-year holding period for long-term treatment.

§ 3.8 TAX BASIS IN PARTNERSHIP INTEREST

(a) Loss Limitation

p. 233. *Insert the following at the end of footnote 162:*
The Tax Act added § 704(d)(3) to provide generally that the limitation takes into account the borrower's share of charitable contribution as defined in § 170(c) and foreign taxes described in § 901.

(b) Basis

(ii) Partnership's Basis in Its Assets (Inside Basis). p. 236. *Insert the following as footnote 169.1 to the first sentence of the second paragraph of this subsection:*
[169.1] Proposed regulations (January 2014) provide that, if a partnership has a substantial built-in loss immediately after the transfer of a partnership interest, the partnership is treated as having a § 754 election in effect for the taxable year in which the transfer occurs, but only with respect to that transfer. Prop. Reg. § 1.743-1(k) (1)(iii).

(c) Liabilities and Economic Risk of Loss

p. 239. *Insert the following as footnote 171.1 at the end of the first full paragraph on this page:*

[171.1] Proposed regulations would overhaul this safe harbor by permitting partners to specify their interests in partnership profits only if those interests are based on the partners' "liquidation value percentages." A partner's liquidation value percentage is determined under a "liquidation value test," which looks to the amount a partner would be entitled to receive if all of the partnership property were sold for fair market value and each partner received his or her proportionate share of the proceeds. Once that amount is determined for each partner, the figure is converted to a percentage by dividing the liquidation value to be received by each partner by the combined liquidation value to be received by all partners.

p. 240. *Add the following to the end of footnote 182:*

Due to the IRS's concern that "some partners or related persons have entered into payment obligations that are not commercial solely to achieve an allocation of a partnership liability to such partner," on January 30, 2014, the IRS proposed new regulations under § 752, Notice of Proposed Rulemaking, REG-119305, 2014-9 I.R.B. 524, 523. The proposed regulations eliminate the presumption that partners will be called upon to satisfy their contractual payment obligations. Instead payment obligations will be respected for § 752 purposes only if the partner satisfies a host of conditions, which include maintenance of reasonable net worth, commercially reasonable documentation, and reasonable arm's-length considerations, inter alia. Prop. Reg. § 1.752-2(b)(3)(ii).

§ 3.9 PARTNERSHIP OPERATIONS

(d) Transactions between Partner and Partnership.

(i) Payments to Partner Acting in Capacity as Nonpartner. p. 246. *Insert the following to the end of footnote 206:*

See subsection 16.7(e).

(ii) Sale of Property between Partnership and Related Party. p. 248. *Insert the following at the end of the second full paragraph on this page:* Moreover, the transfer of tax credits in exchange for capital contribution may also be treated as a disguised sale.[215.1]

p. 249. *Add the following to the end of footnote 217:*

In July 2015, the IRS issued proposed regulations under § 707 to provide guidance on when certain partnership arrangements should be treated as disguised payments for services rather than distributive shares of partnership income. Generally, the proposed regulations apply a "facts and circumstances" test to determine whether certain transactions are disguised payments for services. Prop. Reg. § 1.707-2. It appears that the most important factor is whether the arrangement lacks significant entrepreneurial risk to the service provider relative to the overall entrepreneurial risk of the partnership at the time the parties enter into or modify the arrangement. Prop. Reg. § 1.707-2(c).

[215.1] *231 LLC v. Commissioner*, No. 14-1983 (4th Cir. 2016). The appellate court found that a transfer of state tax credits to a partner who had contributed $3.8 million to the partnership was a disguised sale requiring the partnership to recognize income from the transfer.

§ 3.10 PARTNERSHIP DISTRIBUTIONS TO PARTNERS

p. 251. *Insert the following new paragraph after the first full paragraph on the page:*

The term "waterfall" is often used relative to the distribution section in partnership agreements and limited liability company agreements to define the manner in which distributions flow from the investment to the limited partners/members, and dictate the terms of the sponsor's incentive fee or carried interest. Agreements also frequently include "claw back" provisions that may come into effect when subsequent circumstances are inconsistent with the prior distributions. There are many different structures and variations for defining waterfalls and claw backs, each leading to different economic consequences for limited partners/members. The partners need to understand how these mechanisms work, as an unfavorable waterfall can tilt risk toward the limited partners/nonmanaging members, including exempt organizations. Variations in the structure can alter the economic results and can impact the overall economic deal.

§ 3.11 SALE OR OTHER DISPOSITION OF ASSETS OR INTERESTS

(c) Termination of the Partnership

p. 258. *Insert the following at the end of the subsection:*

The Tax Act eliminates the "technical termination" under former § 708(b)(1). In effect, the partnership will no longer be terminated by the sale of a partnership interest, assuming the entity continues to have more than one partner.

(d) Liquidating Distributions

p. 259. *Insert the following as footnote 261.1 at the end of the first full paragraph on this page:*

[261.1] Proposed regulations (January 2014) provide that, if a liquidating distribution results in a substantial basis reduction (greater than $250,000), the partnership is treated as having an election under § 754 in effect for the year in which the distribution occurs, but only with respect to the distribution to which the substantial basis reduction relates. Prop. Reg. § 1.734-1(a)(2).

(f) Application of Bargain Sale Technique to "Burned Out" Shelters

p. 260. *Insert the following as footnote 266.1 at the end of the second sentence in the first paragraph of this subsection:*

[266.1] See discussion regarding contributions of LLC partnership interest to charities in subsection 2.11(f).

§ 3.12   OTHER TAX ISSUES

(c)   Passive Activity Loss Rules

p. 269. *Insert the following at the end of the subsection:*
The Tax Act added new § 461(l), which disallows a current deduction for "excess business losses" of individuals who are noncorporate taxpayers. This limitation applies after the application of the passive activity loss rules of § 469 and applies to partners who materially participate in a business activity that operates at a loss. The limitation applies at the partner level, to the partner's distributive share of all tax items from trades or businesses attributable to the entity. See § 461(l)(4). However, any disallowed excess business loss may be carried forward and treated as part of the taxpayer's net operating loss carryforward in subsequent years, subject to the new rule allowing NOLs up to 80 percent of taxable income for losses arising in taxable years beginning after December 31, 2017.

(f)   Unified Audits and Adjustments

p. 272. *Insert the following at the end of this subsection:*
New Partnership Audit Rules.[319.1] The new Bipartisan Budget Act of 2015 repealed the current TEFRA unified partnership and electing large partnership (ELP) rules with a new streamlined audit approach, the effect of which is that adjustments of income, gain, loss, deduction, or credit determined at the partnership level and the taxes attributable thereto will be assessed and collected at the partnership level. The new law is effective for taxable years beginning after January 1, 2018; however, small partnerships may opt out, and any partnership may elect to apply the new law before such date.

CAVEAT

There are two critical definitions: (a) "Reviewed Year," which relates to partnership items of income, gain, loss, deductions, or credit and a partner's distributive share for a particular year under audit, and (b) "Adjustment Year," which is the year in which the adjustments are taken into account by the partnership (i.e., when the audit or any judicial review is completed).

[319.1]The author acknowledges contribution to this subsection of the materials prepared by Marks, Paneth, written by Mark Baran, Principal Tax, a copy of which is on file with the author.

The final regulations, which were published in February 2019, provide that a partnership will not be eligible to elect out of the new partnership regime if it has a partner that is itself a partnership or disregarded entity, such as a disregarded single-member LLC or grantor trust.[319.2]

CAVEAT

A partnership that is interested in electing out of the Bipartisan Budget Act ("BBA") rules and is eligible to make this election may want to consider restricting the number, type of partners, and the ability of the partners to change their tax status.

The partnership may also have to substantiate the tax status of the partners, including shareholders that are S Corporations, to make this election.

CAVEAT

The IRS decided not to expand the definition of eligible partners to include persons or entities other than those listed in the statute, even though it has received numerous comments requesting it to exercise its discretionary authority to do so. As a result, an eligible partner does not include partnerships, trusts, disregarded entities, nominees, or other similar persons that hold an interest on behalf of another person, foreign entities that are not eligible foreign entities, and estates that are not estates of a deceased partner.

In order to elect out of the partnership audit regime for a particular tax year, the partnership must make the election on a timely filed partnership return (including extensions) for the tax year in which the election relates. In addition, the partnership must provide:

- Name
- Taxpayer Identification Number
- Federal Tax Classification for each partner and shareholder of the partner that is an S Corp

In addition, a partnership that is electing out of the regime must notify each of its partners of the election within 30 days thereof.

The IRS will need to make assessments against all of the partners in a separate partner-level proceeding if a partnership elects out of the BBA rules. Thus, if a partnership makes the election out, its partners should confirm that they will have sufficient access to the partnership's books and

---

[319.2] All eligible foreign partners, even those with no U.S. filing requirements, must apply for and obtain a valid U.S. TIN for the partnership to file a valid election out of the new budget act rules.

records in order to substantiate the amounts allocated by the partnership in an IRS audit, as stated above. A more crucial aspect is the fact that if a partnership makes a valid election out, the applicable statute of limitations of assessment of tax will be determined at the partner level and is further determined separately for each partner.

(i) Partnership Representative It is important for the parties to select a "partnership representative"; the individual does not need to be a partner but, if so, should not have a potential conflict, which may arise if the partner's interest is changed from one year to the next. The partnership representative will be able to make an election as to which partners will be taxed on any adjustments for a given taxable year if it is in the best interest of the partnership relative to the reviewed year.

CAVEAT

It is important to note that the partnership representative now has the absolute right to bind the partnership in any settlement or audit.

CAVEAT

It is critical when an exempt organization is involved in a joint venture structure that these provisions be carefully reviewed and that the exempt organization consider placing one of its officers (e.g., CEO, CFO) as the "partnership representative" to protect the rights of the exempt organization from the tax standpoint.

CAVEAT

The tax deficiency relative to a partnership level of adjustment will be calculated using the maximum statutory income rate and assessed and collected from the partnership in the year that the audit is completed plus any related penalties and interest; but the partnership's imputed underpayment may be reduced if the partners file amended returns, if they pay any tax due for the audited year, or if the partnership shows that the items are allocable to partners, or are not subject to tax, such as a tax-exempt entity, or are taxed at a reduced corporate or capital gains rate.

EXAMPLE

XYZ Partnership has 50 partners in the 2013 tax year (the reviewed year). In 2015, A and B join the partnership while 13 partners withdraw. On March 1, 2016, the IRS proposes a $10 million adjustment to XYZ Partnership's 2013 tax return. On March 21, 2018, the "partnership representative" negotiates a settlement with the IRS and makes an election to have the adjustment made at the partner level in 2013, the reviewed year. XYZ Partnership needs to furnish adjusted Schedule K-1s to each partner who was a partner in the reviewed year, even if the person is no longer a partner in the adjustment year. The partners are obligated to file amended returns for the reviewed year, in this case 2013. They will be responsible for paying their respective shares of the net adjustment agreed to by the partnership representative in 2018.

CAVEAT

The changes in the Budget Act will require partnerships to consider the impact of the new law on existing agreements and transactions, as well as perform due diligence of partnerships before moving forward in a particular transaction. It requires review of existing agreements when a new partner anticipates joining the entity.

CAVEAT

It is now important to focus on the drafting of contractual provisions as to which partners (including exempt organizations) will be responsible for tax obligations in the partnership context, during initial formation, or subsequent thereto. The IRS will be issuing interpretative guidance as well as new forms, which will lead to additional administration.

It is important to emphasize that the current partners in a partnership could bear economic responsibility for improper tax reporting in prior years. Negotiations are necessary to determine how the partnership will elect to pay the tax due. In addition, the IRS needs to provide guidance on how multitiered partnership structures will be handled in the future.

The partnership representative serves in a similar role as the tax matters partner under TEFRA in that the partnership representative has the sole authority to act on behalf of the partnership; however, there are two important differences between the tax matters partner and the partnership representative. First, whereas the tax matters partner must be a general partner and may be an individual or an entity, the partnership representative can be any person or entity, including a nonpartner, so long as the partnership representative has a substantial presence in the United States. A substantial U.S. presence is required so that the partnership representative is available to communicate with the IRS during an audit.

It should be noted that a partnership may elect out of the new rules if it meets the following criteria:

- All partners are individuals, estates of a deceased partner, S corporations, or C corporations (or foreign entities taxed in the United States as a C corporation), including nonprofits organized as corporations.
- It is not required to issue more than 100 Schedule K-1s.
  - Note: If a partnership furnishes more K-1s than are actually required by § 6031(b), then these additional K-1s are not taken into account when determining whether this criterion is met.
- The election is made on a timely filed partnership return (including extensions) for that taxable year.

If a partnership elects out of the new rules, it must notify each of its partners that it made the election within 30 days of making the election (i.e., within 30 days of submitting the tax return).

CAVEAT

The default rule under the centralized partnership audit regime is that partnership adjustments (the imputed underpayment) are made at the partnership level, and the underpayment must be paid by the partnership; however, the partnership representative may make a "push out" election; that is, the partnership representative may elect to have the partners in the partnership for the reviewed year pay any tax and penalties due as a result of the imputed underpayment.

CHAPTER 4

Overview: Joint Ventures Involving Exempt Organizations

§ 4.1 INTRODUCTION

p. 294. *Insert the following at the end of this section:*

The use of joint ventures by charities is becoming critical in view of the recent tax legislation:

- Reduction in tax rates, especially C corp rates to 21 percent (permanent). C corps have been the largest investor in low-income housing tax credits and new market tax credits.
- Increase in standard deduction and reduction in individual rates.
- Significant estate tax relief through doubling of exemption.
- Estimated $1.45 trillion cost for the 10-year period of tax reform.
- Limit on or elimination of certain itemized deductions.
- All of which will affect charitable giving and therefore make joint ventures even more attractive as a fundraising device.

However, the 2017 Tax Act (Pub. L. No. 115-97) has retained the low-income housing tax credit, and the new market tax credit was not repealed.

QUERY
With corporate tax rates being reduced to 21 percent, will there be less interest by C corps in investing in low-income housing tax credit or new market tax credits? However, the creation of the opportunity zone funds could attract substantial investment in qualified census tracts. See Section 13.11.

Moreover, charities are likely to receive even less support from budget-constrained governmental agencies and contributions from the private sector. As a result of so many natural disasters, charities have needed to develop new avenues and structures to attract partners to conduct their programs. Not often enough, nonprofits have joined forces to accomplish fundraising or program-related goals. Increasingly, nonprofits of all sorts are forging partnerships and other co-investment relationships with for-profit entities to access otherwise unavailable capabilities, capital, and resources.

§ 4.2 EXEMPT ORGANIZATION AS GENERAL PARTNER: A HISTORICAL PERSPECTIVE

(d)   The Two-Prong Test: IRS Adopts *Plumstead Theatre* Doctrine

(ii) Application of the Two-Prong Analysis. p. 309. *Insert the following at the end of footnote 76:*

Low-income housing project, which was run by LLC and whose activities would be attributed to EO/private foundation, met Rev. Proc. 96-32, 1996-1 CB 717 safe harbor requirements and would continue to do so after EO's acquisition of all LLC membership interests, where activities furthered its Code § 501(c)(3) charitable purpose of providing affordable housing for those of low and moderate income. PLR 201603032, January 15, 2016.

(h)   A Road Map

p. 350. *Insert the following after the first full paragraph of this subsection:*

In order to overcome certain negotiating challenges, it is important for counsel of the charity to educate the for-profit organization's representatives regarding structural issues, control factors, bond covenants, and private benefit limitations. This is because often the for-profit counsel is not knowledgeable as to the reasons why the tax-exempt organization is required to structure a transaction to meet the IRS guidelines under Rev. Ruls. 98-15 and 2004-51 and the case law, including St. David's regarding the "control" factors. Understanding the significance of these relevant factors will facilitate negotiations and the structuring of the venture.

(ii) Unfavorable Factors. p. 357. *Insert the following before the Note:*

It is critical for the tax-exempt organization to negotiate an exit strategy at the initial phase in the structuring of the transaction so that there isn't impermissible private benefit at the back end in the event that the nonprofit board determines that the transaction has failed and it needs to unwind. Accordingly, language should be provided to allow for reasonable and comparable terms as to an "exit strategy" option, which needs to be retained by the charity.

	Caveat
Flexibility will also be required even if it is important to "pivot" to "nonexempt" purposes in order to avoid financial losses or pursue greater financial returns depending upon how the project develops. Thus, the exempt organization needs to retain the right to trigger an unwind of the original transaction, especially if it doesn't fulfill its mission or it generates UBIT.	

The mechanics of the unwind and the term need to be set out in the operating agreement. It would include the potential use of a third-party appraisal to validate costs of the unwind, a period during which the unwind can be initiated, say at least five years, along with indemnification provisions and virtual releases. Finally, the charity should retain a power to initiate and expand exempt activities, including mediation or even binding arbitration as part of the exit strategy.

p. 357. *Insert the following after the Note:*

Recent IRS PLR 201744019. A general acute care hospital was founded as a community hospital; it was operated by a § 501(c)(3) hospital system when it applied for tax exemption. Years later, management of the hospital was turned over to a for-profit organization. The agreement with the for-profit required the hospital to provide charity care as previously rendered with no enforcement mechanism. The hospital reported changes on Form 990 annually but did not seek a ruling that its operations continued to be consistent with 501(c)(3) purposes.

On analysis of the relationship between the 501(c)(3) hospital and the for-profit entity using the control criteria of Rev. Rul. 98-15 and similar precedents, the IRS determined that the hospital was not operated exclusively for 501(c)(3) purposes because it allowed a for-profit organization to have complete "control" over its operations and did not "exercise adequate discretion and control as required by IRC 501(c)(3)." This language implies that the control criteria of Rev. Rul. 98-15 is embedded in IRC 501(c)(3) as if it were in the regulations or statute itself.

The IRS also ruled that although the 501(c)(3) provided information on its Forms 990 and did not omit or misstate a material fact, it operated in a manner "materially" different from that which was originally represented in its application. The organization "did not formally notify the Service of the changes in activities, nor did it seek an affirmation letter or private letter ruling to confirm that it continued to qualify for exemption."

In other words, the Form 990 disclosure was not enough.

The PLR confirms that:

1. Rev. Proc. 98-15 is alive and well;
2. It is a facts and circumstances determination; and

3. The 990 disclosure of operational changes does not mean that the IRS has sanctioned any changes. If an organization doesn't seek a ruling regarding continued exemption, any prior Form 990 disclosure is insufficient.

We therefore now have to inform our clients not only about the importance of Form 990 disclosure and evaluate whether—and at what point in time—they should apply for a ruling as to continued exemption.

§ 4.6 REVENUE RULING 2004-51 AND ANCILLARY JOINT VENTURES

(c) Factual Scenarios 1 through 4: Joint Venture Is a "Substantially Related" Charitable Activity (See Exhibit 4.1)

3. Scenario 3: p. 380. *Insert the following footnote at the end of this scenario:*
    [228.1] See subsections 6.5(a) and 10.4(a).

§ 4.9 CONVERSIONS FROM EXEMPT TO FOR-PROFIT AND FROM FOR-PROFIT TO EXEMPT ENTITIES

p. 397. *Insert the following footnote at the end of the last paragraph on this page:*
    [282] See subsection 2.10(c), Strategies in the Event of a Proposed Revocation of § 501(c)(3) Status, for a discussion of procedures involving conversions from one provision of § 501(c) to another after revocation of exemption on conclusion of an audit.

p. 397. *Insert the following new section after Section 4.9:*

§ 4.10 ANALYSIS OF A VIRTUAL JOINT VENTURE

In view of the extensive reach of the IRS published Rev. Rul. 2004-51 as applicable to ancillary joint ventures, this commentator believes that the rationale should apply in a case in which the IRS proposes revocation of an existing § 501(c)(3) organization, alleging impermissible private benefit following an examination of its relationship with a for-profit entity (notwithstanding the fact that no formal joint venture agreement exists between the parties).

Assume a hypothetical case in which an educational or scientific property, such as a magazine or journal, is owned 100 percent by FP, a for-profit business. This magazine attracts and retains members to C, the charity, which provides high-quality educational content related to its charitable goals, including reports of the research supported by FP. FP attracts customers to its business through educational articles and related product placement. The board of C collaborates with FP regarding the educational content of the magazine and oversees the research—in effect, an unconventional "upside down" transaction.

Assume further that the IRS challenges the relationship of the charity and for-profit organization, arguing that there is impermissible private benefit to the FP's business—in effect, that C is operating for substantial nonexempt purpose (i.e., it is acting as a "tool" to enhance the sale of products for FP). This is so notwithstanding the fact that FP provides significant services and pays all expenses related to the production of the monthly periodical and its health products aid C's members in its charitable mission. The educational articles discussing the health benefits of its products, many of which are cutting edge and difficult to find, are followed by product information providing readers with the information necessary to be able to purchase the products for their own use. Some of the advertisements, in essence, produce a summary of the educational article that immediately precedes each advertisement. The advertisements also provide a method for the reader to fulfill C's purpose of helping readers and members extend healthy human life spans.

Even though the magazine is funded and published by FP, the IRS has alleged that the activities of FP in promoting its products in the magazine justify revocation of C's exempt status. Even if the magazine and its advertisements of products are imputed to C, those activities are substantially related to C's exempt purpose, and thus it can be argued, in reliance on Rev. Rul. 2004-51, that there is no justification for revocation. C is operated solely for the exempt purpose of funding scientific research and extending the healthy human life span.

Amounts paid by FP to C are structured to be "reasonable" as determined by independent parties (e.g., royalties, analogous to the facts in Situation 1 of Rev. Rul. 98-15, where management contract fees were deemed reasonable). Royalties are paid by FP to C to be used exclusively to fund research and education.

C retains ownership and control of its name, logo, trademarks, related goodwill, and assets, the use of which are crucial to FP activities; this is analogous to the university retaining ownership of the course curricula and materials in Rev. Rul. 2004-51.

FP donates administrative, accounting, legal, and fundraising information technology to C and performs all marketing functions and sales, analogous to the for-profit partner in Rev. Rul. 2004-51 who handled the administrative/business functions of the venture.

Although there is no formal joint venture structure, C, the § 501(c)(3) organization, should be able to rely on the "bifurcated" control test pursuant to Rev. Rul. 2004-51. This is so even though there is no provision in any agreement dealing with the distribution of net proceeds, but, in fact, substantial royalties are paid by FP to fund C's educational scientific research.

CHAPTER 5

Private Benefit, Private Inurement, and Excess Benefit Transactions

§ 5.1   WHAT ARE PRIVATE INUREMENT AND PRIVATE BENEFIT?

(a)   Introduction

p. 409. *Delete of the Internal Revenue Service Code ("the Code"), Internal Revenue Service, and the parentheses around IRS in the first paragraph.*

p. 411. *Insert the following after the first paragraph on this page:*

In 2019 there were some major news stories involving tax-exempt organizations. One involved the National Rifle Association, an IRC § 501(c)(4) organization, and its related foundation, an IRC § 501(c)(3) organization. Reported allegations include claims that the NRA's CEO, Wayne LaPierre, spent approximately $274,000 over a 13-year period on clothing purchased from designer boutiques through an arrangement with the NRA's advertising agency, Ackerman McQueen, and that he also charged alleged lavish vacations through a credit card from the agency, which he then submitted for reimbursement from the NRA. In addition, there are claims that the NRA made $185,000 in undisclosed donations to a charity run by Mr. LaPierre's wife, whose exempt purposes are unrelated to the NRA's mission.

In addition, accusations of impropriety were made in regard to the relationship between the NRA Foundation, which is controlled by the NRA board, and the NRA. Even though a charity may be controlled by an IRC § 501(c)(4) organization, as is the case here, there are strict rules governing transfers of money or other assets from a charity to a related IRC § 501(c)(4) organization, as charities must devote their assets and revenue toward charitable purposes. Published stories allege that the NRA Foundation made millions of dollars of purchases from a shooting supply company that is controlled by a former NRA director and president, which could be deemed improper inurement or private benefit to an insider. (See subsection 5.1(b).) In 2017, the NRA Foundation purchased $3.1 million of ammunition and other supplies from this entity, which it later donated to local shooting groups.[8.1] In addition, since 2012, the NRA Foundation has reportedly transferred more than $100 million to the NRA and allegedly lent the NRA $5 million in 2017.[8.2]

CAVEAT

"Scandal" was a term also used in connection with the University of Maryland Medical System (UMMS) and the former mayor of Baltimore, who wrote and self-published a series of children's books called "Healthy Holly." While serving on the board of UMMS, Mayor Catherine Pugh sold UMMS 100,000 Healthy Holly books over a number of years for $500,000. It is reported that the mayor did not fully disclose this income, some of which UMMS had apparently labeled as grants. During the time of these sales, UMMS was seeking a $48 million contract to provide health benefits to Baltimore city employees. The mayor resigned from the board and as mayor.

News stories regarding the so-called "Healthy Holly" matter resulted in an audit of UMMS, which, in turn, led to numerous board resignations following disclosure of self-dealing among board members and officers whose businesses benefited from contracts with UMMS. The hospital network has reportedly adopted a new conflict of interest policy that bars it from granting sole-source contracts to board members or their businesses, and precludes it from having any business with certain board leaders. Under new legislation, all board members must submit their resignations by year-end; the Governor has said he does not expect to reappoint "many—if any."[8.3]

[8.1]See generally Mark Maremont, "NRA Awarded Contracts to Firms with Ties to Top Officials," *Wall Street Journal* (Nov. 30, 2018), https://www.wsj.com/articles/nra-awarded-contracts-to-firms-with-ties-to-top-officials-1543590697 (describing previously unreported financial arrangements with consultants and third-party contractors).

[8.2]Danny Hakim, "N.R.A. President to Step Down as New York Attorney General Investigates," *New York Times* (Apr. 27, 2019), https://www.nytimes.com/2019/04/27/us/oliver-north-nra.html.

[8.3]http://www.baltimoresun.com/maryland/baltimore-city/bs-md-kelly-profile-20190329-story.html; http://www.baltimoresun.com/politics/bs-md-umms-resignations-20190606-story.html.

(b) Private Inurement and "Insiders"

p. 412. *Delete* **in this case** *on line 5 in the first paragraph of this subsection.*

(c) Distinction between Private Benefit and Private Inurement

p. 416. *Insert the following after the first sentence in footnote 28:*
Private inurement is a subset of private benefit. See PLR 201044025.

p. 417. *Delete the first citation in footnote 36 and replace it with the following:*
Kentucky Bar Foundation, 78 T.C. at 923.

p. 418. *Insert quotation marks around* **DLC** *in footnote 40.*

p. 419. *Insert quotation marks around* **NRCC** *in the first paragraph on this page.*

§ 5.2 TRANSACTIONS IN WHICH PRIVATE BENEFIT OR INUREMENT MAY OCCUR

(a) Compensation for Services

(i) Introduction. p. 425. *Insert the following at the end of footnote 66:*
The IRS's official position is that nonprofit governance guidance is best reflected in the reporting requirements contained in the revised Form 990. However, many of the good governance principles contained in this publication continue to apply.

p. 426. *Insert the following before the first full paragraph on this page:*

CAVEAT

A public charity, even if complying with the letter of § 501(c)(3), must always consider the spirit of § 501(c)(3) and how its fundraising and spending will appear to the general public. Most recently, the Wounded Warrior Project ("Wounded Warrior"), a charity organized to support veterans of military actions after September 11, 2001, has drawn the attention of media outlets and the ire of Senator Charles Grassley.

In 2016, the *New York Times* reported that Wounded Warrior was spending lavishly on staff retreats, travel, and lodging, with nearly 40 percent of contributions spent on overhead.[69.1] Although this percentage is not as high as some tax-exempt organizations, other veterans services organizations spend approximately 8 percent of their contributions on overhead.[69.2] As a result of the article, Senator Grassley sent a letter to Wounded Warrior

---

[69.1]Dave Phillips, "Wounded Warrior Project Spends Lavishly on Itself, Insiders Say," *New York Times,* Jan. 27, 2016.
[69.2]*Id.*

> requesting "an account of spending not listed on tax forms, including expenses for travel and meetings as well as public relations,"[69.3] among other things. Although Wounded Warrior is not under any legal obligation to respond, there is the risk of additional bad press if it does not. Moreover, other nonprofits, such as the Red Cross and the Nature Conservancy, have responded to Senator Grassley's requests for similar information in the past.

p. 427. *Delete the language in footnote 75 and replace it with the following:*
Russ Buettner, "State Seeks Date on Pay of Leaders at Nonprofits," *New York Times*, Aug. 11, 2011.

(c) Joint Ventures with Commercial Entities

p. 435. *Delete* United Cancer Council *and the parentheses around* UCC *and insert quotation marks around* W&H *in the fourth full paragraph on this page.*

(e) Asset Sales to Insiders

p. 439. *In the third paragraph on this page, insert quotation marks around* APC *in parentheses.*

p. 440. *Delete* private letter ruling *and the parentheses around* PLR *on line 8 on this page. In the first full paragraph, insert quotation marks around* AMH.

(f) Valuation of New-Economy and Internet Companies

p. 442. *In the first full paragraph on this page, insert quotation marks around* IPO.

(ii) Income-Based Approaches—Discounted Cash Flow. p. 444. *In the first paragraph, insert quotation marks around* DCF; *in the second paragraph, insert quotation marks around* EBITDA *and* EBIT.

p. 445. *In the first paragraph on this page, insert quotation marks around* NOPAT, NOPLAT, *and* EVA.

p. 447. *In the second* Caveat, *first sentence, insert quotation marks around* CAPM.

(iii) Other Earnings-Based Valuation Methods. p. 448. *In the first sentence of this subsection, insert quotation marks around* EPS.

(vi) Market Value-Based Approach. p. 451. *In the first sentence of this subsection, insert quotation marks around* M&A.

[69.3]Dave Phillips, "Senator Wants Data on Wounded Warrior Project, a Charity under Fire," *New York Times*, Mar. 18, 2016.

(g) § 501(c)(3) Bonds

p. 454. *In the first paragraph on this page, insert quotation marks around* EP/EO.

§ 5.3 PROFIT-MAKING ACTIVITIES AS INDICIA OF NONEXEMPT PURPOSE

(a) Operations for Profit

p. 456. *In the second paragraph, insert quotation marks around* UBIT.

§ 5.4 INTERMEDIATE SANCTIONS (REVISED)

p. 460. *Delete the last citation in footnote 183 and replace with the following:*
21 The Exempt Org. Tax Rev. 287, 291 (1998).

p. 460. *Insert footnote 186.1 after* **Decision 9390,** *on the second line of the last paragraph on this page:*
186.1 T.D. 9390, 2008-18 I.R.B. 855.

p. 461. *Insert the following paragraph before subparagraph (a):*
Most Chapter 42 taxes may be abated.[188.1] If the foundation is able to establish that (1) the event that caused the tax to be imposed was due to reasonable cause and not willful neglect and (2) the event was corrected, then the tax may be abated;[188.2] however, whether a tax will be abated is completely up to the discretion of the IRS. The mere fact that a foundation relied on the advice of its counsel will not be enough, on its own, to establish that the taxable event was due to reasonable cause.[188.3]

(c) Compensation

p. 470. *Insert, as footnote 223.1, at the end of the first paragraph of this subsection:*
223.1 In specific reference to this issue, the 2017 Tax Law added § 4960, an excise tax on tax-exempt organization excess compensation. See subsection 2.1(1)(F) for a discussion of this new tax.

p. 473. *Insert the following at the end of this section and before subparagraph (i):*
In January 2022, the Chairman of the House Ways and Means Committee on Oversight expanded the probe of the Committee into college

---

[188.1]See § 4962.
[188.2]See § 4962(a).
[188.3]See TAM 201503019 (Jan. 16, 2015).

coaching contracts with a statement that "recent reports about compensation that [your school] will pay its football coaches have raised significant concerns about whether the University is operating consistent with its exempt status." In this regard, letters were written to the presidents of Michigan State University and the University of Miami, stating that it was unclear how such lucrative compensation contracts contributed to the overall educational mission and benefited the student body as a whole. There was specific reference to Michigan State's extension, which will pay coach Mel Tucker $95 million over 10 years, and coach Mario Cristobal, who is being paid $89 million by the University of Miami.

NOTE

The letters raised numerous questions about the compensation package that was paid in the men's football and basketball programs, raising specifically the question as to why the federal government should subsidize the University's athletic programs and escalating coaches' salaries and other noncash benefits. It also questioned the increasing "commercialism" of the university's football and basketball programs; how does the university distinguish its activities from professional sport teams? See, in this regard, the new subsection on NILs in Chapter 14.

Specific questions were raised about the revenue and expenses of the athletic department and the governance of the athletic departments and facilities.

Statistical information garnered from Forms 990 reveal that executive pay at nonprofits is rising, paralleling the trend at for-profits. According to analysis of IRS data of 100,000 tax-exempts from 2014, approximately 2,700 employees of organizations classified as charities earned at least $1 million or more in that year.[237.1] The analysis also revealed an increase in bonus and deferred compensation arrangements similar to those in the for-profit sector and that approximately three-quarters of the charities that provided compensation packages in the million-dollar range were "involved in health care."[237.2] What is not known is the impact of the rebuttable presumption safe harbor on the rise—that is, is the safe harbor of Treas. Reg. § 4958-6 facilitating the ability of nonprofits to pay higher compensation?

[237.1]"Charity Officials Are Increasingly Receiving Million-Dollar Paydays," *Wall Street Journal*, Jan. 6, 2017, https://www.wsj.com/articles/charity-officials-are-increasingly-receiving-million-dollar-paydays-1488754532.
[237.2]*Id.*

1. 2019 Interim Guidance[237.3]

Under section 4960, in tax years beginning after 2017, an employer[237.4] is liable for an excise tax equal to the product of the rate of tax under section 11 [currently 21 percent], and the sum of (1) so much of the remuneration paid (other than any excess parachute payments) by an applicable tax-exempt organization (ATEO) for the taxable year[237.5] with respect to employment of any covered employee in excess of $1,000,000, plus (2) any excess parachute payment paid by such an organization to any covered employee.[237.6]

Section 4960(c)(1) defines an ATEO as any organization that is exempt from taxation under § 501(a)[237.7] or has income excluded from taxation under § 115(1).[237.8] Moreover, § 4960(c)(4)(A) provides that

---

[237.3]The author acknowledges the excellent analysis of section 4960 prepared by Isak Khorets. This material is based on a paper submitted by Mr. Khorets in the graduate tax program at Georgetown University Law Center, entitled "If an Employee Looks Like a Volunteer and Acts Like a Volunteer, Is the Employee a 'Bona Fide Volunteer'?" (Apr. 23, 2019), a copy of which is on file with the author.

[237.4]See Interim Guidance IRS Notice 2019-09, at 5 (providing that the "common-law employer, as determined generally for federal tax purposes, is liable for the excise tax" and that a payment to an employee on behalf of the common-law employer, such as a payment from a related ATEO, "is considered paid by the common-law employer for purposes of section 4960").

[237.5]237.5 See id. (stating that because section 4960(a)(1) refers to a remuneration paid "for the taxable year, but does not specify which taxpayer's taxable year is used, the remuneration to be paid 'for' a taxable year, or how to measure remuneration if an ATEO and a related organization have different taxable years," the report provided that "the excise tax imposed on excess remuneration . . . is determined based on remuneration paid . . . in the calendar year ending with or within the taxable year of the employer").

[237.6]See American Benefits Council Comment Letter, *supra* note 2 (pointing out that "it is not clear from this provision whether remuneration includes (1) any remuneration paid by any related person or governmental entity with respect to the employee's employment by the ATEO, or (2) any remuneration paid by any related person or governmental entity *with respect to the employee's employment by the related person or governmental entity*") (emphasis added).

[237.7]See generally IRC § 501(a) (2019). Organizations exempt under § 501(a) include § 501(c)(3) organizations, such as religious, charitable, and educational organizations, § 501(c)(4) organizations, such as social welfare organizations, or § 501(c)(6) organizations, such as business leagues. See generally *id.* Also, the J.C. Rep. clarifies that a governmental entity that has a determination letter recognizing its tax-exempt status under § 501(c)(3) "may relinquish this status pursuant to the procedures described in section 3.01(12) of Rev. Proc. 2018-5, 2018-1 I.R.B. 233, 239." J.C. Rep., *supra* note, at 6.

[237.8]See generally IRC § 115(1) (2019). Section 115(1) generally exempts "income derived from any public utility or the exercise of any essential governmental function and accruing to a State or any political subdivision thereof . . ." *Id.* With this, the IRS has held that a state university is not a "political subdivision" under § 115(1) because a state university lacks the power to tax, the power of eminent domain, or traditional state police powers (Rev. Rul. 77-165, 1977-1 CB 21). Therefore, the IRS concluded that a state university's income is not exempt from federal income under § 115(1). See *id.* However, state universities' income has been exempted from taxation because of the doctrine of intergovernmental immunity. See Rev. Rul. 87-2, 1987-1 CB 18. The doctrine states that unless Congress specifically enacts legislation that overrides intergovernmental immunity, the federal government will not impose taxes on state universities, despite possessing the power to do so. See IRC § 511(a)(2)(B) ("Without this express directive, the unrelated business income of a state college would be exempt from federal income tax under the doctrine of intergovernmental immunity."). Therefore, a state university that relies on the doctrine of intergovernmental immunity rather than § 501(a) will not be subject to the excise tax imposed by § 4960.

remuneration paid to a covered employee by an ATEO includes any "remuneration paid with respect to employment of the employee by any related person or governmental entity."[237.9]

Further, under § 4960, a covered employee is "any employee (including any former employee) of an [ATEO] if the employee: (A) is one of the five highest compensated employees of the organization for the taxable year, or (B) was a covered employee of the organization (or any predecessor) for any preceding taxable year beginning after December 31, 2016."[237.10]

CAVEAT

Once an employee is considered a covered employee, the employee continues to be considered as such for all subsequent tax years.[237.11] Further, determining whether an employee is one of the five highest-compensated employees is "determined separately for each ATEO, and not for the entire group of related organizations; thus, each ATEO has its own five highest-compensated employees."[237.12] As a result, a group of related ATEOs will most likely have *more than five* covered employees.

Inherent within the covered employee definition is also the notion that an individual cannot be an ATEO's covered employee unless the individual is first established to be an ATEO's employee. However, § 4960 does not provide a definition for "employee." The Interim Guidance states that "only an ATEO's common law employees (including officers) can be one of an ATEO's five highest-compensated employees."[237.13] In determining the existence of a common-law employer-employee relationship, "the crucial test lies in the right of control, or lack of it, which the employer may exercise respecting the manner in

---

[237.9]See generally § 4960(c)(4)(A) (2019).

[237.10]See generally IRC § 4960(c)(2); see also Interim Guidance, *supra* note 8, at 17 (providing that a "remuneration that was vested before the effective date of section 4960 is not subject to excise tax under section 4960 because it is treated as having been paid at vesting"). In June 2020, REG-122345-18 provided an exception that an employee will be disregarded for purposes of determining the tax if neither the ATEO nor any related ATEO, nor any organization controlled by the ATEO, pays the employee for services performed.

[237.11]See Interim Guidance, *supra* note, at 7 (stating that there "is no minimum dollar threshold for an employee to be a covered employee"); see also *id.* (rejecting the proposition that a covered employee ceases to be a covered employee after a certain period of time).

[237.12]Interim Guidance, *supra* note, at 8 (rejecting proposed commentary that suggested a group of related ATEOs "should have only five highest-compensated employees among all the related ATEOs" because this position "is not consistent with a good faith, reasonable interpretation of section 4960").

[237.13]*Id.*; see also Spencer Walters, Comment Letter on Notice 2019-09 and Section 4960 (Apr. 2, 2019), https://www.regulations.gov/contentStreamer?documentId=IRS-2019-0001-0006&attachmentNumber=1&contentType=pdf ("This could be read to imply that officers are common law employees.").

which the service is to be performed and the means to be employed in its accomplishment, as well as the result to be obtained."[237.14]

	CAVEAT
Practitioners are concerned that the common-law definition of "employee" is overly broad and overstates Congressional intent.[237.15]	

A. *Amount of Remuneration Paid.* Section 4960's excise tax is based on the remuneration paid by an ATEO for the taxable year in respect of any remuneration paid to a covered employee in excess of $1 million.[237.16] Section 4960(c)(3)(A) defines "remuneration" as wages (as defined in section 3401(a)).[237.17] Further, a remuneration is treated as paid when there is no substantial risk of forfeiture of the rights associated with the remuneration.[237.18] For the purposes of § 4960(a), a "substantial risk of forfeiture" is defined by cross-reference to § 457(f)(3)(B), which itself cross-references Proposed Treasury Regulation § 1.457-12(e)(1).[237.19] Under § 1.457-12(e)(1), compensation is subject to a substantial risk of forfeiture "only if entitlement to the amount is conditioned on the future performance of substantial services, or upon the occurrence of a

---

[237.14]*Porter v. C.I.R.*, 88 T.C. 548, 554 (1997) (quoting *Reed v. Commissioner*, 13 B.T.A. 513 (1928)).

[237.15]Walters, *supra* note, at 3 (believing that the "Service should conclude that 'covered employees' under Section 4960 must be common law employees and that 'officer' status is not presumptive of common law employee status").

[237.16]See Interim Guidance, *supra* note 8, at 9 (noting that the $1 million threshold is not adjusted for inflation).

[237.17]See IRC § 3401(a) (2019) ("For purposes of this chapter, the term 'wages' means all remuneration (other than fees paid to a public official) for services performed by an employee for his employer, including the cash value of all remuneration (including benefits) paid in any medium other than cash. . . ."). IRC § 4960(c)(3)(A) ("The term 'remuneration' shall not include the portion of any remuneration paid to a licensed medical professional (including a veterinarian) which is for the performance of medical or veterinary services by such professional."). When a covered employee is compensated for both medical services and services not related directly to the performance of medical work, the employer "must allocate remuneration paid to such employee between medical services and such other services." Interim Guidance, *supra* note, at 11. To allocate remuneration paid for medical services and for other services, the employer may use any "reasonable, good faith method." *Id*. However, the Interim Guidance indicated that it would like to receive comments regarding how remunerations "should be reasonably allocated between medical services and other services, including how reasonable allocations can be made taking into account comparable salaries, time spent performing medical services and other services, and any applicable employment agreements." *Id*. at 45.

[237.18]See Interim Guidance, *supra* note 8, at 9 (stating that the flush language at the end of § 4960(a) provides for such an interpretation).

[237.19]See generally Prop. Treas. Reg. § 1.457-12(e)(1) (June 22, 2016).

condition that is related to a purpose of the compensation if the possibility of forfeiture is substantial."[237.20]

B. *Excess Parachute Payment.* Under § 4960, an "excess parachute payment means an amount equal to the excess of any parachute payment over the portion of the base amount[237.21] allocated to such payment."[237.22] Section 4960's excess parachute payments rules are modeled after § 280G.[237.23]

CAVEAT

However, § 4960 and § 280G define "parachute payment" differently. Section 4960's definition refers to payments that are contingent on an employee's separation from employment, while § 280G's definition refers to payments contingent upon a corporation's change in ownership or control.

Under Section 4960, a payment is contingent on an employee's separation from employment when a payment is subject to a substantial risk of forfeiture as defined under § 457(f). The Interim Guidance limited payments contingent on a separation from employment to "payments contingent on an involuntary separation from employment" as opposed to payments contingent on a voluntary separation from employment.[237.24]

CAVEAT

The Interim Guidance provided a series of steps that an employer must use to determine the amount of excise tax under § 4960 as it relates to excess parachute payments. See Interim Guidance, *supra* note, at 13. First, the employer must determine "if a covered employee is entitled to receive payments in the nature of compensation that are contingent on an involuntary separation from employment and are not subject to an exclusion." *Id.* Second, the employer must calculate the "total aggregate present value of the contingent payments, taking into account the special valuation rules that apply when an involuntary separation

---

[237.20]*Id.*; see also Interim Guidance, *supra* note, at 9 (noting that the amount of "remuneration treated as paid at vesting is the present value of the remuneration in which the covered employee vests").

[237.21]§ 4960(c)(5)(D) states that rules similar to the rules of § 280G(b)(3) shall apply for purposes of determining the base amount. See IRC § 4960(c)(5)(D).

[237.22]See generally IRC § 4960(a)(2) (2019).

[237.23]See Interim Guidance, *supra* note, at 12 (stating that section 280G disallows a deduction for any excess parachute payment).

[237.24]See Interim Guidance, *supra* note 8, at 14 (noting that "if an employee may voluntarily separate from service and still be entitled to a payment, then the payment either is not subject to a substantial risk of forfeiture or the forfeiture condition is not related to the separation from employment").

from employment accelerates payment or vesting of a right to a payment." *Id*. Third, the employer must calculate the employee's base amount with respect to the base period. See *Id*. Fourth, the employer must determine "if the contingent payments are parachute payments." *Id*. Fifth, the employer must "calculate the amount of excess parachute payments." *Id*. Lastly, the employer must "calculate the amount of excise tax under § 4960(a)(2)." *Id*.

C. *Reporting on Form 4720*. Lastly, on November 7, 2018, the Treasury Department and the IRS issued proposed regulations under § 6011 and § 6071 that state § 4960's reporting requirements and due date for paying the excise tax.[237.25] The proposed regulations state that § 4960's excise tax must be reported on Form 4720, which is the common form used to report Chapter 42 taxes.[237.26] Each employer that is liable for § 4960's excise tax, regardless of whether the employer is an ATEO or a related organization, must separately report and pay its share of the excise tax.[237.27] Finally, the payment under § 4960 is due when Chapter 42 taxes are ordinarily due—"the 15th day of the 5th month after the end of the taxpayer's taxable year."[237.28]

2. Bona Fide Volunteer Exception

Currently, many practitioners are concerned that the IRS's future guidance regarding § 4960 will stipulate that an ATEO's volunteer officer, who is compensated by a for-profit entity and does not receive additional compensation from the for-profit entity for serving as a volunteer officer in an ATEO, will be nevertheless treated as an employee of the ATEO.[237.29] Because of the practitioners' concern as to § 4960's potential daunting consequences on ATEOs, they suggested that "the most straightforward approach . . . for purposes of avoiding severe harm to ATEOs with volunteer officers is for Treasury to clarify that individuals who serve as officers of an ATEO and do not receive any compensation, directly or indirectly, for their volunteer services are not considered employees of the ATEO for purposes of Section 4960."[237.30]

[237.25]See generally Regulations to Prescribe Return and Time for Filing for Payment of Section 4960, 4966, 4967, and 4968 Taxes and to Update the Abatement Rules for Section 4966 and 4967 Taxes, 26 C.F.R. § 53 (2018).
[237.26]See generally *id*.
[237.27]*See id*.; see also Walters, *supra* note, at 2–3 (believing that amount of tax liability should be determined "based only on amounts paid for employment with the ATEO").
[237.28]*Id*.
[237.29]See American Benefits Council Comment Letter, *supra* note (stating that its ATEOs are "concerned that any additional guidance issued by the Treasury Department and the IRS" must address the remaining lack of clarity regarding whether volunteer officers are considered employees of the ATEO).
[237.30]American Benefits Council Comment Letter, *supra* note.

Further, the Interim Guidance attempted to alleviate the problem by stating that "only an ATEO's common law employees (including officers) can be one of an ATEO's five highest-compensated employees."[237.31] In determining the existence of a common-law employer-employee relationship, "the crucial test lies in the right of control, or lack of it, which the employer may exercise respecting the manner in which the service is to be performed and the means to be employed in its accomplishment, as well as the result to be obtained."[237.32]

The initial IRS guidance raised a concern that an individual with limited involvement in an EO, such as volunteers who worked for corporations but provide services that are related to charity or individuals who do limited work at a nonprofit, could end up triggering the tax. The proposed rules (REG-122345-18) offered a number of important exceptions to limit the 21 percent tax so long as the nonprofit doesn't compensate the person for such services; the proposed rules provide a "limited hours" exception so that the tax will only be triggered if the individual spends more than 10 percent of his or her time or more than 100 hours per year at the nonprofit, whichever is greater. This should cover the typical volunteer at a charitable organization who receives no compensation and works for a limited number of hours.

CAVEAT

Generally, corporate officers at for-profit organizations who volunteer should not be taxed under this rule. However, the limited hours exception should be reviewed closely, especially in a case in which the foundation reimburses the company for the time that the executive spends, which could inadvertently trigger the tax. Moreover, it is critical that adequate record keeping be kept.

The proposed regulations also provide a "nonexempt funds" exception for employees who spend more than 10 percent, but less than 50 percent, of their time providing services to a nonprofit organization. The measurement is by hours or days.

CAVEAT

For these purposes, the proposed regulations provide that a member of the board of trustees is not an employee, assuming the services are solely in their capacity as a board member.

[237.31] Interim Guidance, *supra* note, at 8 (clarifying that an ATEO's common law employees can be one of the ATEO's highest-compensated employees in respect to the definition of a covered employee).
[237.32] *Porter v. C.I.R.*, 88 T.C. 548, 554 (1997) (quoting *Reed v. Commissioner*, 13 B.T.A. 513 (1928)).

Nonprofit organizations affiliated with for-profit entities need to carefully examine their shared services agreements to confirm that the arrangement qualifies as an exception to the application of the section 4960 21 percent excise tax.

To determine whether an employee is a "bona fide volunteer," the Supreme Court has defined a volunteer as one who "without promise or expectation of compensation, but solely for his personal purpose or pleasure, worked in activities carried on by other persons either for their pleasure or for profit."[237.33] The crux of this "bona fide volunteer" definition centers around whether an employee possesses a "promise, expectation or receipt of compensation for services rendered."[237.34]

CAVEAT

It is noted that a "Determination of Service to Be Credited to Employees" method described in § 2530.200b-3[237.35] is an objective standard that would assist both ATEOs and the IRS in differentiating between a "bona fide volunteer" and an employee. It is important to create a more structured approach in determining whether an ATEO's volunteer officer is treated as an employee of the ATEO by establishing a "bona fide volunteer" exception and by including a mechanism used to differentiate between a "bona fide volunteer" and an employee.

---

3. Final Regulations: Section 4960

In January, 2021, Treasury and the IRS released final regulations under section 4960. The final regulations retain the basic approach and structure of the proposed regulations, with certain revisions.[237.36]

Commentators expressed concern that highly paid employees of a non-ATEO performing services for a related ATEO without receiving compensation from the ATEO may be subject to the excise tax.

[237.33]*Tony & Susan Alamo Found. v. Sec'y of Labor,* 471 U.S. 290, 295 (1985) (quoting *Walling v. Portland Terminal Co.,* 330 U.S. 148, 152 (1947)); see also *Purdham v. Fairfax Cty. Sch. Bd.,* 637 F.3d 421, 428 (4th Cir. 2011) (stating that "objective facts surrounding the services performed to determine whether the totality of the circumstances establish volunteer status, or whether, instead, the facts and circumstances, objectively viewed, are rationally indicative of employee status").

[237.34]29 C.F.R. § 553.101(a) (2019).

[237.35]See 29 C.F.R. § 2530.200b-3 (2019) (providing a means to determine the "hours of service which must be credited to an employee for a computation period").

[237.36]The final regulations affect an estimated 261,000 ATEOs and 77,000 non-ATEO related organizations of ATEOs that in historical filings report substantial executive compensation. Of the roughly 261,000 such ATEOs based on filings for tax year 2017, 239,000 are section 501(a) exempt organizations (including 23,000 private foundations), 19,000 are section 115 state and local instrumentalities, 2,000 are section 527 political organizations, 600 are exempt farmers' cooperative organizations described in §521(b)(1), and 200 are federal instrumentalities (although the Treasury Department and the IRS will continue to consider whether federal instrumentalities are ATEOs).

To avoid the excise tax, individuals could cease performing such services, or ATEOs might dissolve their relationships with related non-ATEOs, reducing donations from related non-ATEOs. As a result, the final regulations include exceptions to the definitions of "employee" and "covered employees" (specifically to the rules for determining the five highest-compensated employees for purposes of identifying covered employees) to address such situations. With respect to the first exception, the regulations define "employee" consistent with section 3401(c), in particular adopting the rule that a director is not an employee in the capacity as a director and an officer performing minor or no services and not receiving any remuneration for those services is not an employee.

The general rule provides that employees of a related non-ATEO are not considered for purposes of determining the five highest-compensated employees if they were never employees of the ATEO. In addition, individuals who receive no remuneration from the ATEO or a related organization cannot be among the ATEO's five highest-compensated employees.

Changes to the proposed regulations include:

- "Volunteer" exceptions. Under the exceptions, an ATEO's five highest-compensated employees also exclude an employee of the ATEO who receives no remuneration from the ATEO and performs only limited hours of services for the ATEO.

- A modification to the nonexempt funds exception to covered employee status that expands the measurement period from one applicable year to two applicable years (that is, the current applicable year and the preceding applicable year are treated as a single measurement period). This allows organizations more flexibility for determining whether an employee provided services to the ATEO and all related ATEOs for not more than 50 percent of the employee's total hours worked as an employee of the ATEO and all related organizations. Therefore, in situations where an employee "rotates" to an ATEO for a period that extends longer than six months, or when an employee unexpectedly provides services beyond six months in an applicable year, that employee could still be excluded as a covered employee.

- Taxpayers may use a reasonable, good faith method to allocate remuneration between medical services that are excluded from section 4960 and other services.

The final regulations reserve the question as to whether a federal instrumentality for which an enabling act provides for exemption from all current and future federal taxes is subject to tax under section 4960. Until further guidance is issued, such an instrumentality may treat itself as not subject to tax under section 4960 as an ATEO or related organization. However, if that federal instrumentality is a related organization of an ATEO, remuneration paid by the instrumentality must be taken into account by that ATEO.

The final regulations also reserve the coordination of sections 4960 and 162(m) in circumstances where there is a difference in timing between vesting and payment of remuneration. Until future guidance is issued, taxpayers generally may use a reasonable, good faith approach with respect to the coordination of sections 4960 and 162(m) in circumstances in which it is not known whether a deduction for the remuneration will be disallowed under section 162(m) by the due date (including any extension) of the relevant Form 4720.[237.37]

§ 5.7   STATE ACTIVITY WITH RESPECT TO INSIDER TRANSACTIONS

(a)   State Activity

p. 488. *Insert the following at the end of this subsection:*

In May 2015 the Federal Trade Commission ("FTC") and the attorneys general of all 50 states and Washington, D.C., charged the Cancer Fund of America, Inc. ("CFA"), Children's Cancer Fund of America, Inc. ("CCFOA"), The Breast Cancer Society, Inc. ("BCS"), and Cancer Support Services, Inc. ("CSS"), all of which were run by James T. Reynolds, his family and friends (collectively the "sham charities"), and their managers, with fraud.[284.1] Between 2008 and 2012, the sham charities raised more than $187 million under the auspices that they would fund research or pay for cancer treatment. However, the vast majority of the money raised went to professional fundraisers, the foundation managers, and their families,

---

[237.37]The final regulations will apply to taxable years beginning after December 31, 2021 (with the first applicable year generally being the 2022 calendar year). Until the applicability date, taxpayers may rely on the guidance provided in Notice 2019-09 in its entirety or on the proposed regulations in their entirety. Alternatively, taxpayers may choose to apply the final regulations to taxable years beginning after December 31, 2017, provided they apply the final regulations in their entirety and in a consistent manner. Until the applicability date of the final regulations, taxpayers may also base their positions upon a reasonable, good faith interpretation of the statute that includes consideration of any relevant legislative history.

[284.1]FTC, *50 States and D.C. v. Cancer Fund of America, Inc., et al.* Complaint. Available online at: https://www.ftc.gov/system/files/documents/cases/150519cancerfundcmpt.pdf.

including paying for cars, college tuition, gym memberships, concert tickets, and trips to Las Vegas and the Caribbean.[284.2] To mask this from the authorities and watchdog groups, the sham charities utilized an accounting scheme involving the shipment of pharmaceuticals and other goods to developing countries to report over $223 million in revenue and program spending that did not exist. In reality, the people that the sham charities purported to aid received "boxes of sample-size soap, seasonal greeting cards and Little Debbie Snack Cakes."[284.3]

CFA, CSS, and their founder agreed to settle the charges. The founder is banned from profiting from any charity fundraising in the future, and both charities have been permanently dissolved and their assets liquidated. Additionally, CCFOA and BCS will be dissolved, and their managers are banned from fundraising, charity management, and oversight of charitable assets.

This represented one of the largest and most comprehensive investigations into fraudulent charities to date and was the first time that the FTC and the attorneys general of all 50 states and Washington, D.C., filed a joint enforcement action against a fraudulent charity.

[284.2]Susan Taylor Martin, "Here's Where Cancer Fund of America Donations Went While Dying Kids Got Little Debbie Snack Cakes," *Tampa Bay Times,* May 19, 2015.
[284.3]*Id.*

CHAPTER 6

Engaging in a Joint Venture: The Choices

§ 6.1   INTRODUCTION

p. 490. *Insert the following new subsection at the end of this section:*

(a)   Impact of the 2017 Tax Act (Pub. L. No. 115-97) of Choice of Entity and Partnership Taxation

Although the core infrastructure of Subchapter K was left in place by the 2017 Tax Act (Pub. L. No. 115-97), there are significant implications on the choice of entity for business as well as compensation policy. First, Congress lowered the corporate income tax rate to 21 percent, which is a 40 percent decrease from the 35 percent top rate previously in effect. Accordingly, although the corporate rate is now significantly lower than the highest individual marginal rates that apply to pass-through businesses, there is still remaining a double tax in the corporate structure.

Nevertheless, even with the double tax, it may be an attractive structure if business is willing to leave the earnings in the corporation to compound at the preferential rates by being taxed at 21 percent rather than distribute its earnings to its shareholders (or otherwise compensate them). Other issues arise such as the case where the shareholders also are employed by the company and are to be receiving reasonable compensation; there are also employment tax issues and tax-deferred benefits issues to be considered. In any event, it is important to examine how the new 20 percent deduction of qualified business income (§ 199A) will apply to the particular business strategy.

§ 6.2 LLCs

(b) Comparison with Other Business Entities

p. 449. *Insert the following new subparagraph at the end of this subsection:*
  (vi) "Philanthropic" LLCs vs. Public Charities and Private Foundations. The phrase "philanthropic or charitable LLC" is an informal term without a legal definition. It follows the Chan Zuckerberg announcement about their Initiative. See subsection 6.8(c).

Forgoing Tax Exemption. Public charities and private foundations are tax-exempt organizations, whereas LLCs act as pass-through entities (as to profits, losses, gains, etc.) and provide limited liability to their members. While public charities typically fundraise from a broad section of the general public, private foundations are typically funded by a single family or corporation. All private foundation and public charity expenditures must be made for a charitable purpose. This is in contrast to an LLC, whose members may benefit from a charitable contribution deduction only when the LLC contributes to a charity, and not when the members contribute funds to the LLC.

CAVEAT

As far as advocacy, public charities are subject to a no-substantial-part test relative to lobbying while private foundations may not lobby at all. Neither can participate in partisan political activities. However, an LLC can engage in more advocacy than a tax-exempt organization can, including lobbying and partisan political activities, which often proves decisive when an organization is exploring its options. See subsection 2.3(c).

Private foundations, in contrast to public charities and LLCs, are required to make annual distributions of 5 percent of their prior year's average net investment assets, that is, minimum investment return. There are further limits as to the income tax deduction for contributions to private foundations, in addition to a 2 percent tax on its net investment income. An LLC, on the other hand, has no requirement to make a minimum distribution and is not required to publicly disclose information regarding its activities or the compensation of its highest-paid officers. However, private foundations and public charities are required to make such disclosures on their IRS Forms 990-PF and 990, respectively. Finally, one of the major concerns in using an LLC is that the members will be taxed in the event that the LLC generates net income and will only receive a charitable contribution deduction in the year the LLC actually makes the contribution to a charity.

(c)   Exempt Organizations Wholly Owning Other Entities

(iii) Wholly Owned S Corporation   p. 500. *Insert the following at the end of footnote 53:*

Income from an S Corporation is per se UBTI. Accordingly, an S corporation should only be considered as an entity in a joint venture structure if the net income would be treated as UBTI to the charity absent such a rule.

(d)   Private Foundations as Members of LLCs

p. 505. *Insert the following at the end of this subsection:*

NOTE
At the 2016 Georgetown Nonprofit Tax Conference, senior IRS officials acknowledged Rev. Rul. 98-15 and 2004-51 and invited practitioners to request private letter rulings regarding private foundation investments in LLCs; the IRS admits that such investments raise a host of issues in the partnership context and that the IRS is willing to reexamine this subject, especially in view of issuance of new examples that facilitate the expanded use of program-related investments. They suggested that the IRS may issue a public ruling providing rules that govern a joint venture complying with § 4944(c).

§ 6.3   USE OF A FOR-PROFIT SUBSIDIARY AS PARTICIPANT IN A JOINT VENTURE (REVISED)

(a)   Reasons for Use of a Subsidiary

(iii) Provides Flexibility in Operations   p. 511. *Insert the following at the end of footnote 98:*

A subsidiary can often be used to provide compensation to former senior employees of the tax-exempt parent. Of course, the intermediary sanction provisions, including the five-year lookback rule, need to be reviewed in this regard. See Section 5.4.

p. 511. *Insert the following after the first paragraph on the page:*
PLR 9722032 states that the transfer of stock in a for-profit 501(c)(3) affiliate to the employees of the affiliate is permissible. PLR 200225046 sanctions grants of stock options in a subsidiary owned by a 501(c)(3) to employees of the 501(c)(c)(3), as long as the compensation is reasonable. The following language from the 2002 PLR is relevant:

> The payment of reasonable compensation, including the issuance of stock options to N's officers, employees, and directors, will not result in the inurement

of M's net earnings within the meaning of section 1.501(c)(3)-1(c)(2) of the regulations. Similarly, such payment will not result in the serving of private interests under section 1.501(c)(3)-1(d)(1)(ii). N's use of stock-based compensation plans is not incompatible or inconsistent with M's carrying out of its exempt purposes, in view of the fact that M and N are separate legal entities, and the benefits derived by N's officers, employees, and directors constitute reasonable compensation for the services they have rendered. The compensation to be paid N's officers, directors, and employees should be determined by a compensation consultant to help ensure that it is reasonable.

In addition, M's use of N stock to compensate its own employees will not result in the inurement of M's net earnings within the meaning of section 1.501(c)(3)-1(c)(2) of the regulations or serve private interests under section 1.501(c)(3)-1(d)(1)(ii). An exempt organization may cause shares of its taxable subsidiary to be issued as compensation without contravening the prohibition against inurement and private benefit, so long as the total compensation to be paid by M to an employee is reasonable in amount. (See subsection 5.2(a)(ii), Reasonableness Requirement.) In accordance with the facts presented, the use of N's stock or an option to acquire such stock will not adversely affect M's tax-exempt status as an organization described in section 501(c)(3) of the Code.[98.1]

(b) Requirement for Subsidiary to Be a Separate Legal Entity

p. 516. Insert the following new subsections (iv), (v), (vi), and (vii) before paragraph (c):

(iv) In September 2015, National Geographic Society ("NGS") formed a joint venture with 21st Century Fox called National Geographic Partners, a for-profit media joint venture. In this new venture, Fox has paid $725 million to National Geographic for the contribution of the charity's assets, including its television channels, related digital and social media platforms, as well as travel, location-based entertainment, catalog, licensing, and e-commerce businesses. National Geographic's purpose is to allow it to focus on its fundamental exempt goals of increasing knowledge through science, exploration, and research as to which its endowment will increase to approximately $1 billion. National Geographic received a 27 percent interest in the venture (which will be held by a second-tier, for-profit subsidiary). Fox received a 73 percent interest; in addition to its cash investment, it will provide expertise in global media platforms. There will be an eight-member board of directors, which will have equal representation from the parties; the chair of the board will alternate annually, the initial chair having been chosen by National Geographic. It is understood that the charity obtained opinions of counsel regarding the valuation of the assets that transferred as well as the tax aspects of the underlying transaction.

[98.1] See also Meyer, *A Blueprint for Creating a Taxable Subsidiary,* The Exempt Org. Tax Rev., August 2002.

CAVEAT

Although the $725 million payment will increase National Geographic's endowment to nearly $1 billion, Fox will gain access to millions of new customers, including 6.2 million magazine subscribers, 100 million Facebook followers, 120 million Twitter followers, and 30 million Instagram followers. NGS will receive a revenue stream that is taxable at the subsidiary level but tax free as a dividend when received by the charity.

QUERY

Does the National Geographic structure resemble an exempt-only venture similar to a whole hospital one, in which all or substantially all of the assets have been transferred to the joint venture?[112.1] If so, what is the impact? Perhaps that could explain why a second-tier for-profit subsidiary was used to hold the charity's economic interest in the venture.

CAVEAT

It should be noted that the use of a taxable subsidiary in the National Geographic venture made the issue of UBIT moot. Since there is a for-profit subsidiary used as a blocker, there is no need for the venture to file a Form 990T, which would be available for public review.

(v) The IRS issued a favorable ruling[112.2] in a case where a § 501(c)(3) private school formed a taxable for-profit subsidiary to hold intellectual property. The subsidiary developed software for online educational programs and granted the free license to the parent but could also license the IP to other schools for a royalty. The key issue was whether there was any attribution of the subsidiary to the parent following the *Moline Properties* analysis. The IRS concluded that the structure did not jeopardize the parent's § 501(c)(3) status and ruled that the income from the activity was not unrelated business income. The facts indicate that although the parent owned 100 percent of the taxable subsidiary, it did not control the day-to-day affairs of the subsidiary. It respected the corporate formalities. The subsidiary intended to license the software to unrelated schools; accordingly, the subsidiary was respected as separate from the parent. Neither the activities nor the income of the subsidiary was attributed to the parent.

The IRS determined that the subsidiary was not a mere instrumentality of the institution because the majority of its governing board is independent and does not have a relationship with the school. Moreover, the

---

[112.1]See subsection 4.5(a).
[112.2]PLR 201503018 (Oct. 24, 2014).

institution did not actively participate in the day-to-day affairs of the for-profit organization. The IRS also based its ruling on basic factors such as separate bank accounts, financial records, facilities, and telephone listings. Thus, the IRS concluded that the tax-exempt status of the school would not be adversely affected by its ownership of the for-profit.

We note that although a discussion of the use of equity-based compensation was not included in the analysis or holding of the ruling, it would not affect the institution since the two organizations were determined to be separate entities for tax purposes, and therefore the for-profit would not be subject to § 4958 of the Code regarding excess benefit transactions, because § 4958 is applicable only to organizations described in §§ 501(c)(3) and (c)(4) of the Code.

The IRS also ruled on the UBIT implications of the school's ownership of the for-profit. The IRS determined that since the for-profit's activities could not be attributed to the institution, the subsidiary's gross income would not be UBIT to the institution under § 512(a)(1) of the Code.[112.3]

Section 512(b)(13) provides that if a controlling entity receives or accrues a specified payment from another entity it controls, the payment would be included in the UBIT of the parent to the extent it reduces the net unrelated income of the controlled entity. However, dividend income is not a specified payment and therefore is not subject to UBIT. Thus, any dividends paid by the for-profit to the institution would not be subject to UBIT.

(vi) Other Rulings of Note. PLR 201644019. Although the IRS will not issue rulings on joint ventures *per se*,[112.4] it will issue rulings as to whether particular activities are in furtherance of exempt purposes. As the fact pattern of PLR 201644019 demonstrates, counsel can carefully structure a ruling request that does not focus on a joint venture *per se*, but on other issues, including future charitable activities and use of for-profit subsidiaries to block attribution of for-profit activities to the § 501(c)(3).

In the ruling, a Charity's wholly owned for-profit subsidiary ("Subsidiary") formed an LLC (Partnership) with an unrelated party (X). Charity sold certain assets to Partnership for cash to use to expand its charitable/educational programs. X also indirectly transferred assets to Partnership in exchange for membership interests held through a for-profit subsidiary of X.

Subsidiary also transferred assets to Partnership through two disregarded entities in exchange for Partnership interests. The Charity and Partnership entered into a trademark license agreement whereby the Partnership would pay royalties for the use of the Charity's trademarks,

---

[112.3]See subsection 6.3(d)(ii).
[112.4]Section 3.01(76), Rev. Proc. 2017-3, 2017-1 I.R.B. 130 (12/29/16).

domain names, and social media handles. Of particular importance was Charity's representation that it would not directly or actively participate in the day-to-day management of Subsidiary or any subsidiary or affiliate of Subsidiary, including the Partnership.[112.5]

The IRS ruled that:

1. Charity's use of proceeds from the asset sale would further its § 501(c)(3) missions and purposes.

2. The sale of assets would not generate UBI because the sale was not a business regularly carried on within § 512(a) but rather was a one-time sale.

3. Payments by Partnership to Charity under the trademark license agreement constituted royalties under § 512(b)(2).

4. Subsidiary would be respected as an entity separate from Charity as it satisfied the business activity requirement of *Moline Properties*. As a result, Subsidiary's involvement in the Partnership would not be attributed to Charity.[112.6]

NOTE

Neither Rev. Rul. 98-15 nor 2007-51 were cited because the Charity was not directly participating in the Partnership's activities; it was an indirect equity owner through Subsidiary. IRS determined that the Subsidiary was *in effect* successfully functioning as a blocker entity.

CAVEAT

Although this private letter ruling was favorable to the charitable organization, it did reflect careful planning and significant expenditures—the fee for a PLR is $28,000 for larger organizations. Rev. Proc. 2017-1[112.7] addresses procedures for private letter ruling requests, including a presubmission conference, whereby an organization can discuss the issues with IRS representatives before paying the appropriate fee. The conferences are usually by telephone, and the IRS requires submission of a written submission outlining the proposed requests prior to scheduling the presubmission conference.[112.8] Presumably, the presubmission conference will provide insight as to whether a favorable outcome is likely.

[112.5]These facts are under a section titled "Representations Regarding Attribution."

[112.6]Although there is no discussion of Partnership's programs and activities, it is presumed that those activities would not be charitable/exempt in nature.

[112.7]2017-1 I.R.B. 1 (12/29/2016).

[112.8]Transcript of February 24, 2017, remarks of Janine Cook, TE/GE Deputy Associate Chief Counsel, as delivered at the Washington Nonprofit Legal and Tax Conference as reported in *EO Tax Journal* 2017-68, April 7, 2017.

(vii) The IRS recently issued a private letter ruling that raises concerns as to whether the traditional structural model is being reexamined and may be troublesome for the EO community.[112.9] In the ruling, a § 501(c)(3) hospital system parent requested rulings that certain political activities, including operating a PAC, conducted by its wholly owned for-profit corporation would not adversely affect the parent's 501(c) status. In addition, the parent requested rulings related to a shared services agreement between the parent and the for-profit corporation, the provision of the parent's employee mailing list to the for-profit, and board and officers' overlaps pertaining to the parent and for-profit with regard to political activities.

The § 501(c)(3) parent also requested the IRS to rule that:[112.10]

- The operation of a PAC will not constitute participation or intervention in a political campaign by the parent.
- Its provision of services and other resources (facilities and equipment) to the subsidiary and PAC pursuant to a shared services and facilities agreement, in which the parent was reimbursed for costs, will not constitute participation or intervention in a political campaign by the parent.
- The shared services and facilities agreement will not cause the parent to be operated for private benefit or private inurement.

The parent was the sole shareholder of the subsidiary, which owned interests in two joint ventures and was sole member of an LLC that provides management services to the hospital system. The parent may elect all of the subsidiary's directors and may remove any director with or without cause. The parent may elect or appoint the subsidiary's officers and assistant officers or permit the directors of the subsidiary to do so; it is important to note that the subsidiary does not have any employees who are not also employees of the parent.[112.11]

The parent planned to form a section 527 PAC and select the PAC's board of directors, which, in turn, will select the PAC's officers; the individuals may serve concurrently as officers or directors of the subsidiary or employees of the parent; the PAC will not have its own employees.

[112.9]PLR 202005020 (January 31, 2020).

[112.10]This subsection is based upon materials prepared by Ronald Schultz for presentation at Georgetown Law Center, Special Topics in Exempt Organizations (2020).

[112.11]In addition, under the subsidiary's bylaws, the parent has certain reserved powers to:

- Approve or reject executive and administrative leadership.
- Establish general guiding policies.
- Approve or disapprove annual operating and capital budgets.
- Direct the placement of funds and capital.
- Approve or disapprove salary rates for administrative and department head personnel.

The subsidiary and PAC will solicit voluntary contributions to the PAC from employees of the parent, the subsidiary, and joint ventures/LLC in the system. In addition, the parent's employees will engage in fundraising services pursuant to the shared services agreement on behalf of the subsidiary. The parent will also provide a mailing list (names, titles, etc.) of its employees to be used by the subsidiary/PAC to comply with federal and state campaign finance laws.

CAVEAT

Following examination of the agreement terms and representations, it was argued that the following proves separateness of the subsidiary and the PAC from the parent:

- The parent will not coordinate with the subsidiary or PAC with respect to fundraising efforts.
- The parent will charge fair market value for services it provides.
- The subsidiary and PAC will maintain separate bank accounts, books, and records.
- The subsidiary and PAC will prepare separate financial statements and tax returns.
- The subsidiary and PAC will have separate letterhead and email addresses.
- The parent will adopt a board resolution prohibiting its board/officers/employees from PAC involvement in its official capacity.
- Individuals will track time providing services to the subsidiary and PAC to allocate costs between the two.
- The subsidiary shall have dominion and control over services and facilities used by PAC.

The IRS held that providing the parent employee information to the subsidiary solely to allow the subsidiary/PAC to comply with campaign finance laws so that the PAC may make expenditures to support or oppose candidates for public office is political intervention; reimbursement at fair market value is not enough.

Secondly, the parent's employees are being used to provide services to the subsidiary/PAC. And despite representations and agreement terms, there are no "guardrails or limitations" with respect to services that might be inconsistent with the parent's exempt purposes. Furthermore, there is no demonstration that employees should be treated as employees of the subsidiary rather than the parent for this purpose since the parent's employees will be soliciting contributions to the PAC at the parent's offices during regular business hours, making the activities inseparable from the parent's own operations. Finally, reimbursement at cost or fair market value is not enough to satisfy the separateness standard.

Accordingly, the mailing list and shared services agreement, in this context, result in political intervention and impermissible private benefit to the subsidiary.

- The subsidiary's operation of the PAC will constitute participation or intervention in a political campaign by the § 501(c)(3) parent.
- The parent's provision of services and other resources (facilities and equipment) to the subsidiary and PAC pursuant to the services agreement will constitute participation or intervention in a political campaign by the parent.
- The services and facilities agreement will cause the parent to be operated for the benefit of private interests (and will not further an exemption purpose).[112.12]

CAVEAT

The IRS does not take at face value what it regards as "self-serving" terms or provisions in agreements; the Service tries to look to the actual practice. Facts and circumstances are critical; there is no single answer for all situations involving the political activities of a (c)(3)'s subsidiary.

Some leading commentators have argued that this decision is a reversal of prior IRS guidance in the area, at least where IRS has approved an exempt parent creating a (c)(4) subsidiary. The decision may have implications beyond political activities:

- There are similar governance overlap issues without safeguards that may arise and demonstrate that the parent § 501(c)(3) is arguably controlling the potentially nonexempt activities in question; thus, the activities may be attributed to the exempt parent (e.g., lobbying, unrelated trade or business).
- This may be the case even if there is no shared services agreement or mailing list rental.

When using a shared services agreement in any context involving an exempt organization and a related taxable entity, the practitioner needs to look beyond whether the exempt entity is being treated fairly and at

---

[112.12]The IRS did not rule on inurement, although it was requested by the parent.

fair market value (i.e., review the terms relative to governance overlap and control).

(d) UBIT Implications Applicable to the Use of a Subsidiary

(i) General Rule. p. 518. *Add the following to the end of footnote 119:*
See PLR 20153018 (Oct. 24, 2014), § 6.3(b)(iv), *supra.*

p. 525. *Add the following new subparagraph:*

(iv) Use of C Corporation Blocker.[151.1] It is often beneficial to use a C corporation as a blocker that can be inserted between an exempt organization and the potentially damaging activity to "block" the attribution of the activity to the exempt organization. This is especially useful for blocking excess UBI, as well as political activity, excess lobbying, or conduct of an activity that would jeopardize exemption if conducted directly by the exempt organization. This is so because under section 512(c) and the partnership flow-through of income (see Chapter 2), a partnership's trade or business regularly carried on would be unrelated trade or business with respect to the exempt organization partner. See in this regard the potential of foreign withholding tax.

The C corporation blocker has been respected in PLR 200405016, PLR 200518081, and PLR 201409009. However, the C corporation blocker has not been respected in PLR 200842050.

CAVEAT

The critical factors include the books and records, the extent of board overlap, officer overlap, whether separate accounts are used, board records, and formalities, but most important is the control of the day-to-day affairs of the corporate subsidiary.

The following five diagrams prepared by Amanda Nussbaum, tax partner at Proskauer, were presented in Georgetown University Law School class, Special Topics in Exempt Organizations (Spring 2021); they illustrate how a C corporation could be beneficial in blocking UBTI. (There is presently a 21 percent tax on net UBIT revenue. See Sections 8.7 and 14.6, Scenario 4.)

[151.1]See Section 8.7.

Structure One: Basic Investments in Flow-Throughs Basic Structure to Block UBTI

- UBTI flows to Blocker Corp.
- If Blocker Corp is a U.S. entity, Blocker Corp pays corporate tax on all income allocated by Operating LLC.
- Only Blocker Corp has to file a U.S. tax return.
- Unless Fund can sell stock of Blocker Corp, exit triggers 21 percent tax on gains.
- Tax-inefficient for GP and U.S. taxable investors, who would have paid only 20 percent tax.
- Also tax-inefficient for tax-exempt investors because gains on exit (unlike operating income) generally would not have been subject to U.S. tax.

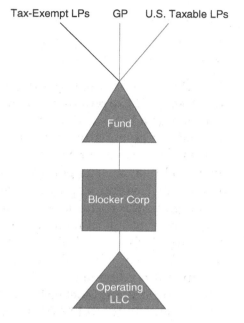

Structure Two Alternative Structure: Investment Directly and Indirectly Through Blocker Corp

- Eliminates the inefficiency for U.S. taxable investors and the GP.

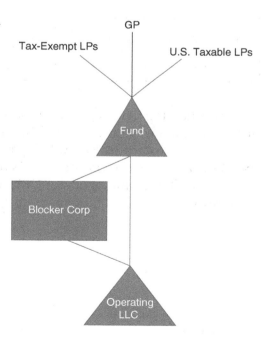

Structure Three Alternative Structure: Parallel Fund for Electing Tax-Exempt Investors

- Blocker pays corporate tax on LLC income allocations and files returns.
- Tax-efficient for U.S. taxable investors. May be tax-efficient for the GP if it is able to receive its carried interest through a partnership below the blocker corporation.
- Blocker incurs 21 percent tax on asset sale.
- Tax-inefficient for tax-exempt investors, unless stock of blocker can be sold (which would only be possible if the parallel fund sets up a separate blocker for each operating partnership investment).
- No ability for tax-exempts to elect into blockers on a deal-by-deal basis (unless the parallel fund sets up a separate blocker for each operating partnership investment).

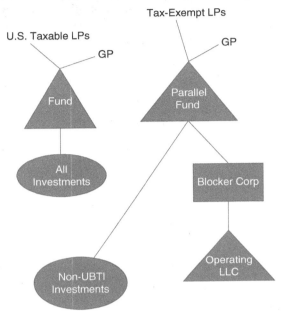

Structure Four:
Parallel AIV

- Blocker pays corporate tax on LLC income allocations and files returns.
- Tax-efficient for U.S. taxable investors and GP.
- Blocker incurs 21 percent tax on asset sale.
- Tax-inefficient for tax-exempt investors, unless stock of blocker can be sold.

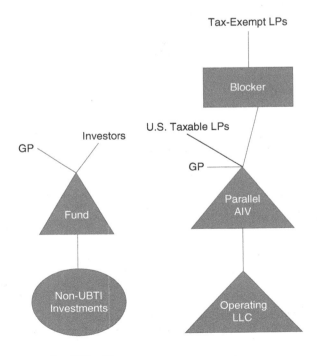

Structure Five:
Unrelated Debt-Financed Income (§ 514(c)(1): "UDFI" – Flow-Through Treatment)

- UDFI flows through partnerships. It doesn't matter how many partnerships there are, whether they are U.S. or non-U.S., or what level the debt is at.[151.2]

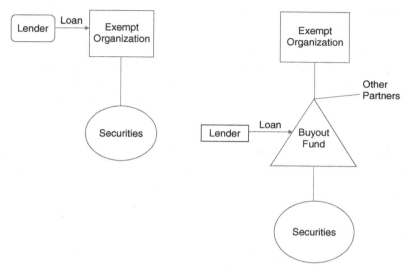

UDFI—Blockers

- Corporations block UDFI.

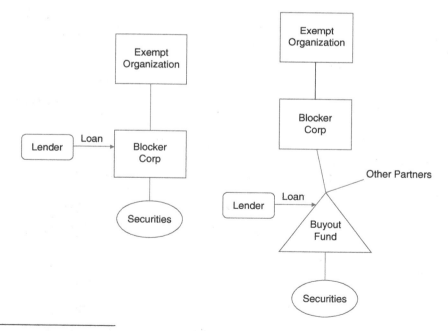

[151.2]TAM 9651001 finds that sale of partnership with acquisition indebtedness generates UDFI.

UDFI—REIT Structures

- REIT structures are often used to block UDFI/UBTI.
- These structures are ineffective for pension trusts that hold 10 percent of a pension-held REIT.

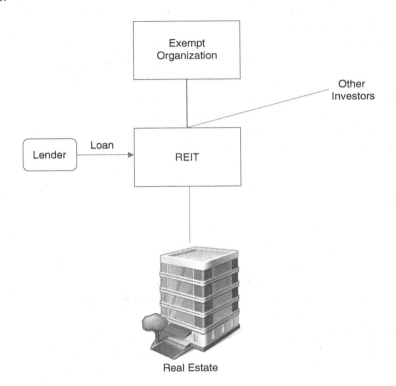

§ 6.5   PRIVATE FOUNDATIONS AND PROGRAM-RELATED INVESTMENTS (REVISED)

(a)   Program-Related Investments

p. 536. *Insert the following after the first full paragraph on this page:*

A private foundation may make an investment that meets the PRI requirements; however, in the event that it takes the form of an equity investment in a functionally related business, such as an LLC with a for-profit member, it may nevertheless need to meet Rev. Rul. 2004-51. Otherwise, the unrelated business income rules could apply to the foundation's share of profits. See p. 380 and Section 10.4. The concern is raised because Rev. Rul. 2004-51 does not provide clarity on these issues. In fact, the IRS may conclude that the for-profit's control over the venture could convert an otherwise related activity into an unrelated activity, causing the exempt partner to be liable for unrelated business income tax.

p. 536. *Delete the second full paragraph on this page and replace with the following:*

Though the IRS's definition of jeopardizing investments explicitly excludes program-related investments, there is no such exception for mission-related investments (MRIs), which are made to generate a profit and to further a foundation's mission. Because MRIs may offer lower returns than non-MRI investments, many have questioned whether this could cause them to be treated as jeopardizing investments. However, on September 16, 2015, the IRS issued Notice 2015-62, which made clear that foundation managers may consider the relationship between an investment and the foundation's mission in making prudent, profit-driven investments. The Notice also implies that MRIs will not be considered imprudent because they offer an expected return that is less than what could be earned on other investments.[198.1]

For an investment to qualify as a PRI under § 4944(c), three requirements must be met:

p. 537. *Insert the following after the first full paragraph on this page:*

In Notice 2015-62,[200.1] the IRS addresses questions that have arisen about whether an investment made by a private foundation that furthers its charitable purposes, but is not a PRI because a significant purpose of the investment is the production of income or the appreciation of property, is subject to tax under § 4944.

Although the regulations list some factors that managers generally consider when making investment decisions, the regulations do not provide an exhaustive list of facts and circumstances that may properly be considered. When exercising ordinary business care and prudence in deciding whether to make an investment, foundation managers may consider all relevant facts and circumstances, including the relationship between a particular investment and the foundation's charitable purposes. Foundation managers are not required to select only investments that offer the highest rates of return, the lowest risks, or the greatest liquidity so long as the foundation managers exercise the requisite ordinary business care and prudence under the facts and circumstances prevailing at the time of the investment in making investment decisions that support, and do not jeopardize, the furtherance of the private foundation's charitable purposes.

[198.1]IRS Notice 2015-62 (Sept. 16, 2015). Specifically, the IRS Notice provides that an investment made by a private foundation will not be considered to be a jeopardizing investment "if, in making the investment, the foundation managers exercise ordinary business care and prudence (under the circumstances prevailing at the time the investment is made) in providing for the long-term and short-term financial needs of the foundation to carry out its charitable purposes."
[200.1]2015-39 I.R.B. 411 (Sept. 15, 2015).

EXAMPLE

A private foundation will not be subject to tax under § 4944 if foundation managers who have exercised ordinary business care and prudence make an investment that furthers the foundation's charitable purposes at an expected rate of return that is less than what the foundation might obtain from an investment that is unrelated to its charitable purposes.

This standard is consistent with investment standards under state laws, which generally provide for the consideration of the charitable purposes of an organization or certain factors, including an asset's special relationship or special value, if any, to the charitable purposes of the organization, in properly managing the organization's investments. See, for example, Unif. Prudent Mgmt. of Institutional Funds Act §§ 3(a), 3(e)(1)(H) and accompanying comments, 7A pt. III U.L.A. 21–22 (Pocket Pt. 2015).

(b) Proposed Regulations: Additional Examples of PRIs

p. 540. *Insert the following after the first full paragraph on this page:*

In April 2016 the Treasury responded to comments to the philanthropy community and recognized that the existing regulations do not represent the diversity of investment opportunities available to foundations. New examples now make clear that PRIs are an applicable tool in advancing all charitable purposes. Original regulations that were published decades ago served as a tool to support economic development; however, in the present economy foundations are using them to support programs in science, technology, education, arts, and the environment. The examples further clarify that the PRIs can be used to support for-profit enterprises, individuals, and international recipients. The final regulations track closely to proposed regulations.

The preamble to the publication of the additional examples sets forth the principles that the IRS intends to post on its website:

1. An activity conducted in a foreign country furthers an exempt purpose if the same activity would further an exempt purpose if conducted in the United States;

2. The exempt purposes served by a PRI are not limited to situations involving economically disadvantaged individuals and deteriorated urban areas;

3. The recipients of PRIs need not be within a charitable class if they are the instruments for furthering an exempt purpose;

4. A potentially high rate of return does not automatically prevent an investment from qualifying as a PRI;

5. PRIs can be achieved through a variety of investments, including loans to individuals, tax-exempt organizations, and for-profit organizations, and equity investments in for-profit organizations;

6. A credit enhancement arrangement may qualify as a PRI; and

7. A private foundation's acceptance of an equity position in conjunction with making a loan does not necessarily prevent the investment from qualifying as a PRI.

CAVEAT

The proposed examples demonstrate that PRIs may accomplish a variety of exempt purposes (and are not limited to situations involving economically disadvantaged individuals and deteriorated urban areas), may fund activities in one or more foreign countries, and may earn a high potential rate of return. The proposed examples also illustrate that a PRI may take the form of an equity position in conjunction with making a loan, and that a private foundation's provision of credit enhancements can qualify as a PRI. In addition, the examples illustrate that loans and capital may be provided to individuals or entities that are not within a charitable class themselves, if the recipients are the instruments through which the private foundation accomplishes its exempt activities.

---

p. 543. *Change the current subparagraph (c) to (d) and insert new subparagraph (c) as follows:*

(c)   **Final Regulations: Additional Examples 11–19**

Example 11 involved a private foundation's investment in a subsidiary of a drug company for the development of a vaccine to prevent a disease that predominantly affects poor individuals in developing countries. Under the investment agreement, the subsidiary is required to distribute the vaccine to the poor individuals in developing countries at a price that is affordable to the affected population and to promptly publish its research results; the example has been modified to make it clear that the subsidiary can also sell the vaccine to those who can afford it at fair market value prices. This clarification is appropriate given that the example also specifies that Y's primary purpose in making the investment is to fund scientific research in the public interest and no significant purpose of the investment involves the production of income or the appreciation of property.

Example 13 involved a private foundation that accepts common stock in a business enterprise as part of a loan to the business and that plans to liquidate the stock as soon as the business becomes profitable or it is established that the business will never become profitable. The sentence in the example regarding the liquidation of the stock has been removed to clarify that the foundation does not need to sell its stock in a business that becomes profitable for the investment in that stock to be a PRI. It is noted, however, that the establishment, at the outset of an investment, of an exit condition that is tied to the foundation's exempt purpose in making the investment can be an important indication that a foundation's primary purpose in undertaking the investment is the accomplishment of the exempt purpose.

Example 15 involved loans by a private foundation to two poor individuals living in a developing country where a natural disaster has occurred. The final regulations amend Example 15 to eliminate the reference to a natural disaster.

CAVEAT

One commenter suggested modifying Example 15 to refer to a "foreign country" rather than a "developing country," noting that providing disaster relief to a foreign country, whether or not it is a developing country, furthers the accomplishment of exempt purposes. Several examples in the proposed regulations illustrate the principle that an activity conducted in a foreign country furthers an exempt purpose if the same activity would further an exempt purpose if conducted in the United States. This principle applies equally to all foreign countries. However, the final regulations did not change the reference to a developing country in Example 15, because the example illustrates PRIs in the context of microloans, which are currently more common in developing countries. In addition, because organizations making microloans often provide loans to many individuals, the final regulations modify the example to reference loans to a group of individuals, rather than two specific individuals with identified business endeavors.

CAVEAT

The proposed regulations include one example involving a loan to an LLC; the results of that example would be the same if the limited liability company described in the example were an L3C. Similarly, the results of examples in which the PRI recipient is a corporation would apply equally if the recipient were a benefit corporation. Treasury sees no need to amend the examples to refer more narrowly to an L3C or benefit corporation when such status is not determinative of the examples' conclusions. Accordingly, the final regulations did not adopt these comments.

The Section on Taxation of the ABA requested that the IRS issue a revenue ruling under section 4944 regarding the qualification of an equity investment in a "non-section 501(c)(3)" limited liability company as a program-related investment.

§ 6.6 NONPROFITS AND BONDS

(b) The Social Impact Bond: Impact Investing

p. 546. *Add the following to the end of this subsection:*

The following two diagrams illustrate the participating parties and flow of funds in these transactions.[208.1] The CohnReznick presentation describes social impact bonds as a "pay for success" financing structure; "pay for success" being a category of contracts that looks to "result/outcomes" versus "activity/imputs."[208.2] The first diagram, "Overview of the PFS Process," identifies the participants and their roles. The second, "PFS Financing: How It Works," explains how the funds flow from the initial funding, usually by a for-profit, to a service provider through an intermediary, with payment by the government to the initial funder(s) if the evaluator determines that the delineated goals for the "population to be served" (which might in other contexts be identified as the "charitable class") have been met.

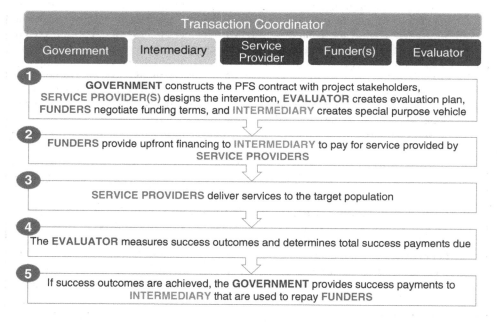

The success of social impact bonds has been mixed and controversial.[208.3] The first U.S. social impact bond involving New York City and Goldman Sachs did not achieve the goal of generating a reduced recidivism

---

[208.1]"Social Impact Bonds and Pay for Success—What Is It?," prepared and presented by CohnReznick at the CohnReznick 5th Annual New Markets Tax Credit Summit, May 2016.
[208.2]*Id.*
[208.3]Kenneth A. Dodge, "Why Social Impact Bonds Still Have Promise," *New York Times,* Nov. 13, 2015.

rate, relieving the government of its obligation to repay the investors. The second program, a "pay for success" program in Utah, provided support to struggling students in prekindergarten years with the expectation that early intervention would reduce the number of students needing special education assistance later on. That program was deemed a success, resulting in repayments to both the for-profit and the nonprofit investors, only to be followed by criticism of the metrics used in determining the program's achievements.[208.4] "The concerns about the program are a reminder of how hard it is to properly structure public-private partnerships like social impact bonds, which depend on easily verifiable and commonly agreed-upon methods of measuring success for goals that can be hard to define. Finding such measurements is increasingly important as government programs face cutbacks and public officials look to find private investors willing to address the funding gap." It remains to be seen whether the inherent challenges in this innovative approach to lessening the burdens of government will ultimately be viable.[208.5]

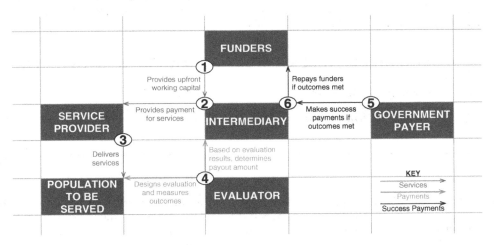

In an article entitled "Balancing Public and Private Interests in Pay for Success Programs: Should We Care About the Private Benefit Doctrine?" written by Sean Delany and Jeremy Steckel,[208.6] the authors analyze how the private benefit doctrine might affect the structure of PFS programs in the United States and might limit or encourage their expansion in the future. At the time the article was written in Spring 2018 there were at least 13 domestic PFS projects underway in nine states as well as Riker's Island, addressing issues such as incarceration, recidivism, early childhood

---

[208.4]Nathaniel Popper, "Success Metrics Questioned in School Program Funded by Goldman," *New York Times*, Nov. 3, 2015.

[208.5]*Id.*

[208.6]See *New York University Journal of Law and Business* 14, no. 2 (Spring 2018).

special education, foster care, homelessness, unemployment, and substance abuse, all of which are outlined in a chart describing the projects' objectives, individuals served, issue area, and initial private investment. The authors argue that the boundaries that tax-exempt organizations must observe when engaging with for-profit entities in the joint venture context to achieve their charitable missions are far from clear, because the private benefit doctrine has evolved in piecemeal fashion without a coherent conceptual framework. As PFS programs continue to develop, the exempt organizations need to ensure that they are not violating the private benefit doctrine. (See Chapter 5.)

CAVEAT

The authors state that "[D]espite the inconsistent jurisprudence surrounding the private benefit doctrine, applying it to PFS programs demonstrates that it protects against valid concerns not addressed elsewhere in the Code, and offers a cost-benefit framework which we use to draw conclusions about the desirability of funding social services through PFS programs."

---

§ 6.7 EXPLORING ALTERNATIVE STRUCTURES (REVISED)

(b) A New Legal Entity—the L3C—a Low-Profit LLC

p. 548. *Add the following to the end of this subsection:*

CAVEAT

Although the IRS has not approved the L3C structure as a vehicle for meeting § 4944(c) of the Code, this commentator recommends that the IRS issue a public ruling that sets forth certain criteria that would enable it to rule favorably as to a particular structure. Such criteria could include the L3C entity keeping separate accounts for each PRI, which would enable the IRS to audit the structure with ease, and definitive rules on governance, including how management could operate to fulfill its dual mission of primary charitable purpose, including control and the definition of a "social mission" for benefit corporations. Such an approach would relieve the IRS from having to do a case-by-case review and issuance of rulings. This is especially important in facilitating the expanded use of PRIs in the context of the recent IRS issuance of final regulations with additional examples tended to encourage the charitable community to take advantage of this vehicle. See, in this regard, Section 6.5.

(c) Benefit and Flexible Purpose Corporation—A Legislative Approach

p. 551. *Insert the following at the end of this subsection:*

As of 2018, 37 states and the District of Columbia had passed some form of flexible purpose business legislation, and "approximately 7,000 businesses were organized as either L3Cs or benefit corporations."[233.1] These numbers should be analyzed in the context of the 30 million businesses in the United States.[233.2] Thus, benefit corporations in their pure form have had good, but minimal, impact. Nevertheless, the limited number of benefit corporations and mere speculation about joint venture possibilities with these triple-bottom-line entities should not minimize the social impact that they promise.

CAVEAT
While B corporations were intended to improve the options for diverse funding for non-profits and allow for-profits to be holistic in their considerations of business deals, their impact may extend beyond corporate and tax law.

Some scholars have argued that "[i]nstead of providing new sources of finance and protecting board members from liability, they have played a large part in an important conversation on the role of business in our country—namely, shifting the focus from shareholder maximization toward a more holistic and community-minded view of the role of business in society."[233.3]

The goal of a benefit corporation is to compel entrepreneurs to do social good while they make a profit. It is a hybrid between nonprofit and for-profit; it pays taxes and may have shareholders; however, there is protection from being sued by shareholders for not maximizing profits:[233.4]

[233.1] The material added in this subsection is based upon research prepared by Michelle Gough, JD, PhD from her graduate tax paper at Georgetown University Law Center, Special Topics in Exempt Organizations, entitled "Benefit Corporations: Are the New State Created Entities Creating Both New C-Corps and New Possibilities in Joint Ventures?" Elizabeth Schmidt, *New Legal Structures for Social Enterprises: Designed for One Role but Planning Another*, 43 Vt. L. Rev. 675 (2019). In addition to L3Cs and benefit corporations, four states have a social purpose corporation (Washington, California, Florida, and Texas) and three recognize the benefit limited liability company. *Id.* For other sites that track social enterprise legislation, see *State by State Status of Legislation*, Benefit Corporation, http://benefitcorp .net/policymakers/state-by-state-status.

[233.2] *Id.* Citing "Quick Facts United States," U.S. Census Bureau, https://www.census.gov/quickfacts/ fact/table/US/PST045217 (calculating that in 2016, the United States had 7,757,807 businesses with employees and 24,813,048 without employees).

[233.3] See Schmidt, footnote 54.

[233.4] The materials added in this subsection are based upon a lecture given by Ronald Schultz at Georgetown Law Center, Special Topics in Exempt Organizations (2022).

(i) Nonprofits may form B corporations but cannot be one itself.

CAVEAT
Chief Counsel Advice (ILM) 201543013 (Section 162 v. Section 170 deduction for payments made to B Corporation—B corporation is not a section 170 charitable organization). See https://www.irs.gov/pub/irs-wd/201543013.pdf.[233.5]

(ii) **Certification.** Certification is a process undertaken through completion and review of the "B Impact Assessment" that is administered by the nonprofit B Lab (see subsection 6.7(d)) and impacts on workers, customers, community, and environment. The legal documents need to be amended to require balance of purpose and profit and to make B Impact Report transparent on bcorporation.net.[233.6]

B corporations may be publicly held.[233.7] The article discusses the voting thresholds for opting in/out, elimination of statutory appraisal rights, director protections being strengthened, aligning derivative suits with conventional corporations, as well as some recent developments with Delaware B corporations.

(iii) **In examining a B corporation "conversion" checklist (business corporation to B corporation), the basic action items are as follows:**

- Governing state public benefit corporation statute and organization's own certificate of incorporation and bylaws

- PBC certificate of incorporation include specific public benefits; other optional provisions

- Board approval—per certificate and bylaw vote provisions

- Shareholder approval

[233.5] As of January 22, 2022, there are 4,520 certified B corporations reported in 78 countries and 153 industries.

[233.6] Examples of B Corporations include:

- Patagonia, Inc. (outdoor apparel)
- Ben & Jerry's (ice cream)
- Kickstarter (fund projects)
- Community development banks
- Insurance companies
- Educational organizations including universities
- Community organizations including in promotion of improved public health.

[233.7] See Harvard Law School forum on corporate governance article by Michael R. Littenberg, Emily J. Oldshue, and Brittany N. Pifer, Ropes & Gray LLP (Aug. 31, 2020): https://corpgov.law.harvard.edu/2020/08/31/delaware-public-benefit-corporations-recent-developments/.

- ○ File amendments of certificate with Secretary of State
- ○ New stock certificates
- ○ Name change—file and impact on other documents

(iv) With regard to converting a subsidiary to a B corporation, the key considerations are as follows:

- ○ State law ease of transition—need a statute permitting it—both states if changing domicile from one to another.
- ○ Statute may treat the entity as the same, so are the converting entity's obligations and assets transferred by operation of law? If so, the entities don't need approvals by third parties to assign existing agreements.
- ○ Are there tax consequences? Under section 351 treatment of contribution of converting entity's assets (e.g., if formerly a SMLLC) to a newly formed B corporation in exchange for interests (which differs from state law treatment); possible tax-free reorganization treatment otherwise.
- ○ Balancing control by 501(c)(3) parent to protect its exemption against the separateness of a B corporation. (See Section 6.3(b).)

  To convert a subsidiary to a B corporation, the documents generally required are as follows:

- ○ Plan of conversion
- ○ Certificate of conversion
- ○ New articles of incorporation and bylaws of the B corporation
- ○ Resolutions: approval documentation by the board of the parent organization and by the "converting entity"
- ○ Other transaction documents as the case may be: intercompany services; shared-services agreement; IP; other
- ○ Third party consents[233.8]

(v) B corporations, Delaware versus Model Act: Summary of Differences. Delaware requires a B corporation to have as a purpose the promotion of a specific public benefit that is set forth in its certificate. The Model Act requires a benefit corporation to have as a purpose the creation of a general public benefit, but permits a specific public benefit purpose in its certificate.

[233.8] A summary of the B Corporations Model Act can be found at https://benefitcorp.net/attorneys/model-legislation and https://benefitcorp.net/sites/default/files/Model%20benefit%20corp%20legislation%20_4_17_17.pdf for the model legislation.

The Model Act requires a B corporation's "public benefit" performance to be reported and assessed against an independent third-party standard. Delaware does not require measurement against a third-party standard.

The Model Act allows a B corporation to appoint a benefit director and a benefit officer. The benefit director is required to prepare a statement of opinion as to whether the corporation has been successful in pursuing its public benefit purposes. (A publicly traded B corporation is required to have a benefit director.) It also permits the appointment of a benefit officer, who is responsible for preparing the annual benefit report. Delaware does not provide for either of these requirements.

The Model Act requires directors to consider the effects of any action or inaction upon seven groups or interests—shareholders, employees, customers, community and societal factors, local and global environment, the corporation's long- and short-term interests, and the ability of the corporation to accomplish its beneficial purposes. Delaware requires a B corporation's directors to balance three factors—the pecuniary interests of stockholders, the best interests of those materially affected by the corporation's conduct, and the specific public interests identified in its certificate.

Under the Model Act, a person must bring a claim against a benefit corporation or its directors or officers through a "benefit enforcement proceeding." Under Delaware law, shareholder derivative suit provisions apply when bringing a cause of action.

The Model Act requires benefit corporations to prepare an annual benefit report, provide a copy to its shareholders, and also make it available to the public. Delaware requires a biennial report that is not required to be made public, but permits an annual report and public disclosure.[233.9]

§ 6.8 OTHER APPROACHES

(c) Forgoing Tax Exemption

p. 553. *Add the following at the end of this subsection:*

The LLC has been used as a vehicle to fulfill charitable objectives for entrepreneurs seeking more flexibility in their philanthropic activity,

---

[233.9] See article by Sandra B. Feldman, Publications Attorney for CT Corporation, Choosing an Incorporation State. https://www.wolterskluwer.com/en/expert-insights/your-benefit-corporation-options-incorporate-in-delaware-or-elsewhere.

including investing in and with for-profit partners.[248.1] A for-profit LLC is not granted tax exemption and donations to it are not deductible, but there are potential tax benefits, particularly for successful entrepreneurs who own appreciated stock.[248.2] This occurs because, as explained in Section 6.2, unless a special election is made, an LLC is a default pass-through entity whereby all financial activity passes through the LLC to the owners.[248.3] If an entrepreneur donates appreciated stock to an LLC formed for charitable purposes, upon the sale of the stock by the LLC, any resulting capital gains taxes would flow through to the donor.[248.4] On the other hand, if the LLC donated the appreciated shares to a § 501(c)(3) tax-exempt charitable organization, the donor would not only receive a deduction at fair market value of the stock, limited to 30 percent of adjusted gross income, but would also avoid the capital gains tax.[248.5]

A philanthropist-owner of an LLC can mitigate the financial consequences of sacrificing an immediate tax deduction for contributions made to a philanthropic LLC by having the LLC make an immediate charitable contribution to a qualifying charity.[248.6] However, for wealthy philanthropists, such as Mark Zuckerberg, the disadvantage of forgoing an immediate charitable deduction is unlikely to dissuade them from organizing as a philanthropic LLC rather than a private foundation.[248.7]

A prominent example of forgoing tax exemption is the "Chan Zuckerberg Initiative," whereby Mark Zuckerberg, founder of Facebook, and his wife, Priscilla Chan, are donating 99 percent of their Facebook shares (valued at approximately $45 billion at the time of the announcement) to advance their numerous charitable objectives, which initially included personalized learning, curing disease, and building strong communities.[248.8]

[248.1]Garry W. Jenkins, *Who's Afraid of Philanthrocapitalism?*, 61 Case W. Res. L. Rev. 753, 756 (2011); most LLC statutes permit LLCs to engage in any lawful activity. See Mohsen Manesh, *Legal Asymmetry and the End of Corporate Law,* 34 Del. J. Corp. L. 465 (2009).

[248.2]This analysis is based on research prepared by Caroline Koo and is adapted from her graduate tax paper at Georgetown University Law Center, Advanced Topics in Exempt Organizations.

[248.3]See Section 3.5.

[248.4]See IRC §§ 1221–1223.

[248.5]See Section 2.1.

[248.6]This comment is based upon a paper submitted by Eunice Lim from her graduate tax paper at Georgetown University Law Center, Special Topics in Exempt Organizations.

[248.7]See Dana Brakman Reiser, *Disruptive Philanthropy: Chan-Zuckerberg, the Limited Liability Company, and the Millionaire Next Door,* 70 Fla. L. Rev 921, 951 (2018) ("In theory, the percentage limits and lack of a full-market-value deduction for donations to private foundations could enable a transfer of appreciated assets to a philanthropy LLC followed by a speedy donation to a public charity to yield a greater tax benefit than the same transfer to a private foundation."). Barbara Benware, *Donating Appreciated Publicly Traded Securities to Charity,* Schwab Charitable, https://www.schwabcharitable.org/public/charitable/nn/noncash_assets/appreciated-public-traded-securities.html.

[248.8]"A Letter to our Daughter," Dec. 1, 2015, available at facebook.com.

While media outlets referred to their investment vehicle as a charitable foundation, the couple created an LLC for the flexibility of being able to make political contributions,[248.9] which private foundations are prohibited from doing, and for-profit investments, which are permissible investments for private foundations under defined circumstances.[248.10] Mr. Zuckerberg explained that they sought "to pursue our mission by funding nonprofit organizations, making private investments and participating in policy debates. . . ."[248.11]

In regard to assertions that the structure would allow avoidance of taxes on the stock, Mr. Zuckerberg explained that he and his wife did not receive the charitable tax deduction allowed upon transfer of the stock to a charity and that they would pay capital gains tax when the LLC sells the stock.

Another example is the "Emerson Collective," founded by Laurene Powell Jobs, widow of Apple CEO Steve Jobs. The Emerson Collective is also structured as a for-profit LLC. Jobs explains that the LLC structure furthers her personal interest in "deploying capital in the most effective way to create the greatest good that we can."[248.12] Demonstrating the flexibility of operation through an LLC are Emerson Collective's purchase of the majority shares in a magazine, *The Atlantic*, and airing a political advertisement on television explaining its position in regard to U.S. immigration policy.[248.13]

Other examples include the Downtown Project, a $350 million privately funded, for-profit LLC dedicated to revitalizing downtown Las Vegas, established by Zappos CEO Tony Hsieh;[248.14] and the Omidyar Network, a $1.29 billion charitable for-profit LLC operating with an affiliate § 501(c)(3) foundation, established by eBay CEO Pierre Omidyar and his wife Pamela Kerr Omidyar.[248.15] Others have elected to leverage their

---

[248.9]"Mark Zuckerberg Is Giving Away His Money, but with a Twist," Dec. 2, 2015, available at fortune.com.

[248.10]See subsection 6.5(b).

[248.11]"Mark Zuckerberg Defends Structure of His Philanthropic Outfit," Dec. 4, 2015, https://mobile.nytimes.com/2015/12/04/technology/zuckerberg-explains-the-details-of-his-philanthropy.html?smprod=nytcore-iphone&smid=nytcore-iphone-share.

[248.12]Ruth McCambridge, "The Atlantic to Be Sold to Jobs' Social Investment LLC," *Nonprofit Quarterly*, July 31, 2017, https://nonprofitquarterly.org/2017/07/31/majority-shares-atlantic-sold-jobs-emerson-collective.

[248.13]*Id.*; Theodore Schleifer, "Laurene Powell Jobs Is Airing Political Ads in the Wake of Trump's DACA Decision," CNBC, Sept. 5, 2017, https://www.cnbc.com/2017/09/05/laurene-powell-jobs-airing-ads-after-trump-daca-decision.html.

[248.14]About Us, DOWNTOWNPROJECT, Mar. 9, 2018, downtownproject.com.

[248.15]Financials, Omidyar Network, https://www.omidyar.com/financials (last visited May 15, 2018) [hereinafter Omidyar Network].

philanthropic power by combining assets (Warren Buffett)[248.16] and forgo "branding" their charitable activities.[248.17]

Social Entrepreneurship and Venture Philanthropy. Other trends in philanthropy include:

1. Donors who view themselves as entrepreneurs, combining charitable goals with approaches typically found in the for-profit sector; examples:

    i. Tony Hsieh (Zappos)—$350 million in LLC to transform downtown Las Vegas.

    ii. Pierre Omidyar (eBay)—uses § 501(c)(3) and LLC to operate Omidyar Network (approximately $1 billion); invests in entrepreneurs and various social missions.

    iii. Gates Foundation—uses private foundations but heavy focus on mission-driven investments.

2. Donors elect to leverage their philanthropic power by combining assets (Warren Buffett and the Bill and Melinda Gates Foundation) and forgo "branding" their charitable activities.

(d)   Hybrid Structures

p. 554. *Add the following at the end of footnote 253:*

After significant lobbying, § 4943 was revised in 2018 to add new § 4943(g), which, as explained in Section 10.2, provides an exemption from the provisions requiring sale of stock in a situation whose circumstances mirror those of Newman's Own Foundation.

p. 555. *Add the following to the end of this subsection:*

In a recent Supreme Court case, *Burwell v. Hobby Lobby Stores, Inc.*, the Supreme Court cited this page in the book, which described Google.org's advancing its charitable goals while operating as a for-profit corporation. See footnote 24 of the *Hobby Lobby* decision, 134 S.Ct. 2751 (2014) at p. 24. It recognized that while operating as a for-profit corporation, it is able to invest in for-profit endeavors, lobbying, and tap Google's innovative technology and workforce. The Supreme Court stated that:

> In fact, recognizing the inherent compatibility between establishing a for-profit corporation and pursuing nonprofit goals, States have increasingly adopted laws formally recognizing hybrid corporate forms. Over half of the States, for instance, now recognize the "benefit corporation," a dual-purpose entity that seeks to achieve both a benefit for the public and a profit for its owners. [Internal footnote omitted.]

[248.16]"In 2006, Buffett pledged most of his fortune to the Gates Foundation and to four charitable trusts created by his family. . . . His gift to the Gates Foundation of 10 million shares of Berkshire Hathaway stock, to be paid in annual installments, was worth approximately $31 billion in June 2006." *Leadership, Warren Buffett, Trustee,* Bill & Melinda Gates Foundation, https://www.gatesfoundation.org/Who-We-Are/General-Information/Leadership/Executive-Leadership-Team/Warren-Buffett.

[248.17]See Chapter 8 discussion on Royalties and Branding.

(f)   Cause-Related Marketing

p. 559. *Add the following new subsection (g) at the end of this subsection and renumber the current (g) and (h) to (h) and (i), respectively.*

(g)   Commercial Co-Venture

A commercial co-venturer involves a for-profit person or company who regularly conducts a charitable sales promotion or underwrites, arranges, or sponsors a sale, performance, or event of any kind that is advertised to benefit a charitable organization.

CAVEAT

Commercial co-ventures have become a popular way for consumer products and services companies to support charitable causes while generating commercial goodwill.

A nonprofit may make an arrangement with a business to receive a percentage of sales; however, in at least 22 states, it is a regulated activity that may require a special registration filing. This activity is sometimes referred to as a "charitable sales promotion" or a "commercial co-venture." State regulators have an interest in protecting charitable nonprofits from being taken advantage of and protecting consumer's expectations that the money will benefit charitable causes.

The law surrounding charitable sales promotions/cause-related marketing and commercial co-ventures is evolving. The state charitable solicitation registration laws often require nonprofits to file a copy of the contract governing the arrangement before any sales take place. Failure to register can lead to fines and in some states even criminal penalties. If the event is a one-time-only sales event, state law is less likely to require registration than if the sales promotion is ongoing. Furthermore, some states require nonprofits to file written reports on units sold and income received; consequently, the nonprofit may need detailed sales reports from the for-profit/other partner.

CAVEAT

The arrangements with the for-profit need to be documented so that there is accountability for the sales promotions.[274.1]

[274.1]In addition, the corporate sponsorship rules under § 501(i) need be reviewed. See Section 8.4.

It is important to note that commercial co-ventures may also exist if one nonprofit agrees to sell products jointly with another nonprofit and agrees that a percentage of the sales will benefit one or the other of the nonprofits. The transaction may be structured as a license agreement involving royalties.

CAVEAT

Of course, the agreement should be formalized such that the nonprofit and the other party commit the arrangement to writing in order to memorialize the responsibilities of each party, and how the contributions/revenue will be split between the two (or more) parties. The parties need to include in the written agreement each of the parties' responsibilities in connection with promoting the sales. The nonprofit should have the discretion to approve any communications about the sales promotion.

CAVEAT

The nonprofit needs to determine if there are conflicts of interest with board members and other "insiders" who also have an interest in the for-profit business. Any transaction resulting in private benefit/private inurement can trigger penalties for the nonprofit and those receiving excess benefit. (See Section 5.4.)

(h)   Impact Investing (as renumbered above)

p. 559. *Insert at the end of the subsection:*

Impact investing may be defined as investments made in companies, organizations, and funds with the intention of generating measurable "social and economic impact" alongside a financial return. Investments typically target some level of financial return from below-market to risk-adjusted market rate and can be made, of course, in asset classes. It should be noted that impact-oriented investors can have different priorities which may fall either into a (1) "return first," where the investors prioritize a financial return with an additional focus on impact; or (2) as a market or industry investment strategy, such as renewable industry.

CAVEAT

This category can include funds with a "negative screen," that is, selecting companies to invest based on social or environmental performance and excluding companies that don't meet the appropriate standards.

The second priority would be investors that prioritize both financial and impact returns, often accepting a lower rate of return, if and when impact goals are achieved. In this category companies would be selected that show leadership and innovation in social and/or environmental areas; finally, the third category would be investors that are typically foundations or public charities that prioritize impact returns over any financial return.

1. Impact Investing and the Commercialism Doctrine. In October 2020, the IRS released PLR 202041009, which denied federal tax exemption under §501(c)(3) to a nonprofit organization that structured and managed "double-bottom-line" impact investment funds.

This ruling is a "warning" to charities engaged in developing impact investing opportunities and may discourage foundations who seek to make program-related investments (see Section 6.5) that intend to invest in certain impact funds. According to the facts, a nonprofit corporation was formed separately from its tax-exempt "parent" organization. The two entities were operationally integrated; the newly formed nonprofit ("manager") applied for tax exemption and provided that it was formed exclusively for charitable purposes, intending to deploy capital into projects that perform a social good and need financing in the capital markets. Its focus was on those organizations that develop and operate affordable housing for the economically and physically disadvantaged and community facilities, such as schools and community health centers; businesses providing access to healthy foods; sustainable energy products, among others. In essence, the manager was focusing on enhancing economic opportunities in the low-income and underserved communities.[278.1]

The organization proposed to charge a substantially-below-market management fee intended primarily to cover its costs. The manager did not take a percentage of profits, that is, a "carried interest" from the funds.

The IRS did not view the fund's investment activity to be sufficiently charitable to overcome the "commercial" aspects of the organization's fund management activities. It concluded that the organization failed the operational test because a substantial portion of its activities consist of managing funds for a fee in order to provide market or near market returns for investors. It cited Rev. Rul. 69-528 that providing investment services for a fee to an unrelated organization is an unrelated trade or business. The IRS focused almost entirely on the organization's expectation of market (or near-market) returns for the investors and did not consider whether the charitable purpose prevailed over the potential rate of return. In effect,

---

[278.1]The manager registered as a state-registered investment advisor and planned to register with the SEC once they satisfied the eligibility requirements.

the IRS holding turned on the "commerciality" doctrine, concluding that a number of factors demonstrated that the manager was primarily engaged in a noncharitable commercial trade or business, that is, receiving a fee for a substantial purpose of providing market or near-market returns to investors. This was so notwithstanding the fact that the manager's activities were not commercial because its fees were lower than market and it cannot share in profits in contrast to commercial managers who receive a percentage of profits. The IRS was also concerned that the manager did not receive donations, grants, or contributions from the public. Finally, the IRS described the organization as "operationally integrated" with the parent, an existing 501(c)(3) organization. The IRS apparently concluded that using a nonprofit to offset costs and increased returns for investors was not an exempt purpose.

CAVEAT

Many practitioners view the IRS denial as making it more difficult for impact investment to qualify as a charitable activity. Accordingly, the author recommends that in many cases, the investment fund activity should be placed in a taxable subsidiary or "blocker." (See Section 6.3.)

CAVEAT

It should be noted that in the private foundation context, making a program-related investment is a charitable activity, while a mission-related investment or MRI is not. The distinction is often muddied between the primary charitable activity, that is, a PRI structure, and the case in which an investment activity is in an MRI that is also socially beneficial, but not charitable.

CAVEAT

An MRI is generally understood as a prudent investment that does not meet the requirements of the PRI, but the charitable mission is at the very least a "positive" factor. (See Section 6.6.)

It is understood in the marketplace that the anticipated value of a PRI (a risk-adjusted return) needs to be distinguishable from that of a "return-seeking" investment.

CAVEAT

In examining the structure, judgment needs to be made with regard to the impact fund as to whether it is the social and/or environmental goals or the investment return that is the primary consideration.

CAVEAT

Some practitioners have viewed PLR 202041009 as suggesting that charities, in considering proposed impact investment activity, should be mindful of the PRI/MRI distinction. Both private foundations and public charities need to classify PRIs on their tax return; there are additional important consequences for private foundations under section 4944(c). (See Section 6.5.)

CAVEAT

Some practitioners have requested additional guidance and regulations that foster use of PRIs and MRIs, pointing out that an area of confusion arises from the borrowing of the definition and name for PRIs from the jeopardy investment rules of IRC 4944 for purposes of determining if certain grants—such as recoverable grants—count toward the mandatory minimum investment return payout requirements under § 4942. Additional confusion exists within the philanthropic community, as discussions encouraging MRIs are confused with program-related investment grants. In other words, is a PRI an investment decision to which IRC 4944 applies and over which an investment committee and its policies are applicable, or is the PRI a grant decision to which IRC § 4942 applies and over which a grants committee has oversight? It is suggested that clarity could be provided if the Treasury Regulations found that "mission-related investments" are investment decisions under IRC § 4944 and "program-related investment" are grant decisions under IRC § 4942.

In addition, clarifying that presence of possible market rates of return do not disqualify an investment or grant as an MRI/PRI. While Treasury recently attempted to make this clear, private foundations remain reluctant to find market rate investments as permissible in MRI/PRI decisions even when the primary reason for the decision is not the rate of return.[278.2] See PRL 202041009.

[278.2]See comments of Council on Michigan Foundation to IRS, dated May 28, 2021, with regard to matters to be included in the 2021–2022 Priority Guidance Plan.

CHAPTER 7

Exempt Organizations as Accommodating Parties in Tax Shelter Transactions

§ 7.2   PREVENTION OF ABUSIVE TAX SHELTERS

(b)   Reportable Transactions

(ii)   Listed Transactions

p. 568. *Add footnote 32.1 at the end of the second sentence in the first paragraph:*

[32.1] In 2015 the Treasury Department issued final regulations that address the proper tax treatment of the transaction described in Notice 2008-99. Consequently, transactions that are the same as, or substantially similar to, transactions described in Notice 2008-99 are no longer considered "transactions of interest," effective for transactions entered into on or after January 16, 2014. 2015-35 I.R.B. 221 (Aug. 11, 2015).

p. 568. *Add the following to the end of the first paragraph:*

In IRS Notice 2017-10[36.1] the IRS now treats as a listed transaction a conservation easement arrangement involving the syndication of conservation easements that purport to give investors charitable deductions significantly greater than the amounts invested. The notice identifies certain conservation easement arrangements as taxable in this transaction and designates them as listed transactions for purposes of Treas. §§ 1.6011-4(b)(2), 6111, and 6112.[36.2]

(vii)   Reporting Requirements.   p. 570. *In the second paragraph of this subsection, add the following before the last sentence:*

[36.1] IRS Notice 2017-10, I.R.B. 2017-4 (Jan. 23, 2017) (https://www.irs.gov/irb/2017-04_IRB/ar12.html).
[36.2] 36.2 For more detailed discussion, see subsection 16.3(g).

■   135   ■

In 2014 the Form 990's Schedule A was expanded to require Type III organizations to complete a list of questions related to compliance with the detailed rules pertinent to supporting organizations, and the instructions to Schedule R, "Related Organizations and Unrelated Partnerships," were amended to clarify that transactions with disregarded entities do not need to be reported on Part V, "Transactions with Related Organizations."

§ 7.3 EXCISE TAXES AND PENALTIES

(c) Disclosure Requirements

p. 573. *Delete the last sentence (and footnote) of the first full paragraph and replace it with the following:*

If the exempt organization fails to do so, the IRS imposes a further penalty of $100 for each day of nondisclosure, up to a maximum penalty of $50,000 for any one disclosure.[67]

---

[67]IRS Publication 557, "Tax-Exempt Status for Your Organization," 21 (Feb. 2015).

CHAPTER 8

The Unrelated Business Income Tax

§ 8.1 INTRODUCTION

(a)   The Rising Tide of Commercialism

p. 578. *Insert the following in the body of the text after footnote 3, before the last sentence in the first paragraph:*

During the COVID-19 pandemic,[3.1] as families sheltered in place, Christian streaming services in particular have seen a rise in viewership and membership.[3.2]

> **EXAMPLE**
>
> RightNow Media, an online streaming platform that features hundreds of hours of Christian teaching and Bible-focused content for children, had 10,000 new subscribers join in April 2020.[3.3] The ministry specifically markets its streaming service to churches and the church leaders then offer their congregants free access.[3.4]

Accordingly, a UBIT issue may arise for the churches if the so-called "donations" are viewed by the IRS as equivalent to subscription fees

---

[3.1]The materials added to this subsection are based on a paper written by James A. Maroules, Esq., "Thoughts and Prayers 3.0—The New Normal?," and is adapted from his graduate tax paper at Georgetown University Law Center, Special Topics in Exempt Organizations.

[3.2]See Jeannie Law, "Christian Streaming Services See Spike in Viewers as Families Turn to Faith-Based Shows in Lockdown," *Christian Post*, May 8, 2020, https://www.christianpost.com/news/christian-streaming-services-see-spike-in-viewers-as-families-turn-to-faith-based-shows-in-lockdown.html.

[3.3]*Id.*

[3.4]*Id.*

for digital goods. Not only may there be UBIT, but many states now tax the streaming of digital goods for state and local tax sales and use tax purposes.[3.5]

(b) Impact of UBIT and Reporting Trends

p. 579. *Delete the first three sentences of this subsection and replace with the following (note that footnote 8 is deleted):*
According to the Fall 2014 Statistics of Income Bulletin, reporting on information for the 2010 reporting year, 43,184 exempt organizations filed Form 990-T with $11 billion received as gross UBI, offset by $10.8 billion in deductions.[5] Two percent more tax-exempt organizations filed the Form 990-T for 2010 and reported $341.3 million in unrelated business income tax liability.[6] Total unrelated business income tax liability increased 28 percent from 2009.[7]

p. 579. *In footnote 9, delete* www.irs.gov.

p. 579. *Insert the following to the end of the paragraph:*
The primary reasons for the increases were disallowing expenses that were not connected to unrelated business activities, lack of profit motive, improper expense allocation, errors in computation or substantiation, and reclassifying exempt activities as unrelated. The majority of the adjustments came from the following activities: fitness, recreation centers, and sports camp; advertising; facility rentals; arenas; and golf.[9.1]

§ 8.3 GENERAL RULE

(b) The Definition of "Unrelated Trade or Business"

(i) Trade or Business. p. 585. *Insert the following at the end of footnote 45:*
The exemption for low-cost articles is indexed annually for inflation and is set at $10.60 for 2016. See Rev. Proc. 2015-53.

[3.5]The majority of states tax digital goods based on the end consumer's billing address, which may create a multitude of complications requiring collection, reporting, and remittance of sales tax in multiple states. Indeed, each state has its own definition of what is considered a digital product. However, many states exempt certain 501(c)(3)s from their sales and use tax; it should be noted that aside from federal tax law, there are other state statutory definitions and case law should be consulted. *See also* James W. Gordon, *Religion and the First Justice Harlan*, 85 Marq. L. Rev. 317 (2001); Ruth, *The Supreme Court's Historical Errors in City of Boerne v. Flores*, 43 B.C.L. Rev. 783 (2002).
[5]Fall 2014 Statistics of Income Bulletin, available at https://www.irs.gov/pub/irs-soi/soi-a-eoub-id1403.pdf.
[6]*Ibid.*
[7]*Ibid.*
[9.1]*Ibid.*

(A) SEGREGATING A BUSINESS FROM WITHIN AN EXEMPT ACTIVITY

p. 589. *Insert the following at the end of footnote 64:*

See, for example, *Losantiville Country Club v. Commissioner,* T.C. Memo 2017-158 (investment income held to be UBI when losses from nonmember sales activities not conducted with profit motive, inasmuch as they generated losses to offset income) citing *Portland Golf Club v. Commissioner,* 497 U.S. 154 (1990) (losses from nonmember sales may offset investment income only if sales were entered into for profit).

(iii) "Regularly Carried On."
(A) THE REGULATIONS

p. 591. *Insert the following at the end of footnote 75:*

PLR 201644019 (a one-time sale of assets by a charity's wholly owned subsidiary LLC to an unrelated party was not UBI because the activity was not "regularly carried on").

(iii) "Substantially Related."
(A) THE REGULATIONS

p. 600. *Insert the following Example after the first Example on this page:*

EXAMPLE
M, an organization described in § 501(c)(3), is an alumni association for N, a two-year community college, and provides financial and civic support for the benefit of N. M derives substantially all of its revenue from the operation of a weekly event held in the parking areas of N's campus every Saturday and Sunday year-round. The event features vendors offering arts and crafts, entertainment, a farmer's market, and refreshments. Although the event is free for the public to attend, the vendors must pay a one-time application fee and monthly space fee for the ability to offer their wares at the event. Because the event does not contribute importantly to M's exempt purposes other than through the production of income, the activity is an unrelated trade or business subject to UBIT.[114.1]

§ 8.4 STATUTORY EXCEPTIONS TO UBIT

(b) Activities for the Convenience of Members

p. 604. *Insert the following at the end of footnote 139:*

Cf. Tax-exempt organization received fees from vendors that were held to be unrelated business income; the court rejected argument that funds were royalties or payments made for convenience of members (*New Jersey Council of Teaching Hospitals v. Commissioner,* 149 T.C. 22 (2017)).

(h) Corporate Sponsorship

p. 610. *Insert the following after the Example:*

With regard to links to sponsors' websites referenced in the above example, a link from the university website to the sneaker manufacturer

---

[114.1]TAM 201544025 (Oct. 30, 2015). The organization at issue here, College of the Desert Alumni Association, Inc., has appealed the IRS's decision to the Tax Court. *See College of the Desert Alumni Association, Inc. v. IRS.*

with no promotion or advertising would be viewed as a "qualified sponsorship payment" and not subject to UBIT. However, the inclusion of a statement that the university endorses the sneakers and gives permission for the endorsement to appear in its website could be viewed as a substantial return benefit and be subject to UBIT.

p. 612. *Insert the following at the end of the first paragraph on the page:*
In this regard, pay-per-view or click-through arrangements may be precluded from constituting qualified sponsorship arrangements. A click-through rate is the percentage of people visiting a web page who access a hypertext link to a particular advertisement. A moving banner may be considered advertising rather than sponsorship.

§ 8.5 MODIFICATIONS TO UBIT

(d) Royalties

p. 622. *Insert the following at the end of footnote 246:*
In PLR 201644019, a charity's wholly owned for-profit subsidiary formed an LLC with an unrelated party. The LLC paid the charity royalties for the use of the charity's trademarks, domain names, and social media handles. Because the charity did not directly or actively participate in the day-to-day management of the subsidiary or LLC, payments by the LLC to the charity constituted royalties exempt from UBIT. The subsidiary was in effect successfully functioning as a blocker entity, and the subsidiary's involvement in the LLC would not be attributed to the charity.

(g) Income from Internet Activities

p. 645. *Insert the following at the end of footnote 339:*
In this regard, pay-per-view or click-through arrangements are likely to be characterized as advertising. See subsection 8.4(h).

§ 8.7 CALCULATION OF UBIT

(a) General Rules

p. 659. *Delete the second full paragraph and replace it with the following:*[381]
Before January 1, 2018, tax-exempt organizations could calculate the amount of tax imposed on UBI based on the income of all the unrelated business activities regularly carried on less all the permissible deductions directly connected with the carrying on of these activities.[382] Therefore, losses that were generated by one trade or business could offset the income earned by a different trade or business.

---

[381]The analysis in this subsection is based on research prepared by Nina Roca, Esq. and is adapted from her graduate tax paper at Georgetown University Law Center, Advanced Topics in Exempt Organizations.
[382]IRC § 512 (2017).

Under the new law, a nonprofit must separately calculate the net UBIT for each unrelated trade or business, in effect creating "silos"; accordingly, any loss derived from one unrelated business activity may not offset the income from another unrelated trade or business.[383] Furthermore, net operating loss deductions are only allowed to be used against income from the trade or business from which the loss arose.[383.1] The Joint Committee on Taxation expects this provision will increase revenues from 2018 through 2027 by a total of $3.5 billion.[383.2]

The Act is not clear on how to determine whether an activity would constitute a single or multiple trade or business. There is little guidance as to the meaning of a "separate trade or business" in the Code.

The concept of "separate trade or business" within the realm of exempt organizations was first introduced by the IRS through regulations implementing the fragmentation principle in the mid-1960s.[383.3] This concept was endorsed by the Supreme Court in *United States v. American College of Physicians*, where the court hailed the concept as a "revolutionary approach" to identifying a trade or business.[383.4] See Code § 513(c).[383.5] Although fragmenting income within a business has become a common practice among nonprofits, the concept of separating lines of businesses is novel for exempt organizations and has no for-profit counterpart.

CAVEAT

Under the 2017 Tax Act (Pub. L. No. 115-97) (the "Tax Act") a for-profit corporation is now subject to a 21 percent tax on the taxable income of each year.[383.6] The taxable income of the corporation is the gross income of the corporation less the deductions allowed by Chapter 1 of the Code. As long as all lines of business are owned by the same corporation, all of the corporation's income from the multiple businesses can be offset by losses arising in any of the businesses.[383.7]

Although a for-profit corporation is not required to separate its businesses, it may elect to do so in order to implement multiple methods of

---

[383]TCJA § 13702.

[383.1]TCJA § 13702(b).

[383.2]Joint Committee on Taxation, Estimated Budget Effects of the Conference Agreement for H.R.1, The "Tax Cuts and Jobs Act" (Dec. 18, 2017), (https://www.jct.gov/publications.html?func=startdown&id=5053).

[383.3]Treatment of Income from Unrelated Trade or Business, 32 FR 17657.

[383.4]*United States v. Am. Coll. of Physicians,* 475 U.S. 834 (1986); *Am. Med. Ass'n v. United States,* 887 F.2d 760 (7th Cir. 1989).

[383.5]Tax Reform Act of 1969, Pub. L. No. 91-172, § 121(c). See § 8.3.

[383.6]IRC § 11.

[383.7]See *id.*

accounting. A taxpayer engaged in more than one trade or business may, in computing taxable income, use a different method of accounting for each trade or business.[383.8] No trade or business will be considered separate and distinct unless a complete and separable set of books and records is kept for such trade or business.[383.9] Under these provisions, the default for corporate taxpayers is to treat all lines of business as a single trade or business and apply only one method of accounting. And, if the corporation prefers to use multiple methods of accounting, it would need to demonstrate that the books of each business are separable, that income would still be clearly reflected by the method of accounting that was chosen, and that there would be no shifting of profits and losses by reason of maintaining different accounting methods.[383.10]

CAVEAT

The IRS is not likely to interpret "separate trade or business" in a manner consistent with § 446. It would seem *counterintuitive* for the Service to allow exempt organizations to default into having a single trade or business, which was the law before 2018, when the estimated budget effect of implementing the change in law is to raise $3.5 billion in 10 years. Because the election to treat different activities as separate trade or businesses would result in exempt organizations having to *silo* their gains and losses per business, they are not likely to make this election because it would likely result in a higher tax liability.

Although "separate trade or business" is rarely applicable to corporations, it does arise more often in the context of individual taxpayers.[383.11]

The IRS has previously advocated for a "nature of the business" test when interpreting "separate trade of business" within the context of

---

[383.8]See Code § 446, Treas. Reg. 1.446-1(d)(2).

[383.9]Treas. Reg. § 1.446-1(d)(2).

[383.10]*Id.*

[383.11]The Code embraces the concept of "separate trade or business" for individuals in various provisions, including §§ 130 (1939), 183, 446, and 1348. Some of the clearest guidance is provided in regulation § 1.183-1, which states that the activity or activities of the taxpayer must be ascertained, and, where the taxpayer is engaged in multiple activities, it must first be determined if the activities constitute one undertaking or several undertakings. Ascertaining the activities is a facts and circumstances based test, with the most significant factors, generally, being "the degree of organizational and economic interrelationship of various undertakings, the business purpose which is (or might be) served by carrying on the various undertakings separately or together in a trade or business or in an investment setting, and the similarity of various undertakings." Furthermore, the regulation provides that the Service will generally accept the characterization by the taxpayer of the several undertakings as either a single activity or separate activities, unless the characterization is artificial and not reasonably supported under the facts and circumstances. Further guidance can be found throughout case law. See *Roselle v. C.I.R.*, T.C. Memo 1981-394 (1981); *Californians Helping to Alleviate Medical Problems, Inc. v. C.I.R.*, 128 T.C. 173, 183 (2007).

§ 130.[383.12] The basic theory of the "nature of the business" test is that if two enterprises of an individual are in the same line of business, then those enterprises should be treated as a single trade or business. In *Collins,* the IRS argued that the taxpayer was in the line of business of promoting professional football, so his New York Club and Boston Club should be in the same line of business. The court ultimately found for the taxpayer, stating that although the similarity of the activities may be a fact, this one factor may be outweighed by other considerations, including the separateness of the economic entities; the separate management; the different finance, currency controls, labor, and marketing conditions; and the maintenance of separate books. However, the Service nonacquiesced to the decision.

Although these factors may prove beneficial in determining how the IRS is likely to interpret "separate trade or business," it is important to keep in mind that in all of these cases and statutes, the taxpayer was actively seeking to have the businesses treated as separate because there was a tax benefit in them being distinct. Under existing tax law, the exempt organizations will attempt to do the opposite and aggregate its activities into a single business as opposed to separate businesses. Section 13702 of the Tax Act appears to be the first implementation of "separate trade of business" where having a single business is more beneficial for the taxpayer.

As previously discussed in Section 8.3, the ultimate goal of UBIT was to eliminate unfair competition by taxing the unrelated business activities of exempt organizations on the same basis as their nonexempt competitors.[383.13]

CAVEAT

The new law goes beyond what was originally intended by placing exempt organizations at a disadvantage because only exempt organizations have to "silo" their business and for-profit corporations do not. In keeping as close as possible to this original intent, while also complying with the Congressional intent, the new § 13702 should be read broadly, so as to keep for-profits and nonprofits competitive and have them taxed on a similar basis. The term "separate trade or business" should be interpreted liberally, and the IRS should look to the facts and circumstances, with the most significant factors being the nature of the businesses and the interrelationship of the businesses; indeed the IRS should accept the characterization of the exempt organization, so long as it is not artificial or unreasonable.

Before January 2018, after applying the fragmentation rule and separating out the businesses that produce related income, a nonprofit could

---

[383.12]*Collins v. C.I.R.,* 34 T.C. 592, 594 (1960), nonacq., IRS Announcement Relating to Collins (IRS ACQ Dec. 31, 1964); *Davis v. C.I.R.,* 29 T.C. 878, 887-88 (1958), acq. In part, IRS Announcement Relating to Davis (IRS ACQ Dec. 31, 1959).
[383.13] See § 1.513-1(b), *supra* note 43.

aggregate all the gains and losses from all the unrelated businesses to determine their total net income tax liability. Now, however, an exempt organization must *silo* each separate trade or business. And in determining whether activities constitute separate trade or businesses, the IRS will examine all the facts and circumstances, with the most significant factors being the nature of the businesses and the interrelationship of the businesses; the IRS should accept the characterizations of the exempt organization, so long as they are not artificial or unreasonable.

CAVEAT

It is important to note that if the trade or business were dropped into a blocker corporation, the nonprofit would not be subject to UBIT upon receipt of a dividend, but it would have to pay a 21 percent corporate rate on net sales, rather than just the UBI.

EXAMPLE

An exempt organization whose purpose is the prevention of cruelty to animals, in addition to its charitable purpose, is involved in the business of boarding pets and the business of pet grooming. The organization would be subject to UBIT because the boarding business and grooming business, provided that they were regularly conducted, would not be substantially related to the purpose of preventing animal cruelty. These two businesses would likely be considered a "single" trade or business because the nature of these businesses are identical, the care of animals. If the exempt organization were to characterize them as a single business, the IRS should accept this characterization because it does not appear artificial or unreasonable. Because they would be considered a single business, any income from one of these lines could be offset by losses from the other line.

CAVEAT

However, if the IRS were to challenge the taxpayer's position in the previous example (and argue that these were separate businesses), the exempt organization could respond by dropping both of these businesses into a *blocker* corporation and not pay UBIT on the receipt of the dividends. Whether it was separately incorporated in a blocker corporation or integrated into the exempt organization, the organization would be paying tax at the 21 percent rate. The blocker would be beneficial if the boarding business was operating at a loss and the grooming business was generating income; the loss from the boarding business could be used to offset the gain from the grooming business. Furthermore, if these businesses become a substantial part of the organization, placing them in a blocker corporation would prevent the exempt organization from potentially having its exemption revoked.

In the context of nonprofits investing in private investment funds, if it were not treated as a single business, the exempt organization could use blocker corporations to prevent having to silo each individual portfolio investment.

EXAMPLE

A tax-exempt investor in a private equity fund could request that the investment companies be divided between operating LLCs, which would produce UBI, and the non-UBTI investments. A blocker corporation could then be inserted between the operating LLCs and the private equity fund. In this scenario, only the blocker corporation would pay the corporate tax on the income from the operating LLCs, and dividends to the exempt organization would not be UBIT.

CAVEAT

When determining the extent of the separate businesses, exempt organizations will likely be able to aggregate their unrelated business activities by the nature of the businesses and the interrelationship of the businesses and have the IRS respect this characterization. Although the new tax law seems to disregard the original intent of imposing UBIT, this interpretation of the code provision appears to reach a balance between the legislative intent of imposing UBIT and the existing case law, while still raising the expected revenues predicted by the Joint Committee on Taxation.

To conclude, despite the new code provision that requires exempt organizations to calculate UBIT for each separate trade or business, tax-exempt organizations still have multiple options when it comes to reducing their tax liability. Although exempt organizations may have more income in total that is subject to UBIT, the reduction of the corporate rate from 35 percent to 21 percent may result in an overall lower tax liability. Furthermore, exempt organizations can also take advantage of lower corporate rates by dropping their unrelated business activities into for-profit subsidiaries. By using blocker corporate subsidiaries, the exempt organizations can net all their gains and losses without having to silo the income and losses from separate businesses. Furthermore they can receive dividends without incurring UBIT. An exempt organization can also place a business that would independently qualify for tax-exempt status into a supporting organization under § 509(a)(3). See Section 6.4.

As previously explained, in the context of the new UBTI "silo" rule, tax-exempt organizations are often partners in partnerships that directly or indirectly conduct more than one trade or business. The IRS recently issued an interim guidance, Notice 2018-67,[383.14] which is effective until

---

[383.14] The Notice requests comments regarding the application of § 512(a)(6) to exempt organizations with more than one unrelated trade or business, including distinguishing between trades and businesses under § 512(a)(6); the provision of administrable model for identifying an exempt organization's separate trades or businesses; and response to the use of NAICS as a method for identifying separate trades or businesses.

Treasury issues regulations on the UBTI silo rules. It provides that a tax-exempt organization may rely on "a reasonable, good-faith interpretation" of sections 511 through 514 in determining whether it has more than one unrelated trade or business based on all facts and circumstances.

CAVEAT
Use of North American Industry Classification System ("NAICS") six-digit codes is considered a reasonable, good-faith interpretation.

A tax-exempt organization that is a joint venture taxed as a partner in a partnership may treat a "qualifying partnership interest" as a single trade or business and may further aggregate all of its qualifying partnership interests together as one trade or business.[383.15]

CAVEAT
If a tax-exempt organization acquired a partnership interest prior to August 21, 2018, the organization may treat each such partnership interest as a single trade or business, whether or not the partnership directly or indirectly conducts more than one trade or business.

A qualifying partnership interest is a partnership interest that satisfies either the de minimis test or the "control" test. Under the de minimis test, the tax-exempt organization may hold directly no more than 2 percent of the profits interest and no more than 2 percent of the capital interest in the partnership. Under the control test, the tax-exempt organization may hold directly no more than 20 percent of the capital interest in the partnership and does not have control or influence over the partnership. For the control test, control or influence exists if (i) the tax-exempt organization is able to require the partnership to perform or prevent the partnership from performing any act that significantly affects the operations of the partnership; (ii) the tax-exempt organization's officers, directors, trustees, or employees have rights to participate in the partnership's management or operations; or (iii) the tax-exempt organization has the power to appoint or remove the partnership's officers, directors, trustees, or employees.

Under both the de minimis test and the control test, a tax-exempt organization's percentage interest is the average of the organization's percentage

---

[383.15]The tax-exempt organization may also aggregate any unrelated debt-financed income (discussed later) that arises in connection with a qualifying partnership interest with other income generated by such qualified partnership interest.

interest held at the beginning and the end of the taxable year specified on the organization's Schedule K-1.[383.16]

CAVEAT

A tax-exempt organization cannot meet the de minimis test if its Schedule K-1 does not specify its profits interest. If the tax-exempt organization owns such interest for a period of less than one taxable year, the organization's percentage interest is the average percentage interest held at the beginning and the end of such period.

According to Notice 2018-67, the IRS does not consider providing fringe benefits as an unrelated trade or business, and thus, UBTI generated by providing such fringe benefits is not subject to the UBTI silo rule. See § 512(a)7.

However, net operating losses (NOLs) arising in a taxable year beginning before January 1, 2018, that are carried forward are not subject to the UBTI silo rule and can be applied to UBTI generally. Notice 2018-67 suggests that post-2017 NOLs may be calculated and taken before pre-2018 NOL carryovers are taken.[383.17]

In April 2020, the IRS released proposed regulations providing guidance on how nonprofits with more than one unrelated trade or business should calculate unrelated business taxable income.

As previously discussed, tax-exempt organizations have two types of NOLs. The first type is NOLs that were generated before 2018. These are not tied to a specific unrelated trade or business and may be used against total UBTI. The second type is NOLs that were generated after 2017. These relate to a specific unrelated trade or business and may only be used against income from that unrelated trade or business. The proposed rules clarify that a tax-exempt organization should use its pre-2018 NOLs against its total UBTI before using its post-2017 NOLs against UBTI for each applicable unrelated trade or business. This rule is consistent with the general ordering rules governing NOLs under section 172 of the Code. It is important to note that no such limitations apply to for-profit companies.

[383.16]The de minimis test and the control test take into account the interest in the same partnership owned by a disqualified person (within the meaning of § 4958(f)), a supporting organization (within the meaning of § 509(a)(3)), or a controlled entity (within the meaning of § 512(b)(13)(D)).

[383.17]Parts of the material in this subsection have been derived from PowerPoints presented by Amanda H. Nussbaum, partner at Proskauer, entitled "UBTI in PE Practice, Qualified Transportation Fringe Benefits and Qualified Sponsorship Payments," a copy of which is held by the author, and was presented to the graduate tax class at Georgetown University Law Center on April 16, 2019.

The proposed regulations provide that the pre-2018 NOLs should be taken against the total UBTI in a manner that results in maximum utilization of the pre-2018 NOLs in a taxable year. However, it is unclear how an allocation method would impact the utilization of the pre-2018 NOLs when they are applied first against total UBTI. The allocation method would likely impact how much of the post-2017 NOLs could be used.[383.18]

The proposed regulations now require nonprofits to generally identify their separate unrelated trades or businesses using the first two digits of the North American Industry Classification System (NAICS) codes (NAICS two-digit codes) that most accurately describe the nonprofit's trade or business. NAICS two-digit codes separate trades or businesses into 20 different sectors.[383.19] The use of two-digit, as opposed to six-digit, codes should obviously minimize the administrative burden for nonprofits with multiple unrelated trades or businesses.

CAVEAT

The use of two-digit codes permits the "aggregation" of broadly similar activities when computing UBTI, and thus, allows nonprofits to offset income from one activity with losses from another activity, as long as the two activities are classified within the same broad section. However, a nonprofit cannot use the two-digit code that describes its "exempt" activities to identify its unrelated trades or businesses.

EXAMPLE

A § 501(c)(3) hospital may not use the NAICS two-digit code for healthcare as an umbrella classification for all of its UBTI-generating activity.

CAVEAT

It is important to note that there is no de minimis exception from the silo rules for nonprofits with relatively small amounts of UBTI; all organizations must report their UBTI consistent with the silo rule requirements.

[383.18]Comments are requested as to other allocation methods, but the unadjusted gross-to-gross method is viewed as unreasonable.

[383.19]Notice 2018-67 had instructed nonprofits to determine separate trade or business activities based on any "reasonable" method, while indicating that the use of NAICS six-digit codes would be deemed reasonable. There are more than 1,000 NAICS six-digit codes, and a requirement to define trades or businesses according to that level of detail would have placed a significant administrative burden on nonprofits and, by extension, the IRS. See IRS Issues New Proposed UBIT "Silo" Regulations for Nonprofits, published by Venable LLP, April 2020.

Consistent with Notice 2018-67, the proposed regulations generally allow the "aggregation" of UBTI-generating investment activities that satisfy either a de minimis test or a "control" test. In this regard, if a nonprofit holds an interest in a pass-through entity (such as a partnership, limited liability company, or S corporation), and the scope of the nonprofit's ownership in such entity satisfies either of these tests, then the nonprofit may aggregate all UBTI that it receives through such pass-through entity—even if those activities would otherwise constitute multiple trades or businesses under the NAICS two-digit codes.

CAVEAT

The nonprofit may aggregate all of its pass-through interests that satisfy one of these tests as constituting a single trade or business, such that all UBTI gains and losses flowing through these interests would be reported together as from a single trade or business.

As to whether a tax-exempt organization in a joint venture taxed as a partnership may treat the investment as a qualifying partnership interest and aggregate all of its qualifying partnership interests together as one trade or business, either the de minimis or control test applies.

De Minimis Test. Pursuant to the de minimis test, the nonprofit may hold directly no more than 2 percent of the profit and no more than 2 percent of the capital interest in a pass-through entity including an interest in an S Corp.

CAVEAT

The proposed regulations eliminated the rule provided in Notice 2018-67 that would have required nonprofits to combine interests held by board members, other related persons, "supporting organizations," or controlled entities in determining whether an interest met the requirements of the de minimis test.

Control Test. The control test is satisfied if the nonprofit (i) directly holds no more than 20 percent of the capital interest in a pass-through entity (including an S-Corp); and (ii) does not have control or influence over the decision making of the entity.[383.20]

[383.20]All facts and circumstances are relevant for determining whether a nonprofit has control or influence.

> **CAVEAT**
>
> For these purposes, interests held by "supporting organizations" or entities controlled by the nonprofit are combined with the nonprofit's interest. However, the proposed regulations eliminated the rule in Notice 2018-67 that would have required nonprofits to combine interests held by board members and other, related persons.[383.21]

> **CAVEAT**
>
> The proposed regulations permit a nonprofit to determine its percentage interest in a pass-through entity by relying on the Schedule K-1 it receives from the entity.[383.22]

For purposes of computing public support relative to "public charity" classification (§ 509(a)), the proposed regulations disregard the silo rules. If the silo rules were applied, it would increase the public support threshold in the context of "total support" under § 509(d), which includes UBTI in the denominator.

> **CAVEAT**
>
> Investment activity constitutes a trade or business, which means essentially that all exempt organizations will have at least one trade or business to begin with. Treasury is requesting comments as to the specific factors that should be considered in determining whether an activity is an investment for these purposes.

> **CAVEAT**
>
> Form 1065 K-1s will be revised, but an issue arises because exempt organizations may not be aware of changes in partnership interests until it receives their K-1 many months after the fiscal year ends, so Treasury may need to allow a higher percentage in such year.

Additional guidance will be needed regarding the impact of the NOL changes due to the CARES Act. For example, under the CARES Act, losses arising in taxable years beginning after December 31, 2017, and before

---

[383.21]The proposed regulations provide a "look-through" rule for nonprofits that hold indirect interests in lower-tier partnerships.

[383.22]The proposed regulations generally permit nonprofits to treat "unrelated debt-financed income" (i.e., "passive" income that is typically not subject to UBTI, such as interest, dividends, or rental income, but is treated as UBTI by virtue of debt financing) as income from investment activities, rather than as income from a separate unrelated trade or business.

January 1, 2021, may be carried back to each of the five taxable years preceding the taxable year of such loss. Also, the 80 percent limitation on NOLs' offsetting taxable income has been suspended and NOLs can offset 100 percent of taxable income for tax years 2018, 2019, and 2020. If a loss arising in 2018 is tied to a specific unrelated trade or business, and that loss is carried back to 2017, can that loss be used against total UBTI or may it only be used against income from the specific unrelated trade or business?

CAVEAT
If the NOLs generated in 2018, 2019, or 2020 can be used prior to 2021, they can be used without the 80 percent limitation. However, if they are used in 2021 or later years, they would be subject to the 80 percent limitation. The carryback is valuable for tax-exempt organizations that are taxed at the corporate rate because of the higher corporate tax rate that applied prior to 2018.

To conclude, during the COVID-19 pandemic, nonprofits need to be able to step up and fund societal needs, but now are forced to furlough or lay off staff and face significant budgetary concerns; yet, § 512(a)(6) creates more problems and complexity (115 pages of proposed regulations), while the only purpose of the legislation was to generate tax revenues from the sector. The rules are even more convoluted since the recent CARES Act legislation. The author believes that § 512(a)(6) should be repealed.

Silo Final Regulations.[383.23] In November 2020, Treasury issued final regulations under § 512(a)(6) that provide guidance on how an exempt organization subject to the unrelated business income tax determines, if it has more than one unrelated trade or business, and, if so, how the exempt organization calculates UBTI.

The regulations clarify the guidance provided in the proposed regulations relating to the NAICS two-digit code and interaction between the silo rule and net operating losses, and adopt without substantial change the proposed regulations relating to allocation of deductions among various activities, interaction between the silo rule and the public support tests under section 509, treatment of debt-financed UBTI, and UBTI from controlled foreign corporations and controlled entities.

The final regulations generally retain the proposed rule that a separate unrelated trade or business is identified by the NAICS two-digit code that most accurately describes an exempt organization's trade or business

---

[383.23] A portion of the material in this subsection has been derived from advisory memos prepared by Steptoe (November 2020) and Ropes & Gray (December 2020).

activity; however, the final regulations provide some additional guidance, including that:

- The determination of which two-digit code most accurately describes an exempt organization's activity is based on the more specific NAICS code, such as at the six-digit level, that describes the activity.
- Descriptions in the current NAICS manual (available at census.gov) of trades or businesses using more than two digits of the NAICS codes are relevant in this determination.
- In the case of the sale of goods, both online and in stores, the separate unrelated trade or business is identified by the goods sold in stores if the same goods generally are sold both online and in stores.
- To the extent that other services are provided in connection with a possible rental activity, income from the use of space may cease to be rent from real property and instead take on the character of the services provided.

The final regulations generally adopt the proposed rules for investment activities as previously discussed, while providing detailed additional guidance on the beneficial aggregation rules provided for qualified partnership interests ("QPIs"). In summary, the final regulations retain the 20 percent ownership limit applicable for determining whether a partnership investment may be aggregated together with other qualifying partnership interests in the organization's "investment activities" silo. They provide organizations with incrementally more flexibility by looking through tiers of partnerships and disregarding certain rights commonly provided to limited partners in partnerships when determining whether a partnership interest can be included in the investment activities silo.

NOTE

In order for a partnership interest to be treated as a QPI, the proposed regulations required an exempt organization to (i) directly hold no more than 20 percent of the capital interest in the partnership; and (ii) not have control over the partnership. However, the final regulations rename the "control" test from the proposed regulations to the "significant participation" test, but generally look to the same factors to make this determination as the factors under the control test in the proposed regulations.[383.24]

[383.24]The final regulations expand a favorable "look-through rule" under the proposed regulations to permit an indirect investment in a lower-tier partnership that meets a de minimis test to be treated as a QPI even if the exempt organization significantly participates in the directly held upper-tier partnership.

The proposed regulations had enumerated four *per se* factors that would cause a partnership interest to fail the control test, but otherwise required the organization to determine whether it controlled each partnership based on all the facts and circumstances. The final regulations retain the four *per se* factors, but discard the "general" facts and circumstances test as being too uncertain and too difficult to administer. Accordingly, an organization is treated as significantly participating in the activities of the partnership if:

- The organization, by itself, may require the partnership to perform or may prevent the partnership from performing any act that significantly affects the operations of the partnership;
- Any of the organization's officers, directors, trustees, or employees have rights to participate in the management of the partnership or conduct its business at any time; or
- The organization, by itself, has the power to appoint or remove any of the partnership's officers or employees, or a majority of its directors.

The final regulations also provide greater clarity regarding how the QPI rules apply to S corporation interests. The final regulations clarify that pre-2018 NOLs are taken against the total UBTI in a manner that allows for maximum utilization of post-2017 NOLs in a taxable year.

The final regulations also expand upon a favorable proposed rule by permitting an exempt organization with more than one unrelated trade or business to determine public support using either its UBTI calculated under the silo rules or its UBTI calculated in the aggregate. The second option is intended to prevent the silo rules from having an adverse impact on the calculation of public support while the first option is intended to reduce the administrative burden of requiring two separate calculations of UBTI.[383.25]

CAVEAT

The Final Regulations adopt a limited grace period rule that permits a partnership interest that fails to meet either the de minimis or significant participation test because of an increase in the organization's percentage interest during a taxable year due to the redemption or other action of another partner, to be treated as meeting the requirements for QPI status if the applicable test was met during the prior taxable year.[383.26]

[383.25]The final regulations are applicable to taxable years beginning on or after December 2, 2020. In addition, an exempt organization may choose to apply the final regulations to earlier taxable years beginning on or after January 1, 2018. Alternatively, an exempt organization may rely on a reasonable, good-faith interpretation of § 512(a)(6) for such taxable years.

[383.26]The transitional rule included in Notice 2018-67 and the Proposed Regulations, which permitted an organization to treat any partnership interest acquired prior to August 21, 2018 as a single trade or business activity, will lapse as of the first day of the organization's taxable year following the issuance of the Final Regulations.

(b) Expenses

(ii) Exploited Activity Rule. p. 663. *Insert the following at the end of footnote 398:*

See, for example, *Fish v. Commissioner* (9th Cir. 2017) (pass-through of UBI losses to an IRA beneficiary's personal tax return not permitted).

p. 663. *Add the following new subparagraph at the end of this subsection:*

(iii) Ownership Change. In the context of an ownership change, an issue arises as to whether the net operating losses of a tax-exempt entity can be used by a surviving tax-exempt corporation in a merger. Code section 382 limits the amount of income that can be offset by NOLs where there has been a change in ownership of the taxpayer with an existing NOL in order for its NOL carryovers to be allowed as deductions (after the ownership change pursuant to the annual section 382 limitation).[398.1] The determination of whether there has been an ownership change is expressed in terms of stock ownership, as the provision was intended to apply to for-profit entities where there is a significant ownership change, that is, more than 50 percent.[398.2] The annual section 382 limitation generally equals the fair market value of the stock of the corporation that experienced the ownership change (calculated immediately before the ownership change) multiplied by the applicable federal long-term tax-exempt rate as of the date of the ownership change.[398.3] In general, an ownership change occurs where more than 50 percent of a corporation's stock is sold within a three-year period,[398.4] as well as changes that occur incident to redemptions, recapitalizations, and reorganizations.[398.5]

The Code section 382 rules and the Treasury Regulations thereunder do not specifically encompass or exclude beneficial ownership of loss corporation stock held by nonstock organizations,[398.6] and there is limited authority that speaks to whether Code section 382 should apply to tax-exempt entities.[398.7] The authority that exists is contained in private letter

---

[398.1]Code § 382; Treasury Regulation § 1.382-2T.

[398.2]Robert Mason, Mark Roundtree, and Howard Levenson, "Applying Section 382 to Loss Corporation Affiliates of Exempt Organizations," *Journal of Taxation of Exempt Organizations* 12, no. 3 (Jan./Feb. 2001) ("Taxation of Exempt Organizations Section 382 Article").

[398.3]Code § 382(b).

[398.4]Code § 382(g); Treasury Regulation § 1.382-2T. Note that the calculation of whether an ownership change has occurred may be subject to more complex rules that are irrelevant for purposes of this memorandum.

[398.5]Code § 382(g). Determination of ownership change is measured by changes in stock holdings of shareholders owning 5 percent or more during the period in question. *Id.*

[398.6]Temp. Reg. § 1.382-2T(h)(2)(iii).

[398.7]Code § 382 appears to measure ownership as referring to owners that participate in corporate growth, a concept inconsistent and inapposite to the fundamental concept of tax-exempt organization principles that no earning can inure to the benefit of individuals ("Taxation of Exempt Organizations Section 382 Article").

rulings issued by the IRS, which technically cannot be relied on as precedent by persons other than the taxpayers requesting the ruling.[398.8] These rulings contain complex fact patterns and, in most cases, little or no reasoning by the IRS. In the rulings, the IRS holds that there was no ownership change under Code section 382 in the context of mergers within related tax-exempt groups where the parent had control of one or more subsidiaries with NOLs.[398.9] In the rulings, the loss entity (the entity with the NOL) was transferred to a tax-exempt entity that was under the same control as the transferor tax-exempt entity. Therefore, based on the private letter rulings, it seems that there should be no ownership change.

For example, PLR 200028005 (July 17, 2000) concerned a healthcare system with three Code § 501(c)(3) entities that were the sole corporate members of one or more exempt subsidiary affiliates, some of which owned the stock of for-profit subsidiaries that performed services[398.10] for the group and that had NOLs at the time certain mergers took place. The number of affiliated entities and the mergers were complex; there was no reasoning or analysis by the IRS, other than a recitation that the entities complied with local law governing distribution of assets upon dissolution by tax-exempt organizations. The ruling held:

> The merger of Tax Exempt 1 with Tax Exempt 3 followed by the merger of Tax Exempt 2 with the surviving entity (together with the changes in the corporate membership and governing instruments of the various tax-exempt entities pursuant thereto) does not result in an ownership change within the meaning of § 382(g) of Parent Corp or any other loss corporation owned by an exempt subsidiary affiliate of the former Tax Exempt 1 or Tax Exempt 2, or Tax Exempt 3 systems.[398.11]

The IRS has issued other PLRs involving similar fact patterns, that is, exempt organizations controlled by one or more exempt parents that implement a merger involving controlled subsidiaries, some of which have NOLs.[398.12] Where state law governing such mergers is satisfied, along with

---

[398.8]Code § 6110(k)(3).

[398.9]PLR 200027013 (no ownership change when one tax-exempt entity transferred a for-profit entity's stock to another tax-exempt entity that was also under the control of the transferor tax-exempt entity); PLR 200227014 (no ownership change when one tax-exempt entity distributed stock of a company, which had NOLs, to another tax-exempt entity, which controlled the transferor tax-exempt entity).

[398.10]The services were "substantially unrelated" to the group's exempt purposes.

[398.11]*Id.*

[398.12]See PLR 9001063 (Oct. 13, 1989) (a §501(c)(3) hospital has four supporting organizations under Code § 509(a)(3). The discussion relates to control of the related entities by the parent and within the group. Subsidiary 1's board must be comprised of at least 60 percent of members of the parent's executive committee or officers of the parent. The board of subsidiary 4 is appointed by subsidiary 1 as its sole member, with 60 percent of the board having to consist of members of the parent's executive committee or officers of the parent. Subsidiary 1 owns all of the outstanding stock of a for-profit loss corporation and is also the sole member of another nonprofit supporting organization of the hospital. The IRS ruled that the transfer of the loss corporation's stock from subsidiary 1 to subsidiary 4 will not constitute an ownership change); PLR 9222028 (Feb. 27, 1992).

compliance regarding requisite dissolution clauses and prohibitions on impermissible inurement or private benefit, the IRS rules that there is no "ownership change."

Based on these facts, the author believes that for U.S. federal income tax purposes, it is more likely than not that a merger that meets the control test will not constitute an "ownership change" within the meaning of Code § 382(g) and Treasury Regulation § 1.382-2T. However, because the only indication of the IRS position is found in private letter rulings, there is a possibility that the IRS may challenge the use of an NOL carryforward by a newly formed exempt organization, depending on the facts as to whether there has, in effect, been no "ownership change."

p. 663. *Insert the new subsection:*

(c) Tax on Transportation Fringe Benefits: Qualified Parking, etc.

The Taxpayer Certainty and Disaster Tax Relief Act of 2019 retroactively repealed the 2017 Tax Act provision by which expenses incurred by tax-exempt organizations in providing certain types of fringe benefits were converted into unrelated business taxable income (§ 512(a)(7)).

CHAPTER 9

Debt-Financed Income

§ 9.1 INTRODUCTION

p. 669. *The last citation in footnote 3, second sentence, should read as follows:*

Reg. § 1.514(c)-2.

§ 9.2 DEBT-FINANCED PROPERTY

(a) Overview

p. 671. *Add the following to the end of footnote 10:*

See TAM 201741019 (Oct. 13, 2017) (a tax-exempt trust's activities incurred UBIT from income generated by debt-financed property held through interests in a partnership when the property's activities were not substantially related to the trust's exempt purpose); PLR 20173005 (Jan. 20, 2017) and PLR 201702002 (Jan. 13, 2017) (a tax-exempt hospital may lease its premises to a state university as part of reorganization without incurring UBIT when the proceeds are used to expand and modernize the premises, an activity in furtherance of charitable purposes. Thus, the underlying property is not unrelated debt-financed property).

(c) Acquisition Indebtedness

pp. 676–677. *Add the following to the end of footnote 29:*

PLR 201418061 (Feb. 6, 2014) (borrowing of stocks by the funds—structured as partnerships, in which charity is invested—and entering into short positions held to not result in acquisition indebtedness incurred by organization, so that none of the distributive shares of funds' income or gain derived from these trading activities is treated as debt-financed property); PLR 201434024 (Aug. 22, 2014) (purchase of long positions in stocks in accounts at one or more affiliates of broker using any cash proceeds from short sales made through funds' accounts at these affiliates held to not result in acquisition indebtedness, so that none of distributive shares of funds' income or gain derived from these trading activities will be treated as debt-financed property); PLR 201434026 (Aug. 22, 2014) (use of long positions in stocks, including those purchased with short-sale proceeds, as collateral to secure performance by funds of their obligations to deliver stock to broker to cover its open short positions will not result in acquisition indebtedness).

§ 9.3 THE §514(C)(9) EXCEPTION (NEW)

p. 679. *Add the following to the end of footnote 43:*

Passive income earned from debt-financed property, however, may be excluded from UBI if the taxpayer is a "qualified organization," defined in IRC §514(c)(9)(C), as including educational organizations described in IRC §170(b)(1)(A)(ii). Specifically, IRC §170(b)(1)(A)(ii) refers to "an educational organization [that] normally maintains a regular faculty and curriculum and normally has a regularly enrolled body of pupils or students in attendance at the place where its educational activities are regularly carried on." The corresponding Treasury regulation generally reiterates the statutory language with regard to an "educational organization," but also specifies that (1) formal instruction must be the "primary function" of the organization (primary-function requirement) and (2) any noneducational activities of the organization must be "merely incidental" to its educational activities (merely-incidental test). See subsection 2.5(d)(i).

In *Mayo Clinic vs. United States* (8th Cir. 2021), the Eighth Circuit reversed and remanded a district court's summary judgment decision for the Mayo Clinic ("Mayo"). Mayo is a tax-exempt IRC § 501(c)(3) organization that, among other things, operates five distinct medical schools. After an audit, the IRS determined that Mayo owed tax on certain income that it received from partnerships because it argued that Mayo is not an "educational organization" because its primary function is not formal instruction. Mayo paid the disputed taxes and sued for refund, totaling approximately $11.5 million.

The district court held that the Treasury regulation is invalid "because it adds requirements—the primary-function and merely-incidental tests—Congress intended not to include in the statute."

The Eighth Circuit concluded that Treasury Regulation 1.170A-9 is valid, but only in part, and that application of the statute as reasonably construed by the regulation to Mayo's tax years in question cannot be determined as a matter of law on summary judgment. Accordingly, the court reversed the district court's invalidation of Treasury Regulation 1.170A-9 to the extent it is not inconsistent with IRC § 170(b)(1)(A)(ii) and remanded for further proceedings.

The Appeals Court said that the issue of whether Mayo qualifies as an educational organization "is a mixed question of law and fact," which neither party directly addressed on appeal. To make such a determination, a three-part analysis is typically applied, the court explained: (1) Is the taxpayer organized and operated exclusively for one or more exempt purposes? (2) Is the taxpayer organized and operated exclusively for educational purposes? And, (3) Does the taxpayer meet the statutory criteria for faculty, curriculum, students, and place? Only the second criterion remained at issue. Concluding that more information was needed to determine whether Mayo meets the second criterion, the court remanded the case to the district court.

Ultimately, by invalidating the specific requirement of "formal instruction" found in the Treasury regulation, decisions as to whether an organization meets the definition under IRC § 170(b)(1)(A)(ii) will become more fact-intensive and decided on a case-by-case review of the facts.

§ 9.6 THE FINAL REGULATIONS

(c) Exceptions to the Fractions Rule for Preferred Returns and Guaranteed Payments

p. 683. *Add the following after the first paragraph of this subsection:*

On November 22, 2016, the IRS and Treasury Department issued proposed regulations addressing allocations of items by partnerships that have debt-financed property and one or more (but not all) qualified exempt organization partners.[64.1] The proposed regulations provide further guidance in determining a partner's share of partnership income or loss.

[64.1] Proposed Amendments to Internal Revenue Code § 514(c)(9)(E), 81 Fed. Reg. 84518 (Nov. 23, 2016).

(iv) Timing Rules

(A) PREFERRED RETURNS

p. 686. *Insert the following after the second paragraph on this page, before the Example:*

The proposed regulations expand the preferred return exception to allow related allocations to be disregarded even if the accompanying distribution is not made currently. The proposed regulations require only that the partnership agreement require that the partnership make distributions first to pay any unpaid preferred return to the extent the unpaid preferred return has not been reversed by an allocation of loss before the distribution.

(d) Chargebacks and Offsets

(i) Disproportionate Allocations.   p. 689. *Add the following at the end of this subsection:*

The proposed regulations modify the chargeback exception to disregard certain additional items in computing overall partnership income or loss for purposes of the fractions rule. Specifically, an allocation of overall partnership income that is made to reverse a special allocation of a partner-specific expenditure or a special allocation of an unlikely loss will be ignored in applying the fractions rule.

(e) Partner-Specific Items of Deductions

p. 691. *Add the following at the end of the last paragraph of this subsection:*

The Proposed Regulations add management and similar fees to the current list of excluded partner-specific expenditures under the existing regulations, to the extent that the fees do not, in the aggregate, exceed 2 percent of the partner's aggregate committed capital.

(f) Unlikely Losses and Deductions

p. 692. *Add the following paragraph at the end of this subsection:*

It should be noted that the preamble to the proposed regulations provides that the IRS and Treasury are considering changing the unlikely loss standard from "low likelihood of occurring" to "more likely than not," or some standard in between.

(g) De Minimis Rules

(i) De Minimis Interests.   p. 693. *Add the following new paragraph at the end of this subsection:*

The proposed regulations increase the $50,000 amount to $1 million.

The proposed regulations provide that certain partnerships in which all partners (other than qualified organizations) own 5 percent or less of the capital or profits interest in the partnership will be exempt from application of the fractions rule.

(ii) De Minimis Allocations p. 693. *Add the following at the end of footnote 119:*

(i) Tiered Partnerships
p. 694. *Add the following paragraph at the end of this subsection:*
The proposed regulations amend the third example provided in the regulations that illustrates application of the tiered partnership rules to eliminate the implication that violation of the fractions rule by a lower-tier partnership can cause the upper-tier partnership to violate the fractions rule unless the upper-tier partnership allocates items from the violating lower-tier partnership separately from other items. Thus, where the allocations of an upper-tier partnership satisfy the fractions rule on a stand-alone basis, an arrangement with a lower-tier partnership should not cause a fractions rule violation with respect to the other investments of the upper-tier partnership.

CHAPTER 10

Limitation on Excess Business Holdings

§ 10.1   INTRODUCTION

p. 697. *Delete the regulations citation in footnote 2 and replace with the following:*

Reg. § 1.501(c)(3)-1.

§ 10.2   EXCESS BUSINESS HOLDINGS: GENERAL RULES (REVISED)

p. 699. *Add the following paragraph at the end of footnote 6:*

Many donors use donor-advised funds ("DAFs") instead of private foundations. However, the donor cannot easily "control" the decision as to who is to receive the funds and control as to when they are used. There is no minimum distribution requirement; however, there is no need to form a separate entity so it is easier to form and maintain a donor-advised fund. It is flexible and quite popular as an efficient charitable giving vehicle. There have been published reports that six of the ten largest charity recipients in 2017 were DAFs. Notwithstanding the above, the public has criticized the use of DAFs as not spending enough in the charitable sector; indeed, the charitable contribution is provided "upfront," but there is often a delay in the charitable spending. Finally, there is concern that this classification benefits the very wealthy and there is skepticism about who has actual control of the spending.

p. 701. *Add the following to the end of footnote 17:*

See discussion in subsection 2.11(f) on contributions of LLC/partnership interest to charities.

pp. 703–704. *Add the following to the end of footnote 29:*

See also PLR 201414031(Apr. 4, 2014) (foundation permitted to correct excess business holdings by granting to public charities requisite amount of stock to bring foundation's holdings to 2 percent de minimis amount).

p. 704. *Add the following at the end of the first paragraph on this page:*

In February 2018 the Enterprise Act of 2017, as part of the Bipartisan Budget Act of 2018, added a provision that allows private foundations to retain 100 percent of a business under certain conditions. This will allow a private foundation to avoid the requirement to divest itself of at least 80 percent of its excess business holdings under § 4943.

New § 4943(g) permits a foundation to own 100 percent of a company provided:

1. There are no other shareholders and the shares have been donated to the foundation or acquired in a manner other than purchase;

2. The company must distribute all of its net operating income to the foundation within 120 days of the end of each fiscal quarter;

3. No substantial donor to the foundation can be a director, officer, or employee of the company and the majority of the company's directors have to be persons who are not also on the foundation's board; and

4. The company may not make loans to substantial donors of the foundation.

CAVEAT

The new section benefits Newman's Own Foundation, which owns 100 percent of No Limits LLC, a for-profit company that produces and sells Newman's branded line of food products. The passage of the new law relieves Newman's Own from the requirement that it must divest itself of a significant portion of the for-profit company.

CAVEAT

The for-profit company needs to be governed by its own board and managed by its own managers so that there is appropriate separation from the foundation. However, the foundation, as its sole shareholder, may appoint the company's board; there may be overlap of the two boards so long as the majority of the company's board is not also on the foundation's board.

CAVEAT

In the case of a pass-through LLC, the unrelated business income tax rules (see Chapter 8) may apply in view of the 2017 Tax Act (Pub. L. No. 115-97) wherever the new rules prohibit a foundation from using losses from one business to offset the profits of another. See Section 8.7.

As referenced above, § 4943(g) was intended to provide a lifeline to the Newman's Own Foundation by allowing it to indefinitely maintain 100 percent ownership of the for-profit company founded by Paul Newman. (This exception has been referred to as the "Newman's Own Exception.")

CAVEAT

A leading commentator has argued that the requirements of the new provision, particularly the independence requirement, may prove quite challenging, if not insurmountable, in most situations. Further, even if a private foundation can meet the new requirements of § 4943(g), the foundation must still have sufficient liquidity to meet the annual 5 percent distribution requirement under § 4942 with respect to the fair market value of its interest in the for-profit company, thereby potentially creating another significant obstacle to a foundation's 100 percent ownership of the business enterprise.[33.1]

Although this new provision providing an exception to the business holding rules may have only limited application, it does provide planning opportunities in certain cases where the donor seeks to transfer control and ownership of a business enterprise to a private foundation. At a time when private sector philanthropy and entrepreneurship has grown, this exception permits a philanthropist to bequeath an entire business to a private foundation, provided, however, that the after-tax profits will be paid to the foundation and other stringent requirements are satisfied.

CAVEAT

It should be noted that a public charity under § 509(a) avoids the minimum distribution requirement under § 4942 and, fundamentally, is not subject to the excess business holding rules. In cases where a § 4943(g) exception is not a viable option, an alternative structure could allow for the funding of the foundation with nonvoting shares and having nondisqualified persons own at least 80 percent of the voting stock as an alternative to a private foundation in order to avoid both the excess business holding rules and the 5 percent minimum investment return requirement. The business can be contributed to a vehicle that is a public charity and allow the family members to serve on the board.[33.2]

---

§ 10.3 TAX IMPOSED

p. 705. *Delete language in footnote 34 and replace with the following:*
§ 4943(a); Reg. § 53.4943-2(a).

[33.1]These comments are based upon the analysis written by Richard L. Fox, the author of a treatise, *Charitable Giving: Taxation, Planning and Strategies* (Thomson Reuters).
[33.2]*Id.*

§ 10.4 EXCLUSIONS (REVISED)

(a) Functionally Related Business

p 706. *Add the following to the end of footnote 44:*
See PLR 201701002 (Jan. 6, 2017) (program providing "technical assistance" to social service nonprofit organizations held functionally related business when services had a primarily charitable purpose, had access to raw data not available to commercial ventures, and were performed by organization's employees).

p. 706. *Add the following after the Example:*
Assume a private foundation makes an equity investment in a functionally related LLC along with a for-profit member; although there would not be an excess business holding issue, the structure may raise unrelated business income tax questions in the event that the control test under Rev. Rul. 2004-51 is not satisfied. In this regard, see page 380.

(c) Income from Passive Sources

p. 708. *Delete language in footnote 54 and replace with the following:*
Passive income includes income from items excluded by § 512(b)(1), (2), (3), and (5). PLR 9412039 (Mar. 25, 1994); PLR 9250039 (Sept. 16, 1992).

p. 708. *Add the following to the end of footnote 55:*
See PLR 201422027 (May 30, 2014).

p. 708. *Insert the following at the end of this subsection:*
A private foundation often jointly invests with members of the family (i.e., disqualified persons) in an investment fund, either at its formation or thereafter. The co-investors may involve individuals, many of whom are descendants of the founder or a substantial contributor of the foundation, as well as certain trusts created by such individuals and/or partnerships or limited liability companies of which such individuals or trusts own more than 35 percent of the voting and/or profits interest. From time to time, the parties may contribute cash and may withdraw cash from the fund as well. There are numerous advantages for the foundation to co-invest with and in entities who may be disqualified persons: access to investment opportunities that have minimum investment requirements, access to the expertise of otherwise unavailable investment advisors, and economies of scale.

In a representative private letter ruling regarding foundations investing with disqualified persons, the IRS stated in part:

> Section 4943 of the Code expressly contemplates and permits joint or co-investments by disqualified persons and private foundations. Numerous joint or co-investment situations exist, as permitted by § 4943, where both the private foundations and the disqualified persons involved either buy or sell interests in the investment entity or make withdrawals from such entity after formation and initial funding. The passive investments contemplated by [foundation] are not considered a "business enterprise"; see § 4943(d)(3)(B). PLR 200420029.

Although the rulings in this area are fact specific, common threads are representations that the foundation is paying reasonable fees for the brokerage, tax, and portfolio services, and that no disqualified person is receiving an impermissible benefit. Thus, fund managers, who may or may not be disqualified persons as to the private foundation, must be paid reasonable compensation for such management services[58] (i.e., comparable to those received by independent unrelated advisors) consistent with § 4958 and/or the self-dealing rules under § 4941(d).[59]

CAVEAT

The Treasury and IRS 2016–2017 Priority Guidance Plan (Aug. 15, 2016) contains guidance regarding private foundations' investment in partnerships in which disqualified persons are also partners; see IRC § 4941.

CAVEAT

In June 2016, ABA Tax Section sent a letter to the IRS regarding topics for additional guidance: First we recommend that the Service clarify, by revenue ruling, situations in which co-investments between a private foundation and its disqualified persons do not constitute acts of self-dealing within the meaning of § 4941.[60] The revenue ruling would provide that a private foundation's participation in a co-investment arrangement structured with certain protective measures, designed to ensure that its participation is for the benefit of the private foundation and to prevent benefits to disqualified persons, does not constitute self-dealing. The revenue ruling would provide that a "co-investment arrangement" is categorically distinct from a "sale or exchange" prohibited by § 4941(d)(1)(A), and that any benefit that accrues to a disqualified person who is a co-investor as a result of a private foundation's contributions to or withdrawals from an investment fund is "incidental or tenuous" within the meaning of Treasury Regulation § 53.4941(d)-2(f)(2). In addition, the revenue ruling would provide that compensation paid by the investment fund to disqualified persons for investment management or other services falls within the personal services exception of § 4941(d)(2)(E), as long as such compensation is reasonable.

---

[58]The compensation formula typically equals a percentage of the increase in the value of the partnership assets.

[59]Other rulings include PLR 200318069 (questions involving contributions to or withdrawals from investment LLC not deemed sale or exchange); PLR 200423029 (sharing of LLC investment expenses and payment of management fees not self-dealing); PLR 200548026 (§§ 4941 and 4943 issues); PLR 201630009 (receiving income from bequeathed commercial real estate properties not UBI, provided no income resulted from debt-financed property); PLR 201723006 (retaining nonvoting interests in LLC whose sole asset is promissory note from disqualified person not self-dealing when note only generates passive income in form of interest); and PLR 201737003 (foreign organization constructively owning no more than 20 percent voting stock of another company not business enterprise).

[60]Details provided at: https://www.americanbar.org/content/dam/aba/administrative/taxation/policy/062216comments.authcheckdam.pdf.

Contribution of Nonvoting LLC Interests to a Private Foundation. The IRS has consistently ruled that a foundation's proposed receipts from a donor (or the donor's estate) of nonvoting units in an LLC or distributions from the LLC will not constitute an act of self-dealing under section 4941 nor subject the foundation to section 4943.[61] In the ruling, a private foundation under section 509(a) would receive nonvoting units in a newly incorporated LLC from a donor (or the donor's estate) and potential distributions from the LLC that will be a proportionate share of payments of principal and interest from certain debtors held by the LLC. The foundation, as a nonvoting unit holder, would have the right to receive such distributions but not have the right to compel the distributions in any way under the proposed transaction.

In these rulings, foundations typically request that: (1) the receipt and continued ownership of nonvoting units in an LLC from a donor or the donor's estate will not constitute an act of self-dealing under section 4941; (2) the receipt of distributions from an LLC of a proportionate share of the payments of principal and interest, and any actions taken by the LLC in connection with enforcement and collection of these payments, will not constitute acts of self-dealing under section 4941; and (3) the receipt from the donor or the donor's estate (and continued ownership of the nonvoting units) will not result in excess business holdings under section 4943.

Under section 4946(a)(1), certain parties would be deemed disqualified persons with respect to the foundation, including substantial contributors, foundation managers, and family members of these individuals. Donors are disqualified persons as both substantial contributors under section 4946(a)(2) and foundation managers under Section 4946(b)(1) and, accordingly, certain relatives of donors are disqualified persons under section 4946(d) as members of donors' family.

An act of self-dealing would occur if any of the foregoing parties directly transferred the promissory note to the foundation. The foundation would become a creditor under the note to a disqualified person. (See Treas. Reg. § 53.4941(d)-2(c)(1).) Under the proposed transaction, however, donors assign the promissory note to the LLC in exchange for nonvoting and voting units in the LLC. The foundation then receives the "nonvoting" units in the LLC from the donor through a gift (or by a testamentary device or bequest from the donor's estate) rather than through a direct self-dealing transaction. Any direct payments the foundation receives in connection with this transaction would be provided by the LLC and not a disqualified person.[62]

---

[61]See PLR 202101002 and PLR 202037009.

[62]Self-dealing may also be present if any of the above parties indirectly transferred the promissory note and foundation is deemed to "control" LLC under Treas. Reg. § 53.4941(d)-1(b)(5). Under this situation, the foundation would be indirectly serving as the creditor under the note by reason of its ownership interest in the LLC. See Treas. Reg. § 53.4941(d)-1(b)(8), Example (1).

As holder of only nonvoting units, however, the foundation does not "control" the LLC within the meaning of Treas. Reg. § 53.4941(d)-1(b)(5). The foundation lacks management rights and the right to vote on the manager(s).[63]

Moreover, the foundation does not have the power to compel dissolution of the LLC. The foundation is only able to prevent such a dissolution, as the LLC may be dissolved with written approval of all unit holders, both voting and nonvoting.[64]

The IRS concluded that the foundation's receipt of nonvoting units in the LLC will not constitute a loan or extension of credit between a private foundation and a disqualified person within the meaning of section 4941(d)(1) and Treas. Reg. § 53.4941(d)-2(c)(1), since the foundation will not acquire an interest in the promissory note. Instead, the foundation will acquire nonvoting units in the LLC, with respect to which it will not have any management rights or control over potential distributions from the promissory note. The timing and amount of any such distributions are uncertain and cannot be compelled in any way by the foundation. Consequently, the proposed transaction will not constitute an act of direct or indirect self-dealing between the foundation and a disqualified person under section 4941.

The IRS also held, relative to section 4943, that in order for the foundation's nonvoting unit holdings in the LLC to constitute excess business holdings under section 4943(c)(1), the LLC must qualify as a business enterprise under section 4943(a). The term "business enterprise" under section 4943(d)(3) does not include a business having at least 95 percent of its gross income derived from passive sources as set forth in sections 512(b)(1), (2), (3), and (5). The LLC's only active holding is the note, which generates interest, a passive source under section 512(b)(1). Therefore, the LLC will not be considered a business enterprise for purposes of section 4943(d)(3) as at least 95 percent of its gross income will derive from passive sources in the form of interest. (See Treas. Reg. § 53.4943-10(c)(1).) Since the LLC is not deemed a business enterprise, and it holds no interest in any business enterprise, the foundation's holdings of nonvoting units in the LLC are not

---

[63]This is particularly noteworthy as the manager holds the power to manage the affairs of the LLC and determine the timing and amount of potential distributions. Only the holder(s) of the voting units in the LLC, anticipated to be a management trust, has the ability to elect and remove the manager. The foundation simply holds a right to receive distributions if the manager chooses to make current distributions or in the event the LLC dissolves.

[64]The power associated with the nonvoting units of an LLC as a necessary party to vote on the entity's liquidation is not considered equivalent to a "veto power" within the meaning of Treas. Reg. § 53.4941(d)-1(b)(5) because the power cannot be exercised over an action relevant to any potential act of self-dealing, including the power to compel distributions from the LLC or influence the managerial decisions of the LLC in any way.

interests in a business enterprise and would not constitute excess business holdings under section 4943.

CAVEAT

A practitioner has reported that a private letter ruling was recently requested (from the IRS) similarly asking for confirmation that the ownership of nonvoting LLC units in which the LLC owned promissory notes from disqualified persons would not be direct or indirect self-dealing. The IRS responded that it is placing a moratorium on indirect self-dealing private letter rulings based on lack of "control" by the private foundation. The IRS indicated that they are aware that there are multiple rulings on this issue, some of which are as recent as 2020, and there have been many consistent rulings over the decades in which taxpayers received rulings that such arrangements were not self-dealing.

In September 2021, the IRS issued Rev. Proc. 2021-4, stating that it would not issue PLRs as to whether certain transactions constitute self-dealing under section 4941(d). The IRS will not rule on whether an act of self-dealing occurs when a foundation, or other entity, subject to section 4941 owns or receives an interest in a limited liability company or other entity that owns a promissory note issued by a disqualified person. The IRS has explained that it is "currently reviewing its prior ruling position on [these] transactions."

CAVEAT

As a result, tax practitioners will need to issue tax opinions to support the position in a particular case depending on the facts and circumstances. And, of course, documentation would be needed in order to defend against any IRS inquiries.

CHAPTER 11

Impact on Taxable Joint Ventures: Tax-Exempt Entity Leasing Rules (New)

§ 11.3 Internal Revenue Code §168(h) (New)   169

§ 11.3 INTERNAL REVENUE CODE § 168(H)

(c) Subsidiaries of Tax-Exempt Organizations

p. 713. *Add the following at the end of paragraph (c):*

To the extent an LLC is wholly owned by the nonprofit and controls the general partner interest, the LLC may elect to be taxed as a corporation rather than be disregarded for tax purposes by submitting IRS Form 8832. The newly formed LLC, which is now taxable as a corporation, would make a § 168(h) election and be treated as a "blocker," the effect of which is that any capital gains and income received by the blocker entity would be considered UBIT and taxable at the corporate level.

CHAPTER 12

Healthcare Entities in Joint Ventures

§ 12.1 OVERVIEW

p. 733. Insert the following after the first paragraph (which begins on p. 732) on this page:

Many of the changes enacted in the 2017 Tax Act (Pub. Law 115-97) applicable to tax-exempt organizations affect the healthcare sector in significant ways. As described in Section 2.1 and subsections 14.1(b)(ii), (iii), and (iv), these new provisions create additional financial burdens, including additional accounting, administrative, and reporting obligations.

In regard to its no-rule on joint ventures, the IRS issued Rev. Proc. 2018-3,[13.1] adding language clarifying that it also will not address whether a joint venture furthers an exempt purpose. The current language states that the IRS will not rule on "whether a joint venture between a tax-exempt organization and a for-profit organization affects an organization's exempt status, furthers an exempt purpose, or results in unrelated business income."

However, the IRS has indicated that it is "interested in thinking about whether we can find some places where we can rule because we know

---

[13.1]Rev. Proc. 2018-3, 2018-1 I.R.B. 118, § 3.01(73).

that's a huge part of your practice and we've been out of the conversation and think it would be helpful."[13.2]

In fact, the IRS did release a PLR, which, although it cannot be cited as precedent, does indicate its position in an area. PLR 201744019 is discussed in subsection 12.3(d)(vi).

p. 734. *Insert the following before the last paragraph of this subsection:*

Even before the COVID-19 pandemic, the scrutiny of nonprofit hospitals has been a focus of the press. The media has argued that a hospital's community benefit should be more defined in terms of tangible medical benefits for local residents. Some have argued that nonprofit hospitals are even more profitable than for-profit ones, especially since private business pays taxes and nonprofit hospitals may receive a charitable contribution from donors and use tax-free financing for capital projects. The press points out that communities are often conflicted relative to this issue since many of the nonprofit hospitals are large employers, but they argue that economic benefits do not always trickle down to the immediate neighborhoods. They also examine the average chief executive's package, which is said to be worth as much as $3.5 million annually. It was stated in a *New York Times* article that from 2005 to 2015, the average chief executive compensation in nonprofit hospitals increased by 93 percent.[18.1] The challenge also is directed at property tax exemption. It was also pointed out that most profitable nonprofit hospitals tend to be part of huge healthcare systems. Some commentators have asked whether these profitable institutions should be exempt from taxes. Should hospitals be allowed to declare Medicaid "losses" as a community benefit? Many policies have noted that the tax exemption is a blunt instrument for struggling hospitals, particularly in communities with a shortage of healthcare resources; in such cases, tax exemption may make sense. On the other hand, in medically saturated areas where profits and executive compensation approach Wall Street levels, tax exemption may raise eyebrows.[18.2]

§ 12.2 CLASSIFICATIONS OF JOINT VENTURES

p. 735. *In footnote 21, delete the second PLR listed.*

[13.2]Comments of Janine Cook, Deputy Associate Chief Counsel, IRS Office of Associate Chief Counsel (TEGE), at "News from the IRS and Treasury Department" panel presentation to the ABA Tax Section Exempt Organizations Committee, February 9, 2018, as reported by *EO Tax Journal*, 2018-42, Feb. 28, 2018; eotaxjournal.com.

[18.1]*See* Danielle Ofri, "Why Are Nonprofit Hospitals So Highly Profitable?," *New York Times*, February 20, 2020.

[18.2]*Id.*

§ 12.3 TAX ANALYSIS

(b) The IRS's Historical Position

(i) Charitable Purpose.   p. 743. *Delete the language in footnote 51 and replace with the following:*
IRS Ann. 92-83, 1992-22 I.R.B. 59 (June 1, 1992).

p. 746. *Delete the language in footnote 68 and replace with* **Id.**; *delete the language in footnote 69 and replace with* **Id.**

p. 747. *Delete the language in footnote 72 and replace with the following:*
IRS Ann. 92-83, 1992-22 I.R.B. 59 (June 1, 1992).

p. 747. *Insert the following at the end of footnote 74:*
PLR 201529013 (July 17, 2015) provided that an organization that conducted programs for members and employees of its subsidiary companies was distinguishable from this fact pattern because the programs were not available to individuals unable to pay the organization's membership fees.

(iii) Private Benefit and Inurement.   p. 753. *Delete* **Ann. 92-83, 1992-22 I.R.B. 59, § 333.3 (June 1, 1992)** *in footnote 108 and replace with the following:*
IRS Ann. 92-83, 1992-22 I.R.B. 59 (June 1, 1992)

p. 754. *Delete* **Ann. 92-83, 1992-22 I.R.B. 59, § 333.2 (June 1, 1992)** *in footnote 110 and replace with the following:*
IRS Ann. 92-83, 1992-22 I.R.B. 59 (June 1, 1992)

p. 754. *Delete* **Ann. 92-83, 1992-22 I.R.B. 59, § 333.2 (June 1, 1992)** *in footnote 114 and replace with the following:*
IRS Ann. 92-83, 1992-22 I.R.B. 59 (June 1, 1992)

p. 754. *Delete* **Ann. 92-83, 1992-22 I.R.B. 59, § 333.4 (June 1, 1992)** *in footnote 115 and replace with the following:*
IRS Ann. 92-83, 1992-22 I.R.B. 59 (June 1, 1992)

(vi) IRS Revocation of Exempt Status of BHS.   p. 768. *Insert the following after the Note:*
The IRS recently issued PLR 201744019, which confirmed the control criteria of Rev. Rul. 98-15 examining the relationship between a charitable hospital and a for-profit hospital system. See subsection 12.5(e) regarding preserving "control" in the 50/50 venture.

(d)   Revenue Ruling 98-15

(iii) Pre/Post-Joint-Venture Control. p. 782. *In footnote 199, the PLRs listed on the second to last line should read* **199913035** *and* **199913051,** *respectively.*

(vi) Whole Hospital Joint Ventures: Inherent Tax Issues. p. 792. *Insert the following at the end of this subsection:*

PLR 201744019 involved a general acute care hospital founded as a community hospital ("Hospital") and operated by a tax-exempt entity when it applied for tax exemption.

Years later, as a result of funding needs, operation of the Hospital was transferred to the local community board, which in turn leased the land, property, and equipment and transferred operational responsibility to a for-profit specializing in operating rural hospitals. The for-profit agreed to provide charity care in a manner consistent with the Hospital's past practices, but the Hospital had no mechanism to enforce that provision.

The ruling states that the Hospital "notified the Service of a proposed change in activities in documentation submitted to the Service" but does not indicate how this notice was provided. The Hospital also disclosed the change in activities on all Forms 990, which reflected its mission as maintenance of an acute care hospital leased to a for-profit to accomplish the stated goal of providing medical care in its rural location. "However, [the Hospital] did not formally notify the Service of the change in activities, nor did it seek an affirmation letter or private letter ruling to confirm that it continued to qualify for exemption."

The IRS revoked the Hospital's exempt status because it was not operated exclusively for charitable purposes. It failed the operational test by allowing an "outside" for-profit to have complete control over its operations without safeguards to require operation for charitable purposes.

The legal analysis focused on the concept of control as found in Rev. Rul. 98-15; that is, a § 501(c)(3) can enter into a management contract with a for-profit so long as it retains ultimate authority to ensure that the managed assets are devoted to charitable purposes:

> Rev. Rul. 98-15 concludes that an IRC § 501(c)(3) organization may enter into a management contract with a private party giving that party authority to conduct activities on behalf of the organization and direct the use of the organization's assets provided that the organization retains ultimate authority over the assets and activities being managed. However, [Hospital] does not retain ultimate control over the activities of the hospital; it concedes total operational control to the for-profit entity. Although the lease agreement states that the for-profit must provide hospital care and related services to residents of the hospital's primary service area without regard to ability to pay, there is no way for [Hospital] to guarantee this occurs because they do not have access to the books and records of the for-profit.

> **NOTE**
>
> One indicia of the Hospital retaining sufficient control was access to books and records. Because the Hospital did not have access to its own books and records, the IRS determined that it could not guarantee that it was providing care and services to its community without regard to ability to pay.

> **CAVEAT**
>
> The IRS stated that the Hospital "did not omit or misstate a material fact, but operated in a manner materially different from that was originally represented in its Application of Exemption." Thus, although organizations must notify the IRS of operational changes on Form 990, they must also assess when changes from those originally presented are so different as to require a separate "formal" submission, such as a private ruling request.

Of course, however, in this situation, the Hospital relinquished control to a for-profit with no ability to require that operations fulfilled its charitable purposes, a material change from being managed by a nonprofit as originally presented in its application for tax exemption. This position is underscored in Rev. Proc. 2018-5,[242.1] which states that an organization cannot "rely on its determination if there's a material change of facts inconsistent with exemption in the character, purpose or method o[f] [sic] operation of the organization."[242.2] The crucial question is whether exemption would have been revoked if there were material changes to operations as originally described if such operations used a different method that nonetheless continued to serve charitable purposes.

(x) Use of a Subsidiary to Protect the Exempt Parent. p. 805. *Delete the first citation in footnote 292 and replace it with the following:*
    483 F.2d 1098.

§ 12.4 OTHER HEALTHCARE INDUSTRY ISSUES

(d)   Federal Healthcare Fraud and Abuse Statutes

p. 822. *In footnote 360, delete the link (first sentence); it is no longer available.*

[242.1]2018-I.R.B. 233, Dec. 29, 2017.
[242.2]Comments of Victoria Judson, Associate Chief Counsel, IRS Office of Associate Chief Counsel (TEGE), at "News from the IRS and Treasury Department" panel presentation to the ABA Tax Section Exempt Organizations Committee, February 9, 2018, as reported by *EO Tax Journal*, 2018-42, Feb. 28, 2018; eotaxjournal.com.

p. 823. *Delete the language in footnote 376 and replace with the following:*
85 F. Supp. 2d (D. Kan. 1999), *rev'd United States v. McClatchey,* 217 F.3d 823 (10th Cir. 2000).

(e)   IRS Policy and the HHS Office of Inspector General

p. 830. *In footnote 399, delete* available at www.senate.go/<finance/press/ Gpress/2007/prg071907a.pdf *(this citation is no longer available).*

(h)   Integrated Delivery Systems, PHOs, MSOs, and HMOs

p. 837. *Delete language in footnote 430 and replace with the following:*
Rev. Rul. 86-98, 1986-2 C.B. 74.

§ 12.5   PRESERVING THE 50/50 JOINT VENTURE

(b)   Expanding Nonprofit Veto Authority in the 50/50 Joint Venture

p. 852. *Delete the language in footnote 492 and replace it with the following:*
See Rev. Rul. 98-15, Situation 2.

(e)   Preserving "Control" in the 50/50 Venture

p. 860. *Insert the following after paragraph 5:*
The IRS has recently ruled that a general acute care hospital was not operated exclusively for 501(c)(3) purposes when the management of the hospital was turned over to a for-profit and therefore "control" over its operations was ceded to the for-profit system. See IRS PLR 201744019; see also § 4.12(ii).

§ 12.9   GOVERNMENT SCRUTINY

(a)   The IRS Exempt Organizations Hospital Compliance Project

p. 881. *Delete the website information in footnote 580 (citation is no longer available).*

p. 882. *Delete the website information in footnote 587 (citation is no longer available).*

(b)   Congressional Scrutiny

(i) Reporting Requirements.   p. 886. *Delete the website in footnote 607 (citation is no longer available).*

p. 888. *Insert the following new subsection (c):*

(c)   State Action

As state and local governments struggle with budget deficits, several not only have criticized nonprofit hospitals as operating similarly to for-profit hospitals but have sued to revoke their property tax exemption. For example, 26 of New Jersey's nonprofit hospitals are in litigation over their property tax exemption based on a 2015 ruling revoking the property tax exemption of a state charitable hospital.[615.1] This trend is occurring in other states as well and is viewed to be a first step in the challenge to property tax exemption of not only other healthcare organizations, such as nursing homes, but universities as well.[615.2]

§ 12.11   THE PATIENT PROTECTION AND AFFORDABLE CARE ACT OF 2010: § 501(R) AND OTHER STATUTORY CHANGES IMPACTING NONPROFIT HOSPITALS

(a)   Introduction

p. 892. *Insert the following at the end of the last sentence of this subsection:*
   The IRS released final regulations on December 29, 2014.[625.1] The regulations were generally favorably received as reducing and/or simplifying the burdens on hospitals.[625.2]

(d)   Additional Statutory Requirements Applicable to Hospital Organizations

(iv) IRS Periodic Review of Community Benefit Compliance and Annual Congressional Report.   p. 906. *Insert the following at the end of this subsection:*
   Reaction to the first IRS report dated January 28, 2015, was critical for containing numerical data without context.[698.1] Critics, including Senator Grassley, who was one of the forces behind the Affordable Care Act provisions governing charitable hospitals, have asserted that the report lacks the fundamental information to evaluate whether nonprofit hospitals are operating differently from for-profit hospitals and whether they merit retaining their tax-exempt status.[698.2]

[615.1]"Ridgewood Joins Others in Seeking to Tax Nonprofit Hospitals," *The Record,* April 7, 2016.
[615.2]*Id.*
[625.1]TD 9708, I.R.B. 2015-5.
[625.2]75 The Exempt Org. Tax Rev., 115 (2015).
[698.1]"Senator Grassley Says IRS Report on Hospitals' Charity Care 'Disappointing,'" 49 DTR G-2, Mar. 10, 2015.
[698.2]*Id.*

(e) Implications for Joint Ventures

(i) Analysis.   p. 912. *Insert the following to the end of this subsection (i):*

The final regulations address the questions of operations through partnerships and provide that an organization is deemed to be operating a hospital facility if it owns a capital or profits interest in an entity that operates the hospital facility *where the entity is treated as a partnership* for federal income tax purposes.[706.1] Moreover, the regulations clarify that an organization is deemed to own a capital or profits interest in any entity treated as a partnership where it owns that interest *directly or indirectly* through one or more entities that are treated as partnerships.[706.2] Thus, traditional pass-through and attribution concepts are applied.[706.3]

NOTE

The final regulations delete a reference to joint ventures and LLCs contained in the 2013 proposed regulations on the grounds that "those entities are sufficiently covered by the general phrase 'entity treated as a partnership for federal tax purposes.'"[706.4]

In addition, the final regulations clarify that an organization will not be subject to the requirements of § 501(r) if it is not operating a hospital facility, is operating a facility not deemed to be a hospital (i.e., not required to be licensed as a hospital by the appropriate state), or with respect to any activities that constitute an unrelated trade or business with respect to the hospital organization.[706.5] Other than the addition of the unrelated trade or business exception to application of the § 501(r) rules, the fact that they do not apply to an organization that does not operate a hospital facility or to the operation of a nonhospital facility are exclusions codified in the statute itself.

In summary, an organization that owns a capital or profits interest in an entity that operates a hospital where the operational entity is a pass-through vehicle will be treated as operating a hospital facility whether or not the ownership is direct or indirect through other pass-through entities,

---

[706.1]TD 9708, I.R.B. 2015-5, Summary of Content and Explanation of Revisions, "f. 'Operating' a hospital facility."

[706.2]*Id.*

[706.3]Pursuant to Treas. Reg. § 301.7701-2(a), if a hospital organization is the sole owner of a disregarded entity that is the sole owner of another disregarded entity that operates a hospital facility, the hospital organization will be deemed to operate the facility and be subject to § 501(r). TD 9708, I.R.B. 2015-5, Summary of Content and Explanation of Revisions, "f. 'Operating' a hospital facility," fn. 2.

[706.4]TD 9708, I.R.B. 2015-5, Summary of Content and Explanation of Revisions, "f. 'Operating' a hospital facility," fn. 1.

[706.5]*Id.*

except as to unrelated business activities under § 513, activities that are unrelated to operation of a hospital by definition.

The significance of the pass-through analysis is evident in how the Treasury Decision 9708 applies it to the question of hospital-owned physician practices:

> . . .[a] hospital facility would not be required to meet the section 501(r) requirements with respect to a taxable corporation providing care in the hospital facility, even if the corporation is wholly or partially owned by the hospital organization that operates the hospital facility, because the corporation is a separate taxable entity to which section 501(r) does not apply.[706.6]

> By contrast, if a hospital organization is the sole member or owner of an entity providing care in one of its hospital facilities and that entity is disregarded as separate from the hospital organization for federal tax purposes, the care provided by the entity would be considered to be care provided by the hospital organization through its hospital facility. Accordingly, the hospital organization would be required to meet the section 501(r) requirements with respect to care provided by the disregarded entity in any hospital facility that the hospital organization operates.[706.7]

CAVEAT

These considerations will have to be factored in when structuring hospital joint ventures going forward, as the potential applicability of § 501(r) by application of the pass-through rules will have to be weighed against the tax benefits of using C corporations versus partnerships and LLCs that elect pass-through treatment.

The foregoing point is underscored by the preamble of the Treasury Decision citing Rev. Ruls. 2004-51 and 98-15 and stating that where a hospital organization owns an interest in an entity that is treated as a partnership and provides care in a hospital facility, the activities of the partnership are attributed to the hospital organization for purposes of deciding whether the hospital organization is "operated exclusively for exempt purposes or engaged in an unrelated trade or business under generally applicable tax principles." Accordingly, if emergency or other essential medical services are provided by a pass-through entity in which the hospital organization operating the facility has an interest, the hospital will be subject to § 501(r) in regard to the services provided by that pass-through entity because they are deemed to be related to the hospital's exempt purposes. On the

---

[706.6]TD 9708, I.R.B. 2015-5, Summary of Content and Explanation of Revisions, "g. Providing care in a hospital facility through hospital-owned entities."
[706.7]*Id.*

other hand, as noted earlier, if the care is an unrelated trade or business, the hospital organization will not have to satisfy the provisions of § 501(r) in regard to those services, but it will be subject to the provisions of § 513 as to those services and, potentially, depending on the level of unrelated activity, will have to demonstrate that it is operated exclusively for exempt purposes and that the level of unrelated activity does not jeopardize its tax-exempt status.[706.8]

§ 12.12 THE PATIENT PROTECTION AND AFFORDABLE CARE ACT OF 2010: ACOS AND CO-OPS: NEW JOINT VENTURE HEALTHCARE ENTITIES (REVISED)

(b) ACOs

(ii) Forming an ACO: Participants. p. 916. *Add the following to footnote 716:*

In Notice 2011-20 the IRS solicited comments on the need for guidance for EO's planning to participate in a Medicare Shared Savings program (MSSP) through ACO. See in this regard, in Denial 201615022 and recently issued Denial 202210023, that the ACO had asked for a § 501(c)(4) exemption instead of § 501(c)(3) status.

(vi) Planning. p. 924. *Insert the following at the end of this subsection:*

The IRS has recently issued PLR 201615022 denying a tax exemption sought by an ACO that coordinates care for people with commercial insurance. The IRS said the organization did not meet the test for tax-exempt status because it was not operated exclusively for charitable purposes; it provided private benefits for some doctors in the network. The ruling does not affect ACOs formed solely to participate in Medicare, but it could affect similar entities serving privately insured patients. Many ACOs coordinate care for both Medicare beneficiaries and privately insured patients.

CAVEAT

According to T. J. Sullivan, a national expert in healthcare law, ACOs will face an uphill battle in trying to qualify for federal income tax exemptions if they do not participate in Medicare. The IRS acknowledged that the organization was trying to increase the quality of care, lower costs, and improve the health of the community, but it said it had also negotiated agreements with insurers on behalf of doctors and that is not a charitable activity or one that directly benefits the community as a whole.

[706.8]The final regulations contain a newly defined term, *substantially related entity,* which is an entity treated as a partnership for tax purposes in which a hospital organization has a capital or profits interest or a disregarded entity of which the hospital organization is the sole owner or member and that provides emergency or other essential service in a facility operated by the hospital organization where that service is related to the hospital organization's exempt purpose. *Id.*

CHAPTER 13

Low-Income Housing, New Markets, Rehabilitation, and Other Tax Credit Programs

§ 13.2 NONPROFIT-SPONSORED LIHTC PROJECT

p. 944. *Insert the following before the first full paragraph of this section:*

Some nonprofits that have engaged in LIHTC transactions have asserted somewhat aggressive positions that attempt to, in effect, compel renegotiation of their financial upside in transactions that have closed years before. One scenario occurs where a nonprofit that agreed to a certain financial split with its for-profit partner(s) when entering into a transaction years later asserted that honoring it would provide an undue benefit ("impermissible private benefit") for the for-profit developer.

> Ironically, the nonprofit would be taking the contrary position that it would take if the IRS raised the private benefit issue on audit and by litigating the issue, the nonprofit lays out the IRS's argument in publicly available documents.

Another situation involves LIHTC deals coming to the end of the compliance periods, where nonprofits assert Code § 42(i)(7) rights as to first refusal to purchase below fair market value.[4.1] One case in Massachusetts

---

[4.1] See subsection 13.3(m).

has been litigated. See *Homeowner's Rehab, Inc. v. Related Corp. V. SLP. L.P.,* 99 N.E., 3d 744 (Mass. 2018).

	CAVEAT

This area is fertile for challenges because, as the court noted in *Rehab*, the particular language in every agreement will vary and, of course, because of the competing interests of preserving low-income housing versus providing investors the upside they anticipated.

---

§ 13.3 LOW-INCOME HOUSING TAX CREDIT (REVISED)

(b)   Introduction to the Low-Income Housing Tax Credit

p. 949. *Insert the following at the end of this subsection:*

The fiscal year (FY) 2018 omnibus spending bill provided increases for affordable housing, both on the tax and the appropriations front.

- A 12.5 percent increase in low-income housing tax credit allocation for four years (2018–2021), and
- A new permanent provision on income averaging, which would allow housing credit units to be affordable at up to 80 percent of area median income (AMI), offset by deeper targeting in other units to maintain average affordability in the project at 60 percent AMI.

	CAVEAT

Although the 12.5 percent increase for four years will not fully make up for the negative effects of tax reform, which will reduce production by an estimated 235,000 units over ten years, this increase is an important first step and set the stage for Congress to extend this expansion in the future. It will also bring roughly $2.7 billion in housing credit equity to the market.

The IRS has released Notice 2020-53, which allows certain time-sensitive actions, such as the 10 percent test for carryover allocations, the 24-month minimum rehabilitation expenditure period, and the reasonable period of casualty loss restoration or replacement, that were due from April 1, 2020, through December 30, 2020, to have a new deadline of December 31, 2020.

	CAVEAT
Accordingly, as a result of the Notice, owners are not required to perform certain income rectifications or adjust the eligible basis of a business to temporary closures of common areas or amenities due to the COVID-19 pandemic and state agencies are not required to conduct compliance monitoring of these properties. The Notice also allows medical personnel and other essential workers who provide services during the pandemic to be treated as "displaced individuals" eligible for housing and low-income properties.	

(c)   Utilization of the LIHTC by Tax-Exempt Organizations

p. 949. *Insert the following at the end of footnote 17:*

A low-income housing project whose activities would be attributed to private foundation met Rev. Proc. 96-32, 1996-1 CB 717 safe harbor requirements and would continue to do so after the EO's acquisition of all LLC membership interests, where activities furthered the organization's § 501(c)(3) charitable purpose of providing affordable housing for those of low and moderate income. PLR 201603032, January 15, 2016.

(e)   Tax-Exempt Bond-Financed Project

p. 967. *Insert new footnote 85.1 at the end of the third sentence following "rate.":*

[85.1] The IRS issued a ruling that would ease the applicability of the 4 percent floor under certain circumstances. See also section 201(a) of the "Taxpayer Certainty and Disaster Tax Relief Act of 2020" (Act), enacted as Division EE of the Consolidated Appropriations Act, 2021, Pub. L. No. 116-260, 134 Stat. 1182, 3056 (December 27, 2020).

(g)   Applicable Credit Percentage

p. 974. *Insert the following at the end of the first paragraph on this page:*

The minimum applicable percentage of 9 percent was extended to before January 1, 2014, under the American Taxpayer Relief Act of 2012 (§ 302), and to before January 1, 2015, under the Tax Increase Prevention Act of 2014 (§ 112). Finally, the Protecting Americans from Tax Hikes Act of 2015 (§ 131) permanently extended that minimum applicable percentage of 9 percent as of January 1, 2015.

In addition, a permanent minimum rate for the 4 percent LIHTC was implemented at the end of December 2020 with passage of the Consolidated Appropriations Act of 2021 (Division EE—Taxpayer Certainty and Disaster Tax Relief Act of 2020, § 201, p. 2451) on December 27, 2020 ("2020 Act"). This legislation fixed the applicable percentage for the 30 percent present-value LIHTC (4 percent credit) at 4 percent ("4% floor") regardless of prevailing interest rates. To qualify for the 4 percent floor, new or existing buildings, for which IRC § 42(b)(2) does not apply, must (i) be placed in service after December 31, 2020, (ii) receive a LIHTC allocation after December

31, 2020, and (iii) be financed by a tax-exempt bond issued after December 31, 2021 that is subject to the applicable volume cap.[107.1]

p. 976. *Insert the following after the first full paragraph on this page:*

New section 42(b)(3) provides a 4 percent minimum credit rate for buildings to which the 9 percent floor in § 42(b)(2) does not apply and that are placed in service by the taxpayer after December 31, 2020, which apply to:

1. Any building that receives an allocation of housing credit dollar amount after December 31, 2020, and

2. In the case of any building any portion of which is financed with an obligation described in § 42(h)(4)(A), "any such building if any such obligation which so finances such building is issued after December 31, 2020."

Rev. Rul. 2021-20, 4 Percent Floor Application to Housing Credit Buildings, provided additional guidance as to when the 4 percent floor is applicable. Rev. rul. 2021-20 ("Rev. Rul. 2021-20") considered three factual situations:

1. A state agency issued to the taxpayer a draw-down bond that qualifies as an issue of exempt facility bonds prior to 2021 (with draws occurring in a subsequent year). Reg. § 1.150-1(c)(4)(i) treats bonds issued pursuant to a draw-down loan as part of a single issue.

2. A state agency issued to the taxpayer exempt facility bonds in 2020 to finance the construction of a qualified low-income building. In a subsequent year, the agency issued a different issue of exempt facility bonds (not pursuant to a draw-down loan), in a de minimis amount.

3. A state agency allocated to the taxpayer (under a binding commitment) housing credit dollar amounts in 2020 for the acquisition of an existing building, with an additional housing credit amount for the rehabilitation of the building into a qualified low-income building. The state agency also allocated a de minimis allocation of low-income housing credit dollar amount after December 31, 2020.

[107.1]Specifically, the 2020 Act provides "acquisitions of used buildings provided the credits were allocated after 2020 projects that: (i) are placed in service after 2020, and (ii) in the case of any building any portion of which is financed with an obligation described in § 42(h)(4)(A), any such building if any such obligation which so finances such building is issued after December 31, 2020." See Consolidated Appropriations Act of 2021 (Division EE—Taxpayer Certainty and Disaster Tax Relief Act of 2020, § 201, p. 2451, lines 20–24). This leaves open the question as to whether any 4 percent LIHTC projects utilizing tax-exempt bonds allocated in 2020 will qualify for the 4 percent floor. The issue turns on when such 2020 bonds are deemed to be "issued," specifically, whether tax-exempt bonds will be deemed to be issued on the date that they were allocated, subject to the volume cap in 2020, or on the date that they are drawn, either in full or in part, if such draws occur after 2020. At the time of this publication, the IRS has not issued relevant guidance, so a prudent assumption would be that the 4 percent floor would not apply to such buildings.

The revenue ruling concludes:

- The 4 percent floor does not apply to the building in Situation 1, which is financed in part with a draw-down exempt facility bond issue that was issued in 2020 and on which one or more draws are taken after December 31, 2020.
- The 4 percent floor does not apply to the building in Situation 2, which is financed in part with proceeds of an exempt-facility bond issue that was issued in 2020 and in part with proceeds of a different exempt-facility bond issue that is issued in a de minimis amount after December 31, 2020.
- The 4 percent floor does not apply to the building in Situation 3, which receives an allocation of housing credit dollar amount in 2020 and a de minimis additional allocation after December 31, 2020.

The related revenue procedure—Rev. Proc. 2021-43—provides safe harbors for determining whether an exempt-facility bond issue that is issued after December 31, 2020, or an allocation of a housing credit dollar amount that is made after December 31, 2020, is more than de minimis for purposes of the conclusions in Rev. Rul. 2021-20 with regard to Situations 2 and 3.

(m) Disposition of the Partnership's or Investor's Interest Following the Compliance Period

p. 989. *Insert new footnote 164.1 at the end of the first sentence of this subsection:*

[164.1] Various interpretations of § 42(i)(7) continue to result in uncertainty among nonprofit entities, project investors, and for-profit partners as to the applicability of the right of first refusal. See *Homeowner's Rehab, Inc. v. Related Corp. V SLP, L.P.*, 479 Mass. 741, 99 N.E.3D 744 (2018) (rejecting the project investor's claim that a right of first refusal under § 42(i)(7) was not triggered by a bona fide offer). Industry professionals continue to request guidance from the Internal Revenue Service as to (1) whether a bona fide offer is necessary to trigger the right of first refusal, (2) whether the right of first refusal applies only to the sale of the project or also to the sale of the limited partner's interest in the owner of the project, and (3) what assets are covered by the right of first refusal. These issues are being litigated/settled across the country and have been in the forefront of industry discussions. Also, the *Homeowner's Rehab* case has been widely reviewed in the industry and includes a lengthy discussion of the legislative history of § 42(i)(7). (The materials referenced in this footnote were contributed by Carolyn Scogin, an attorney at Blanco Tackabery, who specializes in LIHTC transactions.)

(n) LIHTC 15-Year Issues

p. 991. *Insert the following at the end of the second full paragraph on this page:*

Some allocating agencies require a waiver by the project owner of the right to request a Qualified Contract ("QC") as part of the LIHTC application process. The Qualified Allocation Plan ("QAP") for an allocating agency may also disqualify from participation any principal involved in a project for which a Qualified Contract has been requested. Preliminary consideration and review should be given to both of the foregoing prior to commencing the Qualified Contract process with an allocating agency.

	CAVEAT

Many parties make the error of starting the QC process without realizing that (1) the QC right has already been waived for the project with the state agency (i.e., the boilerplate partnership agreement language includes the QC option but it isn't actually permitted for the deal because of the waiver) and (2) there could be unintended consequences with the allocating agency of requesting the QC even if the right has not been waived. It appears that more agencies are including or expanding these limitations of the QC in QAPs.[168.1]

§ 13.4 HISTORIC INVESTMENT TAX CREDIT

(f) Profit Motive Requirement

p. 1006. Add **(i)** *to the beginning paragraph of this subsection.*

p. 1009. Add the following new subsection **(ii)** *before paragraph (g):*

(ii) *Historic Boardwalk* **Guidance.** In January 2014, Treasury and the IRS issued Revenue Procedure 2014-12, 2014-3 I.R.B. 414, which established a safe harbor for federal historic tax credit investments made within a single tier or through a master lease pass-through structure. This guidance was issued in response to the Third Circuit decision in *Historic Boardwalk* discussed earlier. Although the Revenue Procedure does not establish substantive tax law, it does create a safe harbor for structuring HTC-advantage transactions.[201.1]

According to the revenue procedure, either an investor may hold a direct partnership interest in the lessor entity that holds fee ownership of the project or, where an election is made by a lessor to pass through the HTCs to the lessee of the project, an investor may hold an indirect partnership interest in the lessor through the lessee, provided, however, that the investor does not also hold any other interest in the lessor.

The guidance makes clear that there is no minimum amount of cash that is required to be distributed to the investor in order to be respected as a partner, so projects that do not generate substantial cash returns can satisfy the upside return requirement of the guidance even if the aggregate cash generated by the investment will not exceed the investor's capital

---

[168.1]The materials referenced in this footnote were contributed by Carolyn Scogin, an attorney at Blanco Tackabery, who specializes in LIHTC transactions.

[201.1]Article in *Tax Notes* 146 (12), p. 1545, "Tax Credits: *Historic Boardwalk* Guidance, Recommended Practices" by Jerry Breed and Scott DeMartino.

contribution. The investor, however, must receive a reasonably anticipated value, exclusive of tax benefits, commensurate with the investor member's percentage interest in the partnership.

Caveat
The IRS and Treasury have informally indicated that an investor does not need to receive current cash flow from operations of the project and may derive a portion of the reasonably anticipated value from its interest in the project's residual.

Caveat
The emphasis is on ensuring that the economic value of the investor's interest is not reduced through fees, lease terms, or other arrangements that are "unreasonable" compared to the terms found in real estate development projects that do not qualify for the HTCs.

1. At least 20 percent of an investor's total expected capital contribution must be contributed to the partnership prior to placement in service of the project and maintained for the duration of the investor's ownership of an interest in the partnership. Moreover, at least 75 percent of the investor's expected capital contribution must be fixed before placement in service. The contribution of the "fixed" portion of the investor's investment may be subject to contingencies such as placement in service, stabilization, or receipt of a Part 3 approval from the NPS. This requirement is intended to establish "downside" risk.

2. Funded guaranties are prohibited, and there is a defined range of "impermissible" guaranties. Impermissible guaranties include any guaranty of partnership distributions or other economic return and any guaranty for which the guarantor agrees to maintain a minimum net worth. It is also impermissible for any guaranty of tax structural risk or other disallowance or recapture events that are not due to an act or omission of the managing member or its affiliate. Similarly, no person involved in the HTC-advantaged transaction may pay the investor's costs or indemnify the investor for expenses incurred with respect to an IRS challenge of the HTCs.

Caveat
There is no prohibition against an investor procuring insurance covering risk associated with "impermissible" guaranties from persons not involved with the rehabilitation or the partnership.

3. Unfunded guaranties may cover 100 percent of the amount of the HTCs or the capital contributed to the partnership with respect to the HTCs. Unfunded guaranties may also cover all of the loss due to failure to complete the project as well as environmental liabilities. Further, an operating deficit reserve not in excess of 12 months of operating expenses may be established, and an operating deficit guarantee capped at 12 months of operating expenses may be provided to the investor.

4. According to the guidance, although a managing member or its affiliates may not hold a "call" option to acquire the investor member's interest in the partnership, the investor may hold an option to "put" its interest to the managing member or its affiliate for an amount that does not exceed fair market value.

CAVEAT

Abandonment of an investment is not permitted under the guidance, and an investor that abandons its interest will be deemed to have acquired its interest with the intention of abandoning it, unless the facts clearly establish that its interest is worthless.

The revenue procedure does not address other types of federal or state credits or transactions that combine HTCs with federal low-income housing or federal new markets tax credit transactions.

CAVEAT

It is important that the fees, lease terms, and other arrangements meet a "reasonableness" test as compared to other real estate development projects that do not qualify for § 47 rehabilitation credits. In this regard, a third-party opinion that substantiates the reasonableness should be addressed based on "comparables" from nontax credit advantage transactions from a firm that is not otherwise involved in the structure of the transaction. Furthermore, development fees should be tested under a reasonableness analysis, including any deferred portion and the deferral of the fee payments. This is an area of concern for the IRS.

The guidance provides that the value of the investors' interest may not be diluted by "disproportionate rights to distribute distributions." Preferred returns and special tax distributions to investors are permitted and, if not paid currently, may accrue. There will need to remain some meaningful amount of variable cash distributions after payment of deferred returns.

The guidance authorizes "flips" in the partnership interest after the end of a five-year HTC recaptured period. At all times, however, the principal's interest must be at least 1 percent of each material item of partnership income, gain, loss, deduction, and credit, and the investor's interest in such must be at least 5 percent of the largest investment percentage of such material items in the tax year for which the investor's percentage interest is the largest.

(g)   Recapture Provisions

p. 1010. *Add the following at the end of the subsection:*
The 2017 Tax Act amended the 20 percent HTC, which now needs to be claimed "ratably" and impacted the application of the recapture provisions. See, in this regard, new subsection 13.4(i).

p. 1010. *Renumber the current subsection (h) to (j) and insert the following as new subsections (h) and (i):*

(h)   The Treatment of 50(d) Income and Qualified Leasehold Improvements

The IRS issued Chief Counsel Advice 201505038, which clarified that, in a lease pass-through transaction, the lessee must include ratably in gross income an amount equal to 100 percent of the HTC claimed (rather than 50 percent).
The IRS plans to issue additional guidance shortly that will clarify various issues, including:

i.   whether § 50(d) income is an item of partnership income at the lessee level that increases a partner's outside basis in its partnership interest (§ 705(a));

ii.   whether an investor's distributive share of § 50(d) income can be reduced (along with its distributive shares of other partnership tax items) in a partnership "flip" of the kind described in Rev. Proc. 2014-12;

iii.   whether, upon the sale of an investor's interest in the lessee, an investor's share of any unrealized § 50(d) will be accelerated, or whether it would be allocable to the remaining partners in the lessee over the remainder of the applicable recovery period; and

iv.   the consequences of a termination of a lease after the expiration of the HTC recapture period.[201.2]

[201.2]The author acknowledges the excellent analyses of the § 50(d) income and qualified leasehold improvements issues presented by John Dalton, partner at Bryan Cave at the CohnReznick NMTC conference (May 2016).

Generally, in HTC deals, the recovery period for nonresidential real property is 39 years. There are exceptions, however, including an exception for "qualified leasehold improvement property" ("QLIP"), which has a 15-year recovery period.

QLIP is any improvement to an interior portion of a building that is nonresidential real property, if:

i. the improvement is made under or pursuant to a lease, by the lessor, the lessee, or a sublessee of such portion of the building;

ii. such portion of the building is used exclusively by the lessee (or any sublessee) of such portion; and

iii. such improvement is placed in service ("PIS") more than three years after the date the building was first PIS.[201.3]

CAVEAT

The treatment of certain QREs as QLIPs will have the effect of accelerating a portion of the investor's § 50(d) income because § 50(d) income has to be recognized over the shortest recovery period that could be applicable under § 168. So, if some portion of QREs are depreciated over 15 years rather than 39 years, then a portion of § 50(d) income should be recognized over a 15-year period. Investors would prefer to minimize the QLIP in their deals or eliminate it altogether if possible.

(i) The 2017 Tax Legislation and Issuance of the Proposed Regulations[201.4]

Under[4] the 2017 tax legislation, the 10 percent rehabilitation tax credit was repealed, and the 20 percent HTC discussed in subsection 13.4(b) was modified. The new law amended the 20 percent HTC to require it to be claimed "ratably" over a five-year period. The proposed regulations added sections 1.47-7(a) through (e) to provide rules for calculating the new ratable share and the determination of the HTC. The proposed regulations also coordinate with IRC section 50 (see subsection 13.4(h) with regard to the treatment of section 50(d) income) as well as recapture in the event of a disposition and the income inclusion related to lease property when the lessee is treated as the owner.

[201.3]Section 168(e)(6)(A). Under § 168(e)(6)(B), QLIP does not include any improvement for which the expenditure is attributable to (i) the enlargement of the building, (ii) any elevator or escalator, (iii) any structural component benefiting a common area, or (iv) the internal structural framework of the building.

[201.4]The author acknowledges the summary of the proposed regulations written by Roy Chou and Thomas Boccia and published in a Novogradac Historic Tax Credit Resource Center article, "IRS's Proposed Rehabilitation Tax Credit Regulations Provide Welcome Clarity," June 4, 2020.

The term "ratable share" is the amount equal to 20 percent of HTC determined with respect to the qualified rehabilitated building ("QRB"), as allocated ratably to each taxable year during the five-year credit period. The term "rehabilitation credit determined" is an amount equal to 20 percent of the qualified rehabilitation expenses taken into account for the taxable year the QRB is placed in service. The proposed regulations clarify that the HTC is determined in the taxable year the QRB is placed in service and allocated over a five-year period for each of the next five taxable years, rather than creating five separate rehabilitation credits for a single QRE.

CAVEAT
This is an important distinction, as it provides the foundation for how the changes to IRC 47 under the TCJA interact with certain other provisions within the Code, primarily section 50. Initially, it was unclear if the language meant there were multiple tax credit periods, with each tax credit period commencing when the HTC is claimed; in effect, five separate tax credit periods. Such an interpretation would lead to an aggregate tax credit period of 10 years, which the Treasury determined would be inconsistent with the written text of the statute as well as the intent of Congress. Therefore, the proposed regulations clarify that there is only one five-year tax credit period, which starts from the placed-in-service date of the QREs.

As to the timing, that is, the year the section 50(c) basis adjustment is to apply to investment credit property (in a direct investment structure), the proposed regulations provide examples to clarify the section 50(c) basis adjustment (see subsection 13.4(h)) that is accounted for in the year the QRB is placed in service for the full amount of the HTC determined rather than recorded as the credits are claimed. When the lessee is treated as owner and subject to an income inclusion requirement (in a lease pass-through structure) due to the HTC being claimed over five years, the section 50(d) income, similar to section 50(c) basis adjustment, is also calculated on the full amount of HTC determined in the year the QRB is placed in service and amortized ratably into income over the shortest depreciable recovery life of the QREs that gave rise to the HTC.

As to recapture provisions under section 50(a) (see subsection 13.4(g)), the proposed regulations clarify that there is one five-year tax credit period, which starts from the placed-in-service date of the QREs.[201.5] The proposed

---

[201.5] See Prop. Reg. § 1.47-7(b), (c). Taxpayers may rely on the proposed regulations for QREs paid or incurred after December 31, 2017, in taxable years beginning before the date of the Department of the Treasury decision adopting these regulations as *final regulations* is published in the Federal Register, provided the taxpayers follow the proposed regulations in their entirety and in a consistent manner.

regulations provide an example to illustrate how to calculate tax credit recapture in the event of a disposition.

EXAMPLE

X incurs $200,000 of qualified rehabilitation expenditures and the building is placed in service October 15, 2021. X is eligible to claim total HTCs of $40,000 ($200,000 × 0.20). In 2021 and 2022, X claimed the full amount of the ratable share allowed, or $8,000 per taxable year. X's total allowable ratable share for 2023 through 2025 is $24,000 ($8,000 allowable per taxable year). On November 1, 2023, X disposes of the qualified rehabilitated building. Because the period between the placed-in-service date and the recapture event is more than two, but less than three, full years,[201.6] the applicable recapture percentage is 60 percent. Based on these facts, X has an increase in tax of $9,600 ($16,000 of credit claimed in 2021 and 2022 × 0.60) and has $3,200 of credits remaining in each of the years 2023 through 2025, after forgoing $4,800 in credits in each of the years 2023 through 2025 ($8,000 × 0.60). Thus, a QRB that generated $40,000 of HTCs that was disposed of after two full years caused a recapture of $9,600 (HTC recapture percentage × original amount of credits claimed). However, the taxpayer may continue to claim credits of $3,200 for three more tax years on investment tax credit property that has been disposed of for the remaining three tax years of the original five-year tax credit period.

(j) State Tax Credits (as renumbered). p. 1012. *Insert the following new paragraphs at the end of this subsection:*

The Tax Court maintained this position when it decided *SFW Real Estate, LLC v. Commissioner.*[205.1] The case involved the sale of Virginia state tax credits, and the Court again determined that the sale of the Virginia state tax credits was a disguised sale and the taxpayer was appropriately taxed on the economic benefit of funds received from the sale of the Virginia state tax credits.[205.2]

In *Gateway Hotel Partners, LLC v. Commissioner,*[205.3] the Tax Court determined that two of the transfers of Missouri Historic Preservation Tax Credits were partnership distributions, but that a portion of the third credit transfer was a taxable sale.[205.4] The Tax Court considered whether three transfers made by a partnership resulted in taxable sales under the disguised sale rules, substance over form principles, or otherwise.

[205.1] *SFW Real Estate, LLC v. Comm'r*, T.C. Memo 2015-63 (Apr. 2, 2015).

[205.2] *Id*. See also *Route 231, LLC v. Comm'r*, 810 F.3d 247 (4th Cir. 2016) (affirming the Tax Court's determination that the transfer of Virginia state tax credits from the taxpayer LLC to the member constituted a sale and the funds received by the LLC were taxable income).

[205.3] See *Gateway Hotel Partners, LLC v. Commissioner,* T.C. Memo 2014-5. The author recognizes Kendra H. Merchant for her contribution to this subsection.

[205.4] *Id*.

In *Gateway*,[205.5] the Tax Court considered whether the transfer of tax credits to an indirect owner of the partnership constitutes income to the partnership. No disguised sale under § 707(a)(2)(B) was found where a partner (Washington Avenue Historic Developer ("WAHD")) contributed the proceeds of a bridge loan to a partnership (Gateway Hotel Partners, LLC ("Gateway")) formed to engage in a historic real property development project in exchange for a preferred interest in Gateway and later received a distribution of state tax credits generated by the project. IRS took the position that Gateway was the bridge loan borrower and Gateway repaid the bridge loan by transferring the tax credits. However, the Tax Court found that the borrower was an upper-tier entity that borrowed the funds and then contributed the proceeds to Gateway through several tiers of entities, including WAHD.

The Tax Court then held that the distribution of the tax credits was not a disguised sale because (i) the transfer was made after the two-year period during which transfers are presumed to be a sale under Reg. § 1.707-3(d), so there was a presumption against a disguised sale; and (ii) the facts and circumstances indicated that the transaction was not a sale. In so holding, the Tax Court rejected the IRS's argument that the transfer of the credits was a disguised sale. The Tax Court primarily focused on the fact that the timing and amount of the subsequent transfer of the tax credits were not reasonably certain at the time of the bridge loan contribution and that WAHD/HRI did not have a legally enforceable right to the tax credits: since Gateway could have satisfied WAHD's preferred return with cash, instead of distributing the credits, WAHD had no right to the credits, so its preferred return was subject to the entrepreneurial risks of Gateway's business.

The IRS has listed facts and circumstances, each of which indicates that a transaction is a disguised sale because, at the time of the earlier transfer, the later transfer was not dependent on "entrepreneurial risks" of partnership operations (and, conversely, if the facts and circumstances show that, at the time of the earlier transfer, the later transfer may or may not occur, the transaction will not be treated as a disguised sale):[205.6]

- The timing and amount of a subsequent transfer are determinable with reasonable certainty at the time of the earlier transfer.[205.7]
- The transferor has a legally enforceable right to the subsequent transfer.[205.8]

[205.5]*Id.*
[205.6]Treas. Reg. § 1.707-3(f), Ex 3.
[205.7]Treas. Reg. § 1.707-3(b)(2)(i).
[205.8]Treas. Reg. § 1.707-3(b)(2)(ii).

- The partner's right to receive the transfer of money or other consideration is secured in any manner, taking into account the period during which it is secured.[205.9]
- Any person has made or is legally obligated to make contributions to the partnership so it can make the transfer of money or other consideration.[205.10]
- Any person has loaned or agreed to loan the partnership the money or other consideration it needs to make the transfer, taking into account whether any such lending obligation is subject to contingencies related to partnership operations.[205.11]
- The partnership has incurred or is obligated to incur debt to acquire the money or other consideration needed to make the transfer, taking into account the likelihood that the partnership will be able to incur the debt (including factors such as whether any person has agreed to guarantee or otherwise assume personal liability for the debt).[205.12]
- The partnership holds money or other liquid assets beyond the reasonable needs of the business that are expected to be available to make the transfer (taking into account the income that will be earned from those assets).[205.13]

In *Gateway*, even though WAHD had a disproportionately large allocation of the tax credits and did not have to return the tax credits to the partnership, the transaction was not a disguised sale (i.e., the transaction was not a disguised sale because, at the time of the earlier transfer, the later transfer was dependent on "entrepreneurial risks" of partnership operations).

So long as developers of historic rehabilitation projects recognize the importance of proper documentation and adherence to contractual arrangements, the *Gateway* decision should provide comfort to developers that their tax reporting of such credits is likely to be respected.[205.14] Further note that to avoid recharacterization of such a transfer of tax credits as

---

[205.9]Treas. Reg. § 1.707-3(b)(2)(iii).
[205.10]Treas. Reg. § 1.707-3(b)(2)(iv).
[205.11]Treas. Reg. § 1.707-3(b)(2)(v).
[205.12]Treas. Reg. § 1.707-3(b)(2)(vi).
[205.13]Treas. Reg. § 1.707-3(b)(2)(vii).
[205.14]This subsection is based on an article in Bloomberg BNA, State Tax Blog, written by Kathleen Caggaino, following an interview with Philip Karter, an attorney at Chamberlain Hrdlicka. *Gateway Hotel* examined the tax treatment accorded to the distribution of saleable state tax credits as well as guidance on the circumstances under which a capital contribution from a partner to a partnership should be recharacterized as a taxable sale or exchange under a § 707(a)(2)(B) disguised sale. See subsection 3.9(e).

a disguised sale under the disguised sale rules, real estate partnerships should ensure that partners do not have a right to receive tax credits specifically at a particular point in time.

CAVEAT

With respect to responding to the IRS claim of a disguised sale, it should be noted that the disguised sale presumption in Treas. Reg. § 1.707-3(c) provides that if the transfer has occurred more than two years from the sale, it is presumed not to constitute a disguised sale. Not every rehabilitation project can plan around this presumption but, if the timing of the credit distributions can be made after the two-year threshold, it may be advantageous to the taxpayer. Otherwise, the disguised sale presumptions can be rebutted by either of the parties based on the relevant facts and circumstances (including, but not limited to, those factors indicative of a disguised sale in Treas. Reg. § 1.707-3, which are listed above).

CAVEAT

The court also found that one of the tax credit certificates was issued in the wrong amount in the name of the partner (treated as a tax-free return of capital), which reflected the partnership's intention to sell the balance of the credits earned (i.e., the difference between the face value of the credits and the erroneously discounted value) directly to a third-party tax credit buyer in the taxable transaction.[205.15] Another takeaway to emphasize from *Gateway* is the need for accurate and clear accounting of tax credits.

However, the Tax Court determined that Gateway had sold excess tax credits with respect to a certain portion of the credits transferred. Gateway was not entitled to rescind the transaction since it did not attempt the rescission until the subsequent year. Accordingly, Gateway was required to include as income the proceeds from this transfer. It should be noted that the court imposed a 20 percent negligence penalty with regard to this small portion of the credits determined to have been sold by the taxpayer. The court's determination that the proceeds should have been applied to partnership's income deemed unreported is a warning to taxpayers as to what can happen when the documentation is not complete.

[205.15]Philip Karter of Chamberlain Hrdlicka has concluded that if the partnership had recognized the error and corrected it before the end of the taxable year, the court would have accepted the properly reissued certificates as controlling under the rescinding doctrine, resulting in a 100 percent victory for the taxpayer.

	CAVEAT

If the credits had been distributed to the 1 percent partner followed by liquidation of its partnership's interest, that partner would have been entitled to step up its cost basis in the historic credits to an amount equal to its outside basis (the amount of money it contributed to the partnership). In that case, the subsequent sale of the credits would have produced no gain because the amount realized in cost basis would have been equal in amount. However, the 1 percent partner was not liquidated at the time it received the distribution of tax credits and was not entitled to use its outside basis.

§ 13.6 NEW MARKETS TAX CREDITS (REVISED)

(b)   Allocation of New Markets Tax Credits

p. 1023. *Delete the second full paragraph on this page and insert the following in its place:*

In July 2020, the CDFI Fund awarded more than $3.5 billion in new markets tax credit allocation to 76 CDEs through the calendar year (CY) 2019 round. The CDFI Fund selected the 76 awardees from a pool of 206 applicants requesting an aggregate $14.7 billion in allocation authority. The award recipients are headquartered in 30 states and the District of Columbia. In their applications, awardees estimated that they would make more than $898 million in total investment in rural areas. Through 16 NMTC rounds, the CDFI Fund has made 1,254 allocation awards totaling $61 billion in tax credit authority.

(d)   Allocation Process

p. 1026. *Delete the second full paragraph on this page and insert the following in its place:*

The New Markets Tax Credit (NMTC) program was extended through 2025 with a $5 billion annual appropriation as part of the Consolidated Appropriations Act, 2021, signed by President Trump on December 28, 2020. Before the extension, the NMTC was set to expire at the end of 2020. The NMTC appropriation increased from $3.5 billion per year for calendar years 2010 to 2019 to $5 billion per year for calendar years 2020 through 2025. Additionally, the legislation permits any unallocated funds less than the $5 billion appropriation to be carried forward through 2030, instead of 2025 as under prior law.

(g) Qualified Low-Income Community Investments

p. 1032. *Insert footnote 299.1 at the end of the last sentence of the last paragraph on this page.*

[299.1] See Compliance, Monitoring, and Evaluation FAQs 42, 43, and 44, discussed in subsection 13.6(x), *infra.*

(i) Qualified Active Low-Income Community Business p. 1036. *Insert the following at the end of this subsection:*

CAVEAT

In the event a QALICB anticipates entering into a subsequent phase two development in NMTC funding to an operating business, such as an expansion of a plant or purchase of equipment in a manufacturing facility, it is important to negotiate specific language at the inception of the first phase so that the initial equity investor and CDEs cannot "control" (and veto) subsequent expansion. It is also essential that the forecasts do not include phase two costs in the phase one forecasts, and the legal opinions need to be consistent; often these transactions involve the "portions of the business" (POB) criteria. (See Reg. § 1.45D-1(E)(2)(iii).)

(v) Exiting the NMTC Transaction: The Unwind

(i) Tax Issues: Use of the A and B Notes by For-Profit QALICBs

(2) RELATED-PARTY ACQUISITION

p. 1064. *Insert the following at the end of this subsection:*

In a case where an affiliate of the QALICB steps into the shoes of the investor at the time when either the put or the call is exercised, COD income may be generated to the members of the QALICB. Accordingly, the QALICB often looks for alternatives to minimize the impact of §§ 6(a)12 and 108(e)(4)(A). In this regard, it may consider making a charitable contribution of all of its rights, title, and interest under the put/call agreement; however, there is an issue as to whether the members of the QALICB will be entitled to a charitable contribution deduction. Moreover, before accepting the donation a charity would need to get board approval and potentially be prepared to fund the put or call.

CAVEAT

It is important to recognize that the board of the charity would need to approve any modification of the terms of the B Note, which would have to satisfy the impermissible private benefit rules. See Chapter 5.

CAVEAT

At best, the charitable deduction will be measured by the difference between the fair market value of the equity members' interest less the put price, say $1,000 (which would be based on the likelihood of the put being exercised in view of historical experience). However, the investor should not exercise the put in advance of the assignment because in that case it could be treated by the IRS as an acceleration of COD to the QALICB. It is more likely, however, that the IRS would claim that the deduction on the exercise of the call option is based on the purchaser acquiring the equity interest at fair market value; because the charity would receive the C Note equal to its fair market value but be required to pay fair market value (the call price) for it, the deduction would theoretically be equal to zero.

CAVEAT

If we assume that the purchaser is comfortable taking a charitable contribution deduction on its tax return based on the difference between the fair market value and the put price, it is likely to raise an IRS audit issue in view of the significant amount of the deduction. However, the members of the purchaser could decide to report a reduced charitable contribution to lessen the likelihood of an IRS examination of the contribution.

It is important to note that debt restructuring, which is common among financially troubled debtors, may have income tax consequences to the QALICB. It may result in a deemed taxable exchange of the old debt instrument for the new debt instrument triggering recognition of COD income. In this regard, § 1.1001-3 of the Treasury Regulations provides various tests to analyze whether debt modification is significant and will often be triggered by changes in yield, changes in payment, and timing, among others. In this regard, a change in yield is most important because it will occur if the yield varies from the annual yield on the unmodified debt (determined as of the modification date by more than the greater of (1) one-quarter of 1 percent (25 basis points) or (2) 5 percent of the annual yield of the unmodified debt (0.05 × annual yield)). See Reg. § 1.1001.

Assuming that the purchaser under the put or call assigns all of its interest to a § 501(c)(3) organization, it may propose to modify the terms, especially in the case where the B Note has more than 20 years before principal is due following the end of the compliance period.

In summary, as to the members of the QALICB, any significant reduction that is a moratorium on annual interest or a deferral of interest payments for a number of years is likely to be treated as a significant debt modification (because it would be greater than 25 basis points or 5 percent of the annual yield). The effect of this may be to trigger COD income to the debtor unless it can be shown that the adjusted payments on the modified debt would not result in a reduced yield over the remaining life of the B Note.

To conclude, there are five alternatives in the event that the QALICB members are unwilling to recognize COD income in the year following the end of the compliance period:

1. See the qualified real property business indebtedness exception under § 108(a)(1)(D), discussed in § 13.6(e)(iii)(B); however, the exclusion requires that the value of the property has declined below the mortgage debt; it would also have an impact on depreciation deduction of future years.

2. The purchaser may be able to negotiate with the charity a reduction in the annual interest for, say, the first five years, with an increase in the rates at the back end of the term, so that the overall yield on the debt remains the same.

3. The members may be able to negotiate a deferral as to the exercise date in the put/call agreement with the equity investor—in effect, be able to "kick the bucket."

4. The affiliate could consider contributing its rights to a trust for the benefit of the QALICB members' children, but not only would there be a gift tax issue, but also the trust would be treated as a related party with all COD implications.

5. The affiliate could assign the put/call agreement to an unrelated party (at least 50 percent owned by an unrelated party such as a brother-in-law or sister-in-law, with the members' children owning 49 percent or less); however, this would have gift tax implications both at the initial assignment and subsequently if the majority owner attempts to reassign ownership of the B Note to the members at a later date.

(w) Nonprofits' Use of NMTC (Revised)

p. 1068. *Add the following to the end of footnote 370:*

See also Michele D. Layser, "Nonprofit Participation in Place-Based Tax Incentive Transactions (opportunity zones and the promise of investment and economic development), *Fordham Urban Law Journal* (October 2021). The author states that, as a practical matter, in NMTC transactions, almost all qualified low-income community investments take the form of loans—usually at below-market interest to a business or developer. Some of the loans are extended to nonprofit borrowers who can use the loans to pursue their charitable activities, including many mission-driven projects, such as homeless shelters, food kitchens, religious missions, and so forth. With regard to nonprofits as QALICBs (see page 1070), nonprofits may reach out directly to CDEs or hire consultants who can connect them with CDEs who have allocations available if a nonprofit's project is consistent with the CDE's investment strategy.

(ii) Multiple Roles

(B) As QALICB. page 1071. *Insert the following after the last Example:*

Nonprofit QALICBs, in contrast to for-profit QALICBs, are more likely to produce human capital amenities including employment training centers, childcare centers, school facilities, and, most frequently, healthcare facilities. Park, open space, and recreation and community centers are the most common quality-of-life amenities, followed by art museums, cultural institutions, and public libraries, all of which are more likely to be provided by nonprofit QALICBs. Project improvements to public infrastructure most often include parking lots and garages sponsored by for-profit QALICBs.[374.1]

(iii) Board Approval. p. 1074. *Add the following after the Caveat under this subsection:*

Traps for the Unwary. Finally, the board of the charity needs to be educated by counsel with regard to five possible traps for the unwary involving UBIT, an advance agreement to forgive the leveraged loan, the CDE fee structure, the allocation of COD income, and the use of a "straw party" as a party to the unwind.

1. There is a potential UBIT concern on exit by the nonprofit charity, after the seven-year compliance period expires, if the project is not "substantially related" to the exempt function of the organization, such as relief of the poor or underprivileged or relieving the burdens of the government. The location in a QCT isn't enough.[381.1]

2. It is critical that there is no agreement in advance that the leveraged loan will be forgiven at the end of the compliance period; otherwise, the basic structure of the NMTC may be defective.

3. In most cases, there may be a need for multiple CDEs in order to direct their allocations to the project; it is important that the board of the nonprofit examine the proposed CDE fees because the fees fluctuate and in certain cases may be above market.

4. If the QALICB is structured as an LLC with multiple parties or members, including a nonprofit, and is taxed as a partnership, the operating agreement should contain specific language covering the allocation among the partners of the COD income, if any. It is important

---

[374.1]See generally Martin D. Avravanel et al., "New Markets Tax Credit Program Evaluation," Urban Institute, April 2013. See also paper drafted on reforming the new markets tax credit by Connor Kratz as a graduate student at Georgetown University Law Center, a copy of which is retained by the author.
[381.1]See Rev. Rul. 85-1, 1985-1 C.B. 177; Rev. Rul. 85-2, 1985-1 C.B. 178.

to define narrowly the section on "Refinancing Proceeds" relative to exercise of a put.

5. A straw party should not be used by a QALICB to acquire the equity interest pursuant to the exercise of the put or call. The approach may backfire on the QALICB under the related-party rules (i.e., direct or indirect acquisition of debt, which could generate COD income for the taxpayer).[381.2]

p. 1075. *Delete the last two sentences of the first full paragraph on this page and add the following new subsections after subsection (iv):*

(v) Questions a Nonprofit Board Should Consider in the Context of New Market Tax Financing.[382.1]

1. What capital investments is the organization planning over the next 12 to 18 months?
    ◦ Real estate development/construction
    ◦ Asset purchases
    ◦ New lines of business/service
    ◦ Capital investments in the ordinary course of business

2. Does the organization plan on increasing headcount or services over the next 12 to 24 months?

3. Does the organization plan any potential reduction in community services issues over the next 12 months due to lack of funding?

4. Does the organization have projects/services that have been postponed or canceled due to capital costs and lack of funding through traditional capital campaign activities?

5. The board needs to examine the following issues before approving the structure:
    ◦ What is the minimum deal size that is practicable, considering overall costs and recognizing that leveraged funds are difficult to obtain?
    ◦ How does the organization go about attracting allocation?
    ◦ Deals can take six months or longer, so it may be beneficial to begin as long as a year in advance of an allocation to "market" with prospective CDEs and equity investors.

[381.2]See subsection 13.6(v)(i)(2).

[382.1]This subsection is adapted from a PowerPoint presentation prepared by Myriam Simmons, Director, Credits and Incentives Consulting at Ryan Company.

- Will there be continuity in management during the project development period and compliance period (seven years)?

- Donors to a 501(c)(3) QALICB may want to have certain controls over the project and site selection.

- There is often a perception that pledges are to be used to pay interest rather than providing a new service consistent with the exempt function of the charity.

(vi) Using a Title-Holding Corporation as a QALICB.[382.2]   A QALICB charter school may use a title-holding corporation both as an asset protection vehicle and as a means of obtaining financing from a CDE in connection with an NMTC transaction.

A, a charter school (§ 501(c)(3)) located in a low-income area, in order to protect its valuable real property, establishes a tax-exempt title-holding corporation and transfers a school property subject to a 50-year ground lease with a governmental agency. The title-holding corporation may then sublet to Charity A the school property in exchange for annual rental payments. After paying its expenses, including its payment of rent to the governmental agency, the title-holding corporation will remit its remaining income to Charity A.

To finance improvements on the property, the title-holding corporation may borrow funds from a third-party lender. If the title-holding corporation otherwise qualifies as a QALICB, it may borrow the required funds from a CDE as part of an NMTC transaction. The title-holding corporation may use a portion of the rent it receives from Charity A to repay the loan from the CDE. Despite the limitations imposed by § 501(c)(2) of the Code, the activities undertaken by the title-holding corporation in this example—holding a leasehold interest in improved real property in a low-income area, using loan proceeds to improve that property, leasing that property to another party, and paying all remaining income over to Charity A—are consistent with its qualifications both as a tax-exempt organization described in § 501(c)(2) of the Code and as a QALICB described in § 45D(2) of the Code.

[382.2]See paper on title-holding corporation in the NMTC structure drafted by Brendan Wilson, as a graduate tax student at Georgetown University Law Center, a copy of which is retained by the author.

CAVEAT

Although the aforesaid example focuses on a charter school, a wide variety of other non-profit organizations that hold valuable real property in low-income areas may also benefit from this type of arrangement. For example, community health clinics, hospitals, community colleges, and religious organizations often conduct their activities in low-income communities using property they own or lease from third parties. Like the charter school described earlier, these and other nonprofit organizations may be able to use title-holding corporations to hold and protect their tax-exempt real property while also gaining access to additional financing as QALICBs in NMTC transactions.

---

p. 1075. *Add the following new subsections (x) and (y), after subsection (w):*

(x) CDFI Fund Frequently Asked Questions (FAQs). The CDFI Fund has issued a series of New Markets Tax Credit Compliance and Monitoring Frequently Asked Questions (FAQs) since September 2011, by adding, revising, or updating select questions, some of which are highlighted here:[382.3]

1. When a CDE has received principal repayments on a QLICI and reinvests those proceeds in a new QLICI, the new QLICI is subject to the same requirements found in § 3.2 of the allocation agreement (i.e., types of QLICIs, service area, etc.).

   To the extent a CDE reinvests repayments of principal as new QLICIs, the CDFI Fund is required to check compliance for all reported QLICIs against the requirements specified in the allocation agreement.

[382.3]See recently issued FAQ 17, regarding an allocatee's use of QLICIs to finance housing units if section 3.2(k) of the allocation agreement is listed as "not applicable"; FAQ 18, the definition of "affordable housing" for purposes of meeting section 3.2(k) of the allocation agreement; FAQ 19, the definition of "substantial rehabilitation threshold" for purposes of meeting section 3.3(h) of the allocation agreement; FAQ 20, the exception for acquisition costs in connection with new construction in cases where the QALICB's principal business activity is the rental to others of real property (section 3.3(h)(iv) of the allocation agreement); FAQ 21, the meaning of "innovative investments" for purposes of section 3.2(l) of the allocation agreement; FAQ 33, the definition of "support health-related services" as it relates to QALICBs in federally designated medically underserved areas; FAQ 34, the determination of whether a project is located in a Food Desert using USDA's Approved Access Research Atlas; FAQ 35, the definition of other similar federal/state/local programs targeted toward particularly economically distressed communities; FAQ 41, the restrictions on the use of bond proceeds under the CDFI bond guarantees program in NMTC-related activities; FAQ 42, the restrictions on the use of QLICI proceeds to repay or refinance any debt or equity provider, or an affiliate of any debt or equity provider, whose capital was used, directly or indirectly, to fund a QEI; and FAQ 43, how the fund would monitor the restriction on the use of QLICI proceeds to directly or indirectly repay or refinance any debt or equity provider, or affiliate to any debt or equity provider, whose capital was used, directly or indirectly, to fund the QEI required under the 2015–2016 NMTC application.

EXAMPLE
If an allocatee is required to invest 85 percent of its QLICIs in its approved service area, the CDFI Fund will measure compliance against all reported QLICIs that are currently outstanding, whether original investments or reinvestments, to ensure that 85 percent of its QLICIs are in the approved service area. (See FAQ 16.)

2. **The six-month cure period is available to correct a CDE's or subsidiary CDE's failure to invest substantially all of its QEI proceeds.**

   The six-month cure period[382.4] is available to correct a CDE's or subsidiary CDE's failure to invest substantially all of its QEI proceeds in QLICIs within the 12-month period.[382.5]

   However, the 6-month cure period is not automatically added to the 12-month period. The rules state that the six-month cure period begins on the date the CDE becomes aware (or reasonably should have become aware) of the failure to invest substantially all of the QEI proceeds in a QLICI within the 12-month period. (See FAQ 17.)

3. **Supporting documentation that an allocatee needs to retain in order to demonstrate compliance with investing in areas of higher distress as reflected in § 3.2(h).**

   In addition to CIMS, which provides non-metropolitan status, poverty rate, median family income (MFI) percentages, and unemployment rates, the CDFI Fund has provided several links on its website to assist allocations. (See the "Compliance Monitoring and Evaluation" link for details.)

   Allocatees are advised to retain all relevant information in support of its decision to invest in such areas. Supporting documentation for the areas of higher distress requirement may include statistical indices of economic distress such as poverty rates, median family income, or unemployment rates at the census tract level based on the 2006–2010 ACS; materials from other government programs (e.g., HUD Renewal Communities or EPA Brownfields) demonstrating the area qualified for assistance under those programs; and others.

   The "Compliance Monitoring and Evaluation" section on the CDFI Fund's website has links to the following sites:[382.6]

   ° Federally Designated Empowerment Zones, Enterprise Communities, or Renewal Communities

   ° Brownfield Sites

[382.4]Section 1.45D-1(e)(6).
[382.5]As required by § 1.45D-1(c)(5)(iv).
[382.6]See FAQ 28.

- ◦ SBA-Designated HUB Zones
- ◦ Medically Underserved Areas (Department of Health and Human Services)
- ◦ Food Desert
- ◦ Promise Zone

4. All allocatees are required to invest substantially all (generally 85 percent) of their QEIs as QLICIs. Section 3.2(j) of the allocation agreement may require an allocatee to invest an even higher percentage of QEIs (e.g., 95 percent or 100 percent) as QLICIs, based on representations made by the allocatee in its allocation application.

   A. All allocatees must be able to demonstrate that they initially made QLICIs in the amount specified in their allocation agreements.

EXAMPLE

If an allocatee received QEIs totaling $1 million and is required in its allocation agreement to invest 100 percent of its QEIs as QLICIs, then it must be able to demonstrate that $1 million was initially invested as QLICIs.

   B. If an allocatee subsequently receives repayments of principal from the QLICIs (e.g., amortizing loan payments), but consistent with applicable IRS regulations does not reinvest these proceeds into other QLICIs, then the allocatee will be treated as fulfilling the requirements of § 3.2(j)—notwithstanding the fact that the allocatee is no longer "fully invested" at the initial percentage.

EXAMPLE

An allocatee received QEIs totaling $1 million and is required in its allocation agreement to invest 100 percent of its QEIs as QLICIs. It makes a loan of $1 million to a QALICB. In accordance with the terms of the loan, the QALICB makes interest-only payments for two years, and, beginning in year 3, some small payments of principal along with the interest payments. At the end of the seven-year compliance period, the principal payments total less than $150,000—or 15 percent of the $1 million loan to the QALICB. This amount of repayment is sufficiently minimal as to not trigger reinvestment requirements under the IRS regulations, and the allocatee is in compliance with § 3.2(j).[382.7]

[382.7] See FAQ 35.

C. If an allocatee subsequently receives repayments of principal from the QLICIs that are sufficient enough to trigger reinvestment requirements under the IRS regulations, the allocatee is required to reinvest those proceeds in the same percentage as is required in the allocation agreement.

EXAMPLE

An allocatee received QEIs totaling $1 million and is required in its allocation agreement to invest 100 percent of its QEIs as QLICIs. It makes a loan of $1 million to a QALICB. The QALICB repays the entirety of the loan after two years. The allocatee must reinvest the entire $1 million into a QLICI within the time frames required under IRS regulations in order to be compliant with § 3.2(j).

NOTE

Consistent with IRS regulations regarding reinvestment, the CDFI Fund will not require allocatees to reinvest principal repayments that are received in year 7 of the compliance period.

---

5. Section 6.9 of the allocation agreement requires CDEs to report Material Events to the CDFI Fund within 20 days of the occurrence.

An updated Material Events Form can be found on the CDFI Fund's website. An allocatee should use this form to identify the nature of the event so that the CDFI Fund can determine whether it is material and affects the CDE's ability to retain certification as a CDE or remain compliant with its Allocation Agreement.[382.8]

The CDFI Fund defines a "Material Event" as an occurrence that affects an organization's strategic direction, mission, or business operation and, thereby, its status as a certified Community Development Financial Institution (CDFI) or Community Development Entity (CDE), and/or its compliance with the terms and conditions of the Allocation Agreement. The following list provides examples of Material Events that should be reported to the CDFI Fund on the Certification of Material Event Form.

- An Event of Default as that term is defined in Section 8.1 of the allocation agreement, or any event that upon notice or lapse of time, or both, would constitute an Event of Default.

[382.8] See FAQ 38.

- A merger, acquisition, or consolidation with another entity.

- A change in the Controlling Entity identified in any allocation agreement or where the Controlling Entity will no longer have any ownership or management interest in the Allocatee and/or will no longer have control over the day-to-day management and operations (including investment decisions) of the Allocatee.

- A change in the organization legal status (e.g., dissolution or liquidation of the organization, bankruptcy proceedings, receivership, etc.).

- An event that materially changes the strategic direction, mission, or business of the organization such that the organization no longer meets one or more CDFI or CDE certification requirements such as no longer providing loans or equity investments.

- Changes in business strategy that might have influenced the merits of awarding the application to the extent that such changes result in the allocation use being generally inconsistent with the strategies (including, but not limited to, the proposed product offerings and markets served) set forth in the Allocation Application.

- An event that materially changes the organization's tax and/or corporate structure (e.g., changing from for-profit to nonprofit status).

- An event that results in a change in control of the organization (e.g., control by, controlling relationships, loss of control—as such term is defined in the allocation agreement—by any entity that is a party thereto).

- A change in the composition of the organization's Board of Directors (or other governing body) such that the percentage of the governing or advisory board members representing the organization's Service Area is diminished or altered.

- Relocation of the organization's primary office to another state, which alters the organization's ability to serve or be accountable to its Service Area (based on its most recent certification prior to the relocation).

- A proceeding or enforcement action instituted against the allocatee in, by, or before any court or governmental or administrative body or agency, which proceeding or its outcome could have a material adverse effect on the financial condition or business operations of the allocatee.

- A proceeding instituted against a regulated Affiliate of an allocatee by or before any court or governmental or administrative body or agency, which proceeding or its outcome could have a material adverse effect on the financial condition or business operations of the allocatee.

○ A material adverse change in the condition, financial or otherwise, or operations of the allocatee that would impair the allocatee's ability to carry out the authorized uses of the allocation.

○ The debarment, suspension, exclusion, or disqualification by the Department of Treasury, or any other federal department or agency, of any individual or entity (or principal thereof) that received any portion of the allocation in a procurement or nonprocurement transaction, as defined in 31 C.F.R. § 19.970.

○ The replacement of any key management official(s) (e.g., the Executive Director, the Chief Financial Officer, the Board Chairperson, or their equivalents) who had been named in the Allocation Application.

○ The receipt of an Adverse Opinion, Qualified Opinion, or Disclaimer of Opinion in audited financial statements of the allocatee.

6. An allocatee may request an amendment to its allocation agreement.
An allocatee may request an amendment to its allocation agreement by submitting a written request on the CDE's letterhead to the CDFI Fund. The request, at a minimum, must:[382.9]

1. identify the name and control number of the allocatee;

2. identify the portion(s) of the allocation agreement that needs to be modified;

3. state the reasons why the allocatee is making the request; and

4. explain the extent to which the proposed modifications are consistent with what the allocatee had proposed in its initial application to the CDFI Fund, and will help to further the goals of the New Markets Tax Credit Program.

The request can be submitted by email to ccme@cdfi.treas. gov with subject line: NMTC: Allocation Agreement Amendment Request. The request can also be submitted by mail to:

Attention: Compliance

U.S. Department of the Treasury

Community Development Financial Institutions Fund

1500 Pennsylvania Avenue, NW
Washington, DC 20220

[382.9]See FAQ 61.

Justification for approving an amendment to an allocation agreement includes, but is not limited to, a determination that the amendment request is:

1. consistent with the intent of the NMTC Program statute and regulations and furthers the goals of the NMTC Program;

2. consistent with (or not a substantive departure from) the business strategy proposed in the initial application for an allocation; and

3. sufficiently narrow in scope that it does not disadvantage other allocatees or other applicants from the same allocation round.

   Although an amendment request can be submitted at any time, it must be submitted no later than 90 calendar days before the allocatee needs the determination.

7. There are new QALICB use restrictions that relate to QLICI proceeds being used to repay or refinance any debt or equity provider (or an affiliate of any debt or equity provider). Beginning with the CY 2015–2016 round, any debt or equity provider, or affiliate of any debt or equity provider, whose capital was used, directly or indirectly, to fund a QEI may receive QLICI proceeds to repay or refinance reasonable expenditures that are incurred by the debt or equity provider (or affiliate) and that are directly attributable to the qualified business of the QALICB if the expenditures (i) were incurred no more than 24 months prior to the date on which the QLICI transaction closes or (ii) represent no more than 5 percent of the total QLICI proceeds from the QEI.[382.10]

CAVEAT

Reasonable expenditures are expenditures for a legitimate business purpose that occur during the normal course of operation, and must be similar in amount and scope when compared to expenditures by a similar entity for a similar project under similar circumstances. Refinance includes transferring cash or property directly or indirectly to the debt or equity provider or affiliate of the debt or equity provider.

[382.10]See FAQs 44, 45, and 46 (April 2017).

CAVEAT

Of note, the IRS has not issued guidance on what costs can be repaid or refinanced with QLICI proceeds under IRC § 45D. Until such guidance is issued, the CDFI Fund supports the use of the aforementioned parameters for transactions involving the repayment or refinancing of expenditures.

EXAMPLE

A is a debt or equity provider, or affiliate of a debt or equity provider, whose capital was used, directly or indirectly, to fund a QEI, the proceeds of which were used to make a QLICI. Within 24 months prior to the closing of the QLICI transaction, A expends $1 million to obtain development permits, begin construction, acquire or install equipment, and acquire other property related to the project, all of which represents reasonable expenditures directly attributable to the qualified business of the QALICB, and for which A has retained documentation (i.e., invoices, receipts, proof of payment, etc.). More than 24 months prior to the closing of the QLICI, A expends $700,000 of documented, reasonable expenditures directly attributable to the qualified business of the QALICB. The QALICB receives $10 million in total QLICIs from the QEI funded by A.

24-month provision

Out of $10 million in total QLICIs, up to $1 million of the QLICI proceeds can be used to repay the entity for these documented expenditures and to directly or indirectly repay sources used to fund QEI (e.g., a leveraged loan). The remaining QLICI proceeds ($9 million) could be used for additional expenditures such as operating needs, working capital needs, equipment, additional construction expenditures, or other needs related to the project of business of the QALICB.

5 percent provision

The QALICB may use no more than 5 percent of QLICI proceeds to reimburse documented, reasonable expenditures that are directly attributable to the qualified business of the QALICB regardless of when those expenditures were incurred. In this scenario, if the total QLICIs to the QLICB were $10 million, the QALICB could use up to $500,000 to reimburse expenditures that were incurred prior to the QLICI closing.

In summary, of the $1.7 million in documented, reasonable expenditures directly attributable to the qualified business of the QALICB incurred by A, the QALICB may elect to either reimburse the full amount of reasonable expenditures incurred within 24 months of the QLICI closing date ($1 million) or reimburse reasonable expenditures that represent up to 5 percent of the QLICI proceeds incurred at any time prior to the QLICI closing date ($500,000). It may not do both.

The CDFI Fund will need to monitor the restriction on the use of QLICI proceeds to directly or indirectly repay or refinance any debt or equity provider, or affiliate to any debt or equity provider, whose capital was used, directly or indirectly, to fund the QEI required under the CY 2015–2016 NMTC application.[382.11]

A QALICB may use QLICI proceeds to repay or refinance any debt or equity provider, or affiliate of any debt or equity provider, and to monetize an asset owned by, contributed, sold, or otherwise transferred to the QALICB (or an affiliate of a QALICB) but not including the accreted value of an asset.

Under the CY 2015–2016 round, a QALICB is permitted to use QLICI proceeds only to repay or refinance a debt or equity provider (or affiliate of a debt or equity provider) whose capital was used directly or indirectly to fund the QEI, subject to the provisions referenced in this section. The QALICB may use QLICI proceeds to repay or refinance expenditures incurred by the debt or equity provider (or their affiliate) for the acquisition of any asset contributed, sold, or otherwise transferred to the QALICB to the extent such asset represents a reasonable expenditure directly attributable to the qualified business for the QALICB. However, the amount that can be repaid or refinanced for such an asset is limited to the asset's original cost and not to any accreted value obtained by appraisal or other valuation methods. Such transactions remain subject to the aforesaid 24-month rule or 5 percent rule.

EXAMPLE

B is a debt or equity provider, or affiliate of a debt or equity provider, whose capital was used, directly or indirectly, to fund a QEI, the proceeds of which were used to make a QLICI. B acquired property for $700,000 less than 24 months prior to the QLICI closing, which represents a reasonable expenditure directly attributable to the qualified business of the QALICB; the current appraised value of the property is $1 million. More than 24 months prior to the closing of the QLICI, B acquired equipment for $500,000 (currently appraised at $600,000), which represents a reasonable expenditure directly attributable to the qualified business of the QALICB. The QALICB receives $10 million in total QLICIs from the QEI funded by B. The QLICI's proceeds could only be used to

---

[382.11]CDEs must include such covenants in financing agreements with QALICBs as may be necessary to reflect this restriction. The agreements containing such covenants must be available for inspection by the CDFI Fund. In addition, the CDE should collect such information as may be necessary and maintain documentation to trace the use of QLICI proceeds by the QALICB at the time the initial QLICI is made and at least annually thereafter. In situations where the QALICB will directly or indirectly repay or refinance any debt or equity provider or affiliate of any debt or equity provider, whose capital was used, directly or indirectly, to fund a QEI under the 24-month or 5 percent exception rules, the CDE should maintain documentation demonstrating that the reimbursements can be directly traced to actual expenditures by the debt or equity provider (or its affiliate) and are directly attributable to the qualified business of the QALICB. Documentation to support compliance with this restriction must be retained for the entire period of the QLICI in the QALICB plus three years or the seven-year compliance period plus three years, whichever is shorter. See FAQ 45.

reimburse up to the original cost of acquisition (not the appraised value) of both the property and equipment ($700,000 + $500,000 = $1.2 million) subject to the 24-month or 5 percent limitations. The QALICB may elect to either reimburse the full amount of reasonable expenditures incurred within 24 months of the QLICI closing date ($700,000) or reimburse reasonable expenditures that represent up to 5 percent of the QLICI proceeds incurred at any time prior to the QLICI closing date ($500,000). It may not do both. See FAQ 46 (April 1, 2017).

(y) Future of the NMTC Program

CAVEAT

PATH Act and Potential Impact of Tax Reform
During 2017, in the likely attempt to enact tax reform legislation, there is obvious concern that the NMTC provisions may be repealed or significantly modified. However, because the PATH Act provided $3.5 billion in annual allocation authority to the CDFI Fund through 2019,[382.12] it is unlikely that the program will be terminated prior to 2020 as part of tax reform.[382.13] Unlike the low-income house tax credit and historic tax credit, the NMTC is not permanently codified in the Internal Revenue Code. Thus, some legislators may be tempted to propose eliminating the NMTC program to pay for other items (e.g., lowering corporate tax rates).

§ 13.10 THE ENERGY TAX CREDITS

(a) Overview

p. 1093. *Add the following footnote at the end of the second sentence:*

[402.1] Community solar projects enable low-income residents in the District of Columbia and elsewhere to have access to the benefits of solar energy with the goal of reducing by at least 50 percent the electric bill of low-income households with high energy burdens. The program is part of the Renewable Portfolio Standard Expansion Amendment Act of 2016, funded by the Renewable Energy Development Fund (REDF). Community solar programs allow multiple energy customers to subscribe to the shared solar projects. After solar panels are installed, they convert the sun's energy into direct current (DC) electricity, which is sent to a converter that then converts the DC electricity into an alternating current (AC) so that it can be used in homes and businesses. A meter measures the amount of electricity produced by the solar panels before the electricity is fed into the utility grid. The utility company keeps track of how much electricity (kilowatt hours) is fed into the grid by the solar panels. The value of this electricity provides a cash credit to specified low-income residents' monthly electric bills. Although there are significant challenges in order to implement community solar projects, the innovative program has been developed by Herb Stevens of Nixon Peabody. The author retains a copy of a PowerPoint presentation titled "Innovative Thinking and Lawyering for Community Solar Projects" (March 2017) written by Herb Stevens and Carolyn Lowery, which was presented to a Georgetown Law School graduate tax class, Advanced Topics in Exempt Organization.

[382.12] The Protecting Americans from Tax Hikes Act of 2015, P.L. 114-113 (Dec. 18, 2015).
[382.13] On February 15, 2017, congressmen Pat Tiberi (R-OH) and Richard Neal (D-MA) introduced bipartisan legislation in the House to make the NMTC a permanent part of the Internal Revenue Code. See The New Markets Tax Credit Extension Act of 2017, H.R. 1098 (2017).

p. 1097. *Add the following new subsection following subsection (f):*

(g)   2015 PATH Act

In December 2015, Congress passed the Protecting Americans from Tax Hikes (PATH) Act, which contained a long-awaited multiyear extension of solar and wind tax credits together with one-year extensions for a range of other renewable energy technologies. Prior to this extension, Congress would only renew the credits in one- and two-year extensions. This discouraged technology development and building of facilities.

The PATH Act amended §§ 48(a) and 48(a)(5)(C) of the Code to provide that the investment tax credit is extended for wind energy facilities beginning construction in 2015 and 2016, subject to a phaseout as follows:

1. Credit is reduced by 20 percent for projects that begin construction in 2017;
2. Credit is reduced by 40 percent for projects that begin construction in 2018; and
3. Credit is reduced by 60 percent for projects that begin construction in 2019.

The Act also amended § 48(a)(2)(A)(i) of the Code to extend the investment tax credit for solar energy projects beginning construction prior to 2022, subject to a phaseout as follows:

1. Credit is reduced to 26 percent for projects that begin construction in 2020; and
2. Credit is reduced to 22 percent for projects that begin construction in 2021.

In the case of projects that begin construction prior to 2022 and are not placed in service before 2024, the credit is reduced to 10 percent.

p. 1097. *Insert the following new section at the end of Section 13.10:*

§ 13.11   THE OPPORTUNITY ZONE FUNDS: NEW SECTION 1400Z-1 AND SECTION 1400Z-2[431] (REVISED)

Similar to the enactment of the New Market Tax Credit, the 2017 Tax Act (Pub. L. No. 115-97) (the "Tax Act") provided a new provision to encourage economic growth and investment in distressed communities. It provides two main tax incentives to encourage investment in qualified

---

[431]Added by § 13823 of 2017 Tax Ct.

opportunity zones. First, it allows for the temporary deferral of inclusion in gross income for capital gains that are invested in a qualified opportunity fund. The second main tax incentive in the bill excludes from gross income the post-acquisition capital gains on investments in opportunity zone funds that are held for at least 10 years (Act § 13823(a); see also new IRC §§ 1400Z-1, 1400Z-2).

CAVEAT

The provision allows wealthy investors to defer taxes on gains that are invested in qualified Opportunity Funds that, in turn, invest in distressed communities (similar to the NMTC) designated by the governor of the state. The provision provides for the temporary deferral (up to nine years) of inclusion in gross income for capital gains reinvested in a qualified opportunity fund and the permanent exclusion of capital gains from the sale or exchange of an investment in the qualified opportunity fund. The provision allows for the designation of certain low-income community population census tracts as qualified opportunity zones, where low-income communities are defined in § 45D(e).

Opportunity funds must be certified by the U.S. Department of Treasury and are required to hold at least 90 percent of their assets in qualified opportunity zone businesses and/or business property.

The definition of low-income community is similar to that used in the new market tax credit structure. Governors are responsible for identifying areas in their states to be designated as opportunity zones. The Tax Act generally allows for 25 percent of the states' low-income community population census tracks to be so designated.

Although opportunity zones are similar to new market tax credits in that they still bring investments to low-income areas, there is a benefit in that total amount of investments that qualify for the subsidy are not limited by annual allocation amounts.

CAVEAT

In view of the record high sales and gains in the stock market, this new provision could attract significant investment to low-income communities.

The rules are very technical, and Treasury needs to develop rules on how the Opportunity Funds are certified and meet the criteria. Once that occurs, new capital should begin to flow into the area, similar in effect to the new market tax credit, to incentivize the low-income community.

(a)   Introduction

The 2017 Tax Act allows individuals and corporate investors to defer capital gains on the sale of stock business assets or other property (wherever located) by investing in a qualified opportunity zone (which must invest at least 90 percent of its assets, directly or indirectly, in businesses located in designated opportunity zones, i.e., low-income communities). But the deferral does not apply to gains generated on the sale to the fund itself.

The proceeds must be invested within 180 days beginning from the initial sale or exchange in the amount equal to the gain to be deferred. Moreover, there is partial forgiveness of the deferred capital gain if held for five or seven years; and furthermore, any future gain on the investment in an opportunity fund may be excluded if the investment is held for ten years.[432]

The deferred portion of the gain is taxable when the investment in the opportunity fund is sold or, if sooner, on December 31, 2026, unless the date is subsequently extended. So if the opportunity fund investment is held for 10 years, beyond 2026, the tax basis of the new investment is deemed to be its fair market value on sale. In effect, further appreciation on the investment, but not the deferred gain, is eliminated permanently. As a result, leveraged investments generating depreciation during the hold may not be recaptured. It is important to note that the original property sold need not be located in or connected in any way with a qualified census tract.

CAVEAT

Taxes that would otherwise need to be paid to Government (IRS) can work for the investor over the deferral period and potentially generate cash distributions, losses, even tax credits.

This is a remarkable opportunity for high-net-worth individuals to defer gain and subsequently exclude further gain based upon the appreciation of their investment in an opportunity zone. Moreover, and most important, it allows and incentivizes investments in qualified census tracts.

---

[432]See Steven Mount, "New Program Allows Deferral and Possible Forgiveness of Capital Gains Invested in Low-Income Community Business," *Real Estate Journal* (Feb. 2018); see also paper written by Kevin Winters, in Georgetown Law Graduate Tax, Advanced Topics in Exempt Organizations ("Opportunity Zones: Questions and Applications," a copy of which is retained by author).

(b)   Operations of QOZ Business

An opportunity fund may be sponsored by CDFIs as well as banks that are presently involved in the new market tax credit program as well as other individuals, corporations, or nonprofits. The opportunity fund needs to invest in qualified opportunity zone property ("OZP"), which would include *qualified* stock, partnership interests, and business property. In all cases, to qualify as an opportunity zone business, *substantially all* of the tangible assets of the business must be used in an opportunity zone. A qualified opportunity fund must hold at least 90 percent of its assets in qualified opportunity zone properties (which does not include another opportunity fund). The 90 percent requirement is determined by the average percentage of two OZP held by the Fund measured on the last day of the first six-month period of the taxable year of the Opportunity Fund and the last day of the taxable year (for calendar year taxpayer would be June 30 and December 31, but there could be a short-year issue). If the Fund fails the 90 percent test in any year, it is not disqualified but is required to pay a penalty for each month it fails to meet the requirement in an amount equal to the excess of the 90 percent of its aggregate assets over the amount of qualified opportunity zone property held by the Fund multiplied by the underpayment rate under § 6621(a)(2) of the Code. If the opportunity fund is a partnership or a pass-through entity, each partner must pay his proportionate share of the penalty. There is an exception if the opportunity fund can demonstrate that its failure to meet the 90 percent test is due to reasonable cause.

The qualified opportunity zone stock or partnership interest must be acquired from the corporation or partnership by the fund after December 31, 2017, solely in exchange for *cash*. (It is an equity investment structure.) During substantially all of the holding period of the qualified opportunity stock or partnership interest, the corporation or partnership must continue to qualify as an opportunity zone business.

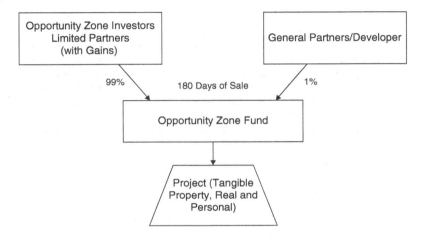

Similar limitations with regard to the qualified opportunity zone business are based upon the new market tax credit rules relative to active businesses such as the 50 percent of gross income and the limitation on intangibles and nonqualified financial property and "sin" uses. See subsection 13.6(i).

Investments in qualified opportunity zone business property must be tangible property used in a trade or business acquired by purchase (see § 179(d)(2)) in which the related party rules apply, but substitute a 20 percent test instead of 50 percent). Second, and most important, the original use in the qualified opportunity zone must commence with the zone business *or* the business must substantially improve the property, which means during any 30-month period beginning after the acquisition of the property, additions to basis of the property must exceed an amount equal to the adjusted basis of the property at the beginning of the period. In effect, the improvements must exceed the adjusted basis of the purchase of the property.

CAVEAT

Gains (cash) generated by transfer to the OZF do not qualify for the deferral and exclusion benefits in view of the "related party" issue; a sale to an unrelated party is required;

one cannot combine the sale and investment in the fund. Moreover, the investor needs to hold his interest in the OZF for seven years for the full 15 percent increase in basis, so the December 2019 investment date is critical.

CAVEAT

The tax deferral may apply as to all gains, including 1250 recapture gain. If the investor has a negative capital account and sells for little cash, he may need to fund the investment with additional monies in order to cover full gain on transfer. In addition, during the operation of OZF, assuming there is leveraging in the fund through nonrecourse financing (wherein losses are generated through depreciation in the early years), because the basis is zero, the investor may need to wait until years 5 to 7 to establish and rebuild basis in order to take the losses.

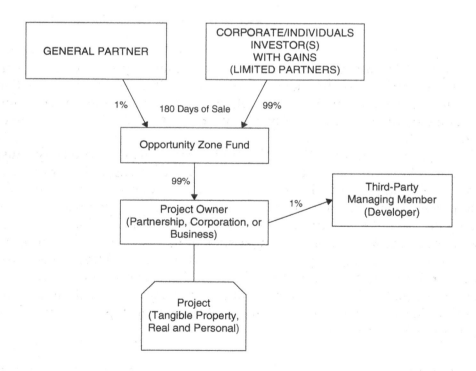

(i) Combining with Other Tax Incentives.[433]

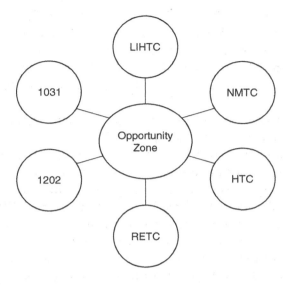

(c)   Pairing Opportunity Zone Incentives with NMTCs

Through the NMTC structure, the investor can take advantage of the leveraging structure and generate tax credits over a seven-year period. So not only can the capital gains be deferred for a seven-year period, including an increase in basis with partial forgiveness after five- and seven-year holding periods, but the taxpayer can receive incremental benefit through the tax credit regime. However, the investor is likely to be a C corporation in view of the AMT, which was retained in the 2017 Tax Act as to individuals. Nevertheless, sufficient basis is needed to absorb the required NMTC basis adjustment. Accordingly, the OZ deferral election will generally be limited to the QEI less the sub-CDE fees and the NMTCs that are generated.

CAVEAT

It is important to note that QALICB must also be a qualified opportunity zone business (which should be relatively easy to accomplish in view of the similarities of the programs). Sub-CDEs will need to obtain the status of a QOF; however, they may now self-certify, pursuant to Frequently Asked Questions issued by the IRS. Moreover, the QLICIs need to be equity investments under the OZ rules; as a result, the investors may not be able to rely on the reasonable expectation safe harbor test (which affects the issuance of tax opinions). The existing CDEs may need to get approval from the CDFI Fund if making equity QLICIs is not consistent with their approved business strategy in the executed NOAA with the CDFI Fund.

---

[433]Diagram published by Novogradac & Company.

(d)   Use by Tax-Exempt Organizations: Win-Win

Opportunity funds may be purchased and sold similar to mutual funds. A fund could invest in all aspects of mixed-use development in designated qualified census tracts beneficial to low-income exempt organizations. It incentivizes urban renewal as well as rural development, allowing developers to create and expand communities with new multifamily housing and retail venues.

It may also attract "angel" investors and incubators, along with venture capitalists, thereby attracting companies to locate in opportunity zones, where, after a 10-year hold, a liquidation may generate millions of dollars in capital gains with permanent exclusion from taxation.

There are many reasons why a nonprofit should form joint ventures or a for-profit subsidiary to directly partner with the OZF to operate in the designated low-income high-unemployment zones, consistent with its exempt function. Because the law favors *new* businesses, new construction, startups, and incubators may be motivated by the incentives. Thus, an opportunity fund could operate or fund a new technology or healthcare business in the zone. A successful tech startup could experience significant growth over a decade, allowing the investor a large permanent exclusion from taxation. Community healthcare and food deserts are also sorely needed in many low-income communities, and walk-in clinics and urgent care facilities, already growing in popularity, may also be attractive projects for opportunity funds.[434]

(e)   Preliminary Steps in Formation of Opportunity Fund

1. Formation of Opportunity Zone Fund (OZF) as a corporation or a partnership for purposes of investing in Qualified Opportunity Zone Property ("QOZF"): use of an LP/Query: will an LLC qualify as an OZF?

2. General Partner of the LP: formation of the limited liability company; operations of OZF. (See 90 percent test, discussed in subsection 13.11(b).)

3. Management Company: formation of the limited liability company that will act as a management company.

4. Terms of the Investment Management Agreement.

5. Overall fee structure, which needs to be competitive in the marketplace, with return of capital and preferred annual distributions; minimum ten-year hold, claw back, etc.

---

[434]See Kevin Winters, "Opportunity Zones: Questions and Applications," Georgetown Law Graduate Tax, Advanced Topics in Exempt Organizations.

6. Confirmation of designation as QCT by Governors, approved by Treasury.

7. Self-certification of OZF based upon IRS Frequently Asked Questions. To self-certify, a taxpayer merely completes a form (to be released in summer 2018), which is attached to taxpayer's federal income tax return.

8. Preparation of OZF Business Plan (to be reviewed by counsel), including land and building acquisition, timing. Need to "tie-up" properties within designated zones.

9. Draft of private placement memorandum.

10. Draft of the subscription agreement.

11. Review of exemptions under the Securities Act, state blue sky laws, and the Investment Advisers Act.

12. Proposed liquidation of fund, cash-out of investors, redemption, etc., after ten years.

(f)   Treasury Publishes Opportunity Zone Proposed Regulations

The First Important Step in the Structuring of OZ Funds. As part of the 2017 Tax Act, a new tax incentive program was created to spur economic growth and investment in designated distressed communities (each an "opportunity zone" or "OZ"). Not only does the OZ incentive program allow for the deferral of certain capital gains to the extent that such gain is invested in a qualified opportunity fund ("QOF"), but it also allows for income exclusion for gains on investments in QOFs that are held for at least ten years. While the OZ incentive program was well received, both practitioners and potential investors had many questions about the program that seemed to be unanswered by the initial provisions provided for in the Tax Act.

As such, on October 19, 2018, the Treasury Department issued additional guidance for the OZ incentive program. Specifically, the Treasury Department issued a set of proposed regulations and a revenue ruling, both of which can be relied on by taxpayers. In addition to the proposed regulations and the revenue ruling, the Treasury Department provided a draft Form 8996, the self-certification form for QOFs, and corresponding instructions for the form. Although the additional guidance answers many questions that investors and practitioners have about the OZ incentive program, there were still a number of unanswered questions, some of which were addressed in the second tranche of guidance issued from the Treasury Department in April 2019.[435]

---

[435]See subsection (g), *infra*.

A highlight of the guidance from the proposed regulations is as follows:

i. **Eligible Taxpayers.** Taxpayers who are eligible to defer gain under the OZ incentive program are those that recognize "capital gain" for federal income tax purposes. As such, individuals, C corporations (including REITs and RICs), partnerships, common trust funds, qualified settlement funds, disputed ownership funds, and certain other types of entities should qualify.

ii. **Gain Issues.** The OZ incentive program provides gain deferral for capital gains only; however, unrecaptured 1250 gain (depreciation recapture) should be eligible for deferral. More IRS guidance is needed to clarify this issue. The gain to be deferred must be gain that would have been recognized (assuming that deferrals under the OZ incentive program were not permitted) no later than December 31, 2026. In the case of a taxpayer who made an election to defer with respect to some but not all eligible gains, the term "eligible gain" includes the portion of the eligible gain for which no election has been made.

    The gain to be deferred must not arise from a sale or exchange with certain related persons. Generally, the OZ incentive program adopts the related-party rules found in § 267(b) and § 707(b)(1) of the Internal Revenue Code (the "Code"), except that it substitutes "20 percent" in place of "50 percent" each place it occurs in § 267(b) or § 707(b)(1). For example, a partnership and a person owning, directly or indirectly, more than 20 percent of the capital interest, or the profits interest of such partnership, are considered to be related parties.

    Except as otherwise provided for in provisions of the OZ incentive program, the first day of the 180-day period during which an investment of capital gains must be made into a QOF is the date on which the gain would be recognized for federal income tax purposes.

iii. **Gains of Partnerships and Other Pass-Through Entities.** A partnership may elect to defer all or part of a capital gain to the extent that it makes an eligible investment in a QOF. If so, no part of the deferred gain is required to be included in the distributive shares of the partners. If the partnership does not elect to defer capital gain, a partner may elect to defer gain with respect to its distributive share under the OZ incentive regime (provided that all other requirements have been met). A partner's 180-day period generally begins on the last day of the partnership's taxable year. A partner may also choose to begin its own 180-day period on the same date as the start of the partnership's 180-day period (in situations in which the partner knows both the date of the partnership's gain and the partnership's decision not to elect deferral).

iv. **Inclusion in Income When Deferral Ends.** All of the deferred gain's tax attributes are preserved through the deferral period and are taken into account when the gain is included. If a taxpayer disposes of less than all of its fungible interests in a QOF, the interests that are disposed of are identified using a first-in, first-out method.

v. **QOF Qualification.** A QOF must be classified as a corporation or partnership for federal income tax purposes. Thus, it seems that limited liability companies also should qualify, since Reg. § 1.1400Z-2(d)-1(a) states that it is "qualified as a corporation or partnership for federal tax purposes." A QAOF must be created or organized in one of the 50 states, the District of Columbia, or a U.S. possession. If organized in a U.S. possession, then an entity must be organized for the purpose of investing in qualified opportunity zone property that relates to a trade or business operated in the possession in which the entity is organized. There is no prohibition to using a "preexisting" entity as a QOF, provided that all other requirements of the OZ incentive program are satisfied, including that QOZ property is acquired after December 31, 2017.

vi. **Investment in QOF.** To qualify for the OZ incentive program, an investment in a QOF must be an equity interest in the QOF, including preferred stock or a partnership interest with special allocations (i.e., such investment cannot be a debt instrument within the meaning of § 1275(a) and Reg. § 1.1275-1(d)). Thus, convertible debt should not qualify for the OZ incentive program, but query whether certain types of debt instruments may also qualify, as some of these instruments may be classified as equity for federal tax purposes. Provided that the eligible taxpayer is the owner of the equity interest, status as such is not impaired by the taxpayer's use of the interest as collateral for a loan. Deemed contributions of money under § 752(a) of the Code do not qualify as an investment in a QOF, which is a beneficial result.

vii. **Designating When a QOF Begins.** It is expected that Form 8996, the self-certification form, will be attached to a QOF's federal income tax return for the relevant tax years. On Form 8996, it appears that the penalty for nonqualification is calculated monthly, but such penalty does not apply to any months before the first month in which an eligible entity is a QOF. On Form 8996, a QOF is allowed to identify both (1) the taxable year and (2) the first month in that year in which the entity becomes a QOF. If an eligible entity fails to specify the first month it is a QOF, then the first month of its initial tax year as a QOF is designated as the first month that the eligible entity is a QOF. The "first six-month period of the taxable year of the fund" under the 90 percent test means the first six-month period composed entirely of months that are within the taxable year and during which the entity is a QOF. For example, if a calendar-year entity was created in February and chooses April as its first month as a QOF, then the 90 percent test dates are the end of September (which is six months from April 1) and the end of December. This means that if a calendar-year QOF chooses a month after June as its first month as a QOF, then the only testing date for that first taxable year is the last day of the QFO's taxable year. But see the second tranche under subsection (g).

viii. **Valuation Method for Applying the 90 Percent Asset Test.** For purposes of the 90 percent asset test of a QOF, the QOF is required to use the asset values that are reported on the QOF's applicable financial statement for the taxable year (namely, a financial statement within the meaning of Reg. § 1.475(a)-4(h), which, generally, includes a financial statement filed with the SEC or one that has significant business use). (But see modification in the second tranche of proposed regulations under subsection (g).) This may present a problem for certain QOFs if GAAP financial statements are used, since GAAP accounting takes into account impairment, depreciation, and so forth, which could strain the 90 percent asset test. If there is no applicable financial statement, then the QOF should use "cost of the asset." Presumably, this means the original cost basis, without regard for depreciation.

ix. **Working Capital Safe Harbor.** A new working capital safe harbor is established for QOF investments in QOZ businesses that acquire, construct, or rehabilitate tangible business property, which includes both real property and other tangible property used in a business operating in an OZ. The safe harbor allows QOZ businesses to hold a reasonable amount of working capital (generally, cash, cash equivalents, or debt instruments with a term of 18 months or less) for 31 months if (1) there is a written plan that identifies the financial property as property held for the acquisition, construction, or substantial improvement of tangible property in the OZ, (2) there is a written schedule consistent with the ordinary business operations of the business that the property will be used within 31 months, and (3) the QOZ business complies with such schedule. Solely for purposes of applying the 50 percent "active" conduct test in § 1397C(b)(2), as required by the definition of a QOZ business, if any gross income is derived from a reasonable amount of working capital, then such gross income is counted toward satisfaction of such 50 percent test.

x. **Basis Step-Up Election.** Taxpayers may make the election for a step-up in their QOF investments after the QOZ designation expires. Specifically, such election is preserved until December 31, 2047 (essentially allowing all QOF investments to qualify for the step-up).

xi. **QOZ Business Qualification.** Generally, to qualify as a QOZ business, "substantially all" of a corporation or partnership's tangible property owned or leased must be QOZ business property. In this context, "substantially all" means at least 70 percent. Note that this means that if $100 were invested in a QOF, and the QOF decided to invest through a partnership or corporation, the proposed regulations dictate that a minimum of $63 must be QOZ business property (90 percent × 70 percent × $100). If the QOF operates a trade or business directly and does not invest equity in any QOZ business, then the 90 percent asset test would apply (i.e., $90 must be QOZ property). Thus, there is an incentive for QOFs to invest in a QOZ business rather than holding QOZ business property directly.

xii. **QOZ Stock.** Certain redemption transactions will cause stock acquired by a QOF to not be treated as QOZ stock. For example, stock issued by a corporation is not treated as QOZ stock if, at any time during the two-year period beginning on the date one year before the issuance of such stock, the corporation made one or more purchases of its stock with an aggregate value exceeding 5 percent of the aggregate value of all of its stock as of the beginning of the two-year period.

xiii. **Revenue Ruling: Exclude Basis of Land.** New Revenue Ruling 2018-29 primarily addresses the concept of "original use" as follows:

> If a QOF purchases an existing building located on land that is wholly within a QOZ, the original use of the building in the QOZ is not considered to have commenced with the QOF, and the requirement that the original use of the tangible property in the QOZ commence with a QOF is not applicable to the land on which the building is located. If a QOF purchases a building wholly within a QOZ, a substantial improvement to the building is measured by the QOF's additions solely to the adjusted basis of the building. Measuring a substantial improvement to the building by additions to the QOF's adjusted basis of the building does not require the QOF to separately improve the land upon which the building is located.

By excluding the basis of land, the rules facilitate repurposing vacant buildings in QOZs. But see the second tranche of proposed regulations under subsection (g).

xiv. **Key Issues Not Addressed.** Key issues not addressed in the initial October 2018 guidance include many critical subjects that are described below. There has been further clarification, however, in the second tranche referenced in subsection (g):

- The term "substantially all" is used in various places of the OZ incentive program. For example, for property to qualify as QOZ business property, during substantially all of the QOF's holding period for such property, substantially all of the use of such property must be in a QOZ. Further, for definitions of "qualified opportunity zone stock" and "qualified opportunity zone partnership interest" during substantially all of the QOF's holding period for such interest, such interest is qualified as a QOZ business. What does this term "substantially all" mean as it is used in these other references? See subsection (g), *infra*.

○ How long is the "reasonable period" for a QOF to reinvest proceeds from the sale of qualifying assets without paying a penalty? The OZ incentive program provides that a QOF has "a reasonable period of time to reinvest the return of capital from investments in qualified opportunity zone stock and qualified opportunity zone partnership interests, and to reinvest proceeds received from the sale or disposition of qualified opportunity zone business property." For example, if a QOF sells QOZ property shortly before a testing date, such QOF should have a reasonable amount of time in which to bring itself into compliance with the 90 percent asset test. See subsection (g), *infra*.

○ In calculating the value of a QOF's assets, Form 8996's instructions allow the use of a certified audited financial statement that is prepared in accordance with GAAP. However, the proposed regulations' requirements are a bit more complex. Additional guidance was necessary to reconcile this conflicting guidance. See subsection (g), *infra*.

○ Will there be any relief for a taxpayer who fails to reinvest eligible gain into a QOF within 180 days of the transaction that produced such gain? Currently, there is no such relief.

○ Do section 1231 gains need to be aggregated with section 1231 losses in order to be an "eligible gain"? Section 1231 gains are only capital gains to the extent that they exceed section 1231 losses. See subsection (g), *infra*.

○ There does not appear to be guidance on whether a new building built on unimproved land satisfies the "original use" and "substantial improvement" requirements for QOZ business property. See subsection (g), *infra*.

○ The additional guidance does not appear to address leased property. How such property is accounted for may put pressure on the 90 percent asset test. This subject is discussed in subsection (g), *infra*.

○ How are interim gains—that is, gains recognized at the QOF level—treated? For example, will such gains be eligible for deferral to the extent that they are invested? This subject is answered favorably in the second tranche. See subsection (g), *infra*.

- ◦ Is carried interest a qualifying investment in a QOF? Currently, there is no distinction for interest received for cash versus services. See subsection (g), *infra*.

- ◦ What other information reporting requirements are necessary under the OZ incentive program? For example, what are the forms and instructions by which an eligible taxpayer may elect to defer eligible gains?

- ◦ What are some examples that will lead to an entity's decertification as a QOF?

(g)   Treasury Publishes the Second Tranche of Proposed Opportunity Zone Regulations

On April 17, 2019, the Treasury Department issued a second tranche of proposed regulations, which again can be relied on by taxpayers. This additional guidance provides answers to open issues related to the definition of "substantially all," the use of qualified OZ business property, the treatment of leased tangible property, the sourcing of gross income in a QOZ, a reasonable period for a QOF to reinvest proceeds from the sale of a qualifying asset without paying a penalty, and various other topics. However, as was the case with the first set of regulations, there are still a number of unanswered questions (some of which the Treasury Department solicited additional comments on).

A highlight of the guidance from the second tranche of proposed regulations is as follows:

i. **Qualified Opportunity Zone Business Property.** *Definition of "Substantially All" for Purposes of Code Sections 1400Z-2(d)(2) and (d)(3).* After the first tranche of proposed regulations, the term "substantially all" remained undefined in a number of places in the OZ incentive program. "Substantially all" is clarified to mean (i) 70 percent as it relates to usage of tangible property in an OZ and (ii) 90 percent as it relates to the holding period of tangible property used in an OZ, an interest in stock, or a partnership interest (which qualifies as qualified OZ stock or qualified OZ partnership, respectively).

ii. **Special Rules for Section 1231 Gains (Depreciable Real Estate Held Over One Year).** Only net section 1231 gains are eligible for the deferral under the OZ incentive program. The 180-day period for investing capital gain income from section 1231 property in an QOF *begins* on the last day of the taxable year. This rule may present a trap for unwary taxpayers, since gain on the sale of depreciable real estate held for more than one year is a 1231 gain treated as a long-term capital gain. But the IRS stated that it is necessary to wait for the end of the taxable year to open the 180-day period for investment, in order to see if such gains are reduced by netting against 1231 losses during the year (attributable to the taxpayer; e.g., an individual may have such losses through other partnerships or individually). A delay in receiving a Form K-1 could also create difficulties for a partner in a partnership wanting to roll over gain allocated to him from a partnership. There is no election provided as in subsection (f)(iii) in the partnership context.

iii. **Original Use of Tangible Property by Purchase.** The "original use" of tangible property acquired by purchase starts on the date when that person (or a prior person) first places the property in service in a qualified OZ for purposes of depreciation of amortization (i.e., tangible property located in a qualified OZ that is depreciated or amortized by a taxpayer other than the QOF or qualified OZ business would not be of "original use"). Tangible property (other than land) located in a qualified OZ that has not yet been depreciated or amortized by a taxpayer (other than a QOF or qualified OZ business) would satisfy the original use requirement.

CAVEAT

When a building or other structure has been vacant for at least five years prior to being purchased by a QOF or qualified OZ business, such property will satisfy the original use requirement.

Improvements made by a lessee to leased property would satisfy the original use requirement and are considered purchased property for the amount of the unadjusted cost basis. The determination of whether the substantial improvement requirement is satisfied for tangible property that is purchased is made on an asset-by-asset basis and not on an "aggregate" basis. The IRS indicated that it is considering applying the rule on an aggregate basis, but it has not done so at this point. This may raise critical issues for many businesses.

Safe Harbor for Testing Use of Inventory in Transit. Inventory (including raw materials) of a trade or business does not fail to be used in a qualified OZ solely because the inventory is in transit from a vendor to a facility in the trade or business that is in a qualified OZ, or from a facility of the trade or business that is in a qualified OZ to customers of the trade or business that are not located in a qualified OZ.

iv. **Treatment of Leased Tangible Property.** *Status as Qualified Opportunity Zone Business Property.* Leased tangible property can satisfy the

90 percent asset test for a QOF and the "substantially all" requirement for a qualified OZ business if (1) such leased tangible property is acquired under a lease entered into after December 31, 2017, and (2) substantially all of the use of such leased tangible property is in a qualified OZ during substantially all of the period for which the business leases the property. There is no original use requirement with respect to leased tangible property. Further, leased tangible property can be leased from a related lessor (see below for additional limitations applied to related parties). All leases under which a QOF or qualified OZ business acquires rights with respect to any leased tangible property must be a "market rate lease," as determined under the regulations under section 482.

As noted above, the lessor and lessee of tangible property may be related. If a lessor and lessee are related, leased tangible property shall not be qualified OZ business property if, in connection with the lease, a QOF or qualified OZ business at any time makes a prepayment to the lessor (or a person related to the lessor) relating to a period of use of the leased tangible property that exceeds 12 months. Further, if a lessor and lessee are related, leased tangible property shall not be qualified OZ business property unless the lessee becomes the owner of other tangible property that is qualified OZ business property and that has a value not less than the value of the leased tangible property. Such acquisition must occur during a period that begins on the date that the lessee receives possession of the property under the lease and ends on the earlier of (1) the last day of the lease or (2) the end of the 30-month period beginning on the date that the lessee receives possession of the property under the lease.

CAVEAT

There is an anti-abuse rule to prevent the use of leases to circumvent the substantial improvement requirement of real property (other than unimproved land). For example, warehousing of land or "land banking" is unacceptable, and modification of many existing lease arrangements to meet this test will be required.

---

v. **Valuation of Lease Property.** On an annual basis, leased tangible property may be valued using either an applicable financial statement method or an alternative valuation method. Once a QOF or qualified OZ business selects one of the valuation methods, it must apply such method consistently to all leased tangible property with respect to the taxable year.

CAVEAT

A QOF or qualified OZ business may select the applicable financial statement valuation method if they actually have an applicable financial statement (within the meaning of Reg § 1.475(a)-4(h)). Under this method, the value of leased tangible property is the value of such property as reported on the applicable financial statement for the relevant reporting period. Such applicable financial statements must be prepared in accordance with U.S. generally accepted accounting principles, and there must be recognition of the lease of the tangible property.

Under the alternative valuation approach, the value of leased tangible property is determined based on a calculation of the "present value" of such tangible property—that is, the sum of the present values of the payments to be made under the lease for such tangible property. For purposes of this calculation, the discount rate is the applicable federal rate under § 1274(d)(1). Under this alternative valuation approach, once the value of the leased property is fixed at the outset of the lease, it does not change over the course of the lease; under the GAAP method above, it is expected that the valuation of the leased property will decline over time.

vi. **Qualified Opportunity Zone Businesses.** *Real Property Straddling a Qualified Opportunity Zone.* If the amount of real property based on square footage located within the qualified opportunity zone is substantial as compared to the amount of real property based on square footage outside of the qualified opportunity zone, and the real property outside of the qualified opportunity zone is contiguous to part or all of the real property located inside the qualified opportunity zone, then all of the property is deemed to be located within a qualified opportunity zone.

CAVEAT

The meaning of the term "continuous" in this context is subject to interpretation without further guidance.

---

vii. **50 Percent of Gross Income of a Qualified Opportunity Zone Business.** There are three safe harbors and a facts and circumstances test for determining whether sufficient income is derived from a trade or business in a qualified OZ for purposes of the 50 percent test in Code section 1397C(b)(2).

- **Hours:** The first safe harbor requires that at least 50 percent of the services performed (based on hours) for a business by its employees and independent contractors are performed within the qualified OZ.

- **Amounts Paid:** The second safe harbor requires that at least 50 percent of the services performed, based on the amounts paid for such services, for the business by its employees and independent contractors are performed within the qualified OZ.

- **Tangible Property and Management:** The third safe harbor provides that a trade or business may satisfy the 50 percent test if: (1) the tangible property of the business that is in a qualified OZ and (2) the management and operational functions performed for the business in the qualified OZ are each necessary to generate 50 percent of the gross income of the trade or business.

- **Facts and Circumstances Test:** Finally, the 50 percent test may be satisfied if, based on all facts and circumstances, at least 50 percent of the gross income of a trade or business is derived from the active conduct of a trade or business in the qualified OZ.

viii. **Use of Intangibles (40 Percent).** The term "substantial portion" as it relates to the usage of intangible assets in the active conduct of a trade or business in a qualified OZ means at least 40 percent.

ix. **Active Conduct of a Trade or Business.** The ownership and operation (including leasing) of real property used in a trade or business is treated as the active conduct of a trade or business for purposes of the OZ incentive program. However, merely entering into a triple-net lease with respect to real property owned by a taxpayer is not the active conduct of a trade or business by such taxpayer. This provision will likely impact the conventional leasing of industrial properties.

x. **Working Capital Safe Harbor.** Expanding on the first tranche of the proposed regulations, the written designation for the planned use of working capital includes the development of a trade or business in the qualified OZ as well as the acquisition, construction, and/or substantial improvement of tangible property. There is an example of such a written plan to create a restaurant business, but without a specifically identified site yet. This example indicates that a QOF need not have "identified" the specific property within the qualified OZ in order to benefit from this working capital safe harbor.

	CAVEAT
Exceeding the 31-month period does not violate the safe harbor if the delay is attributable to waiting for government action, the application for which is being completed during the 31-month period.	

xi. Relief with Respect to the 90-Percent Asset Test. *Relief for Newly Contributed Assets.* A QOF may apply the 90 percent asset test without taking into account any investments received in the preceding six months.

	CAVEAT
This provision is very favorable and may, in certain circumstances, allow almost a year before the 90 percent test will be applied.	

QOF Reinvestment Rule. Proceeds received by a QOF from the sale or disposition of: (1) qualified OZ business property, (2) qualified OZ stock, and (3) qualified OZ partnership interests are treated as qualified OZ property for purposes of the 90 percent requirement, so long as the QOF reinvests the proceeds received by the QOF from the distribution, sale, or disposition of such property during the 12-month period beginning on the date of such distribution, sale, or disposition. Such proceeds must be held in cash, cash equivalents, or debt instruments with a term of 18 months or less. A QOF may reinvest proceeds from a sale of an investment into another type of qualifying investment.

xii. Amount of an Investment for Purposes of Making a Deferral Election. A taxpayer may make an investment for purposes of the gain deferral election under the OZ incentive program by transferring cash *or* property to a QOF. There are special rules for determining the amount of an investment for purposes of the deferral election if a taxpayer transfers property other than cash to a QOF in a carryover basis transaction. In such a case, the amount of the investment equals the lesser of (1) the taxpayer's adjusted basis in the equity received in the transaction or (2) the fair market value of the equity received in the transaction, both of which are determined immediately after the transaction. In the case of a contribution to a partnership QOF, the basis is calculated without regard to any liability that is allocated to the contributor under § 752(a).

xiii. Events That Cause Inclusion of Deferred Gain. *In General.* Generally, an inclusion event (i.e., an event that causes the recognition of gains deferred under the OZ incentive program) results from a transfer of a qualifying investment in a transaction to the extent the transfer reduces a taxpayer's equity interest in the qualifying investment. However, except as provided elsewhere in the regulations, a transaction is also an inclusion event to the extent a taxpayer receives property from a QOF in a transaction that is treated as a distribution for U.S. federal income tax purposes.

Inclusion events include, but are not limited to:

- A taxable disposition of all or part of a qualifying investment;

- A taxable disposition of interests in an S corporation that is the direct investor of a QOF;

- A transfer by gift of a qualifying investment;

- A redemption of qualified QOF stock that is treated as an exchange of property for the redeemed qualifying QOF stock under Code section 302;

- A liquidation of a QOF corporation to which section 331 applies; and

- Certain nonrecognition transactions.

Certain disregarded transfers and certain types of nonrecognition transactions (e.g., an acquisitive asset reorganization under Code section 381) are not inclusion events. Debt-financed distributions from a QOF partnership are generally not inclusion events, subject to two limitations:

1. Such distribution will trigger inclusion of deferred gain to the extent the distribution exceeds the investor's basis (which includes such investor's share of liabilities); and

2. If such distribution generally occurs within the first two years of an investor's contribution of cash/property to the QOF (or in some cases later), there are certain rules that could recharacterize the original contribution as an investment that does not qualify for the benefits of the OZ incentive program (under the "disguised sales" rules of section 707(a)(2)(B)).

Timing of Basis Adjustments. The 10 percent and additional 5 percent basis step-up on a taxpayer's investment in a QOF as of the end of 2026 is basis for all purposes. The basis adjustment upon recognition of deferred gain is made immediately after the amount of deferred capital gain is taken into income. For dispositions after 10 years of qualifying QOF partnership interests, by the equity investor, the bases of the QOF partnership's assets are also adjusted with respect to the transferred qualifying QOF partnership interest, with such adjustments calculated in a manner similar to the adjustments that would have been made to the partnership's assets if the selling partner had purchased the interest for cash immediately prior to the transaction and the partnership had a valid section 754 election in effect. This treatment should prevent recapture of depreciation taken by the partner on assets of the QOF partnership over the ten-plus years of holding the investment. It is an important technical fix that should allow taxpayers to realize substantial benefits.

Partnership and S Corporation Provisions. The transfer by a partner of all or a portion of its interest in a QOF partnership will generally be an inclusion event. However, a transfer in a transaction governed by Code § 721 or § 708(b)(2)(A) is generally not an inclusion event, provided there is no reduction in the amount of the remaining deferred gain that would be recognized by the transferring partners in a later inclusion event.

The conversion of an S corporation that holds a qualifying investment in a QOF to a C corporation (or vice versa) is not an inclusion event. If an S corporation is an investor in a QOF, the S corporation must adjust the basis of its qualifying investment in the same manner as for C corporations, but this rule does not affect adjustments to the basis of any other asset of the S corporation. Solely for purposes of the OZ incentive program, an S corporation's qualifying investments in a QOF will be treated as disposed of if there is a greater than 25 percent change in ownership of the S corporation.

For purposes of investments held for at least ten years, a taxpayer who is the holder of a direct qualifying QOF partnership interest or qualifying QOF stock of a QOF S corporation may make an election to exclude from gross income some or all of the capital gain from the disposition of qualified OZ property reported on Schedule K-1 of such entity, provided the disposition occurs after the taxpayer's ten-year holding period.

xiv. **Treatment of Carried Interest.** Where a partner receives a partnership interest in exchange for services (e.g., carried interest), such portion of such investment is not eligible for the benefits related to qualifying investments of the OZ incentive program. The first set of proposed regulations had stated that a partnership interest with special allocations was an eligible QOF investment, but these new proposed regulations would require restructuring in this area.

xv. **Consolidated Return Provisions.** QOF stock is not stock for purposes of Code section 1504 affiliation. The provisions of the OZ incentive program apply separately to each member of a consolidated group.

xvi. **General Anti-Abuse Rule.** If a significant purpose of a transaction is to achieve a result that is inconsistent with the purposes of the OZ incentive program, the IRS may recast a transaction (or series of transactions) for federal tax purposes as appropriate to achieve the tax results that are consistent with the OZ incentive program.

xvii. **Key Issues Still Not Addressed by the Second Tranche of Proposed Regulations.**

- Should prior use of fully depreciated/amortized property be disregarded for purposes of the original use requirement?

- How should the OZ incentive program treat tangible personal property that is realistically not capable of being substantially improved?

- Should inventory be excluded from the 70 percent test for qualified OZ businesses?

- What are the specific mechanics by which the election for holders of a direct qualifying QOF partnership interest or qualifying QOF stock of a QOF S corporation can exclude from gross income some or all of the capital gain from the disposition of qualified OZ property?

xviii. **Conclusion.** The second tranche of proposed regulations is a significant step forward in providing guidance to QOF investors, developers, and fund managers. It provides clarity on a number of open questions that remained after the October 2018 publication of the initial set of proposed regulations by including the definition of substantially all, the use of qualified OZ business property, the treatment of leased tangible property, the sourcing of gross income in a QOF, a reasonable period for the QOF to invest proceeds for the sale of qualifying assets without paying a penalty, and restrictions as to triple-net leases and carried interests.

CAVEAT
Notwithstanding the "refreshed" regulations, there are still a number of unanswered questions for which Treasury still needs to provide guidance. During 2019, we expect further clarification in the form of IRS guidance (but not in the form of proposed regulations) and, perhaps, revenue rulings.

(h) Opportunity Zone Funds: Application of Final Regulations: The Opportunity Zone Tax Incentive Program in the Wake of the COVID-19 Pandemic (Revised)

In December 2019, the Treasury Department released final regulations for the opportunity zone (OZ) program to refine and clarify certain aspects of the first two sets of proposed regulations[436] and to make the rules easier to follow and understand (the "Final Regulations"). The Final Regulations are examined in this section.

The OZ program is highlighted in light of the unprecedented economic challenges presented by the COVID-19 outbreak. Indeed, taxpayers with short-term or long-term capital gain income generated in 2019, or in early 2020, can use the OZ program to invest the qualified gains in a QOF for a period of time.

As some investors reevaluate their commitments to qualified opportunity zones in the face of the COVID-19 global pandemic, they may enjoy some level of favorable tax treatment in 2020 if they decide to liquidate their capital from the funds. While investors would likely consider multiple variables (i.e., the extent fund withdrawal is allowed, market stability, and investor ability to write off losses) before deciding to take money out of OZs, the Internal Revenue Code has some advantages for those seeking to opt out of funds.

To the extent individuals had deferred capital gains by committing them to QOFs in previous tax years, the gains would be recognized in 2020 if those investors decided to liquidate their investment in 2020. Such liquidation would result in those investors' ability to offset their capital losses generated in 2020, thereby reducing their tax liabilities. While such result may not be the original tax benefit investors were looking for when they invested in opportunity funds, it may be more beneficial than sustaining a capital loss in 2020 because those losses cannot be carried back.

The Final Regulations clarify that individuals would not be subject to interest or other kinds of penalties if they chose to liquidate their investments early.

- Given the market's current volatility, investors may be willing to realize losses in 2020 to offset previously deferred gains. Note that the IRS may challenge attempts to offset gains and losses by liquidating OZ investments to determine if those individuals lacked bona

---

[436]The first set was published in October 2018 and the second set was issued in May 2019. See subsections 13.11(f) and (g). See also "Applying the Opportunity Zone Program in the Wake of the COVID-19 Pandemic," by Michael I. Sanders and Kendra H. Merchant, published in the July/August 2020 edition of the *WG&L Journal of Corporate Taxation* (Vol. 47, No. 4), a Thomson Reuters publication. Reprinted with permission. The author recognizes Kendra H. Merchant for her contribution to this subsection.

fide, good-faith intentions to follow through on those commitments in line with the anti-abuse provisions discussed hereinafter.[437]

- The OZ program was designed to offer tax relief for investments in low-income communities and does not levy interest-laden penalties on investors who choose to withdraw capital gains from funds. The OZ program also allows a restart on the clock on the 180-day window for reinvesting in other funds without losing out on the OZ program's favorable tax treatment.

Once the capital gains have been reinvested into a QOF and then dropped into a qualified opportunity zone business ("QOZB"), taxpayers have up to 62 months to reinvest the proceeds into various qualified opportunity zone projects. This extended reinvestment period is particularly useful in light of the uncertainty in the current markets.

The Final Regulations became effective March 16, 2020. The new rules give taxpayers increased flexibility and extension of time when it comes to determining when the 180-day capital gain reinvestment countdown begins for purposes of meeting the QOF deadline.

- COVID-19 Update: The IRS issued Notice 2020-23, which grants investors whose deadline falls between April 1 and July 15, 2020 automatic relief of the 180-day investment requirement. It followed with Notice 2020-39, which extended the 180-day requirement to December 31, 2020. The Notice also extended the 90 percent investment standard date to December 31, 2020 (as reasonable "cause") and tolled the 30-month substantial improvement period (during April 1, 2020 through December 31, 2020).

Accordingly, QOFs are a remarkable opportunity for high-net-worth individuals to defer gain and subsequently exclude further gain based upon the appreciation of their investment in an opportunity zone. This summary highlights certain major clarifications and additional flexibility found in the Final Regulations. It also points out certain unresolved matters.

(A) Changes Related to Eligible Gains

i. **Deferral of Gross Section 1231 Gains.** "Section 1231 assets" are unique assets for purposes of determining applicable tax treatment—basically, a section 1231 asset is depreciable property held in trade or business (i.e., business property), like a rental building or a piece of machinery.

---

[437]In an example provided in the Final Regulations, the IRS said that individuals who direct their capital gains into opportunity funds they have established, yet have no intention of actually investing in the projects, would not be eligible to participate in the opportunity zone program.

The Final Regulations provide that investors (including pass-through entities) are allowed to invest the entire amount of "gross" section 1231 gains from the sale of business property (without regard to section 1231 losses) in qualified QOFs.[438] This enables more section 1231 gains to be eligible for investment in QOFs because investors are no longer required to "net" their otherwise eligible section 1231 gain against their section 1231 losses. This change also provides investors more flexibility in realizing gains eligible to be invested in a QOF.

ii. **Investment Period Start Date.** The 180-day period to invest section 1231 gains in a QOF now begins the date of the sale of the underlying asset.[439] Investors do not have to wait until the end of the taxable year for the 180-day investment period to begin, eliminating the issue of unnecessarily delay or stalling of planned OZ investments. This flexibility is beneficial for investors.

EXAMPLE

If an investor has $1 million of section 1231 gain on January 7 and $500,000 of a section 1231 loss in March, the deferral of that entire $1 million of section 1231 gain could be invested in a QOF and possible income exclusion for gains on that investment in a QOF if held for at least 10 years. In addition, that $500,000 section 1231 loss that would have otherwise offset capital gain is now going to be an ordinary loss, which is another favorable result for tax purposes.

As to the 180-day investment period for a pass-through entity (including, for example, a partnership), the Final Regulations provide three options for the investment period start date:

1. The date of the sale of the underlying asset;

2. The end of the taxable year; or

3. The due date of the entity's tax return, not including any extensions (which is currently March 15 for pass-through entities).

Though the Final Regulations arguably leave open whether the gross section 1231 gain rules and the 180-day investment period rules both apply to a partnership, a consistent application of the rules under the Final Regulations apply to "eligible gain" of an "eligible taxpayer," which would

---

[438]The Final Regulations provide that a gain is eligible for deferral under Treas. Reg. § 1400Z-2(a) if the gain is treated as a capital gain for federal income tax purposes.
[439]Treas. Reg. § 1400Z-2(a)(1)(A).

include gross section 1231 gain of an eligible taxpayer that is a partnership, S corporation, trust, or decedent's estate.

iii. **COVID-19 Structuring Point.** Individuals interested in "cashing out" their investments in OZs in 2020 may also benefit from the ability to reinvest in other QOFs within a 180-day window—they would effectively be recognizing a capital gain in 2020, and the 180-day window in which investors can place gains into OZs begins whenever a capital gain is recognized. That may be an attractive option for individuals who have become dissatisfied with the funds they have invested in.

There is a reasonable basis for taking the position that a taxpayer may dispose of some or all of its qualifying investment in a QOF in a transaction that constitutes an inclusion event, recognize gain as a result, and defer the amount of gain from the inclusion event by making another qualifying investment of the gain recognized due to the inclusion event in either the original QOF or a different QOF within 180 days of the inclusion event in order to make a new deferral election.

The Code and Final Regulations do not preclude taxpayers from reinvesting in a QOF in this manner and, though the regulatory text itself is not clear, permitting transfers in such a transaction structure would not be inconsistent with the policies underlying the opportunity zone program. The IRS and the Treasury Department have indicated their support by virtue of providing additional flexibility in the Final Regulations that was not present in the proposed regulations. Also note that opportunity zone practitioners are engaging in these types of transactions, which indicates general industry and practitioner support for this transaction structure (which, of course, is not binding on the IRS but it carries weight, particularly with a new program like that created for opportunity zones).

To better illustrate, let's assume that in 2020 a QOF distributes cash to an investor in exchange for all or some of the investor's qualifying investment (i.e., ownership interest) in the QOF. Though not a violation of the Final Regulations, such a distribution to a QOF investor may be an "inclusion event" to the extent that the distributed property has a fair market value in excess of the investor's basis. As a result of inclusion event treatment, the capital gain the investor had deferred by investing the funds in the QOF in a prior tax year would be recognized in 2020 (i.e., the year of the distribution) and would be available to offset the investor's capital gains and losses in 2020. This reduction in tax liability may be a better result for an investor if the investor may otherwise be facing a capital loss in 2020. Such a capital loss cannot be carried back and there is an increased likelihood of a capital loss for 2020 because of the economic impact of COVID-19.

This distribution in exchange for all or some of the investor's interest in the QOF may still be taxable—but the rules in the Final Regulations recognize that the investor may be able to roll this gain into another QOF investment (which could potentially defer gain recognition until December 31, 2026). The Final Regulations do not apply interest or any penalties to an investor for a withdrawal of some or all of such investor's invested capital from a QOF and the 180-day reinvestment period restarts. The related-party rules under the Final Regulations would not change the result for this type of cash out/reinvestment transaction structure.

However, note that there may be diminishing returns if investors repeatedly liquidate gains that are parked in QOFs only to redeploy them into other funds later, since investors may miss out on the increased levels of the five- or seven-year stepped-up basis.

One provision of the original opportunity zone legislation provides a 15 percent step-up in basis for investments made before December 31, 2019, if those investments are held for seven years. After that window closes, investments can qualify for a 10 percent step-up in basis if they are held for five years. The ability to defer capital gains by investing in opportunity funds is set to expire in 2026, so the deadline for claiming a 10 percent step-up in basis is December 31, 2021.

(B) Gains from Sale of Property to an Unrelated QOF or Its QOZB. A recurring question has been to what extent, if at all, an investor may sell property to a QOF or QOZB, then contribute an amount equal to the gain on the sale to the QOF, and treat the gain as "eligible gain" and the purchase as a "purchase" from an unrelated party.

Although the Final Regulations allow the QOZB to sell land to another QOZB, even if they are related parties, any gains would not be eligible to be invested in the second QOZB by investors of QOZBs if related (and possibly by unrelated investors of QOZBs in certain circumstances, as discussed below).[440] With respect to the second QOZB, the land would *not* be considered qualified property in the hands of the second QOZB if purchased from the related QOZB—even if the relatedness happened *subsequent* to the purchase of the land in a series of steps.

---

[440]Note that there is some question under the Final Regulations as to whether there needs to be related parties (i.e., persons related to each other as described in Internal Revenue Code § 267(b) or 707(b)(1), determined by substituting "20 percent" for "50 percent" each place the phrase "50 percent" occurs in those sections) for a recontribution to be ineligible.

CAVEAT
If a taxpayer/investor sold property to an unrelated QOF and then invested the amount of the sales proceeds in the same QOF, that sequence of transactions could be characterized under "circular cash flow" principles as if the taxpayer/investor contributed the property directly to the QOF (and each transfer of the amount of the sales proceeds would be disregarded) and the acquired property would not qualify as qualified opportunity zone business property ("QOZBP").

The Final Regulations confirm that generally applicable federal income tax principles would require this result if, under the facts and circumstances, the consideration paid by the QOF or by a QOZB returns to its initial source as part of the overall plan. Under the step transaction doctrine and circular cash flow principles, the circular movement of the consideration in such a transaction is disregarded and the transaction treated as a transfer of property to the purchasing QOF for an interest therein or, if applicable, as a transfer of property to a QOF for an interest therein followed by a transfer of such property by the QOF to the purchasing QOZB. In other words, property deemed contributed cannot be QOZBP.[441]

The Final Regulations also note that if an eligible taxpayer/investor sells property to, or exchanges property with, an unrelated QOZB as part of a plan that includes the investment of the consideration by the taxpayer/investor back into the QOF that owns the acquiring QOZB, the transaction potentially may be recast or recharacterized as a nonqualifying investment even if the QOF retains the consideration (rather than transferring the consideration to the QOZB).

(C) Structural Benefit to Leasing to a Related Party. Note that the Final Regulations confirm certain structural benefits as to the related-party leasing rules[442]—certain restrictions or prohibitions apply to related-party sale or exchange transactions that do not apply to related-party lease transactions. These benefits should be considered regardless of

---

[441]Accordingly, an eligible taxpayer/investor's gain from a sale to or an exchange of property with an unrelated QOF (acquiring QOF), as part of a plan that includes the investment of the consideration received by the eligible taxpayer/investor back into the acquiring QOF, is not "eligible gain" to the "eligible taxpayer/investor" because the transaction would *not* be characterized as a sale or exchange to an unrelated person for federal income tax purposes. Similarly, an eligible taxpayer/investor's gain from a sale to or an exchange of property with an unrelated QOZB (acquiring QOZB) is not eligible gain to the eligible taxpayer/investor if the sale occurs as part of a plan that includes (i) the investment of the consideration received by the eligible taxpayer/investor back into the QOF that owns the acquiring QOZB, followed by (ii) the contribution by the QOF of that consideration to the QOZB. Furthermore, because the transaction is not treated as a "purchase" of tangible property by the QOZB from an unrelated party, the newly acquired property will not qualify as QOZBP.

[442]Treas. Reg. § 1400Z-2(e)(2).

relatedness of parties to an anticipated transaction(s) based on the open question discussed above of whether there needs to be related parties for a recontribution to be ineligible. To the extent the restrictions in the earlier paragraph affect or possibly affect the intended activities of the QOZBs, the parties may consider structuring their relationship or certain aspects of their relationship as a lessor-lessee (as opposed to a buyer-seller).

EXAMPLE

Possible gain exclusion under the Final Regulations may be available if, instead of a sale of the land, the intended transaction is structured as a lease of the land with an FMV purchase option after 10 years (calculated from the date of the original QOF investment), assuming the land is not considered property sold in the ordinary course of business that would result in ordinary gains not eligible for deferral (as discussed earlier).

In structuring a relationship or certain aspects of a relationship as a lessor-lessee, a key issue is whether the transaction will qualify as a sale or a lease for federal income tax purposes, as certain restrictions or prohibitions apply to related-party sale or exchange transactions that do not apply to related-party lease transactions. If the transaction qualifies as a "lease" for tax purposes, the property leased from a related party may be eligible QOZB property, provided other applicable requirements are satisfied. If, on the other hand, the transaction qualifies as a "sale" for tax purposes, the property acquired in a sale or exchange from a related party would not be eligible QOZB property.

LEGAL BACKGROUND

In *Oesterreich v. Comm'r*, 226 F.2d 798 (9th Cir. 1955), the parties entered into a 68-year "lease" of land that provided the lessee with an option to buy the land for $10.00 upon expiration of the lease. The agreement provided for larger rental payments in earlier years and decreasing rental payments in later years. The lessee agreed to (1) pay all taxes and similar charges on the property; (2) erect a new building on the premises; and (3) take out adequate insurance related to the property.

The IRS asserted that the parties entered into an agreement for the sale of the land rather than a lease. To determine whether the transaction was a lease or sale, the test was not what the parties called the transaction, but what the *intent* of the parties was when entering into the transaction; that is, what they intended to happen.

It was clear from the facts that the parties intended the title to the premises to pass to the lessee at the end of the 68-year term. The following facts also led the court to conclude that the parties intended a sale rather than a lease: (1) the option to buy was for a nominal amount; (2) the payments were front-loaded; and (3) the lessee would forfeit a $350,000 building if it did not exercise the $10.00 option. The court recognized that while the mere option to buy at the expiration of a lease did not in and of itself turn a lease into a sale, the fact that there was virtually no question that the option would be exercised weighed heavily in favor of being a sale.

In *A.J. Concrete Pumping, Inc. v. Comm'r*, TC Memo 2001-42, the court analyzed the sale-versus-lease issue in the context of an equipment lease. The parties entered into "leases" ranging from 36 to 60 months, each with an option to buy for $1.00 upon expiration of the lease. The court pointed to four factors used to determine whether a sale had occurred: (1) whether the seller transferred legal title; (2) whether the benefits and burdens of ownership passed to the buyer; (3) whether the owner had a right under the agreement to require the other party to buy the property; and (4) how the parties treated the transaction.

The court analyzed the intent of the parties and held that they intended the transactions to be sales of the equipment for the following reasons: (1) most of the payments for the leases were received in a single or lump-sum payment; (2) the lessee had the option to buy the equipment for $1.00 upon the expiration of the lease; (3) the lessee was required to pay for all of the expenses to repair the equipment; and (4) the lessee had to maintain insurance for the equipment. While there was no evidence that title had actually passed to the lessees, the fact that the lessees bore the benefits and burdens of ownership led the court to conclude that a sale was intended.

In *Saghafi v. Comm'r*, TC Memo 1994-238, the court provided a list of factors to be used in determining whether a sale was intended for tax purposes. The factors included:

1. Whether legal title passes;
2. How the parties treat the transaction;
3. Whether an equity is acquired in the property;
4. Whether the contract creates a present obligation for the seller to execute and deliver a deed and a present obligation for the purchaser to make payments;
5. Whether the right to possession is vested in the purchaser;
6. Which party pays the property taxes;
7. Which party bears the risk of loss or damage to the property;

8. Which party receives the profits from the operation and sale of the property; and

9. Whether the sales price of an asset reflects its fair market value at the time of its alleged sale. (citations omitted)

The court rejected the taxpayer's purported sale because none of these factors were present and the taxpayer could not provide a nontax business purpose for the purported sale.

In *M & W Gear Co. v. Comm'r*, 446 F.2d 841 (7th Cir. 1971), the purported lease constituted a sale for tax purposes. The parties to the transaction initially agreed to the sale of farmland for $358,000. However, the documents were drafted as a lease agreement with an option to purchase for $342,700 less all monies paid pursuant to the lease.

The court looked to the intent of the parties and found that a sale was intended. The following factors led to the court's conclusion: (1) the option price was considerably less than fair market value; (2) the buyer had an economic obligation to buy the farm; that is, the buyer spent over $100,000 to improve the property and bought farm equipment; (3) the documentation surrounding the transaction evidenced that a sale was intended; (4) the rent exceeded fair market value, indicating that the buyer was building equity in the property; and (5) through its lease payment, the buyer reimbursed the seller for land taxes and insurance.

In *Frank Lyon Co. v. United States*, 435 U.S. 561 (1978), a bank ("Bank") and Frank Lyon Company ("Lyon") entered into a sale-leaseback arrangement for a building. The Bank initially hoped to construct and own the building, but could not obtain the necessary regulatory approvals. The regulators approved of a sale-leaseback transaction, whereby the building would be owned by a third party, so long as the Bank had an option to purchase the leased property at the end of the fifteenth year.

The Bank and Lyon entered into a ground lease, a sales agreement, and a building lease. Under the ground lease, Lyon leased the site for 76 years and 7 months. Pursuant to the sales agreement, Lyon purchased the building from the Bank. The purchase money was financed by Lyon and a third-party bank, except for $500,000 invested by Lyon. Under the building lease, the Bank leased back the building. The building lease provided the Bank with an option to purchase and also held the Bank responsible for all expenses associated with the maintenance of the building, taxes, and insurance. The purchase option equaled the sum of the unpaid balance of the mortgage, Lyon's $500,000 investment, and 6 percent interest on that investment.

Lyon took deductions on its tax returns as if it was the owner of the building. The IRS argued that Lyon was not the owner of the building for tax purposes and that the entire transaction was a sham designed to provide economic benefits to the Bank and a guaranteed return to Lyon. The Court found that the transaction was not a sham, but that it was compelled by valid business reasons. The various factors comprising the substance and economic realities of the transaction drove the Court's decision that Lyon was the owner for tax purposes. Some of the factors included:

1. Lyon was primarily liable on the mortgage (in the event anything should go awry);

2. Lyon was exposed to real and substantial risk;

3. Lyon's financial position was substantially affected due to the presence of the long-term debt and the use of $500,000 of working capital; and

4. The bank was compelled to use the sale-leaseback transaction due to regulatory constraints; that is, there was a nontax business motive.

In closing, the court stated:

> [W]here . . . there is a genuine multiple-party transaction with economic substance which is compelled or encouraged by business or regulatory realities, is imbued with tax-independent considerations, and is not shaped solely by tax avoidance features that have meaningless labels attached, the Government should honor the allocation of rights and duties effectuated by the parties.. . . So long as the lessor retains significant and genuine attributes of the traditional lessor status, the form of the transaction adopted by the parties governs for tax purposes.

Rev. Proc. 2001-28, 2001-1 CB 1156, provides guidelines to be used in determining whether a transaction qualifies as a sale or lease for federal income tax purposes. The procedure applies to "leveraged leases," which generally involve three parties and terms covering a substantial part of the useful life of the leased property. If, under the facts and circumstances of the transaction, all of the general guidelines are met, the leveraged lease will be respected as a lease and will not be deemed a sale for tax purposes.

The following is a general description of the guidelines:

1. The lessor must incur and maintain a minimum unconditional "at risk" investment in the property of at least 20 percent;

2. The lease term must include all renewal or extension periods, except those at the option of the lessee at fair rental value at the time of the option or renewal;

3. No lessee may have a contractual right to purchase the property from the lessor at a price less than fair market value;

4. Except for limited circumstances, no part of the cost of the property or the cost of improvements, modifications, or additions to the property may be furnished by any lessee (note that the exceptions provide further conditions; for example, the improvement must not be required

in order to complete the property for its intended use and the furnishing of the cost of the improvement must not constitute an equity investment by a lessee);

5. No lessee may lend to the lessor any of the funds necessary to acquire the property, or guarantee any indebtedness created in connection with the acquisition of the property by the lessor; and

6. The lessor must represent and demonstrate that it expects to receive a profit from the transaction, apart from the value of or benefits obtained from the tax deductions, credits, allowances, and other tax attributes arising from such transaction.

At the risk of the recharacterization of a transaction by the IRS, due consideration must be given to structure the transaction as a lessor-lessee relationship (as opposed to a buyer-seller relationship), based on all facts and circumstances and those factors set forth above. As noted, certain restrictions or prohibitions apply to related-party sale or exchange transactions that do not apply to related-party lease transactions—consideration must be given to the transaction documents so that the transaction qualifies as a "lease" for tax purposes. There must be a genuine multiple-party transaction with economic substance that is compelled or encouraged by business or regulatory realities, imbued with tax-independent considerations, and not shaped solely by tax avoidance features that have meaningless labels attached. The lessor must retain significant and genuine attributes of the traditional lessor status in substance for the form of the transaction adopted by the parties to be honored by the IRS and govern for tax purposes.

(D) Impact of "Step Transaction" Doctrine and "Circular Cash Flow" Principles. The preamble to the Final Regulations warns that if such transaction were successfully challenged under the "step transaction" doctrine and "circular cash flow" principles, the transaction would be treated for federal income tax purposes as a transfer of property to the purchasing QOF for an interest therein or, if applicable, as a transfer of property to a QOF for an interest therein, followed by a transfer of such property by the QOF to the purchasing QOZB.[443] In either case, the investor would *not* be treated as investing eligible gain in the QOF, and the property would not be QOZBP.

To reiterate, there is confusion about whether this could be the result regardless of whether the taxpayer became "related" to the QOF following its investment in the QOF because the preamble discussion does not

---

[443]The step transaction doctrine is generally not applied if a step has independent economic significance, is not a sham, and was undertaken for a valid business purpose. Property sales can occur between a taxpayer and a QOF or its QOZB with valid business purpose and independent economic significance from taxpayer's following investment in the QOF.

address whether the taxpayer became related. (Although the preamble discussion does make reference to an example in the anti-abuse section of the Final Regulations whereby the taxpayer does become related following its investment. This example implies that the transaction was not valid because of the unitary plan to become related.)

However, note that the application of the step transaction doctrine and circular cash flow principles depends on the facts and circumstances of each case. If a step has independent economic significance, is not a sham, and was undertaken for a valid business purpose, the substance of a series of steps would generally be respected under federal tax law and by the IRS.

To conclude, the step transaction and circular cash flow principles are generally not applied if a step of the transaction has independent economic significance, and gains from sales or exchanges with QOFs or QOZBs should be able to be invested into QOFs or QOZBs where the seller-investor is not "related" after its investment.

(E) Changes Related to Qualified Opportunity Zone Business Property.
  i. **Working Capital Safe Harbor.** In order for the QOZB to be a "qualified opportunity zone business" as described by the Final Regulations, the QOZB must show that (i) substantially all of its tangible property (owned or leased) is "qualified opportunity zone business property" as described by the Final Regulations, (ii) at least 50 percent of the total gross income derived by the QOZB comes from the active conduct of a qualified business within an OZ, (iii) less than 5 percent of its property is attributable to nonqualified financial property ("NQFP"), and (iv) a substantial portion, which means at least 40 percent, of the QOZB's intangible property is used in the active conduct of its business within an OZ.[444]

The "substantially all" threshold with respect to both the required amount and use of tangible property owned or leased by a QOZB is 70 percent. Although not certain under the Final Regulations, the preamble seems to make clear that working capital is treated as tangible property for purposes of applying the 70 percent tangible property standard. More precisely, the preamble makes clear that unexpended amounts of working capital are "not, following the conclusion of the final safe harbor period, tangible property for purposes of applying the 70 percent tangible property standard." Accordingly, working

---

[444]Solely for purposes of applying Internal Revenue Code § 1397C(e)(1) to the definition of a qualified opportunity zone business under Treas. Reg. § 1400Z–2(d)(3), working capital assets are treated as reasonable in amount for purposes of Internal Revenue Code § 1397C(b)(2) and Treas. Reg. § 1400Z–2(d)(3)(A)(ii), if all of the requirements in Treas. Reg. §§ 1400Z–2(d)(3)(v)(A) through (C).

capital may be treated as tangible property during the safe harbor period, but this interpretation is not without doubt.

The 2021 Corrective Amendments resolved any ambiguity in the application of the 2020 Corrective Amendment to the safe harbor. As revised by the 2021 Corrective Amendments, section 1.1400Z2(d)-1(d)(3)(vi)(D)(1) now reads as follows (changes shown in italics):

> *For start-up businesses utilizing the working capital safe harbor*, if [the working capital safe harbor] treats property of an entity that would otherwise be nonqualified financial property as being a reasonable amount of working capital because of compliance with three requirements of sections 1.1400Z2(d)-1(d)(3)(v)(A) through (C), the entity satisfies the requirements of *section 1400Z-2(d)(3)(A)(i)* only during the working capital safe harbor periods for which the requirements of sections 1.1400Z2(d)-1(d)(3)(v)(A) through (C) are satisfied; however, such property is not QOZ business property for any purpose.

The revised safe harbor eliminates the cross-reference to the definition of QOZ business property. As revised, the safe harbor now specifically refers to the satisfaction of the 70 percent tangible property requirement in section 1400Z-2(d)(3)(A)(i). Accordingly, under the 2021 Corrective Amendments, it is clear that an entity that qualifies for the safe harbor is deemed to satisfy the 70 percent tangible property requirement while subject to the working capital safe harbor.

QUERY
However, does the 50 percent gross income requirement still apply?

The 2021 Corrective Amendments also specifically limit the availability of the safe harbor to "start-up" businesses. Accordingly, a newly formed entity that has not yet begun its trade or business may qualify for this additional safe harbor to give it time to "grow" out of the bad tangible property that was contributed for development.[445] (How is a "start-up" business defined when a QOZB is engaged in multiple businesses or development activities? Under what circumstances may the businesses be combined?) Thus, as a practical matter, a start-up QOZB can develop property on "bad" land during its working capital safe harbor period. So long

---

[445]The (D)(1) safe harbor would apply to other nonqualifying tangible property, for example, land that is purchased from a related party.

as the QOZB satisfies the 70 percent tangible property requirements, taking into account the developed property and the land, by the expiration of the relevant working capital safe harbor period, the QOZB continues to satisfy its 70 percent tangible property requirement.

CAVEAT
For a non-"start-up" business, this additional time period to cover nonqualifying tangible property is not available. Instead, such entities that are already engaged in a trade or business generally must satisfy the 70 percent tangible property requirement from the time they intend to qualify as a QOZB. However, these entities may be able to use the other safe harbors applicable to property under construction for which working capital is being expended to qualify certain property as QOZ business property during their working capital safe harbor periods even though the property is not yet being used in the trade or business.[446]

There are no restrictions on the QOZB selling land. However, the QOZB's NQFP must be limited to less than 5 percent of unadjusted basis in the assets.[447]

If the land sale can be construed as a sale in the ordinary course of business, then the receivable will not be NQFP (and any gains from such sale will be treated as ordinary gains not eligible for deferral).

Accordingly, the QOZB can sell real property to the second QOZB for cash as long as the QOZB utilizes that cash within the business to pay off existing debt or to fund QOZB operations. If the QOZB were to distribute the cash from the real property sale to the QOF, and then the QOF distributed that cash to investors, it would be viewed as a "return of capital." Though not a violation of the Final Regulations, note that such a distribution to a QOF investor from a land sale could be an inclusion event to the extent that the distributed property has a fair market value in excess of the investor's basis. Also note that a QOF investor's transfer of cash or other property to the QOF partnership in an otherwise eligible contribution may

---

[446]See KPMG LLP analysis of 2021 Corrective Amendments (August 2021).

[447]NQFP includes cash that is not reasonable working capital, cash equivalents, and/or short-term debt (i.e., notes receivable in excess of 18 months). Accounts or notes receivable acquired (seller financing) in the ordinary course of trade or business from the sale of property are not treated as NQFP for purposes of determining whether a QOZB has exceeded this 5 percent NQFP threshold. Note, however, that if determined to be a sale of property in the ordinary course of business, any gains from such a sale would be treated as gains taxed as ordinary income (i.e., "ordinary gains"), as opposed to gains treated as capital gains eligible for deferral under the Final Regulations (i.e., "eligible gains").Note that this 5 percent threshold of NQFP must take into consideration any "sin business": the Final Regulations provide that a business that leases more than a de minimis amount of property to a sin business (as defined and discussed here) is not a QOZB and this de minimis threshold was set at 5 percent. In other words, a QOZB cannot lease more than 5 percent of its real property to a sin business.

be recharacterized as a nonqualifying investment to the extent that any such distribution is treated as a disguised sale under the rules provided under section 707 of the Internal Revenue Code (i.e., made within a two-year period).

(F) Extended 62-Month Safe Harbor.   The Final Regulations provide a 62-month safe harbor—rather than a simple 31-month safe harbor (as was provided under the proposed regulations applicable to OZs), a QOZB can choose to apply a subsequent 31-month working capital safe harbor to tangible property for a maximum 62-month period (i.e., a QOZB can choose to "piggyback" two successive 31-month safe harbor periods).[448]

Under IRS Notice 2020-39 (as a result of the federally declared disaster for purposes of Code § 165(i)(5)(A)), all QOZBs holding working capital assets intended to be covered by the working capital safe harbor before December 31, 2020, receive an additional 24 months to expend the working capital assets of the QOZB, as long as the QOZB otherwise meets the requirements to qualify for the working capital safe harbor. The 24-month period under IRS Notice 2020-39 is extended an additional 24 months under IRS Notice 2021-10 for the Company's working capital assets intended to be covered by the working capital safe harbor before June 30, 2021.

For purposes of qualifying for the working capital safe harbor (whether for the 31-month or the expanded 62-month period), the amount of working capital is treated as "reasonable" if: (1) the amounts of working capital are designated in writing for the development of a trade or business in a qualified OZ, including when appropriate the acquisition, construction, and/or substantial improvement of tangible property in such a zone (the "designated in writing" requirement); (2) there is a written schedule consistent with the ordinary start-up of a trade or business for the expenditure of the working capital assets and, under such schedule, the working capital assets must be spent within 31 months of the receipt by the business of the assets (the "reasonable written schedule" requirement); and (3) the working capital assets are actually used in a manner that is substantially consistent with the writing and written schedule (the "property consumption consistent" requirement).

In April 2021, the IRS issued proposed rules that allow businesses to use the 31-month working capital safe harbor holding as well as directly clarifying that businesses have up to an additional 24 months to deploy cash into projects due to the COVID-19 pandemic. Most importantly the proposed rules also allow businesses to follow a new or revised written

---

[448]Undesignated cash reserves can be held by the QOZB in amounts up to 5 percent of unadjusted assets. Amounts exceeding the 5 percent could be considered excess NQFP, potentially disqualifying the QOZB unless they are designated for use in a written plan as described in the Final Regulations.

plan and schedule for the deployment of cash. The additional time plus the regulatory blessing to directly permit businesses to alter their written time will allow OZ funds to react appropriately to any unexpected planning issues that result from the pandemic.

CAVEAT

Prior to the publication of the proposed rules clients generally composed written plans to cover possible changes and provide flexibility. The only previous guidance was that the written plan had to be contemporaneous and money had to be spent consistently therewith. These new rules recognize that the money may now be deployed into a new project if an existing project goes defunct. This allows companies to revisit their plans and make appropriate adjustments if they are necessary.

Under the proposed rules, the revised or new plan must be completed 120 days after the close of the incident or federal disaster as defined under Title 44, Section 206.32(f) of the Code of Federal Regulations.

Although the effective date of the proposed rules is when the final regulations are published, taxpayers may rely on the proposed regulations for taxable years beginning after December 31, 2019 and must be changes to their written plans.[449]

CAVEAT

To use the working capital safe harbor in accordance with the Final Regulations, the plan for the project must incorporate these requirements, explicitly and in writing, likely needing to be prepared by a professional.

A QOZB must receive multiple cash infusions during the initial 31-month period to qualify for a maximum 62-month safe harbor. Specifically, under the 62-month working capital safe harbor, a QOZB can qualify for a 31-month safe harbor period with respect to this QOZB's "first" cash infusion. Upon receipt of a subsequent contribution of cash (subsequent cash infusion), such QOZB may choose to both (i) extend the original 31-month safe harbor period that covered the initial cash infusion and (ii) receive safe harbor coverage for the subsequent cash contribution for another 31-month period for a maximum 62-month period (that is, a duration equal to two working capital safe harbor periods), provided that such QOZB

---

[449]IRS Notices 2021-10 and 2020-39.

satisfies the following two conditions: (1) the subsequent cash infusion must be independently covered by an additional working capital safe harbor; and (2) the working capital safe harbor plan for the subsequent cash infusion must form an integral part of the working capital safe harbor plan that covered the initial cash infusion.[450]

CAVEAT

Cash received by the QOF from a capital transaction (e.g., sale or refinancing) and then distributed to investors *sooner than two years* could be construed as a "disguised sale," thus invalidating the original deferral to the extent the distribution is treated as a disguised sale. Note, however, that the Final Regulations confirm that a debt-financed distribution of cash to a QOF investor is generally not an inclusion event if made after two years. However, the QOF should be able to distribute any gains from the land sale to investors. For example, if the original cost of the land was $10.0 million and the QOF sold it for $15.0 million, $5.0 million of the proceeds should be distributable without incident.

Also, the monies received by the QOZB from the land sale could be distributed to the QOF and held in the QOF for up to 12 months, provided such monies are converted from NQFP (i.e., held in eligible temporary investments, including debt with a term less than 18 months). The QOF could even lend this cash to the second QOZB if the term does not exceed 18 months.

i. **COVID-19 Update.** If a QOZB is located in a QOZ within a federally declared disaster zone, the QOZB may receive up to an additional 24 months to utilize its working capital assets. Exceeding the 31-month period does not violate the safe harbor if the delay is attributable to waiting for government action, the application for which is completed during the 31-month period.

(G) Anti-Abuse Rules. An additional issue that should be considered is whether an original land purchase may be considered a violation of anti-abuse rules that prohibit holding land for speculative investment provided

---

[450]As indicated in examples provided in the Final Regulations, the rules would allow a QOZB to string together subsequent or overlapping working capital safe harbors with respect to the same tangible property including as illustrated in the following: (a) Example A: a QOZB has a master written plan for the completion of a project over a 55-month period, with such plan providing that in respect of a start-up cash contribution, phase 1 of the project will be completed over a 30-month schedule and upon subsequent receipt of additional equity in cash, and phase 2 of the project will be completed over a 25-month schedule; or (b) Example B: a QOZB writes a plan with a 30-month schedule for the use of the date 1 cash and approximately 18 months after date 1, on date 2, such QOZB acquires additional equity in cash and writes a second plan with a 25-month schedule for this cash received on date 2.

in the Final Regulations.[451] These anti-abuse rules are intended to prevent the acquisition of land for speculative investment in arrangements inconsistent with the purposes of the Final Regulations, such as a parcel of unimproved land that is not accompanied by a new capital investment or is not the subject of increased economic activity or output. Before selling any real property, a good-faith effort should be made to improve the land by more than an insubstantial amount in a way having more than a transitory effect. Any grading, clearing, and/or paving activities undertaken to improve real property under the plan for the project (as well as all other facts and circumstances) would be taken into account in applying the speculative land purchase anti-abuse rules.

(H) Working Capital as Tangible Property. Note that though not certain under the Final Regulations, the preamble seems to make clear that working capital is treated as tangible property for purposes of applying the 70 percent tangible property standard. More precisely, the preamble makes clear that unexpended amounts of working capital are "not, following the conclusion of the final safe harbor period, tangible property for purposes of applying the 70 percent tangible property standard." Accordingly, working capital should be viewed as tangible property during the safe harbor period. The regulatory text itself is not clear on this point, but the preamble text seems to clarify that amounts held as working capital are "good assets," income earned on the working capital is treated as income derived from the active conduct of a trade or business, and any tangible property for which working capital is expended is treated as used in the trade of business and as QOZB property while covered by the safe harbor.

i.   **Intangible Property.** The Final Regulations provide that intangible property is used in the active conduct of a trade or business in a qualified opportunity zone if: (1) the use of the intangible property is normal, usual, or customary in the conduct of the trade or business; and (2) the intangible property is used in the qualified opportunity zone in the performance of an activity of the trade or business that contributes to the generation of gross income for the trade or business. This change in the Final Regulations addresses concerns surrounding valuation of intangible property used in the conduct of trade or business in OZs.

Note that if a QOF invests in a QOZB, there is no overall limit on the amount of intangible property (e.g., intellectual property) that the opportunity zone business can own, but a "substantial portion" of its

---

[451]Treas. Reg. § 1.1400Z2(f)-1.

intangible property must be used in the "active conduct of a business" in a zone (though Treasury will need to further define these terms). As to a QOF that directly owns assets in an OZ, only up to 10 percent of a fund's property (and any cash and property not located in an opportunity zone) can be intangible property, but there is no requirement that a percentage of a fund's intangible property be related to the active business of the fund.

ii. **Cure Period.** The Final Regulations also provide for a six-month cure period for a nonqualifying trade or business. If a trade or business causes the QOF to fail the 90 percent investment test on a semiannual testing date, the QOF may treat the stock or partnership interest in that business as QOF property for that semiannual testing date, provided the business corrects the failure within six months of the date on which the stock or partnership interest lost its qualification. This provides additional flexibility and takes into account practical difficulties businesses may encounter.

(I) Changes Related to Substantial Improvement Requirement: Aggregation Test. Section 1400Z-2(d)(2)(D) requires that if tangible property was already used in an OZ ("non-original use" asset) when purchased by a QOF or QOZB, then it needs to be "substantially improved" by the QOF or QOZB before it can become QOZB property.

Substantial improvement, as defined by section 1400Z-2(d)(2)(D)(ii), requires the QOF or QOZB to more than double the adjusted basis of the property within 30 months after acquiring the property.

Under the proposed regulations, the substantial improvement test was measured on an asset-by-asset basis, making it a practical impossibility to substantially improve (or quantify that substantial improvement) in some instances. The Final Regulations allow some flexibility, permitting investors to measure improvement in aggregate in certain circumstances; the following asset aggregation rules address the issue of how to measure substantial improvement.[452]

i. **Operating Assets.** For purposes of determining whether basis has been doubled to meet the substantial improvement requirement for the non-original use assets, the cost of purchased property that qualifies as QOZB property (i.e., original use property) may be added to the basis of purchased non-original use assets if the original use assets in the same zone (or a contiguous zone) are used in the same trade or business and improve the functionality of non-original use assets being improved (the "functionality" test).

---

[452]Treas. Reg. § 1.1400Z2(d)-2.

EXAMPLE

A developer would just need to show how their purchase of furniture and equipment adds to the "functionality" of the old property they bought to develop. It remains unclear, however, how this rule would apply outside of the real estate context (e.g., how it would apply to a fund that invests in a business with an assembly line and buys a new assembly line).

---

ii.   **Buildings.** For clusters of commonly owned buildings, buildings that are part of an "eligible building group" can be aggregated for purposes of applying the substantial improvement requirement.[453]

Ambiguity remains relative to demolished property because Treasury did not affirmatively clarify that structures in an OZ that will be demolished pursuant to the development of a trade or business should be treated as qualified OZ business property during the period before demolition.

iii. **Vacant Property.** Property in an OZ will qualify as QOZB original use property (meaning it does not need to be substantially improved) if it was vacant one year before the designation of the tract as an OZ (three years for other property). Regarding the definition of "vacant," real property, including land and buildings, is considered vacant if the property is "significantly unused," meaning more than 80 percent of the building or land, as measured by the square footage of useable space, is not being used. This could boost the number of viable real estate projects qualifying under the OZ program, especially in areas overwhelmed with abandoned lots.

iv.   **Land.** The Final Regulations retain the rule that land is not required to be substantially improved. However, the regulations also retain the rule that land should be improved by more than an "insubstantial" amount, which is a fact-intensive inquiry.

When applying the "functionality" aggregation rule to non-original use land, the original use property must improve the land by a more than insubstantial amount. Improvements to the land, including grading, clearing, remediation of contaminated land, or acquisition of related QOZB property that facilitates the use of the land in a trade or business of the eligible entity, will be taken into account in

---

[453]Buildings on a single deeded property may be treated as a single property and buildings on contiguous parcels of land may be treated as a single property as long as they are: operated exclusively by the QOF or QOZB; share business resource elements (e.g., accounting or other back office functions) or employees; and are operated in coordination with one or more of the trades or businesses (e.g., supply chain interdependencies or mixed-use facilities). For two or more buildings treated as a single property, the amount of basis required to be added will be the total basis of each building.

determining whether the land was improved by more than an insubstantial amount.[454]

v. **Nonqualifying OZ Property.** The Final Regulations clarify that improvements made to nonqualifying OZ property (because it was purchased on or before December 31, 2017; purchased from a related party; or lacks substantial improvements) do not satisfy original use requirements as purchased property, unlike lessee improvements to leased property, which are treated as separate property and satisfy the original use requirement as purchased property for the amount of the unadjusted cost basis of such improvements.

The Final Regulations clearly provide that self-constructed property (property manufactured, built, or produced by a taxpayer for its trade or business) is generally eligible to be considered "acquired by purchase" (so not subject to the substantial improvement test).

vi. **QOF Tangible Property.** The Final Regulations made changes related to tangible property that affect various aspects of the OZ program.

Tangible property used in a trade or business of an eligible entity satisfies the "substantially all" requirement of the 70 percent use test if it is qualified tangible property and the Final Regulations provide that tangible personal property can be included for purposes of meeting the substantially improved test.[455]

The Final Regulations did not clarify that reasonable capitalized fees paid to a related party with respect to the development or redevelopment of tangible property are considered an addition to adjusted basis for purposes of measuring the substantial improvement of property and do not cause the property to fail to qualify as QOZB property.

vii. **Substantial Improvement Period.** The Final Regulations clarify that for both QOFs and QOZBs, property in the process of being improved

---

[454]The Final Regulations include both a square footage test and an unadjusted cost test to determine if a project is primarily in a QOZ, and provide that parcels or tracts of land will be considered "contiguous" if they possess common boundaries, and would be contiguous but for the interposition of a road, street, railroad, stream, or similar property. Importantly, the Final Regulations also extend the straddle rules to QOFs and QOZBs with respect to the 70 percent use test, although the application of the rules needs further clarity.

With respect to brownfields, the Final Regulations provide that all property that is part of a brownfield site (including land and structures) is considered original use property (i.e., no substantial improvement requirement) as long as, within a reasonable period of time, investments are made to ensure that the property meets basic safety standards for both human health and the environment. In addition, brownfield remediation will be considered "more than insubstantial" improvement of land.

[455]In addition, the Final Regulations resolved the issue of whether inventory should be excluded from the 70 percent test for qualified OZ businesses by providing taxpayers the option of excluding inventory (including raw materials) from the numerator and denominator of the 70 percent use of tangible property test and the 90 percent investment standard test for QOF direct investments in QOZB property.

is treated as used in a trade or business and satisfies the requirements of the 31-month substantial improvement test (i.e., the QOF or QOZB does not need to wait until the improvements are completed to treat the property as substantially improved for purposes of the 90 percent or 70 percent tests).

To address concerns that the 31-month working capital safe harbor for substantial improvements would be violated by delays caused by projects disrupted by events beyond taxpayers' control, the Final Regulations provide QOZBs located in federally declared disaster areas an additional 24-month period to use working capital after the initial 31-month safe harbor period. This is an expansion of the relief provided by the proposed regulations for delays attributable to waiting periods for government actions (e.g., projects requiring extensive permitting and other types of governmental approvals), which is a toll on the 31-month safe harbor period for a duration equal to the permitting delay.

(j) Changes Related to Type of Entity

i. **Corporate Consolidated Return Rules.** Corporations with one or more subsidiaries are generally treated as a consolidated group and generally file a consolidated return. Treasury provided certain rules in the Final Regulations that are considered favorable changes.

First, the Final Regulations provide that a QOF is also allowed to be a member of a consolidated group, subject to certain conditions. In addition, the Final Regulations allow a member of a consolidated group to make investments in a QOF of the capital gains of another member of the consolidated group.

These changes should be considered in the context of large companies as well as banks, which tend to form community development arms for the sort of investments made in OZs: the Final Regulations allow a member of a consolidated group to be a different party from the member of the group that recognized the gain to invest the gain (e.g., gain recognized from the sale of a capital asset) by one part of a bank and another division of the bank (like the community investment part of such bank) could make the investment.

ii. **10-Year Sale of Interest in a QOF Partnership.** When a partner sells a QOF interest after 10 years and elects to adjust the basis of their partnership interest to FMV, the QOF partnership may adjust partnership assets to the net fair market value (FMV) of the disposed-of interest, plus the partner's share of partnership debt. This clarification is intended to prevent a reduction in an investor's share of partnership debt upon selling a QOF partnership interest from reducing the OZ tax benefits provided by the 10-year basis step-up.

iii. **10-Year Gain Exclusion Provision for Partnerships and S Corporations.** Gain exclusion for asset sales by QOFs and QOZBs was expanded in the Final Regulations: when a QOF partnership or S corporation sells property, if its owners have held their interest for 10 years, such owners can make an election for each taxable year to exclude a QOF's gains from all sales or exchanges (not just capital gains) in the taxable year. This exclusion rule extends to pass-through gains from the sale of property by QOZBs owned by a QOF but does not apply to gains from the sale of inventory by the QOF in the ordinary course of business.

CAVEAT

Note that the Final Regulations did not address the "interim gain problem"; investors must hold qualifying investment for 10 years for gain exclusion.

---

iv. **Special Gain "Inclusion" Rule.** Treasury did not change the special gain inclusion rule that can result in investors in QOF partnerships having to recapture some or all of prior losses, as capital gain income, on December 31, 2026.

The statute generally provides that a QOF investor's deferred gain is not subject to tax until the earlier of: (1) the date the investor sells or exchanges the qualifying investment; or (2) December 31, 2026.

Deferred gain becomes taxable to the extent a transaction reduces the taxpayer's equity interest in the qualifying investment. The regulations provide an extensive list of such transactions, including sales of the taxpayer's interest in the QOF, sales of an interest in an S corporation or partnership that is a QOF investor, and gifts of the QOF interest.

Provided that distributions from QOF partnerships and S corporations do not exceed the partner's or shareholder's basis, there is no inclusion event. Similarly, dividend distributions from C corporations are not an inclusion event, unless the dividends are in excess of basis.[456]

---

[456]When there is an inclusion of the deferred gain, the proposed regulations (which were not changed under the Final Regulations) require the QOF investor to include the lesser of two amounts in income, minus the investor's basis. The first is the FMV of the investment disposed of, and the second amount equals "an amount which bears the same proportion to the remaining deferred gain as" the first amount bears to the "fair market value of the total qualifying investment immediately before the inclusion event." In other words, there is no change under the Final Regulations to the requirement that partnerships and S corporations basically have to recapture their losses at a minimum on an inclusion event.

v.   **Carried Interest.** The carried interest rules are generally retained but the Final Regulations change how the allocation percentage is calculated. The proposed regulations provided that carried interests (i.e., profits interests in a partnership that are received in exchange for services) must be treated as nonqualifying investments under the OZ rules and included rules for determining the "allocation percentage" of a partner's qualifying and nonqualifying interests when a partner made a qualifying capital investment and also received a nonqualifying carried interest.

The Final Regulations provide that the portion of sales proceeds allocated to the nonqualifying carried interest for the percentage is now based on the share of residual profits the mixed-funds partner would receive with respect to the carried interest, disregarding any allocation of residual profits for which there is not a reasonable likelihood of application, and is no longer based on the highest share of residual profits the partner would receive with respect to the carried interest.

(k)   Changes Related to Basis Adjustments

i.   **Effect of Inclusion Event on 10-Year FMV Basis Election.** The Final Regulations include a number of modifications and clarifications to the rules relating to "inclusion events," that is, events that result in an investor recognizing all or a part of their deferred gain.[457]

An inclusion event generally results in a reduction or termination of a qualifying investment's status as a qualifying investment to the extent of the reduction or termination. However, certain types of inclusion events (namely, certain distributions) do not terminate an investor's qualifying investment and do not preclude a subsequent 10-year basis step-up, as long as the investor continues to own the QOF interests.

CAVEAT
Note that a debt-financed distribution of cash to a QOF partnership investor is generally not an inclusion event if made after two years.

---

ii.   **Option to Disregard Recently Contributed Property to a QOF.** The Final Regulations generally retain the rules under the proposed regulations permitting a QOF to disregard recently contributed property for purposes of the 90 percent investment test, expressly rejecting any

---

[457]Treas. Reg. § 1.1400Z2(b)-1.

change to avoid an undefined mathematical result if all of the QOF's property were being disregarded under this rule.

The Final Regulations provide that a QOF has until the fifth business day after a contribution of property to exchange such property into cash, cash equivalents, or short-term debt in order to qualify for the rules. Treasury and the IRS declined to adopt recommendations to expand this rule from 6 months to 12 months, at least during a QOF's initial start-up period, and also declined to adopt recommendations to provide a wind-down period safe harbor for applying the 90 percent investment test.

iii. **Transfer of Qualifying Interest by Reason of Death.** The Final Regulations clarify that Internal Revenue Code section 1014 does not apply to adjust (or "step-up") the basis of an inherited qualifying OZ investment (i.e., interest in a QOF) to its FMV as of the deceased owner's death.[458]

This clarification in the Final Regulations came as a surprise; many commentators anticipated that the Final Regulations would provide for a step-up in basis of the qualifying interest to its FMV at the date of the decedent's death (which would reduce the beneficiary's capital gains tax on inherited qualifying OZ property in a manner consistent with how the Internal Revenue Code treats other inherited property), and instead the Final Regulations confirm that the basis remains at zero with respect to the QOF investment. This rule may complicate estate planning for QOF investors and may discourage certain OZ equity investments by elderly taxpayers.

(L) Changes Related to Property That a QOF Leases

i. **Leased Property.** The Final Regulations limit the requirement of proof of "arm's-length" leasing arrangement to related parties and create a rebuttable presumption that the terms of a lease are market rate for leases between unrelated persons.[459]

A QOF or QOZB may treat leased tangible property as QOZBP for purposes of satisfying the 90 percent investment standard and the 70 percent tangible property standard. To qualify, the leased tangible property must satisfy the following two general requirements: first, analogous to owned tangible property, leased tangible property must be acquired under a lease entered into after December 31, 2017. Second, and also similar to owned tangible property, substantially all of the use of the leased tangible property must be located within a QOZ

---

[458]Section 1.1400Z2(b)-1(c)(4).

[459]The Final Regulations also provide that the requirement for property leases to be arm's-length does not apply to leases with a state or local government, or an Indian tribal government.

during substantially all of the period for which the business leases the property. The Final Regulations confirm that property subject to an existing lease will not constitute QOZBP unless the lease was entered into on or after December 31, 2017.

Neither the original use requirement (i.e., that requires purchased property that qualifies as QOZB property) nor the substantial improvement requirement (i.e., that requires the QOF or QOZB to more than double the adjusted basis of the property within 30 months after acquiring the property) apply to leased property. Also, any improvements made to the leased property can satisfy the original use requirement, so, for example, a QOF or QOZB can be the tenant on a ground lease and build new property that should qualify as QOZBP. Additionally, there is no requirement that the lessor and lessee be unrelated parties, as would be the case for property acquired by a QOF or QOZB by purchase. This provides flexibility in structuring QOF transactions for existing owners of property in an OZ. However, if the lessor and lessee are related, it triggers a few additional requirements, including a prohibition on prepayments.

Note that there is an anti-abuse rule that disqualifies leased property as QOZBP if there is a plan, intent, or expectation that the underlying real property could be purchased for anything other than its fair market value at the time of purchase. If, at the time a QOF or QOZB enters into a lease for real property (other than unimproved land), there was a plan, intent, or expectation for the QOF or QOZB to purchase the real property for an amount of consideration other than the fair market value of the land (as determined at the time of the purchase without regard to any prior lease payments), the leased real property does not qualify as QOZBP at any time.

In light of the foregoing, valuation is a key consideration. The value of each asset that is leased by a QOF is equal to the present value of the leased asset. The "present value" of such leased asset is (i) equal to the sum of the present values of each payment under the lease for the asset, and (ii) calculated at the time at which the QOF enters into the lease for the asset. Once calculated, that present value is used as the value for the asset by the QOF for all testing dates for purposes of the 90 percent investment standard. To determine the present value of the lease payments, the proposed regulations provided that the discount rate is the applicable federal rate (AFR) under Code § 1274(d)(1). The Final Regulations provide that the short-term AFR must be used.

Further note that to qualify as QOZBP, the terms of a lease must be market rate at the time at which the lease was entered into (market-rate lease requirement). For this purpose, whether a lease is market rate (that is, whether the terms of the lease reflect common, arm's-length market pricing in the locale that includes the QOZ) is determined in accordance with the regulations under Internal Revenue Code ("Code") section 482.

Code section 482 provides that the arm's-length standard is met if the results of a transaction are consistent with the results uncontrolled taxpayers would have had if they had engaged in the same transaction under the same circumstances. Whether the arm's-length standard is met is generally determined by reference to the results of comparable transactions under comparable circumstances since identical transactions can rarely be found. Evaluations of a result are made using a method selected under the best method rule. The best method rule generally requires that the arm's-length result of a controlled transaction be determined using the method that, under the facts and circumstances, produces the most reliable measure of an arm's-length result.

This limitation operates to ensure that all of the terms of the lease are market rate. Under the Final Regulations, the market-rate lease requirement applies to leases between related parties. However, the market-rate lease requirement does not apply to leases between unrelated parties; the Final Regulations provide a rebuttable presumption that, with regard to leases between unrelated parties, such unrelated-party leases are arm's-length and the terms of the lease market rate (that is, the lease satisfies the market-rate lease requirement). The Final Regulations also exempt from the market-rate lease requirement leases between an unrelated party and a state or local government and Indian tribal governments. In other words, for purposes of satisfying the market-rate lease requirement, tangible property acquired by lease from a state or local government, or an Indian tribal government, is not considered tangible property acquired by lease from a related party.

As noted above, certain restrictions or prohibitions apply to related-party sale or exchange transactions that do not apply to related-party lease transactions—consideration must be given to the transaction documents so that the transaction qualifies as a "lease" for tax purposes. The lessor must retain significant and genuine attributes of the traditional lessor status in substance for the form of the transaction adopted by the parties to be honored by the IRS and govern for tax purposes.

Lastly, the Final Regulations provide that short-term leases of personal property to lessors using the property outside an OZ may be counted as QOZB property.

ii. **Sin Business 5 Percent Test.** The Final Regulations provide that a business that leases more than a de minimis amount of property to a sin business is not a QOZB; this de minimis threshold was set at 5 percent. In other words, a QOZB cannot lease more than 5 percent of its real property to a sin business.

The Final Regulations also provide clarification that the prohibition on sin businesses only applies to a QOZB; this prohibition does not apply to a QOF. To serve as an example, the FAQs provide that a hotel business of a QOZB could potentially lease space to a spa that provides tanning services.

A "sin business" includes any (i) private or commercial golf course, (ii) country club, (iii) massage parlor, (iv) hot tub facility, (v) suntan facility, (vi) racetrack or other facility used for gambling, or (vii) store, the principal business of which is the sale of alcoholic beverages for consumption off premises.[460]

(M) Foreign Investments in Qualified Opportunity Funds.   Foreign persons are generally subject to U.S. income tax on income that is effectively connected with the conduct of a trade or business within the United States.[461]

i. **General.** Under the FIRPTA Withholding provisions, certain transferees or payors are required to withhold a specified percentage of the sales proceeds, distributions, or other payments that would be payable to foreign persons and pay the same over to the IRS.

CAVEAT

The foreign person must file a U.S. income tax return, claim a credit for the withheld amount, and either pay any additional tax due or claim a refund of all or a portion of the withheld amount.

However, withholding may be less appropriate when the foreign person intends to defer the realized gain in a QOF for several reasons. First, the withholding would reduce the amount of cash payable to the foreign person and thus, make it more difficult for the foreign person to secure and invest in a QOF the amount of cash necessary to achieve full gain deferral. Second, the purpose of the withholding is to approximate the foreign person's tax liability on the transfer or payment and such tax liability will be reduced or

---

[460] As described in Internal Revenue Code § 144(c)(6)(B).
[461] This analysis is based upon a client alert prepared by Seyfarth Shaw LLP, April 2021. See IRC §§1445, 1446(a), and 1446(f).

eliminated if the foreign person makes a timely and proper invest-ment in a QOF.[462]

ii. **Deferral Election:** *Eligibility Certificate.* The "security-required per-sons" (certain foreign persons and certain foreign-owned partner-ships described below) that invest "security required gain" (gain from a "covered transfer," which is generally a transfer subject to withhold-ing) may not make a deferral election unless they obtain an "eligi-bility certificate" with respect to that gain by the date on which the deferral election is filed with the IRS.

NOTE

If a security-required person obtains an eligibility certificate and provides security to the IRS before the transaction giving rise to the gain, then the withholding is reduced or elimi-nated. If a security-required person does not obtain an eligibility certificate for the transfer, then the transfer is subject to normal withholding.

---

iii. **Security-Required Person.** A partnership, whether foreign or domes-tic, is a "security-required person" if it meets three tests: the "owner-ship" test, the "closely-held" test, and the "gain or asset" test.

   A. The ownership test is met if, at the time of transfer, 20 percent or more of the capital or profits interests in the partnership are owned (directly or indirectly through one or more partnerships, trusts, or estates) by one or more nonresident aliens or foreign corporation.

   B. The closely-held test is met if, at any time during a lookback period (the period that begins on the later of the date that is one year before the date of the transfer or the date on which the part-nership was formed, and that ends on the date of the transfer), a partnership has 10 or fewer direct partners that own 90 percent or more of the capital or profits interests in the partnership, with any related partners (within the meaning of Code §267(b) or 707(b)(1)) being treated as a single partner.

   C. The gain or asset test is met if either (i) the amount of security-required gain from the transfer exceeds $1 million or (ii) at any time during a lookback period (same as above), the value of the

---

[462]If withholding were not reduced or eliminated and the foreign person did defer tax by investment in a QOF, then the foreign person may be able to claim a credit for the withheld amount and use the credit to offset other income or claim a refund.

partnership's assets that are U.S. real property interests or assets used in a U.S. trade or business exceeds 25 percent of the total value of the partnership's assets.[463]

(N) Conclusion. The overall response by Treasury has been positive in clarifying many of the open issues at a critical time in view of the COVID-19 pandemic, but many unresolved questions remain. Treasury needs to provide continuing guidance in order to spur economic growth and investment in distressed communities in order for the OZ program to be successful and meet its original legislative goals.

As investors brace for current and possibly future economic instability, the tax treatment surrounding QOFs may play a role in their decisions to maintain with current commitments or terminate their investments and move capital gains into different areas.

The OZ incentive is making its intended impact in struggling communities across the country, but practitioners believe its effectiveness could be enhanced through a number of targeted improvements to both the regulations and underlying statute, especially in view of the need for economic relief and recovery in the wake of COVID-19. Improvements that establish additional guardrails will encourage investment in new and existing businesses, and accelerated market development will position OZs to play an important role in the pandemic recovery.

There is further concern against pursuing major changes to the incentive that may disrupt the fragile and still-developing OZ market.

Practitioners believe that many of the following recommendations would significantly improve the guardrails and incentive without resulting in undue disruption to communities or market participants.[464]

(O) Legislative Recommendations
  i. **Reporting and Transparency.** The immediate establishment of reporting and transparency requirements for OZ investments in a manner

---

[463]To obtain an eligibility certificate, a security-required person must submit an application to the IRS. The application must generally include the following: (i) certain information about the security-required person, including his, her, or its U.S. taxpayer identification number, and the covered transfer; (ii) an agreement for the deferral of tax and provision of security (a "deferral agreement"); (iii) an agreement with a U.S. agent; and (iv) acceptable security (an irrevocable standby letter of credit issued by a U.S. bank that meets certain capital and other requirements) that secures the amount of the security-required gain for which the eligibility certificate is being obtained. The deferral agreement will require the security-required person to: (a) timely file a federal income tax return and pay any tax liability due on the security-required gain when required; (b) report any security-required gain in accordance with the Treasury regulations under Code §1400Z-2; (c) provide security to the IRS with respect to any tax liability due on security-required gain; and (d) appoint a U.S. person to act as the security-required person's agent for certain purposes specified in the deferral agreement.

[464]The recommendations in this section are based upon materials prepared by Economic Innovation Group, March 2021.

that protects confidential information.[465] The IMPACT Act is a comprehensive reporting regime that would significantly enhance efforts to evaluate the OZ policy and guard against abuse, while striking an appropriate balance between the need for more granular measure data and the protection of confidential taxpayer information.[466]

ii. **Sunset of High-Income OZ Tracts.** An early sunsetting of OZ designations for tracts that exceed a certain threshold of median family income after careful consideration of factors, including those in distressed urban cores, and a high poverty rate. In addition, states should have the ability to replace disqualified tracts with new tracts designated as OZs. Any legislation should provide grandfathering rules for QOFs to deploy existing investments and complete existing projects in disqualified tracts. Failure to include reasonable grandfathering rules would upset many existing investments and commitments and undermine investor confidence in the OZ program.[467]

iii. **Allowance of Fund-to-Fund Investments.** Under the current statute, a taxpayer must make an investment directly into a QOF in order to have a qualifying investment, and a QOF is not permitted to invest in another QOF. An intermediary investment structure, such as a "feeder fund," would not only make these small OZ projects possible, but would also allow smaller investors to make direct, diversified investments in QOFs.

iv. **Extension of Deadline for OZ Benefits.** The OZ statute was originally enacted in 2017 with a deadline for investment and realization of gains in 2026. The OZ incentives are also time-driven, providing for exclusion of a portion of the deferred gain for QOF interests held for five and seven years before the 2026 realization event and exclusion of the appreciation in the QOF interest after holding it for ten years. The final regulations, which clarified many open issues, were released two years later. And shortly thereafter, the COVID-19 pandemic had a chilling effect on OZ investments. As a result of these factors, the

---

[465] Senator Tim Scott's bipartisan Improving and Reinstating the Monitoring, Prevention, Accountability, Certification and Transparency Provisions of Opportunity Zones (IMPACT) Act is one proposal that would achieve these goals.

[466] The IMPACT Act requires reporting by QOFs and investors and imposes penalties for failing to comply with the reporting requirements, with allowances made for reasonable cause. The IMPACT Act also provides for Treasury to produce an annual report on national OZ activity that looks at aggregated data, such as the number of funds, total assets, and distribution of investments, and tracks socioeconomic indicators of OZ communities over time.

[467] The IRS has announced in Announcement 2021-10 that the Census 2020 changes will not affect original OZ designations.

OZ subsidy has not had sufficient time to foster investment before the upcoming investment deadline and realization event in 2026. Accordingly, legislation should extend the 2026 deadline for investment and realization of gains.

v. **Interim Gains.** Under the statute, gains realized on the sale of investments in QOFs that have been held for at least ten years are excluded from gross income. Current regulations provide a mechanism for exclusion of gain from the sale of the underlying business assets held at the QOF or a lower-tier entity level after the QOF has been held for ten years. However, gain on the sale of business assets held less than ten years is included in income. If a QOF engages in such activity, the QOF investor will not realize the full ten-year gain exclusion benefit, even if the proceeds are reinvested into subsequent OZ investments. This limitation has discouraged many traditional private equity and venture capital investors from investing in operating businesses in OZs. Accordingly, recognition of gain on the sale of OZ business interests by a QOF should be deferred as long as the sale proceeds are invested into other OZ property within a 12-month period.

vi. **Reporting Requirements.** Treasury and the IRS have implemented reporting requirements for QOFs and investors using Form 8996, *Qualified Opportunity Fund,* and Form 8997, *Initial and Annual Statement of Qualified Opportunity Fund (QOF) Investments.* Treasury and the IRS have authority to require the reporting of additional information to ensure compliance with the OZ requirements. Forms 8996 and 8997 should be amended to capture additional information, such as inclusion events, and to ensure compliance with the OZ requirements.

vii. **Affordable Housing.** The OZ incentive can be a valuable tool to attract private capital to create more affordable rental housing. However, affordable housing developers that intend to rehabilitate or convert existing property to affordable housing projects have a very difficult time meeting the requirement that either "original use" of the property commence in the OZ or that the property be substantially improved. The substantial improvement threshold is even more challenging for affordable housing projects in expensive urban areas, which is often where such housing is most acutely needed. Regulations should be issued allowing property converted from market-rate to affordable rental housing to be considered "original use" property (similar to the special exceptions for vacant property and brownfields in the existing regulations). Regulations could provide that property converted from market-rate to affordable would be considered "original use" provided the property is subject to a recorded Land Use Restriction Agreement ("LURA") requiring a minimum set-aside that at least 40 percent of all units are affordable to households earning 80 percent or less of the area median income.

Regulations could also treat existing affordable rental housing as "substantially improved" if improved by more than an insubstantial amount and subject to a LURA as described above. "More than insubstantial" could be defined as in excess of 20 percent of the unadjusted cost basis of such property, consistent with the low-income housing tax credit ("LIHTC") standard. This change is likely to require legislation.

viii. **Includible Gain Relief for LIHTC Investments.** The existing regulations provide a special computation of deferred gain inclusion for qualifying investments in a QOF partnership or S corporation, which requires investors to recognize a great portion of deferred gain, even if the fair market value of their investments has declined. This will likely impact LIHTC partnerships because LIHTC investments generally do not appreciate in value due to the long-term land use restrictions for these projects. Modifying the inclusion rules for LIHTC partnerships would permit investors to recognize tax benefits for any decrease in value of their investment upon inclusion of the deferred gain, which would increase the value of the incentive and encourage more affordable rental housing investment in OZs. The regulatory computation of includible deferred gain should be modified so as to not adversely affect LIHTC activity.

ix. **New Markets Tax Credit Pairing Fixes.** Although there is overlap between the goals of the OZ incentive and the new markets tax credit ("NMTC") to encourage the flow of capital into low-income communities, it is often difficult for an investor to be eligible for both incentives. This is due to existing NMTC regulations that have the effect of encouraging investments to be made in the form of loans rather than equity investments (because investors in entities making loans have greater protection from recapture under a "reasonable expectations" test). Yet, controlling equity interests are not eligible for the "reasonable expectations" protection. (See Section 13.6(r).) Without reasonable expectations protection from recapture, investors generally perceive the compliance risk as too great and are unwilling to enter into such transactions. The NMTC regulations should relax the controlling equity definition to increase protection from recapture, which would provide the certainty necessary for CDEs to invest in QOFs.

x.   **Certification of QOFs.** Treasury and the IRS should retain the self-certification process that has allowed the rapid creation of new funds and investments. To the extent the Biden administration determines it appropriate to collect additional information as part of the certification process, it is recommended that such requirements continue to be applied on a "self-certification" basis, and any changes apply only prospectively to new QOFs. In addition, there needs to be balance between the usefulness of any additional collection of information against the burden imposed by the additional collection; specifically, to ease any newly adopted certification requirements for small QOFs that have less capital.

xi.   **Preexisting Businesses.** Congress intended existing businesses with expansion and growth potential to qualify for OZ tax benefits.

NOTE
In his press release announcing the introduction of the Investing in Opportunity Act, Senator Tim Scott (R-SC) wrote, "The Investing in Opportunity Act can provide the chance that entrepreneurs and small businesses are looking for to grow, innovate, and create jobs," underscoring that this incentive was intended to draw capital to OZ both to help existing businesses grow and to spur creation of new businesses.

The requirement that OZ business property must have been acquired after December 31, 2017 and used in the OZ for substantially all of the entity's "holding period" makes it difficult for existing businesses to qualify as an OZ business. Such existing business are therefore unable to raise additional equity capital from QOFs. The substantial improvement test should be modified to allow tangible property purchased on or before December 31, 2017 to be treated as qualified property if the business makes other substantial investments, such as the acquisition of new tangible property, that exceed the basis of existing property during the substantial improvement period, similar to the rule for related-party leases of tangible personal property. Regulations would also need to clarify that for purposes of the "substantially all of the use" for "substantially all of the holding period" of the QOZ Property requirement, the holding period requirement begins upon the "certification" of the QOF.

xii.   **Remove Taint of Nonqualifying Property.** Under the statute, property must be purchased after December 31, 2017, and either substantially improved or originally used in the OZ, to be considered qualifying business property. As a result, property acquired before

2018 or property acquired in a nontaxable transaction would not qualify. However, there was some question as to whether, if nonqualifying property was substantially improved, the portion that was substantially improved could be considered qualifying business property. In the preamble to the final regulations, Treasury and the IRS answered that question in the negative because it would impose administrative burdens for both taxpayers and the IRS to track improvements. This rule is inconsistent with the treatment of leasehold improvements and improvements to land, which can qualify under the regulations. In addition, taxpayers generally must track improvements separately for accounting purposes and depreciation purposes, so there is no additional burden. Regulations need to be issued to provide that nonqualifying property does not "taint" any new improvements made by a QOF or OZ business by treating any nonqualifying property incorporated into a new property as a separate asset for purposes of the OZ requirements.

xiii. **New Legislation Proposals (April 2022).** In April 2022, Senate Bill 4065 and House Bill 7467 were introduced with four major provisions:

A. *Modification of Population Census Tracts Designated as Qualified Opportunity Zones:* Disqualification of certain population census tracts: any census tract that was designated as a qualified opportunity zone before the date of the enactment of this subsection, and is either:

  ◦ A "High Median Family Income Tract" (greater than 130 percent of the national median family income), or

  ◦ A census tract for which the chief executive officer of the state submits a request for OZ designation removal.

  Exceptions. Disqualification will not apply if:

  ◦ The non-higher education student population of the census tract has a poverty rate of 30 percent or higher, or

  ◦ The Secretary approves a request by the chief executive officer of the state to retain the OZ designation.[468]

---

[468]Any preexisting trade or business of a QOF or QOZB would still qualify provided that it meets the following:

- Filed a registration statement under the Securities Act of 1933 or prepared comparable offering memorandum showing intent to invest in the disqualified census tract, *and*
- Before the disqualified census tract appears on any list published by the Secretary, has made or entered into a binding investment in the aggregate of more than $250,000 and designated in writing for the use in, or the development of, such trade or business, *or*
- Is determined by the Secretary to have relied on the designation and to have suffered a loss due to the decertification.

B. *Information Reporting Requirements:* New QOF reporting requirements with respect to QOZB interests held by the QOF are as follows:

- The name and address of any QOZB in which the QOF invests.
- North American Industry Classification Code for each business.
- Approximate number of residential units (if any) for real property held.
- Approximate average number of full-time equivalent employees.

With respect to QOZBP held by the QOF:

- North American Industry Classification Code for each business.
- Approximate number of residential units (if any) for real property held.
- Approximate average number of full-time equivalent employees.

Any other such information as the Secretary may require.[469]

C. *Modification of Rules for Investments in Qualified Opportunity Funds.* Extension of deferral period from December 31, 2026 to December 31, 2028. Modification of additional 5 percent basis step upholding period from seven years to six years. Modification of the definition of QOF to include qualified "feeder" funds; any investment vehicle that invests in a QOF if:

- Such investment vehicle is organized as a domestic partnership for the purpose of investing in one or more QOF corporations or partnerships, and
- All investments made in the investment vehicle are made in cash; and
- Not less than 95 percent of the assets of which are equity investments in QOF corporations or partnerships.

D. *State and Community Dynamism Fund.* Creation of a fund to support public and private investment, including capital for QOZs, and existing small business and community economic development

---

[469]New QOZB reporting requirements for every applicable qualified opportunity zone business shall furnish to the qualified opportunity fund a written statement in such manner and setting forth such information to enable such qualified opportunity fund to meet the requirements of section 6039(b)(5). Annual report factors include: unemployment rate; number of persons working in the tract; poverty rates; median family income; demographic information; average annual rent paid; number of residences; rate of home ownership; average value of residential property; number of affordable housing units; number and percentage of residents not employed; number of new business starts; and distribution of employees by NAICS.

programs and incentives to underserved business and communities with an annual authorization of $1 billion, and a minimum allocation for states: 0.9 percent of total authorization.

To receive an allocation, states would be required to certify that they will use the funds to:

- Build capacity in underserved communities;
- Advance investment in minority-, women-, and veteran-owned businesses;
- Address workforce development;
- Align priorities to support affordably priced housing.

Funds allocated may be used for any eligible use in a low-income community and eligible "high-impact" projects include:

- Businesses with fewer than 200 employees;
- Project that provide community goods or services;
- Affordable housing.

States will be required to report annually to Treasury.

(P) Open OZ Items: Proposals. Treasury should attempt to clarify certain open issues in order to eliminate some of the potential pitfalls that exist in the program. The following lists a number of items along with proposals for consideration:

1. **QOF Certification/Noncertification**
   - Proposals:
     - **(a)** As to certification, allow established QOFs to be grandfathered and scale newly adopted respective self-certification requirements since smaller funds have less restrictive and burdensome regulatory requirements based upon the amount of capital funds raised.
     - **(b)** Involuntary certification should be warranted only if the QOF exhibits willful and continuous noncompliance over an extended period of time (e.g., a QOF that willfully fails to achieve the 90 percent investments standard for a period of three consecutive testing days).

2. **Stimulate the Investment in Operating Businesses to Promote Job Growth**
   - The regulations make it difficult for existing businesses to qualify for OZ investment due to the treatment of their ownership of

"existing" property as nonqualifying property relative to the 70 percent substantially-all test.

○ Proposals:

(a) Allow tangible property purchased on or before December 31, 2017 to be treated as qualified property if the business acquires new tangible property over a 30-month period that exceeds its aggregate adjusted basis of all existing property at the beginning of such period.

(b) Create a portions of the business rule for QOZBs, similar to the NMTC regulations that maintain separate books and records for the portion of the business that does qualify.

3. **Use of Intangible Property:** The final regulations provide, with respect to any taxable year, that a substantial portion (defined at 40 percent) of the intangible property of a QOZB is required to be used in the active conduct of a trade or business in the QOZB. Tangible property is considered "used in the active conduct" of a trade or business in a QOZB if the use of the intangible property is normal, usual, or customary in the conduct of the trade or business and the intangible property is used in a QOZB in the performance of an activity of the trade or business that contributes to the generation of its gross income.

○ Proposals:

(a) The phrase "used in an act of conduct of a trade or business" should be defined as the commercial use of intangible property for the management, development, manufacturing, and sale or lease of goods and services to generate gross income, which would include the development of intangible for sale so long as a substantial amount (40 percent) of the services to develop the intangible are performed in the OZ.

(b) Provide that the portion of the intangible property used in the active conduct of the business is determined based on the portion of gross income generated by the commercial use of such intangible property over the total gross income from the use of the intangible property.

(c) Provide that the situs where the intangible property is used in the act of conduct of the trade or business is consistent with where the business tangible property is used in the active conduct of such business.

4. **Working Capital Safe Harbor (70 Percent Tangible Property Test):**

    ◦ The regulations do not define what is meant by a "working capital safe harbor." However, the regulations suggest by example that a business only qualifies while it possesses working capital assets that were funded through QOF equity investments. This is a potential trap for the unwary, especially for "start-up" businesses that are required to spend their QOF equity in the early stages of a start-up period, leaving them with no working capital and, therefore, uncertainty of whether they can rely on the benefits of the safe harbor for the remainder of the start-up period.

    ◦ Proposal:

    (a) The regulations should define working capital safe harbor as the 31-month period beginning with the date of the infusion of working capital assets, regardless of when such assets are consumed during that period.

5. **Valuation of Contributed Property:**

    ◦ Proposal:

    (a) For purposes of the 70 percent substantiality test, contributed property should be valued at fair market value at the time the property is contributed. The regulations provide that a QOZB's contributed assets (which are "bad" assets) use a "fluctuating" number for the 70 percent substantiality test. Accordingly, even if the business satisfies the 70 percent on the testing date, it can fail to do so if the local real estate market continues to appreciate. Valuing contributing property that is treated as a bad asset based on increased market values creates uncertainty and is counterintuitive to the objective of the incentive. Accordingly, the regulations should provide that for purposes of the 70 percent test, contributed property is to be valued at a fixed number at each testing date equal to the fair market value of the property <u>at the time</u> it was contributed to the QOZB.

6. **Stimulate Investment in Affordable Housing (typically under long-term land use restrictions):**

    ◦ Proposals:

    (a) Allow properties that are converted from market rate to affordable rental housing to be considered original use property.

    (b) Reduce the substantial improvement threshold for affordable housing to 20 percent of the adjusted basis of the acquired property over a 24-month period or $6,800 per unit, whichever is greater.

(c) Allow investors to recognize tax benefits for any decrease of value of their affordable housing investment at the 2026 inclusion date.

(d) Allow qualified "pre-investments" to be made by QOFs after the QOZ designation expires provided the requirements of low-income community under Section 45D(e) are met.

7. **Related-Party Developer Fees:**

   ◦ Proposal:

   (a) Related party's expenditures for services to construct property (e.g., developer fees) should satisfy the "purchase" requirements, even if paid to a related party. The regulations should include an example where an eligible entity pays reasonable expenditures to a related party for services to construction property do not violate the purchase requirement as defined in Section 179(d)(2).

8. **Treatment of Reimbursements of Predevelopment Expenditures to a Related Party.**

   ◦ Proposal:

   (a) Regulations should clarify that reimbursements to related parties for reasonable expenditures incurred within 24 months of the reimbursement satisfy the purchase requirement as provided by section 179(d)(2).[470]

p. 1100. *Insert the following as Appendix 13B:*

APPENDIX 13B

Tax Compliance Checklist for U.S. Taxpayers' Investment in Qualified Opportunity Funds Pursuant to 26 U.S. Code § 1400Z-2

July 24, 2019. This Appendix has been prepared by Paul Saint-Pierre of PSP Advisors LLC. Mr. Saint-Pierre is the principal advisor of PSP Advisors LLC. He specializes in advising and consulting with business development companies, private equity real estate funds, opportunity

---

[470]See also Blaine G. Saito, "Agency Coordination and Opportunity Zones," *Fordham Urban Law Journal*, Vol. 48, No. 5, September 1, 2021, Northeastern University School of Law Research Paper No. 422. Available at SSRN: https://ssrn.com/abstract=4038534

zone funds, mutual funds (investment companies), real estate investment trusts, institutional co-investment programs, real estate capital investment banking, and secondary market transactions of investment interests issued by alternative assets funds. Any comments and inquiries regarding this federal tax compliance checklist can be directed to Paul Saint-Pierre at Paul@PSP-Advisors.com.

REF	FEDERAL TAX COMPLIANCE ITEM	REFERENCE: INTERNAL REVENUE CODE	REFERENCE: IRS PROPOSED REGULATIONS AND FORMS
	ELIGIBLE GAIN ASSESSMENT		
1	**U.S. Taxpayers Only:** The eligible taxpayer is a person who may recognize gains for purposes of federal income tax accounting, including foreign investors who file U.S. federal tax returns (see Item 8 below).		§ 1.1400Z2(a)-1(b)(1)
2	**Sources of *Eligible Gain*:** The realized capital gain that is an *eligible gain*, and thus eligible for deferral under 26 USC 1400Z-2(a), is any amount treated as a short-term capital gain, long-term capital gain, unrecaptured Section 1250 gain, and capital gain net income in the case of Section 1256 contracts and Section 1231 property, for federal income tax purposes. If a taxpayer receives QOF *eligible interests* in exchange for the provision of services to (i) a qualified opportunity fund (i.e., carried interest) or (ii) a person in which the QOF holds a direct or indirect equity interest, then the QOF *eligible interest* is not a QOF *qualifying investment*. (See Item 11A below for the definition of QOF *qualifying investment* and see Item 11B below for the definition of QOF *eligible interest*.)	The term *eligible gain* is described in 26 USC 1400Z-2(a)(1)	§ 1.1400Z2(a)-1(b)(2)(i)(A)§ 1.1400Z2(a)-1(b)(9)

REF		FEDERAL TAX COMPLIANCE ITEM	REFERENCE: INTERNAL REVENUE CODE	REFERENCE: IRS PROPOSED REGULATIONS AND FORMS
3		**Tax Work Papers:** The realized capital gain, which is earmarked for deferral as an *eligible gain*, is documented in tax work papers with regards to the federal tax recognition date for the capital gain transaction event, transaction facts, transaction documents, its tax attributes (e.g., short-term capital gain, long-term capital gain, etc.), tax reports and statements, and the analysis of related parties in the capital gain transaction event.		§ 1.1400Z2(a)-1(b)(5)
		See Items 4, 5, and 6 below regarding related party compliance requirements. See Exhibit 1 for potential sources of *eligible gain*.		
4		**Related-Party Compliance Rule #1:** The realized capital gain, which is earmarked for deferral as an *eligible gain*, does not arise from a sale or exchange with a person who, within the meaning of 26 USC 1400Z-2(e)(2), is related to the taxpayer who recognizes the capital gain or who would recognize the capital gain if 26 USC 1400Z-2(a)(1) did not apply to defer recognition of the capital gain.	26 USC 1400Z-2(e)(2)26 USC 267(b)26 USC 707(b)(1)	§ 1.1400Z2(a)-1(b)(2)(i)(C)
5		**Related-Party Compliance Rule #2 (Partnerships and Pass-Through Entities Only):** If an *eligible gain* is not deferred by a partnership or other pass-through entities, then a gain in a partner's distributive share is an *eligible gain* with respect to the partner (taxpayer) only if it is an *eligible gain* with respect to the partnership and it did not arise from a sale or exchange with a person that, within the meaning of 26 USC 1400Z-2(e)(2), is related to the partner (taxpayer).		§ 1.1400Z2(a)-1(c)(2)(ii)(C) § 1.1400Z2(a)-1(c)(3)

REF		FEDERAL TAX COMPLIANCE ITEM	REFERENCE: INTERNAL REVENUE CODE	REFERENCE: IRS PROPOSED REGULATIONS AND FORMS
		Therefore, a partner's involvement in a transaction with the partnership that gives rise to a related-party transaction may reduce the amount of *eligible gain* as reported to the partner on Schedule K-1. Review the facts and circumstances.		
6		**Related-Party Compliance Rule #3:** Gain is not eligible for deferral if such gain is realized upon (a) the sale or other transfer of property to a QOF in exchange for an eligible interest or (b) the transfer of property to an eligible taxpayer in exchange for an *eligible interest*. See Item 14C below.		§ 1.1400Z2(a)-1(b)(2)(iv)
7		**Time Period for *Eligible Gain* Recognition:** The *eligible gain* would be recognized for federal income taxes before January 1, 2027, if 26 USC 1400Z-2(a)(1) did not apply to defer recognition of the capital gain.	26 USC 1400Z-2(a)(1)	§ 1.1400Z2(a)-1(b)(2)(i)(B)
8		**Capital Gain Reporting:** The realized capital gain, which is earmarked for deferral as an *eligible gain*, will be reported on, or rolled up onto, one of the following IRS forms in the tax year of the federal tax recognition date:		
8	A	**Individual taxpayer:** IRS Schedule D (Form 1040) Capital Gains and Losses and/or IRS Form 4972 Tax on Lump-Sum Distributions		IRS Schedule D (Form 1040) Capital Gains and Losses and/or IRS Form 4972 Tax on Lump-Sum Distributions
8	B	**Corporate taxpayer** (including corporate tax filers of any of IRS Forms 1120, 1120-C, 1120-REIT, 1120-RIC, 1120S, etc.): IRS Schedule D (Form 1120) Capital Gains and Losses or IRS Schedule D (Form 1120S)		IRS Schedule D (Form 1120) Capital Gains and Losses or IRS Schedule D (Form 1120S)
8	C	**Partnership taxpayer:** IRS Schedule D (Form 1065) Capital Gains and Losses		IRS Schedule D (Form 1065) Capital Gains and Losses

REF		FEDERAL TAX COMPLIANCE ITEM	REFERENCE: INTERNAL REVENUE CODE	REFERENCE: IRS PROPOSED REGULATIONS AND FORMS
8	D	**Estate and Trust taxpayer:** IRS Schedule D (Form 1041) Capital Gains and Losses and/or IRS Form 4972 Tax on Lump-Sum Distributions		IRS Schedule D (Form 1041) Capital Gains and Losses and/or IRS Form 4972 Tax on Lump-Sum Distributions
9		**180-Day Investment Period:** *Eligible gain* will be treated as a *qualifying investment*, provided the *eligible gain* is invested in a qualified opportunity fund during the 180-day period beginning on the date of such asset sale or exchange that resulted in the *eligible gain*. The first day of the 180-day period is the date on which the capital gain would be recognized for federal income tax purposes, without regard to the deferral available under Section 1400Z-2. Other rules apply: Section *1256 Contracts:* The 180-day period for investing capital gain net income from Section 1256 contracts in a QOF begins on the last day of the taxable year. Section *1231 Capital Gain Net Income:* The 180-day period for investing capital gain net income from Section 1231 property in a QOF begins on the last day of the taxable year. Partnership *Partners:* In the case of a taxpayer who is a partner in a partnership, the 180-day period generally begins on the last day of the partnership's taxable year, because that is the day on which the taxpayer/partner would be required to recognize the gain if the gain is not deferred. The proposed regulations, however, provide an alternative for situations in which the taxpayer/partner knows (or receives information) regarding both the date of the partnership's gain and the partnership's decision not to elect deferral under Section 1400Z-2.	26 USC 1400Z-2(a)(1)(A)	§ 1.1400Z2(a)-1(b)(4) § 1.1400Z2(a)-1(b)(2)(iii) § 1.1400Z2(a)-1(b)(2)(iii) § 1.1400Z2(a)-1(b)(4)(ii)(B) § 1.1400Z2(a)-1(b)(4)(ii)(C) § 1.1400Z2(a)-1(c)(2)(iii)(A) § 1.1400Z2(a)-1(c)(2)(iii)(B)

REF		FEDERAL TAX COMPLIANCE ITEM	REFERENCE: INTERNAL REVENUE CODE	REFERENCE: IRS PROPOSED REGULATIONS AND FORMS
		In that case, the taxpayer/partner may choose to begin his or her own 180-day period on the same start date for the partnership's 180-day period. Capital *Gain Dividends Received by RIC and REIT Shareholders.* If an individual RIC or REIT shareholder receives a capital gain dividend (as described in Section 852(b)(3) or Section 857(b)(3)), the shareholder's 180-day period with respect to that gain begins on the day on which the dividend is paid. ***Undistributed Capital Gain Received by RIC and REIT Shareholders.*** If Section 852(b)(3)(D) or Section 857(b)(3)(D) (concerning undistributed capital gains) requires the holder of shares in a RIC or REIT to include an amount in the shareholder's long-term capital gain, the shareholder's 180-day period with respect to that gain begins on the last day of the RIC or REIT's taxable year.		
10		*Eligible Gain* **and** *Qualifying Investment* **Reporting:** The election to defer the recognition of capital gain, and the amount of *eligible gain* invested in QOF *qualifying investment(s)*, is, or will be, recorded on IRS Form 8949 Sales and Other Dispositions of Capital Assets.		See Instructions for IRS Form 8949 (2018) and Form 8949 (2018)
		QUALIFYING INVESTMENTS IN QUALIFIED OPPORTUNITY FUNDS ("QOFs")		
11	A	*Qualifying Investment:* The term *qualifying investment* means an *eligible interest* (as defined in § 1.1400Z2(a)-1(b)(3)), or portion thereof, in a QOF to the extent that a deferral election applies with respect to such *eligible interest* or portion thereof.		§ 1.1400Z2(b)-1(a)(2)(xvi)

REF		FEDERAL TAX COMPLIANCE ITEM	REFERENCE: INTERNAL REVENUE CODE	REFERENCE: IRS PROPOSED REGULATIONS AND FORMS
11	B	*Eligible Interest:* For purposes of 26 USC 1400Z-2, an *eligible interest* in a QOF is an equity interest issued by the QOF, including preferred stock or a partnership interest with special allocations. Thus, the term *eligible interest* excludes any debt instrument within the meaning of Sections 1275(a)(1) and 1.1275-1(d).		§ 1.1400Z2(a)-1(b)(3)
12		**QOF Verification:** Receipt of the QOF's initial self-certification and all semi-annual compliance reports on IRS Form 8996, Qualified Opportunity Fund. This form certifies that the corporation or partnership was organized to operate as a QOF. All of the IRS Forms 8996 may be retained in the taxpayer's tax workpapers. **NOTE:** The QOF completes and files IRS Form 8996 with its annual tax return, including extension periods. The QOF investor/taxpayer is not required to attach IRS Form 8996 to his/her/its federal income tax return. **DUE DILIGENCE NOTE:** It is important to verify (a) that the QOF has executed its self-certification process, (b) the QOF's employer identification number, (c) the first month that the QOF chose to be a QOF, (d) that qualified opportunity zone property ratios are compliant with the minimum 90 percent requirement, (e) any penalties incurred with regard to qualified opportunity zone property noncompliance, and (f) that the QOF has complied with IRS Form 8996 federal filing requirements. Also request and receive the QOF's organization documents (i.e., corporate articles of incorporation, LLC members' agreement, partnership agreement); the organization's		See Instructions for IRS Form 8996 (2018) and IRS Form 8996 (2018)

REF		FEDERAL TAX COMPLIANCE ITEM	REFERENCE: INTERNAL REVENUE CODE	REFERENCE: IRS PROPOSED REGULATIONS AND FORMS
		documents, as filed with the state department of corporations, must include a statement of its purpose for investing in qualified opportunity zone property by the end of its first QOF year. The documents should also include a description of the qualified opportunity zone business(es) that the QOF expects to engage in, either directly or indirectly through a first-tier operating entity.		
13		**Invest in QOF after Certified First Month Election:** The taxpayer's acquisition of QOF *eligible interest* must occur no earlier than the first month the QOF chose to be a qualified opportunity fund. Note the first month election on IRS Form 8996 Part 1 line 4 that the QOF chose to be a qualified opportunity fund.		§ 1.1400Z2(d)-1(a)(1)(iii)(B)
14	A	**Acquisition of QOF *Eligible Interest* from QOF for Cash:** The taxpayer's acquisition of QOF *eligible interest* is (i) an equity interest of corporate shares or partnership units, (ii) newly issued by the QOF, and (iii) was, or will be, effected with (a) cash (from any source) or other property, (b) within 180 days after the capital gain event date (federal tax recognition date), and (c) before June 29, 2027.		§ 1.1400Z2(a)-1(b)(3)(i) § 1.1400Z2(a)-1(b)(4)(i) § 1.1400Z2(a)-1(b)(9)
14	B	**Acquisition of QOF *Eligible Interests* from a Person Other than QOF:** Alternatively, a taxpayer may acquire QOF *eligible interest* from a person other than the QOF that issued the QOF eligible interest. The acquiring taxpayer may treat the investment as a QOF *qualifying investment* (26 USC 1400Z-2(a)(1)(A)) to the extent that the taxpayer/acquirer allocates eligible gain in the secondary market purchase of the QOF *eligible*	26 USC 1400Z-2(c) and 26 USC 1400Z-2(e)(1)	§ 1.1400Z2(a)-1(b)(9)(iii)

REF		FEDERAL TAX COMPLIANCE ITEM	REFERENCE: INTERNAL REVENUE CODE	REFERENCE: IRS PROPOSED REGULATIONS AND FORMS
		interest. The taxpayer-acquirer is required to start its ten-year hold period on the transaction date to access the election under 26 USC 1400Z-2(c). Since the seller of QOF securities may own and hold both QOF *qualifying investments* (26 USC 1400Z-2(e)(1)(i)) and nonqualifying investments in the same QOF (see 26 USC 1400Z-2(e)(1)(ii)), it is imperative that the taxpayer/acquirer conduct proper due diligence to determine that the seller is in fact selling its inventory of QOF *qualifying investments* based on a review of the seller's tax records and the receipt of adequate representations and warranties. Both transaction parties should report the transaction to the QOF to ensure the accuracy of QOF securities ownership records. **TRANSACTION DUE DILIGENCE NOTE: The QOF does not have any tax compliance obligation to distinguish and report between (i) issued QOF** *qualifying investment* **securities and (ii) other issued nonqualifying investment securities, so it is likely that the QOF will be unable to warrant and guarantee the understandings between the transaction parties.**		
14	C	**Acquisition of QOF** *Eligible Interests* **in Exchange for Property Contribution:** The taxpayer may contribute property in exchange for QOF eligible interests. The regulations for determining the amount of, and the tax cost basis of, the QOF eligible interests can be complex and should be interpreted according to the specific facts and circumstances for each taxpayer who intends to contribute property in exchange for QOF *eligible interests.* No deferral for		§ 1.1400Z2(a)-1(b)(10)(i)(B) § 1.1400Z2(a)-1(b)(2)(iv)

REF	FEDERAL TAX COMPLIANCE ITEM	REFERENCE: INTERNAL REVENUE CODE	REFERENCE: IRS PROPOSED REGULATIONS AND FORMS
	gain realized upon the acquisition of an eligible interest: Gain is not eligible for deferral under 26 USC 1400Z-2(a)(1) if such gain is realized upon the sale or other transfer of property to a QOF in exchange for an eligible interest (see Item 14C below) or the transfer of property to an eligible taxpayer in exchange for an *eligible interest*.		
15	**Tax Work Papers:** In the case of (i) acquiring multiple QOF *qualifying investments* over time in one or more QOFs and (ii) the utilization of capital gain as *eligible gain* with various tax attributes, it is recommended that the taxpayer maintain tax work papers to identify and assign each *eligible gain* to each QOF *qualifying investment* to enable proper recognition of deferred capital gain, including basis adjustments, when any QOF *qualifying investment* is disposed of. (See Items 17 and 18, below.)		§ 1.1400Z2(a)-1(b)(5) § 1.1400Z2(a)-1(b)(6) § 1.1400Z2(a)-1(b)(7) § 1.1400Z2(a)-1(b)(8)
	TAX COMPLIANCE MAINTENANCE ITEMS DURING HOLD PERIOD		
16	**Tax Work Papers:** The taxpayer should annually request and receive IRS Form 8996, from each QOF, for all QOF *qualifying investments*, and then review and retain them in tax work papers. Receive confirmation from the QOF that the IRS Form 8996 was timely filed with its federal tax return.		
17	**Tax Work Papers:** It is incumbent on each taxpayer to maintain proper records to track the tax cost basis in each QOF qualifying investment, since the adjusted cost basis is employed to report the recognition amount of capital gain and tax liabilities no later than the tax year ending December 31,	26 USC 1400Z-2(b)(2)	

REF	FEDERAL TAX COMPLIANCE ITEM	REFERENCE: INTERNAL REVENUE CODE	REFERENCE: IRS PROPOSED REGULATIONS AND FORMS
	2026. The initial tax basis for the QOF *qualifying investment* is $0, with periodic step-up in tax cost basis depending on the holding period.		
18	**Recognition of Deferred Capital Gain:** All deferred capital gain is recognized at the earlier of (1) the dates of sale or exchange for a QOF *qualifying investment* or (2) December 31, 2026. The tax attributes of the *eligible gain* is associated with each QOF *qualifying investment*; when the taxpayer recognizes the deferred capital gain in gross income, the tax attributes of the recognized capital gain will be identical to the tax attributes of the *eligible gain* that was deferred. The recognized amount of capital gain is equal to the lesser of (i) the original deferred capital gain or (ii) the fair market value of the QOF *qualifying investment* on the date of capital gain inclusion in gross income, less the taxpayer's tax cost basis in the QOF *qualifying investment*.	26 USC 1400Z-2(b)(2)(A)	§ 1.1400Z2(a)-1(b)(5)
19	**Sale of QOF *Investment Interest* and Reinvestment to Defer Recognition of Capital Gain Prior to January 1, 2027:** If the taxpayer disposes of his or her **entire** QOF *qualifying investment* prior to January 1, 2027, and if the taxpayer wishes to further defer the amount of capital gain that is otherwise to be included in income, then the taxpayer must invest the amount of the Section 1400Z-2(b) recognizable capital gain into the original QOF or into another QOF during the maximum 180-calendar day period beginning on the date when the taxpayer disposed of its **entire** QOF *qualifying investment*. The minimum 10-year hold for the election under 26 USC 1400Z-2(c) is restarted on the reinvestment date.	26 USC 1400Z-2(b) and 26 USC 1400Z-2(c)	§ 1.1400Z2(a)-1(b)(4)(ii)(D)(1) § 1.1400Z2(a)-1(b)(4)(ii)(D)(2)IRS NARRATIVE: Tacking

REF	FEDERAL TAX COMPLIANCE ITEM	REFERENCE: INTERNAL REVENUE CODE	REFERENCE: IRS PROPOSED REGULATIONS AND FORMS
20	**Permitted Transactions Featuring Nonrecognition of Deferred Capital Gain:** The Opportunity Zone regulations stipulate a list of permitted transactions, with the taxpayer acting alone or in concert with the other shareholders in a QOF, that will result in the nonrecognition of deferred gain (i.e., not capital gain inclusion events). These noninclusion events generally include (a) IRC Section 721 contributions, (b) IRC Section 708(b)(2)(A) mergers or consolidations, (c) a partnership's deemed or actual distribution of property and cash, provided the fair market value is less than or equal to the partner's tax cost basis in its QOF *investment interest*, and (d) a transfer of a QOF's assets in an acquisitive asset reorganization described in IRC Section 381(a)(2) (i.e., a qualifying Section 381 transaction).		IRS NARRATIVE: Exceptions for Disregarded Transfers and Certain Types of Nonrecognition Transactions § 1.1400Z2(b)-1(c)(6)(ii)(A) § 1.1400Z2(b)-1(c)(6)(ii)(B) § 1.1400Z2(b)-1(c)(6)(ii)(C) § 1.1400Z2(b)-1(c)(6)(iii) § 1.1400Z2(b)-(c)(7)(iv)(B) § 1.1400Z2(b)-1(c)(11)(i)(B)
21	*Special Rule for Investments Held for at Least Ten Years: In the case of any* QOF qualifying investment held by the taxpayer for at least ten years and with respect to which the taxpayer makes an election under this clause (26 USC 1400Z-2(c)), the tax cost basis of such property shall be equal to the fair market value of such QOF qualifying investment on the date that the QOF qualifying investment is sold or exchanged.	26 USC 1400Z-2(c)	
22	**Sale or Exchange of QOF Qualifying Investment:** A QOF *qualifying investment* must be (i) held for at least ten years after the taxpayer's investment date for each QOF *qualifying investment* and (ii) disposed of prior to December 31, 2047, to qualify for the election under 26 USC 1400Z-2(c). Tax cost basis adjustments are required in the case of QOF partnership *qualifying investments* and QOF partnership assets.	26 USC 1400Z-2(c)	§ 1.1400Z2(c)-1 § 1.1400Z2(c)-1(b) § 1.1400Z2(c)-1(b)(ii)(2)

REF	FEDERAL TAX COMPLIANCE ITEM	REFERENCE: INTERNAL REVENUE CODE	REFERENCE: IRS PROPOSED REGULATIONS AND FORMS
23	**Tax-Free Treatment of Recognized Capital Gain After Ten-Year Hold:** Taxpayers who hold QOF *qualifying investments* for more than ten years are also eligible to tax-free: (a) capital gain reported on Schedule K-1, (b) QOF REIT distributed and undistributed capital gain as reported on IRS Form 1099-DIV and/or IRS Form 2439, (c) capital gain net income from IRC Section 1231 property reported on Schedule K-1, (d) unrecaptured IRC Section 1250 gain reported on Schedule K-1, IRS Form 1099-DIV, and/or IRS Form 2439, (e) capital gain net income from IRC Section 1231 property reported on Schedule K-1, (f) unrecaptured IRC Section 1250 gain reported on Schedule K-1, IRS Form 1099-DIV, and/or IRS Form 2439, and (g) IRC Section 1245 Property Recapture, all of the above in connection with a QOF's sale of qualifying opportunity zone property. **NOTE:** The applicable regulations pertaining to this specific topic matter are complex and merely proposed at this time; § 1.1400Z2(c)-1 applies to taxable years of a taxpayer, QOF partnership, QOF S corporation, or QOF REIT, as appropriate, that end on, or after, the date of publication in the **Federal Register** of a Treasury decision adopting these proposed rules as final regulations. Accordingly, it is advised that taxpayers become familiar with all of the proposed regulations of § 1.1400Z2(c)-1 and to review the final regulations when available and update their compliance programs.		IRS NARRATIVE 1: Special Election for Direct Investors in QOF Partnerships and QOF S Corporations IRS NARRATIVE 2: Ability of QOF REITs to Pay Tax-Free Capital Gain Dividends to Ten-Plus-Year Investors § 1.1400Z2(c)-1

REF	FEDERAL TAX COMPLIANCE ITEM	REFERENCE: INTERNAL REVENUE CODE	REFERENCE: IRS PROPOSED REGULATIONS AND FORMS
24	**Permitted tacking events to extend and protect the ten-year minimum holding period** *Holding period for QOF investment received in a qualifying Section 381 transaction, a reorganization described in Section 368(a)(1)(E), or a Section 1036 exchange.* For purposes of 26 USC 1400Z-2(b)(2)(B) and 1400Z-2(c), the holding period for QOF stock received by a taxpayer in a qualifying Section 381 transaction in which the target corporation was a QOF immediately before the acquisition and the acquiring corporation is a QOF immediately after the acquisition, in a reorganization described in IRC Section 368(a)(1)(E), or in an IRC Section 1036 exchange, is determined by applying the principles of section 1223(1). *Holding period for controlled corporation stock.* For purposes of 26 USC 1400Z-2(b)(2)(B) and 1400Z-2(c), the holding period of a *qualifying investment* in a controlled corporation received by a taxpayer on its *qualifying investment* in the distributing corporation in a qualifying section 355 transaction is determined by applying the principles of IRC Section 1223(1). *Tacking with donor or deceased owner.* For purposes of 26 USC 1400Z-2(b)(2)(B) and 1400Z-2(c), the holding period of a *qualifying investment* held by a taxpayer who received that *qualifying investment* as a gift that was not an inclusion event, or by reason of the prior owner's death, includes the time during which that *qualifying investment* was held by the donor or the deceased owner, respectively.	26 USC 1400Z-2(b)(2)(B) and 26 USC 1400Z-2(c)	§ 1.1400Z2(b)-1(d)(1)(ii) § 1.1400Z2(b)-1(d)(1)(iii) § 1.1400Z2(b)-1(d)(1)(iv)

REF	FEDERAL TAX COMPLIANCE ITEM	REFERENCE: INTERNAL REVENUE CODE	REFERENCE: IRS PROPOSED REGULATIONS AND FORMS
25	*Notification of Section 1400Z-2(c) Election by QOF Partner or QOF Partnership:* A QOF partner (taxpayer) must notify the QOF partnership of an election under section 1400Z-2(c) to adjust the basis of the qualifying QOF partnership interest that is disposed of in a taxable transaction. Notification of the 26 USC 1400Z-2(c) election, and the adjustments to the basis of the qualifying QOF partnership interest(s) disposed of or to the QOF partnership asset(s) disposed of, is to be made in accordance with applicable forms and instructions. Similar requirements are set forth in proposed § 1.1400Z2(b)-1(h)(4) regarding QOF S corporations and QOF S corporation shareholders.	26 USC 1400Z-2(c)	§ 1.1400Z2(b)-1(h)(3) § 1.1400Z2(b)-1(h)(4)

Exhibit 1   POTENTIAL SOURCES OF ELIGIBLE GAIN

	SOURCES OF ELIGIBLE GAIN	IRS FORMS
A	Sale/exchange of liquid and illiquid investment securities (capital assets)	Form 1099-B Form 8949 Schedule D
B	LTCG distributions from REIT and RIC investments	Form 1099-DIV-Box 2a Schedule D
C	Undistributed LTCG from REITs and RIC investments	Form 2439-Box 1a Schedule D
D	Pass-through STCG and LTCG capital gain from partnerships, S corporations, estates, and trusts	Schedule K-1-Boxes 8 and 9a Schedule D
E	Taxable part of gain on sale of personal residence (net of home sales gain exclusion) and other real estate investments	Form 1099-S Form 8949 Schedule D
F	Installment sale income on capital assets	Form 6252 Schedule D

Exhibit 1 POTENTIAL SOURCES OF ELIGIBLE GAIN

	SOURCES OF ELIGIBLE GAIN	IRS FORMS
G	Capital gain net income on IRC Section 1231 property	Form 4797 Form 6252 Form 8824 Schedule K Schedule D
H	Gain from the sale of business property	Form 4797-Part I Schedule K-1- Box 10 Schedule D
I	Gain from casualty and theft	Form 4684 Schedule D
J	Capital gain net income from IRC Section 1256 contracts and straddles	Form 6781 Schedule K-1- Box 11 Schedule D
K	Capital gain or (loss) from like-kind exchanges	Form 8824 Schedule D
L	Unrecaptured IRC Section 1250 Gain (Real Property)	Form 1099-DIV- Box 2b Schedule K-1-Box 9c Form 2439-Box 1a Unrecaptured Section 1250 Gain Worksheet Schedule D
M	Collectibles	Form 1099-DIV- Box 2d Schedule K-1-Box 9b 28% Rate Gain Worksheet Schedule D
N	The taxable part of a gain from a sale of IRC Section 1202 qualified small business stock	Form 2439-Box 1c 28% Rate Gain Worksheet Schedule D

CHAPTER 14

Joint Ventures with Universities

§ 14.1 INTRODUCTION

p. 1111. *Add the following new subsection at the end of this section:*

(b) The 2017 Tax Act (Pub. L. No. 115-97)

The 2017 Tax Act (Pub. L. No. 115-97) ("the Tax Act") made significant changes to the taxation of charitable organizations, including colleges and universities, with one particular provision targeted at certain colleges and universities, some of whom will be subject to an additional new tax on their investment income.

Because of the numerous uncertainties amid likely substantial tax liabilities, some of which must be paid via estimated tax payments, many affected colleges and universities have requested that Treasury delay implementation of this and other new provisions so that they have a reasonable period of time to "estimate our new tax burden" and "budget for this dramatic tax increase."[32.1] In addition to interpretive guidance from Treasury, organizations and practitioners await revised Form 990-T, whereby UBIT, the focus of many of the changes, will be reported, as well as Form 4720, Return of Certain Excise Taxes Under Chapters 41 and 42, in regard to reporting under § 4968 (tax applicable to certain private colleges and universities on investment income) and § 4960 (tax on excessive compensation).

[32.1] "Practitioners, College Groups Endorse Endowment Tax Delay," *Daily Tax Report* (BNA), May 31, 2018.

(i) Tax on Investment Income—§ 4968. The Tax Act imposes a new 1.4 percent excise tax on the "net investment income" of endowments of private colleges and universities with more than 500 students and net assets of at least $500,000 per student. The tax applies to private institutions with at least 500 tuition-paying[32.2] students, more than half of whom are located in the United States, with an aggregate fair market value of assets (other than assets used directly in carrying out exempt purposes) of at least $500,000 per student at the end of the prior tax year. See § 4968(b)(1). The assets and investment income of related organizations are included in the calculations. See § 4968(d)(1). The investment assets language mirrors the language of § 4942, the private foundation payout rules.[32.3]

The provision raises numerous questions, including the definition of "tuition-paying students." In comments to Treasury, it has been suggested that tuition paying be determined by the tuition invoice sent to the student and not be measured by how the tuition is paid (i.e., by scholarship or other assistance).[32.4] In regard to determining net investment income, § 4968 refers to the regulations under § 4940(c), the rules relating to private foundation excise tax on investment income for guidance.

In regard to the meaning of "related organization," § 4968(d)(1) specifies that assets and net investment income of related organizations controlled by it or described in § 509(a)(3) are to be included, except that assets and income not intended or available for the use or benefit of the reporting educational institutions shall not be included. "Related organization" is defined as any organization that controls or is controlled by such institution, is controlled by one or more of the same persons that control the educational institution, is a supported organization under § 509(f)(3), or is a supporting organization under § 509(a)(3).

Illustrating the complexity of identifying related organizations for purposes of determining assets and income to be included is one of many comment letters sent to the Treasury Secretary. In one such letter, an "applicable educational institution" has suggested that:

> related organizations be defined to only include those organizations that are operating organizations (not passive investments) more than 80 percent

---

[32.2]Language specifying "tuition-paying" students was added back in to § 4968 by the Bipartisan Budget Act of 2018 enacted on February 9, 2018, after having been stricken in the debate on the Tax Reform Act of 2018.

[32.3]"News from IRS, Treasury and the Hill" panel presentation at the ABA Tax Section Exempt Organizations Committee meeting, May 11, 2018, as reported by *EO Tax Journal* 2018-111 (June 6, 2018); eotaxjournal.com.

[32.4]May 24, 2018, letter from Emory University to the Secretary of the Treasury, as reprinted in *EO Tax Journal* 2018-108 (June 1, 2018); eotaxjournal.com.

controlled by the [reporting entity] (similar to the rules under IRC Section 368(c) and IRC Section 1563(a)(1) or are Type I supporting organizations under § 509(a)(3)). . . .[32.5]

In other words, this institution is suggesting that control be measured by an 80 percent threshold and that only one type of supporting organization under § 509(a)(3), Type I, be included. This suggestion illustrates the complex structural relationships of colleges and universities that have numerous affiliated organizations that they may not control and/or whose assets are restricted to use in their respective tax-exempt purposes. Unless the suggested definitions are applied, the educational institution asserts that because it can neither direct funds from those related organizations it does not control nor obtain relevant financial information for computational purposes, including the assets and income of such entities would result in the imposition of the § 4968 tax on organizations other than private colleges and universities.[32.6]

In June 2018 the IRS released Notice 2018-55 relating to calculation of gain in regard to the sale of assets under § 4968. Section 3 of the Notice provides that for property held on December 31, 2017, and continuously thereafter to the date of its disposition, the basis of the property for purposes of determining gain is to be not less than its fair market value on December 31, 2017. In other words, in an effort to minimize the impact of the tax, organizations will have a step up in basis for assets that, when sold, will be subject to the tax. The Notice further states that taxpayers can rely on this guidance until further guidance is issued. As the IRS explained in its press release accompanying issuance of the Notice:

> A private college or university, subject to the new 1.4 percent excise tax on net investment income, that sells property at a gain generally may use the property's fair market value at the end of 2017 as its basis for figuring the tax on any resulting gain, the Internal Revenue Service said today. In many instances, this new stepped-up basis rule will reduce the amount of gain subject to the new tax. Normal basis rules will continue to apply for calculating any loss.[32.7]

NOTE

Although modern technology will facilitate an appraisal as of the December 31, 2017, date at the time of a future sale, organizations subject to the tax and contemplating imminent sale of a property may want to consider obtaining an appraisal sooner rather than later.

[32.5]*Ibid.*
[32.6]*Id.*
[32.7]https://www.irs.gov/newsroom.

(ii) The 2017 Tax Act (Pub. L. No. 115-97); Final Regulations; Section 4968. The final regulations, which were published in September 2020, generally follow those proposed in mid-2019 with a few changes based on the comments received by the IRS. They largely track the proposed regulations.

Educational institutions that otherwise meet the requirements of § 4968 need to review their inventory of intangible assets to determine if those assets can be included in the definition of exempt assets and, therefore, be excluded from the educational institution's asset base.[32.8] Similarly, educational institutions should review and thoroughly document whether they can establish a reasonable method to determine a reasonable cash balance, including the calculation of three months of operating expenses, to further increase the amount that is excluded from the asset base.[32.9]

The final regulations generally adopt the "tuition-paying students" definition of the proposed regulations: scholarships awarded by the institution do not constitute tuition paid on behalf of the student, but scholarships from third parties are considered payments of the student's tuition. However, the final regulations add that, in determining whether a student is tuition-paying, government grants—federal, state, and local—are taken into account.

While the final regulations eliminate cross-references to regulations under § 4940(c) and create new terms to define net investment income for § 4968 purposes, organizations must still be aware of § 4940(c) language to determine their gross investment income. The final regulations provide that gross investment income generally means income from interest, dividends, rents, payments with respect to securities loans (§ 512(a)(5)), and royalties, but not including such income to the extent that is included in computing the tax imposed by IRC section 511. Royalties flowing from trademarks on the institution's name or logo, as well as from intellectual property that has been donated to or purchased by the institution, are not excluded.

[32.8]The final regulations outline circumstances in which intangible assets may be treated as being used directly in carrying out an educational institution's exempt purpose; for example, royalty income would be excluded from investment income; patents, copyrights, and so on are treated as assets the institution uses "directly" in carrying out its exempt purpose. But, trademarks on the institution's logo or name and intellectual property that has been donated or sold to the institution will not be considered assets used directly to fulfill exempt purposes. The final regulations include detailed examples of assets considered to be used and not used directly in carrying out an institution's exempt purposes.

[32.9]The final regulations permit an organization to calculate a reasonable cash balance using any reasonable method and replaces the safe harbor in the proposed regulations with one based on three months of operating expenses allocable to the organization's program services.

CAVEAT
Educational institutions should review all calculations of gross investment income, capital gain net income, and their allowable deductions to accurately determine their § 4968 liability.

Educational institutions must be aware of the changes to the definitions of control, attribution, and constructive ownership under § 318(a)(2). The final regulations generally provide that an educational institution controls a nonstock organization if the institution (or at least one of its managers, directors, officers, trustees, or employees) can:

- Appoint or elect more than 50 percent of the nonstock organization's governing body.
- Require the nonstock organization to make an expenditure, or prevent an expenditure.
- Require the nonstock organization to perform any act that significantly affects its operations, or prevent the nonstock organization from performing such an act.

Similar rules apply to determine whether an educational institution is controlled by a nonstock organization.[32.10]

Educational institutions will have to review the applicability of each definition of control based on their particular relationships with other organizations.[32.11]

(iii) Siloing of UBIT Activities—§ 512(a)(6).   As described in subsection 2.1(1), many of the changes in the Tax Reform Act of 2017 that affect this sector involve modifications to UBIT. New IRC § 512(a)(6) requires exempt organizations with more than one unrelated trade or business to separately compute income and losses from those trades or businesses when computing UBIT. In other words, organizations are required to "silo" their revenue and losses for each trade or business so that the losses from one business cannot be used to offset the revenue of another. Although the IRS has added this issue to its Fiscal 2018 Priority Guidance Plan, colleges and

---

[32.10] An organization is controlled by one or more persons that also control the institution if more than 50 percent of the members of the governing body of the other organization are directly or indirectly controlled by persons that comprise 50 percent or more of the governing body of the educational institution. The final regulations also include complex rules for determining control of or by a trust.

[32.11] The final regulations state that any asset of a related organization used directly in carrying out the institution's exempt purpose should be excluded from § 4968(b)(1)(D). The final regulations also provide that an asset of a related organization that is treated as an asset of the educational institution will be considered to be used directly in carrying out exempt purposes if: (1) the related organization is described in § 501(c)(3), and (2) the asset is being used directly in carrying out the related organization's exempt purpose. The analysis in this subsection is based on a client alert published by EY's Exempt Organization Tax Services (September 2020).

universities in the meantime must struggle with determining reasonable approaches, including the allocation of expenses for dual use facilities when making these computations. (The allocation of expense issue has also been added to the FY 2018 Priority Guidance Plan.)

To the extent colleges and universities have not yet "spun off" unrelated activities, such as summertime use of facilities, to a separate for-profit entity, this has now become a front and center issue, particularly because for-profits are not subject to siloing of revenue and expenses.

Of course, spinning off activities presents its own set of issues, such as the computation of UBIT from related entities under § 512(b)(13), the extent to which NOLs from an activity previously under the umbrella of a § 501(c)(3) can be utilized by the successor entity, and so on.

Incident to the question of spinning off one or more activities into a for-profit entity is the choice of entity (e.g., LLC or corporation). It has been suggested that the C corporation may deserve favorable consideration in creating a joint venture for several reasons, including the 21 percent tax rate, the § 1202 gain exclusion, and AMT changes.[32.12] On the other hand, use of a C corporation would mean that an asset sale would be taxable at the entity level; any income that might be related to the exempt organization's charitable purposes could not be excluded from income, nor could interest, rents, royalties, or annuity income that would be exempt if there was pass-through under § 512(b)(13). Other considerations are whether joint venture partners prefer flow-through treatment of income, expenses, and so on, and whether there should be an activity by activity approach to the choice of entity question.[32.13]

Practitioners and organizations are awaiting regulatory or other guidance on the interpretation of trade or businesses so they can make appropriate accounting adjustments; they are awaiting revised Form 990-T as well. Many have requested delay in implementation of this provision.

(iv) Employer-Provided Fringe Benefits—§ 512(a)(7). In the Taxpayer Certainty and Disaster Tax Relief Act of 2019, § 512(a)(7) was retroactively repealed, by which expenses incurred by tax-exempt organizations in providing certain types of fringe benefits were converted into unrelated business taxable income.

(v) Excess Compensation Tax—§ 4960. New § 4960 imposes a 21 percent excise tax on applicable tax-exempt organizations in regard to annual compensation that exceeds $1 million, including excess parachute payments contingent on separation from employment, paid to a covered employee applicable tax-exempt organization and certain 80 percent

---

[32.12]Jim Hasson and Virginia Gross, "Hot UBIT Topics, Tax Cuts and Jobs Act of 2017: Changes to UBI," presented at 2018 Representing and Managing Exempt Organizations, Washington, DC, April 27, 2018.
[32.13]*Id.*

controlled entities.[32.14] The tax applies to organizations exempt from tax under § 501(a) and political organizations under § 527(e)(1).[32.15] Employees are current employees who are one of the five highest-paid employees during the taxable year and former employees during the preceding year. See Chapter 2, subsection 2.1, 1.C.

(vi)   Denial of Deduction for Right to Purchase Stadium Tickets—§ 170(l). One of the more clear-cut changes in the Tax Reform Act of 2017, but one with a dramatic negative impact on the revenue of colleges and universities with athletic programs, is in § 170(l), which disallows a deduction for amounts paid to or for the benefit of an institution of higher education where the taxpayer receives, directly or indirectly, the "right to purchase tickets for seating at an athletic event in an athletic stadium of such institution."

§ 14.3   COLLEGES AND UNIVERSITIES IRS COMPLIANCE INITIATIVE

p. 1119. *Insert the following new subsections at the end of this section:*

(a)   Publication of Nondiscrimination Policy

The IRS issued Revenue Procedure 2019-22, 2019-22 I.R.B. 1260, which updates Revenue Procedure 75-50, 1975-2 C.B. 587, relating to school non-discrimination policies, for the first time in almost 45 years. The revision relates to the manner of publicizing a tax-exempt school's policy prohib-iting discrimination on the basis of race and, in recognition of modern technology, adds a third method for a private school to satisfy the notice requirement by using its Internet website. Now, in addition to publicizing nondiscrimination policies in newspapers, radio, and television, schools can publish their nondiscrimination policy on their primary publicly acces-sible Internet homepage at all times during the taxable year (excluding out-ages and maintenance windows) "in a manner reasonably expected to be noticed by visitors to the homepage." Publicly accessible means that a visi-tor does not have to input information such as a username and password to access the page. A link to a different page where the notice appears or a notice that "appears in a carousel or only by selecting a dropdown or by

---

[32.14]With reference to Treas. Reg. § 1.414(c)-5 relating to the power to appoint 80 percent of the members of an organization's governing body.
[32.15]Also included are organizations under § 521 (farmer cooperatives) and organizations that have excluded tax under § 115(1) income of states and municipalities derived from a public utility or the exercise of any essential governmental function.

hover (mouseover)" is not acceptable. If a hosted website is used, the notice must appear on "its primary landing page" within the hosted website.

(b) Varsity Blues Investigation

The so-called Varsity Blues scandal described in Section 2.11 may lead the IRS to reexamine the practices of colleges and universities to receive contributions from donors whose children attend the schools.[1]

§ 14.5 FACULTY PARTICIPATION IN RESEARCH JOINT VENTURES[131.1]

p. 1130. *Delete the first sentence of footnote 132 and replace it with the following:*
See, for example, Gen. Couns. Mem. 39, 863 (Dec. 9, 1991).

p. 1131. *Add footnote 135.1 at the end of the first paragraph on this page:*
[135.1] At the leading research institutions, a distribution of net royalty income to the faculty member/inventor ranges from 33 percent to 50 percent. Most revenue distributions are net so that the technology transfer offices may recoup the cost of protecting the intellectual property. For example, at MIT, the institution deducts a 15 percent administrative fee from gross royalty income, and then further deducts all costs associated with protecting the intellectual property . . . before finally distributing one-third of what's left to the inventor (http://web.mit.edu/tlo/documents/MIT-TLO/ownership-guide.pdf). In contrast, Yale, after recovery of all out-of-pocket costs incurred to protect the intellectual property, deducts a 10 percent administrative fee, allowing the inventor to receive a 50 percent share on the first $100,000 with a tiered system applying to excess proceeds (https://ocr.yale.edu/faculty/policies/yale-university-patent policy). The materials in this subsection are adapted from a paper submitted by Stephanie Hooper at Georgetown University Law Center, Special Topics in Exempt Organizations, the Ownership and Exploration of Faculty Intellectual Property.

p. 1131. *Insert the following new paragraphs after the first paragraph on this page:*
In the context of the foregoing discussion regarding joint ventures with faculty members such as professors, scientists, or researchers, the following four examples analyze the potential of private inurement or impermissible private benefit.

1. **Scenario 1**
   ◦ Faculty member is not a disqualified person under § 4958.[135.2]
        A university and a researcher who is not in a position of authority, does not directly report, has no role in hiring decisions, and no responsibility for approving the operating budget or capital

---

[131.1]See "Universities and Joint Ventures: Navigating the Rules with Examples" by Javan A. Kline. The following examples are based on Mr. Kline's paper, which was submitted in the Georgetown Law School Special Topics in Exempt Organization graduate tax class.
[135.2]See subsection 5.4(a) regarding disqualifying persons in intermediate sanctions relative to excess benefit transactions.

expenditures of the college, invent a therapeutic drug that is patentable. According to the agreement between the university and the researcher, the university retains ownership of the invention and ultimately receives a patent relative to the invention. The university grants the researcher the right to receive 30 percent of the royalties on the patent consistent with the university standards on a semi-annual basis. In addition, the researcher receives a salary with benefits along with royalties on the invention as incentive base compensation. Both the university and the researcher share in the revenues generated by the invention on a proportionate basis. However, the university maintains control over the patent, how it is used, and the stream of income it generates.[135.3] Under this scenario, since the research is scientific under § 501(c)(3), it should not create impermissible private benefit or private inurement or give rise to excess benefit tax under § 4958, because the researcher is not a disqualified person. The foregoing terms are in accordance with industry standards and the university contains control; therefore, it should not create UBIT for the university nor jeopardize its exempt purpose.

2. **Scenario 2**

   ◦ Researcher is a disqualified person.

   A university enters into a joint venture agreement with a researcher who is the dean of one of the colleges and is in charge of scientific research. As dean, the researcher plays a significant role in faculty hiring, supervising research, and is principally responsible for reviewing the operating budget and capital expenditures at the college. The researcher invents a therapeutic drug that is patentable. According to the agreement between the university and the researcher, the university owns the invention and ultimately receives the patent for the invention. The researcher receives 30 percent of the university's royalties on the patent, which is consistent with university standards. This is in addition to the researcher's salary and benefits. Royalties on the invention is an incentive-based compensation and the parties share in the revenue on a proportional basis. It is critical that the university maintain control over the patent, its use, and the stream of income it generates. Accordingly, the arrangement should not generate private inurement or excess benefit taxes because the arrangement is consistent with the university norms.

[135.3]This example was in large part from proposed Reg. § 53.4958-5(d) (never promulgated).

CAVEAT

It is advisable that the university satisfy the rebuttable presumption required under Treas. Reg. § 53-4958-6, especially since the arrangement is likely to be under greater scrutiny because of the disqualified person's participation.[135.4]

---

3. Scenario 3

° The researcher is a disqualified person and owns the invention.

Assume the same facts as scenario 2, but the researcher owns the invention and ultimately receives the patent thereof. Not only does the university receive only a minority percentage of the royalties with the balance going to the researcher, but the researcher maintains control over the patent, its use, and the stream of income. Accordingly, such an arrangement would not be consistent with university standards, because the researcher is a disqualified person. It is likely that the arrangement would be considered an excess benefit, subjecting both the disqualified person and the university to tax requiring correction under § 4958. Though unlikely, depending upon the scale, the arrangement could be viewed as impermissible private benefit, which could impact on the university's tax-exempt status.

4. Scenario 4

° Use of C corporation blocker.

The university plans to enter into a joint venture with a for-profit entity and forms a 100 percent owned subsidiary (C corporation) to own its interest in the venture ("LLC"). The university will own a 25 percent voting membership interest through its subsidiary, and the for-profit partner will own a 75 percent voting membership interest. The LLC will manufacture clothing, sweatshirts, and other consumer-oriented products of interest to students. The C corporation shall serve as a blocker and be subject to income tax on its share of income from the LLC, while the university should not be subject to UBIT on any dividends received from the C corporation. As a result, the university's exempt status should not be jeopardized because of the use of the corporate blocker. If, however, the activities of the ventures are substantially related to the university's exempt purpose and it retains control, it may be beneficial for the university

---

[135.4]This example was adapted in large part from proposed Reg. 53-4958-5(d) (never promulgated) (see Example 3).

to use a supporting organization as a member of the LLC or otherwise invest directly into the venture, because in such a case there should be no UBIT under the principles of Rev. Rul. 2004-51.[135.5]

§ 14.6 NONRESEARCH JOINT VENTURE ARRANGEMENTS

(a) Basic Functions

p. 1134. *Delete the citation in footnote 155 and replace it with the following:*
Id.

p. 1135. *Delete the citation in footnote 156 and replace it with the following:*
Id.

(b) Entertainment, Sports, and Travel Activities

(v) Travel Tours. p. 1149. *Delete the citation in footnote 229 and replace it with the following:*
See Reg. § 1.513-7, Example 2.

§ 14.7 MODES OF PARTICIPATION BY UNIVERSITIES IN JOINT VENTURES (REVISED)

(c) Distance Learning

(ii) Massive Open Online Courses (MOOCs). p. 1159. *Insert the following after the second full paragraph on this page:*

Between 2012 and 2015, more than 25 million people enrolled in MOOC courses.[279.1] Although the rate of course completion is low (2.1 million as of April 2015), educators are excited about the global reach of MOOCs and are finding that persons in both developed and undeveloped countries are using them not only for academic purposes but for career improvement as well.[279.2] Moreover, both "[e]conomically and academically disadvantaged populations are taking particular advantage of MOOCs."[279.3] Interestingly, although these findings were based on a study by persons affiliated with Coursera, a for-profit entity, they indicate that MOOCs are furthering charitable and educational § 501(c)(3) goals by reaching disadvantaged persons

---

[135.5]See subsection 4.6, Rev. Rul. 2004-51, ancillary joint ventures, page 374, and so on.

[279.1]C. Zhenghao, B. Alcorn, G. Christensen, N. Eriksson, D. Koller, and E. Emanuel, "Who's Benefiting from MOOCs, and Why," *Harvard Business Review*, Sept. 22, 2015; https://hbr.org/2015/09/whos-benefiting-from-moocs-and-why.

[279.2]Id.

[279.3]Id.

across the globe—"[a]mong non-student completers, people with lower socioeconomic status, people with lower levels of education, and people from developing countries are all more likely to report educational benefits."[279.4]

Thus, although MOOCs are at an early stage of development and there are numerous issues that need to be resolved, such as the low rate of completion, it does appear that participating universities are furthering their § 501(c)(3) goals even when partnering with a for-profit company. Of course, potential tax issues will have to be addressed as MOOCs evolve.

During 2020, as a result of the COVID-19 pandemic, distance learning has received increased attention in view of technological advances that have upended educational programs throughout the country. Brandname universities that had previously been immune to the forces that have driven innovation and transformation have had to examine online learning and the remote teaching phenomenon. Indeed, distance learning may be the wave of the future. Many believe that the shutdown is not a temporary problem; it needs to be seized as a chance to pursue innovation to "student-centered" instruction; that is, to make learning more effective. This is especially important in small college towns that can benefit from the new market tax credit structure as well as the opportunity zone legislation (see Chapter 13).[279.5]

[279.4]*Id.*

[279.5]The author acknowledges the excellent analysis of universities and joint ventures prepared by Javan A. Kline. The update that follows is based on a paper submitted by Mr. Kline, in the graduate tax program at Georgetown University Law Center, entitled "Universities and Joint Ventures: Navigating the Rules with Examples." Mr. Kline adds that while Coursera and edX were at the forefront of offering MOOCs from major universities (see generally https://about.coursera.org/ and https://www.edx.org/about-us), such companies now also offer certificates and degrees from major universities; one can earn a Professional Certificate in Data Science from Harvard University on edX.org (see https://www.edx.org/professional-certificate/harvardx-data-science) or a Master of Computer and Information Technology from the University of Pennsylvania on coursera.org (see https://www.coursera.org/degrees/mcit-penn). Also, a number of leading universities also partner with for-profit technology companies such as 2U (see https://2u.com), who are generally referred to as online program management (OPM) providers (see https://www.insidehighered.com/digital-learning/article/2017/10/25/opms-fee-service-growing-revenue-share-models-dominate), to offer online degrees. Generally speaking, the university provides the degree, reputation, professors, and educational components and the for-profit partner provides the technology infrastructure and support to provide the content in an online environment. For example, an OPM provider partners with numerous universities conferring degrees online, including Yale University and Northwestern University (see https://2u.com/partners/). Such arrangements may be based on a revenue-sharing or a fee-for-services model (see https://www.insidehighered.com/digital-learning/views/2019/10/30/shaky-legal-ground-revenue-sharing-agreements-student-recruitment; https://www.insidehighered.com/digital-learning/article/2017/10/25/opms-fee-service-growing-revenue-share-models-dominate; https://www.insidehighered.com/news/2020/02/05/online-program-management-copanies-face-washington-microscope; https://www.insidehighered.com/digital-learning/article/2019/09/13/century-foundation-calls-colleges-take-control-outsourced-online).

EXAMPLE

An illustration of the fast-paced developments surrounding MOOCs is the SPOC (small private online course), a combination of traditional and digital approaches. With SPOCs, students watch MOOC-type lectures independently *and* attend a class that offers traditional student–teacher interaction.[279.6] In this manner, students benefit from the classroom approach of getting feedback and instruction from a teacher as well as interacting with other students, while having the flexibility of viewing MOOC video lectures at a time and place convenient for them. This variation is interesting because it addresses some of the criticisms of MOOCs by supplementing the MOOC Internet lecture with the classroom benefits of personal feedback, interaction, and the human administration of quizzes and tests.

CAVEAT

The revenue-sharing arrangements can provide more than 50 percent of the revenue from the venture to be provided to the for-profit OPM provider; as a result, universities need to make sure that such arrangements do not jeopardize their tax-exempt status or create unexpected UBIT.

(f)   University Endowments

(ii)   Government Scrutiny of University Endowments.   p. 1167. *Add the following to the end of this subsection:*

On December 2, 2015, the Congressional Research Service released a report that provided background information on college and university endowments and summarized various options for changing their treatment.[318.1] Some of the policy changes mentioned in the report include imposing an annual payout requirement on endowment funds, taxing endowment earnings, and reducing the value of the charitable deduction for gifts to endowments on the basis of the lapse of time between an endowment gift and its ultimate use for charitable purposes.[318.2]

Following the Congressional Research Service report, on February 8, 2016, the Senate Committee on Finance and House Committee on Ways and Means sent a letter to the president of Southern Methodist University requesting information regarding the operations of Southern Methodist

---

[279.6]"Education in the Digital Age: What Tax-Exempt Universities Should Consider Before Engaging in a Distance Learning Venture with a For-Profit Company," unpublished paper written by Patricia Spiccia in connection with graduate tax program at Georgetown Law Center. A copy of the paper is on file with the author.

[318.1]Molly F. Sherlock et al., Cong. Research Serv., R44293, "College and University Endowments: Overview and Tax Policy Options" (2015).

[318.2]*Id.*

University and the status of the university's endowment.[318.3] The letter was sent to 56 private universities and colleges with endowments of more than $1 billion for the purpose of assisting the Committees in conducting additional oversight of how colleges and universities are using endowment assets to fulfill their charitable and educational purpose.[318.4] Specifically, the letter expressed concerns that many colleges and universities have raised tuition far in excess of inflation despite their large and growing endowments.[318.5] The questionnaire contained 13 questions, including areas of inquiry such as endowment management, endowment spending and use, donations, and conflicts of interest.[318.6]

	CAVEAT
Committee members are continuing to consider ways to address the rising cost of tuition, but navigating the tax code as it relates to colleges and universities raises complex tax issues.	

As discussed in subsection 14.1(b)(i), Congress did enact a 1.4 percent tax on the net investment income of applicable educational institutions.

p. 1167. *Add the following new subsection:*

(g) Other Commercial Arrangements

A New Jersey property tax case has raised some interest.[318.7] The case involved a property tax exemption claimed by a restaurant operated on the campus of Kean University. The restaurant was located in the University's new science, technology, and math building; the New Jersey Educational Facilities Authority, which held title to the property, financed the building's construction. The Kean University Foundation hired a third party to operate the restaurant and pay the Foundation a $250,000 annual fee and 12.5 percent of the restaurant's gross revenues. The third-party manager had full discretion over all management decisions.

[318.3]Letter from Orrin G. Hatch, Chairman, Senate Committee on Finance; Kevin Brady, Chairman, House Committee on Ways and Means; and Peter J. Roskam, Chairman, House Committee on Ways and Means Oversight Subcommittee, to Dr. R. Gerald Turner, president, Southern Methodist University (Feb. 8, 2016) (on file with tax analysts).

[318.4]*Id.*

[318.5]*Id.*

[318.6]*Id.*

[318.7]*Gourmet Dining, LLC, v. Union Township and New Jersey Educational Facilities Authority*, New Jersey Appellate Division, May 31, 2019 (Docket No. A-4799-17T3).

The local tax authority assessed property tax on the restaurant portion of the building. The restaurant claimed that it should be exempt from property tax on the grounds that, pursuant to New Jersey law, it is "used for public purposes" by attracting people to the campus who otherwise might not have known about the University's particular academic programs; was providing an upscale restaurant choice for visiting parents; had provided more than $259,000 in scholarship funds for University programs (the Foundation was required to allocate at least 10 percent of restaurant revenue to scholarships); and whose staff was principally comprised of university students.

The New Jersey appellate court held that the restaurant was "unique" in that it was located on campus and was viewed by the University as a recruiting tool. The court distinguished the restaurant "because it provides students, other members of the University community, and visitors to the campus an alternative dining experience . . . concept of a public purpose 'must expand when necessary to encompass changing public needs of a modern dynamic society.'"

While an appeal petition has been filed with the New Jersey Supreme Court, the opinion has been cited as potentially heralding the expansion of the concept of "public purposes" where there is some public benefit from a private, for-profit use of government property.[318.8]

CAVEAT

This case involved a local property tax, not a determination by the IRS as to exemption under Code § 501(c)(3). Your author suspects that an IRS analysis could result in a conclusion that the exempt organization may be involved in a joint venture or other partnership or contractual arrangement that is being operated in a manner similar to commercial for-profit restaurants and that the income therefrom is taxable as UBI. Alternatively, depending on whether the restaurant's activity is substantial in comparison to the Foundation's total activity, it could jeopardize the entity's exempt status, but for it having been established as a state educational institution, as it appears from the court opinion.

(h) UBIT Implications for Universities with the Emergence of NIL Deals[318.9] (New)

(i) NIL Policies. In June 2021, the National Collegiate Athletic Association ("NCAA") adopted a name, image, and likeness ("NIL") policy that allows

---

[318.8]Carl Rizzo, "NJ Tax Stop: Private, For-Profit Property May Be Tax-Exempt," *Law* 360, July 16, 2019; https://www.law360.com/articles/1178757/nj-tax-stop-private-for-profit-property-may-be-tax-exempt.
[318.9]This subsection was drafted in substantial part by DyTiesha Dunson and is based on research in her graduate tax paper at Georgetown University Law Center, Advanced Topics in Exempt Organizations (2022).

current student-athletes to be compensated for their NIL as of July 1, 2021, regardless of whether a state has an NIL law in place.[318.10] The NIL policy is broad and has a lot of room for interpretation for states wanting to enact their own NIL laws. The NCAA's NIL policy provides the following guidance:

1. Individuals can engage in NIL activities that are consistent with the law of the state where the school is located. Colleges and universities may be a resource for state law questions.

2. College athletes who attend a school in a state without an NIL law can engage in this type of activity without violating NCAA rules related to name, image, and likeness.

3. Individuals can use a professional services provider for NIL activities.

4. Student-athletes should report NIL activities consistent with state law or school and conference requirements to their school.[318.11]

Prior to the NIL policy adoption, the NCAA had a strict amateurism rule for its participants, the student-athletes. It defined an amateur as "someone who does not have a written or verbal agreement with an agent, has not profited above his/her actual and necessary expenses or gained a competitive advantage in his/her sport."[318.12] This rule meant that, excluding necessities like tuition, meals, books, and room and board, athletes were not able to receive any other compensation. While the adoption of the NIL policy has allowed student-athletes to be compensated, it also may have led to unintended tax consequences for universities. More specifically, universities may now be subject to the unrelated business income tax ("UBIT") for payments received if they are involved in NIL deals with their student-athletes.

(ii) History of NCAA NIL Policy. After World War II, the NCAA adopted a set of principles that were intended to ensure amateurism in collegiate sports.[318.13] These principles were upheld until the policy change in 2021. The NCAA's compensation rule has long been publicly debated and challenged in the courts. For example, in 2014 a California district court ruled that the NCAA's compensation rules were an unlawful restraint of trade and enjoined them from prohibiting member schools from giving student-athlete scholarships up to the full cost of attendance at their

---

[318.10]Michelle Brutlag Hosick, "NCAA Adopts Interim Name, Image, and Likeness Policy," NCAA Media Center, June 30, 2021, https://www.ncaa.org/news/2021/6/30/ncaa-adopts-interim-name-image-and-likeness-policy.aspx.
[318.11]*Id.*
[318.12]*What is amateurism?*, https://ncaa.egain.cloud/kb/EligibilityHelp/content/KB-2219/What-is-amateurism.
[318.13]*History*, https://www.ncaa.org/sports/2021/5/4/history.aspx.

respective schools.[318.14] Furthermore, in December 2020, the U.S. Supreme Court granted certiorari to a class action case against the NCAA that involved current and former student-athletes who alleged that the NCAA rules limiting compensation in exchange for athletic services violated Section 1 of the Sherman Act.[318.15] While the Supreme Court's opinion focused only on a narrow subset of the NCAA's compensation rule, Justice Kavanaugh's concurrence made it clear that the NCAA would soon have to make changes to its compensation rules. Specifically, he writes that the "NCAA's business model of using unpaid student-athletes to generate billions of dollars in revenue for the colleges raises serious questions under the antitrust laws."[318.16]

While the events above are important in discussing the history of the NIL debate, the catalyst in changing the NCAA's NIL policy came in 2019 when California passed the Fair Pay to Play act, which made it illegal for state schools to prohibit student-athletes from making money off their NIL.[318.17] Following the enactment of California's law, 27 other states passed their own NIL laws, with some going into effect as early as July 1, 2021.[318.18] State passage of NIL laws led the NCAA to enact an interim nationwide NIL policy because a failure to do so would allow states that had NIL policies a competitive advantage in recruitment over states that did not. Although the NCAA's policy is temporary, it will remain in place until Congress enacts federal legislation on the topic or until the NCAA adopts a new rule.

(iii) UBIT Issues. Most colleges and universities are tax-exempt because of their educational purpose under § 501(c)(3). See subsection 2.5(d). Furthermore, since student-athletes have traditionally been considered unpaid amateurs engaging in extracurricular activities rather than in profitable professions, collegiate sports, and any necessary expenses paid for and services given to student-athletes, have been deemed an extension of the university's educational mission.[318.19] Tax-exempt organizations are

---

[318.14]*O'Bannon v. NCAA*, 802 F.3d 1049, 1052-53 (9th Cir. 2015). The district court also required that the NCAA hold up to $5,000 per year of deferred compensation in a trust for student-athletes until they leave college. *Id.* at 1053. However, on appeal, the Ninth Circuit held that the district court's ruling allowing students to be paid cash compensation of up to $5,000 per year was erroneous. *Id.*

[318.15]*NCAA v. Alston*, 141 S.Ct. 2141, 2151 (2021).

[318.16]*Id.* at 2168.

[318.17]Dan Murphy, "Everything You Need to Know about the NCAA's NIL Debate," ESPN, Sept. 1, 2021, https://www.espn.com/college-sports/story/_/id/31086019/everything-need-know-ncaa-nil-debate. The law was originally set to become effective in 2023, but was amended to become effective September 1, 2021.

[318.18]*Id.*

[318.19]Mike McIntire, "The College Sports Tax Dodge, *New York Times*, Dec. 28, 2017, https://www.nytimes.com/2017/12/28/sunday-review/college-sports-tax-dodge.html; see Rev. Rul. 67-291, providing that university athletic programs conducted for the physical development and betterment of students are an integral part of the educational process, and thus qualify for federal tax exemption.

generally not required to pay taxes on its activities unless the activities are subject to UBIT. UBIT applies if (1) the business activity income comes from a trade or business, (2) that is regularly carried on, and (3) is not substantially related to the exempt organization's purpose.[318.20] In order for UBIT to apply to a university's income, the venture must not be substantially related to the performance of the school's educational mission and does not constitute a substantial part of the school's overall educational activities.[318.21]

In the past, universities typically have not worried about UBIT in the context of their athletic programs. When UBIT was first considered by Congress in 1950, it concluded that "income of an educational organization from admission to football games is not subject to UBIT because athletic activities of schools are substantially related to its educational program."[318.22] This determination has consistently been used by universities against any potential application of UBIT on their athletic program income. However, now that student-athletes are able to take advantage of NIL deals, there is an argument that income from those NIL deals with university involvement often structured as joint ventures can be subject to UBIT. The following are examples of NIL deal structures with possible UBIT implications.

(1) Structure 1: NIL Deal Tax Implication: Corporate Sponsorship Agreements. Structure 1 involves three parties: the university athletic department, the student-athlete, and a sponsor. In this structure, the sponsor arranges separate deals with both the athletic department and the student-athletes. The deal with the athletic department will typically require the department to promote the sponsor's logo or use the sponsor's product for funding. If accepted, the deal with the student-athletes will require the athlete to promote the sponsor's product, by an agreed-to means, in exchange for pay and/or product.

The sponsorship deal between the athletic department and sponsor could potentially have UBIT implications. There is a specific UBIT exemption for certain sponsorship payments under section 513(i). (See subsection 8.4(h).) However, that exception arguably does not apply to this structure.

The qualified sponsorship payment exception applies if the sponsor does not receive a substantial return benefit for its payment to the university for the use of its name, logo, or product line.[318.23] In Structure 1,

---

[318.20]Section 512(a).

[318.21]See sections 8.3, 511(a), and 513(a).

[318.22]Matthew J. Mitten, "Commercialized Intercollegiate Athletics: A Proposal for Targeted Reform Consistent with American Cultural Forces and Marketplace Realities," *Journal of Intercollegiate Sport*, 202, 213-14 (Dec. 2009) (quoting H.R. Rep. No. 2319, 81st Cong., 2d Sess. (1950), reprinted in 1950-2 C.B. 380, 409; and S. Rep. No. 2375, 81st Cong., 2d Sess. (1950), reprinted in 1950-2 C.B. 483, 505).

[318.23]This exception does not apply to advertisements.

the sponsor can be seen as receiving a substantial return benefit. The sponsor is benefiting not only from the athletic department's use of their logo or product, but also by being able to strike deals with each student-athlete. Many student-athletes will accept the individual deals with the sponsor because of the arrangement between the athletic department and sponsor. Furthermore, the university will likely have heavy involvement in negotiating the transaction between the student-athlete and sponsor.

CAVEAT

Employees of the athletic department will likely provide input on whether the student-athlete should accept the deal. Considering the publicity received by the athletic department for negotiating the deal on behalf of its athletes, with the publicity the sponsor receives for entering the deal, a determination can be made that the deal between the sponsor and athletic department provides the sponsor with a substantial return benefit.

If the qualified sponsorship payment exception does not apply, payments made to the university from the sponsor may be subject to UBIT. One of the requirements for income to be subject to UBIT is that it is not substantially related to the exempt organization's purpose. College athletics are generally viewed as substantially related to a school's educational purpose. However, now that student-athletes are getting paid, college athletics are arguably not furthering an educational mission because they are no longer unpaid amateurs engaging in extracurricular activities. Assuming the other requirements of UBIT are met, the payments made to the university from the sponsor can be subject to UBIT.

(2) Structure 2: NIL Deal Tax Implication: Group Licensing Deals. Structure 2 involves three parties: the university, the student-athlete, and a third party. In this structure, a group of athletes combine their NILs and license them collectively to a third party. The university will also license its official trademark and logos to the third party to place on merchandise. The athletes will receive a share of net revenue from the merchandise based on the use of their NIL and the university will receive a share of the net revenue in exchange for the use of its trademarks and/or logos.

The university should not be subjected to UBIT in the group licensing structure because of the royalty exemption.[318.24] The royalty exemption excludes payments for the use of intangibles such as trademarks, trade names, service marks, or copyrights from UBIT.[318.25] However, based on the

---

[318.24]Section 512(b)(2).
[318.25]See subsection 8.5(d).

facts, if this structure is recharacterized as payment for services, the royalty exemption may not apply.

CAVEAT

If the university agrees to pay royalties to the student-athlete for the use of their NIL on merchandise, the structure will start to look more like payment for services. This alternative structure will more likely subject the university to UBIT.

---

(3) Structure 3: NIL Deal Tax Implication: Booster Collectives. Structure 3 involves an alumni-funded "collective" that is used to provide student-athletes with lucrative endorsement deals in exchange for product promotion. The university or athletic department will not be a party to the transaction between the student-athlete and collective.

While the university is not a party in a Structure 3 deal, there may still be tax consequences. Universities with large amounts of money in the collective can use it as a tool to recruit student-athletes to the university. The collectives can be seen as indirect "pay for play" compensation by the university or payments for services by the university.[318.26]

According to the *Wall Street Journal*, the Kansas Jayhawks Barnstorming Tour is being organized by supporters as a collective that operates <u>outside</u> the normal university and its athletic department.

Collectives are companies, usually founded by well-connected and well-resourced alumni, to pool financial resources of the university's fan base and direct funds to the athletes, who are not able to profit from their name, image, and likeness under the rules set forth above.

CAVEAT

It was projected that the members of the title team could collectively make $1 million during a six-week tour to seven gyms around Kansas; they will sign autographs for fans, auction off game-worn sneakers, and shoot around but not play games or scrimmages during the event.

Some collectives operate using a subscription model that solicits monthly dues from members, while others function as a nonprofit, in fact, even as a 501(c)(3) organization in an attempt to make the donors' contributions tax deductible.

[318.26]See "Booster Collectives Shake Up Athletic Pay," *Wall Street Journal*, May 5, 2022.

Although interactions between boosters and recruits are not allowed in college sports, some collectives are skirting this by dangling lucrative endorsement deals to prospective athletics.

CAVEAT

There is growing fear that the best recruits will go wherever the money is the highest and that, without a collective, the university will miss out on the talent. At least 37 of the 65 schools in the five richest athletic conferences have at least one collective; ten more have similar deal entities.

Although NCAA rules prohibit NIL deals from functioning as an over-inducement to attend the school, and coaches cannot promise specific deals, they can certainly boast to the recruits about the school's collective pot of money or cite six-figure deals that star players have received.

CAVEAT

In Kansas, 6th Man Strategies, a limited liability company, has arranged half a dozen car deals, campaigns with local Wendy's and Applebee's and, in December 2021, added a 501(c)(3) charitable arm, Reaching Champions Joining Hearts Foundation, Inc., that has since raised more the $2 million. The majority of the revenue is anticipated to go to the Kansas basketball players (approximately 70 percent of ticket sales and profits from a series of silent auctions). The tour's first stop in Wichita in April generated about $125,000 in revenue from selling 250 VIP tickets for $75 each, more than 2,500 general admission tickets for $30, and another $30,000 from the auction.

CHAPTER 15

Business Leagues Engaged in Joint Ventures

§ 15.1 OVERVIEW

(a) General Rules

p. 1172. *Add the following to the end of footnote 7:*

See subsection 2.2(a); in May 2020, the IRS issued final regulations on donor disclosure providing for trade associations under § 501(c)(6) to no longer be required to disclose their large donors on Schedule B of Form 990.

p. 1175. *Add the following to the end of footnote 24:*

Rev. Proc. 2017-58 (the reporting exception for associations with nondeductible lobbying expenses is $115 for 2018).

p. 1175. *Delete Rev. Proc. 98-19 from footnote 26.*

(b) § 501(c)(6) and Joint Ventures

p. 1177. *Add the following to the end of the first full paragraph on this page:*

On April 28, 2015, the NFL announced it would be giving up its tax-exempt status.[40.1] The organization stated that the change in filing status made no material difference to the business and had become a distraction; however, many speculated that the league relinquished its tax-exempt status to avoid the requirement that it must publicly disclose its high-level executives' salaries.[40.2]

[40.1]See Darren Rovell, "NFL League Office Relinquishing Tax-Exempt Status," ESPN, Apr. 28, 2015, http://espn.go.com/nfl/story/_/id/12780874/nfl-league-office-gives-tax-exempt-status.

[40.2]Maxwell Strachan, "Why Did the NFL Voluntarily Give Up Its Tax-Exempt Status? Experts Weigh In," *Huffington Post*, Apr. 28, 2015, http://www.huffingtonpost.com/2015/04/28/nfl-tax-exempt-status_n_7166020.html.

(c) Definition of § 501(c)(6) Organizations

p. 1178. *Insert the following after the first sentence of the second full paragraph:*

In addition, the members of the business league must "have a voice in [its] operation" and there must be "meaningful extent of membership support."[45.1]

§ 15.2 THE FIVE-PRONG TEST (REVISED)

(a) Members with a Common Business Interest

p. 1181. *Delete language in footnote 63 and replace it with the following:*

Id. Cf. Rev. Rul. 83-164, 1983-2 C.B. 95 (organization representing diversified businesses that utilize computers manufactured by only one company is not exempt).

p. 1181. *Delete first Rev. Rul. citation in footnote 68 and replace it with the following:*

Id.

(b) Promoting the Common Business Interests

p. 1183. *Add the following paragraph at the end of paragraph (b):*

The IRS has recently released a memo (BNTA 2022-004), concluding that providing pension and health benefits to members do not further § 501(c)(6) common business interest. These activities relieve members of business expense and burden of separately providing for and managing their health and pension benefits; therefore, the activities are generally subject to tax as unrelated business trade or business and not substantially related under section 513. In addition, the IRS released two § 501(c)(6) denial letters (denial 202213010), similar to the organization described in Rev. Rul. 83-164, during which the taxpayer was directing its activities to the uses of specific products and solutions for only a segment of the industry, and not the entire line of business (see subsection 15.2(c)). In denial letter 202214015, the facts showed that the organization was not formed to promote the common business interest of a particular industry or trade, but rather to perform particular services for the members and promote their individual interests. The services to their members included financial analysis of their potential investment opportunities; in fact, an individual can only become a member if they are invited or are "accredited" investors and willing to invest in start-up businesses. The ruling cited *General Contractors Association of Milwaukee* 202 Fed. 2d. 633, 637 (7th Circuit, 1953), stating that the services provided inure to the benefits of the members and are more than substantial.

[45.1]PLR 201242016 (Oct. 19, 2012).

(c)   Activities

(ii)   Limitation on Particular Services for Individuals.   p. 1186. *Delete the General Counsel Memorandum citation at the beginning of footnote 95 and replace it with the following:*
> Id.

(d)   Commercial Activity for Profit

p. 1187. *Delete the language in footnote 100 and replace it with the following:*
> Id. at 420.

p. 1188. *Delete the language in footnote 103 and replace it with the following:*
> Rev. Rul. 58-294, 1958-1 C.B. 244.

§ 15.3   UNRELATED BUSINESS INCOME TAX

(a)   General Rules

p. 1192. *Delete the language in footnote 121 and replace it with the following:*
> PLR 199905031 (Feb. 5, 1999).

(b)   Exception for Indirect Investment in Ancillary Joint Ventures

p. 1193. *Delete the language in footnote 128 and replace it with the following:*
> PLR 200528029 (Apr. 20, 2005).

CHAPTER 16

Conservation Organizations in Joint Ventures

§ 16.1 OVERVIEW

pp. 1200–1201. *Insert the following to the end of footnote 1:*

For the 2013 tax year, the Urban Institute website reports 8,834 organizations classified as "environmental" on the basis of NTEE code classifications, with aggregate gross receipts of $12.2 billion and aggregate total assets of $25.6 billion. The largest organization in the environmental category, in terms of both gross receipts and total assets, is the National Geographic Society, with gross receipts of $686 million and total assets of $1.3 billion for 2013 (http://nccsweb.urban.org/PubApps/showOrgsByCategory.php?close=1&ntee=C, last visited March 29, 2016).

§ 16.2 CONSERVATION AND ENVIRONMENTAL PROTECTION AS A CHARITABLE OR EDUCATIONAL PURPOSE: PUBLIC AND PRIVATE BENEFIT

(a) IRS Ruling Position

p. 1201. *Insert the following to the end of footnote 2:*

PLR 201204020 (organization not exempt under § 501(c)(3) where its lake preservation activities were secondary to promoting the social and recreational activities of residents on the lake); PLR 201210044 (organization providing residential solar energy systems to low- and moderate-income families was not exempt because any environmental benefits to the public would be indirect and tangential); PLR 201221023 (organization denied exemption because its activities did not generate environmental benefits; rather, it acted as an intermediary that purchased carbon offsets from a commercial enterprise and resold them to businesses, which is an activity ordinarily conducted by commercial for-profit ventures); PLR 201405018 (IRS revoked charitable status of organization it determined to be primarily operated to benefit the founder's accounting practice clients by accepting donations of properties for which the clients claimed significant charitable contribution deductions); PLR 201451043 (IRS revoked charitable status of organization initially recognized as a private foundation, in part because grants it made to fund a botanical garden served the private interests of organizational managers; the public had limited access to the garden, which was enclosed by property owned by the organization's officers and was controlled by the officers); PLR 201514009 (IRS revoked charitable status of an organization it found to be primarily operating to facilitate grossly overstated façade easement contribution deductions for donors, citing *New Dynamics Foundation v. United States,* 70 Fed. Cl. 782 (2006), for the proposition that where an organization is actively participating in a scheme designed to facilitate tax avoidance it is not entitled to exempt status, because it is furthering a substantial nonexempt purpose); PLR 201531022 (activity of acquiring claims to clean up fuel spills from underground storage tank for a fee is a financing activity normally engaged in by for-profit entities such as banks and investment companies and not a charitable activity); PLR 201648020 (organization seeking exemption for restoring incorporator's residence, an historic landmark, denied exempt status based on multiple factors including inurement and impermissible private benefit).

(b) Judicial Holdings

p. 1207. *Delete the language in footnote 13 in its entirety and replace with the following:*

The special contribution percentage limitation and carryover rules were extended again by the Tax Increase Prevention Act of 2014 and made permanent by the Protecting Americans from Tax Hikes (PATH) Act of 2015 (Pub. L. 114-113, Div. Q Title I, Sec. 111, Dec. 18, 2015). The PATH Act also enacted a special provision (new Code § 170(b)(2)(C)) for § 170(h) contributions made by Alaska Native Corporations of land conveyed under the Alaska Native Claims Settlement Act, effective for contributions made in taxable years beginning after December 31, 2015.

p. 1208. *Delete the first paragraph following the Caveat.*

§ 16.3 CONSERVATION GIFTS AND § 170(H) CONTRIBUTIONS (REVISED)

(a) Qualified Conservation Easements

p. 1208. *Add the following to the end of footnote 15:*

This has led the present administration to propose revisions to the § 170(h) deduction requirements, including (1) strengthening standards for organizations to qualify to receive deductible contributions of conservation easements by requiring such organizations to meet minimum requirements, specified in regulations, which would be based on the experiences and best practices developed in several states and by voluntary accreditation programs; (2) modifying the definition of eligible conservation purposes for which deductible contributions may be made, requiring that all contributed easements further a clearly delineated federal conservation policy (or an authorized state or tribal government policy) and yield significant public benefit; (3) requiring a donor to provide a detailed description of the conservation purpose or purposes furthered by the contribution, including a description of the significant public benefits it will yield, and the donee organization to attest that the conservation purpose, public benefits, and fair market value of the easement reported to the IRS are accurate; (4) requiring additional reporting of information about contributed conservation easements and their fair market values; (5) prohibiting a deduction for any contribution of a partial interest in property that is, or is intended to be, used as a golf course; (6) disallowing a deduction for any value of a historic preservation easement associated with forgone upward development above a historic building, and requiring all historic structure easements to comply with the 2006 Pension Protection Act provisions applicable to façade easements; and (7) piloting a nonrefundable conservation easement credit. General Explanations of the Administration's Fiscal Year 2017 Revenue Proposals, p. 213 (available at https://www.treasury.gov/resource-center/tax-policy/Documents/General-Explanations-FY2017.pdf).

p. 1209. *Add the following to the end of the Caveat:*

State law may require that the deed of easement be recorded before it is effective, meaning that an untimely recording of a conveyed deed of easement can mean a delayed or denied charitable deduction, depending on the facts and circumstances.[15.1] Further, any attempt to rescind or remove the easement restrictions if the deduction is modified or disallowed by the IRS also raises conditional gift issues that jeopardize the deduction.[15.2]

p. 1209. *Add the following to the end of footnote 16:*

Various court decisions have explored the deductibility under § 170 of cash contributions made by donors of conservation easements to the donee organizations that were solicited, and in some cases required as a condition to acceptance of the easement donation, for the purpose of monitoring and enforcing the easement. The more recent decisions favor deductibility of the cash payments even if made as a condition of the conservation easement donation. See *Scheidelman v. Commissioner*, 682 F.3d 189 (2nd Cir. 2012) ("when a cash contribution (even mandatory in nature) serves to fund the administration of another charitable donation, it is an 'unrequited gift'" and thus deductible as a charitable donation); *Kaufman v. Commissioner*, 136 T.C. 294 (2011) (cash contribution was deductible, as court saw no benefit to the donor other than facilitating the easement donation and an increased deduction by the amount of the cash contributed). In *Glade Creek Preserve, LLC v. Commissioner*, T.C. Memo 2020-148, the United States Tax Court addressed the timing of a deduction for a cash donation accompanying a conservation easement donation, and held that the taxpayer was entitled to take the charitable deduction in the year the taxpayer paid the cash into escrow (2012) rather than the year the escrow closed (2013), because once the funds were deposited in escrow the funds were out of the taxpayer's control and the chance the settlement agent would not pay the funds to the donee was so remote as to be negligible.

p. 1209. *Add the following paragraph at the end of this page:*

The IRS will also challenge the deductibility of a contribution of an easement that does not appear to place restrictions on the property that

---

[15.1]For recent cases interpreting New York State's conservation easement statute, *see Mecox Partners v. Commissioner*, 2016 WL 398216 (S.D.N.Y.) (delay in recording deed until subsequent tax year also caused appraisal to fail to satisfy the "more than 60 days prior" timing requirement of qualified appraisal rules); *Zarlengo v. Commissioner*, T.C. Memo 2014-161, and *Rothman v. Commissioner*, T.C. Memo 2012-163, each of which held that state law determines the nature of the property rights transferred, and because New York's easement law requires recording to be effective, the recording date governs the date of the contribution for federal tax purposes.

[15.2]*Graev v. Commissioner*, 140 T.C. 377 (2012) (holding that side letter agreement to remove the easement in the event the IRS disallowed the deduction was not a remote contingency, and thus there was a conditional, rather than a completed, gift under Treasury Regulation § 1.170A-1(e)).

go beyond those of local ordinances and law. For example, in *1982 East, LLC*,[17.1] the Tax Court held that the easement failed to satisfy § 170(h)(4) because it was local law and the rules of the landmarks preservation commission, not the easement, that preserved the subject property.

pp. 1209–1210. *Add the following to the end of footnote 17:*

In *Bosque Canyon Ranch*, the Fifth Circuit found that the ordinary standard of statutory construction, rather than the usual strict construction standard for "intentionally adopted tax loopholes," applies to analyze tax deductions for conservation easement donations. *BC Ranch II, L.P., also known as Bosque Canyon Ranch II, L.P. v. Commissioner*, Docket Numbers 16-60068 and 16-60069, United States Court of Appeals, Fifth Circuit (Aug. 11, 2017) (vacating and remanding to the Tax Court; the appellate court allowed flexibility in satisfying the perpetuity requirement and the requirements of a baseline report). The taxpayer's receipt of a substantial benefit may result in a disallowance of the entire contribution deduction. In *Wendell Falls Development*, the IRS and the court disallowed the entire $1.798 million claimed deduction because a preponderance of the evidence demonstrated that the taxpayer expected a substantial benefit from the contribution of the easement, which required the property to be used as a park, that being an increase in the value of adjacent lots owned by the taxpayer that resulted from the adjacent property's access to the park within the planned community. *Wendell Falls Development, LLC v. Commissioner*, T.C. Memo 2018-45. In *Triumph Mixed Use Investments III, LLC et al. v. Commissioner*, T.C. Memo 2018-65, the court held that the taxpayer was not entitled to a charitable contribution deduction for a transfer of real property and development credits because it transferred the property in exchange for approval of a concept plan and expected approval of an area development plan as a quid pro quo. The court found that the transfer of real property and development credits was integral to the city's approval of both plans and that the benefit had substantial value and was not reported or valued by the taxpayer in determining the deduction.

p. 1210. *Add the following to the end of footnote 18:*

On May 15, 2020, the Internal Revenue Service Office of Chief Counsel released Memorandum Number 202020002, a charitable contribution case update that lists and describes select charitable contribution cases since 2012. Although the memorandum is not limited to conservation easement cases, many of the cases included in the memorandum involve conservation easement issues such as § 170(h) requirements, valuation, substantiation, and penalties. Select Charitable Contribution Cases 2012 Forward (updated April 15, 2020), Office of Chief Counsel Memorandum Number 202020002 (available at https://www.irs.gov/pub/irs-wd/202020002.pdf).

(b) Exclusively for Conservation Purposes: Enforceable in Perpetuity

p. 1211. *Add the following to the end of the second paragraph of this subsection:*

Courts have held that a conservation easement that permits modification of the boundaries or substitution of properties is not a qualified real property interest because it is not an interest in an identifiable, specific piece of property, as required by the statute.[22.1]

[17.1]T.C. Memo 2011-84. The IRS will also assert that in such cases, the value of the easement is zero or minimal. For a discussion comparing the restrictions under the easement versus local ordinances and laws, see *Gorra v. Commissioner*, T.C. Memo 2013-254 (holding that the façade easement did impose restrictions not imposed under local law and citing prior cases addressing the issue in various fact patterns). In *Kissling v. Commissioner*, T.C. Memo 2020-153, the Court addressed the valuation of a façade easement donation, determined that the easement imposed material restrictions that lowered the property's value when the city's enforcement of its preservation code was largely ineffective, and reduced the claimed deduction by approximately 15 percent after reviewing the experts' valuation methodologies.

[22.1]*Balsam Mountain Investments, LLC v. Commissioner*, T.C. Memo 2015-43 (substitution of 5 percent of the land initially subject to the easement violated the requirement); *Belk v. Commissioner*, 140 T.C. 1 (2013),

p. 1212. *Delete the language in footnote 23 in its entirety and replace with the following:*
Turner v. Commissioner, 126 T.C. 299 (2006).

p. 1212. *Insert this paragraph following the first full paragraph on this page:*

In *Turner v. Commissioner*, the court examined the open space and historic preservation requirements and concluded that the donor did not satisfy either requirement and thus was not entitled to a charitable contribution deduction for a gift of a conservation easement. In that case, an individual bought parcels of unimproved land located within a historical overlay district, with approximately half the land located in a floodplain where development was prohibited.

p. 1212. *Add the following at the end of this page:*

The conservation purpose requirement was recently addressed in *Atkinson*,[24.1] a golf course easement case. In that case the court considered

---

aff'd, 774 F.3d 221 (4th Cir. 2014) (substitution of contiguous land for all or a portion of the initially restricted land violated the requirement). The ability to make such modifications or substitutions may also be violations of the "in perpetuity" requirement and the qualified appraisal requirement, each of which is discussed below. The Fifth Circuit Court of Appeals appeared to take a more liberal view of certain permitted easement modifications in its review of *Bosque Canyon Ranch*, in which it found that the perpetuity requirement was not violated where the easement permitted, with the consent of the easement holder, a relocation of home sites, because the external boundaries of the easement and the maximum sizes of the home sites could not be changed. *BC Ranch II, L.P., also known as Bosque Canyon Ranch II, L.P. v. Commissioner*, Docket Numbers 16-60068 and 16-60069, United States Court of Appeals, Fifth Circuit (Aug. 11, 2017) (vacating and remanding to the Tax Court). In *Salt Point Timber*, the Tax Court found that a qualified conservation contribution was not made because the easement deed provided that if certain conditions were met, the easement could be replaced by an easement encumbering an adjacent property, which was not required to be held by a qualified organization. The easement deed contained no express condition that the holder of a replacement easement was required to be a qualified organization, and the taxpayer failed to provide persuasive evidence that the conditions for replacing the easement were so highly improbable or remote that they would be ignored. *Salt Point Timber, LLC v. Commissioner*, T.C. Memo 2017-145.

[24.1]*Atkinson v. Commissioner*, T.C. Memo 2015-236. Golf course easements have been the source of controversy over the past decade. In *Kiva Dunes Conservation, LLC v. Commissioner*, T.C. Memo 2009-145, the court did not address the conservation purpose requirement but addressed the valuation of the easement and upheld 90 percent of the claimed deduction. More recently, the Tax Court addressed a variety of issues involving golf course easements. In *PBBM-Rose Hill, Ltd., PBBM Corporation, Tax Matters Partner v. Commissioner*, Tax Court Docket No. 26096-14 (Bench Opinion Sept. 9, 2016), the court denied a $15.16 million golf course conservation easement deduction, holding that the value of the easement was $100,000 but denying the entire deduction on the basis that it failed the extinguishment requirement, the "in perpetuity" requirement, and the conservation purpose requirement. With respect to the failed conservation purpose, the court stated that although the reservation of rights by the owner of the property to make certain improvements to the property did not impair the conservation purpose any more than the use of the property as a golf course, and thus those rights alone did not cause the easement to fail, the easement did not create any right of access by the public to the easement area, access was available only by a single road and past a guarded gatehouse after the guard ascertained the car occupant intended to use the facilities, only a small part of the property was visible off the property and the general public was not allowed access, and the easement on the golf course did not protect uncommon habitat or species. In *RP Golf LLC v. Commissioner*, T.C. Memo 2016-80, the court held that the easement was not granted in perpetuity because the property was subject to preexisting unsubordinated mortgages at the time of the grant, and the consents to subordinate were not executed

both the "natural habitat" and "open space" alternative means to satisfy the requirement. The court held that the placement of conservation restrictions on two separate golf courses within a single development did not satisfy the "natural habitat" prong, in part because the use of pesticides and other chemicals to maintain the golf course actually injured or destroyed native natural habitat rather than protecting it. The court also observed that the restrictions did not protect a particular species of tree that was native to the property, and that the developers planted certain grasses to maintain the course that were not native to the property. The court found that the easements did not preserve an open space because the golf courses were located in a private gated community that was not easily accessible or open to view by the general public. The court stopped short of opining as to whether a golf course easement was inherently inconsistent with the conservation purpose requirement.

CAVEAT

Donations of golf course conservation easements have been the subject of much controversy. The Treasury Department has proposed eliminating § 170(h) deductions for golf course easements.[24.2] Taxpayers should expect the IRS to continue scrutinizing golf course conservation easements, both for conservation purposes and for other substantive and valuation issues.

The special "conservation purpose" requirement provisions for contributions of façade easements have also been addressed in litigation. In *61 York Acquisition v. Commissioner*,[24.3] the court found that the façade easement

---

until after the contribution. In that case the court declined to address whether a golf course conservation easement could meet the conservation purpose requirement or whether the value of the easement was appropriate. In *Champions Retreat Golf Founders LLC v. Commissioner*, T.C. Memo 2018-146, the court found that the grant of a conservation easement on a private golf course did not satisfy the conservation purpose requirement and thus did not qualify for a charitable deduction. In that case, the court addressed the taxpayer's arguments pertaining to a relatively natural habitat, open space, and a clearly delineated governmental conservation policy and concluded that the grant did not further any of these conservation purposes. However, the Tax Court memorandum decision was vacated with respect to the conservation purpose requirement and remanded for a determination of the proper amount of the deduction. *Champions Retreat Golf Founders, LLC v. Commissioner*, Case No. 18-14817 (11th Cir. May 13, 2020) (Internal Revenue Code only requires a relatively natural habitat or similar ecosystem, not that the land itself be relatively natural; conservation easement that otherwise satisfies the conservation purposes requirement is not disqualified just because it includes a golf course).

[24.2] General Explanations of the Administration's Fiscal Year 2017 Revenue Proposals, p. 213 (available at https://www.treasury.gov/resource-center/tax-policy/Documents/General-Explanations-FY2017.pdf).

[24.3] *61 York Acquisition, LLC, SIB Partnership, Ltd., Tax Matters Partner v. Commissioner*, T.C. Memo 2013-266. Section 170(h)(4)(B) provides that a contribution that consists of a restriction with respect to the exterior of a certified historic structure shall not be considered to be exclusively for conservation purposes

deed failed to satisfy the conservation purpose requirement because it did not protect and preserve two walls and various other portions of the outside structure and thus did not preserve the "entire exterior" of the building as required by § 170(h)(4)(B).

In *Hewitt* (*Hewitt v. Commissioner of IRS*, 21 F.4th 1336 (11th Cir. 2021)), the Eleventh Circuit Court of Appeals was asked to determine whether the Treas. Reg § 1.170A-14(g)(6)(ii) post-donation improvement regulation was either (1) procedurally invalid under the APA or (2) substantively invalid under the *Chevron v. NRDC* framework. The Court held that Treas. Reg § 1.170A-14(g)(6)(ii) was procedurally invalid under APA § 553(c) for failure to respond to the relevant and significant comment (on the proposed regulation) by the New York Land Conservancy (NYLC) and did not rule on the *Chevron* matter.

The *Hewitt* holding may be interpreted in one of two ways. First, it could be read broadly as invalidating the entirety of the regulation. This reading would allow taxpayers to defend against IRS attacks based on both the post-donation improvements and the proportionate-value formula. If read more narrowly, however, the regulation is only invalid as to the improvement provisions specifically. The Court, by included qualifying language,[24.4] suggested the invalidity of the regulation and the significance of the comment were only in relation to the post-donation improvements issue. However, the Court did not give further guidance to the extent of the ruling's impact. The subsequent *Oakbrook* decision created a Circuit split.

The *Oakbrook* (*Oakbrook Land Holdings, LLC v. Commissioner of Internal Revenue*, 28 F.4th 700 (6th Cir. 2022)) facts mirror *Hewitt*'s. The petitioners in *Oakbrook* were challenging the procedural and substantive validity of Treas. Reg § 1.170A-14(g)(6)(ii). However, unlike in the Eleventh Circuit, the Sixth Circuit held that the regulation *complied* with the APA's procedural requirements. The Court concluded that NYLC's comments were not significant in light of the entire regulation.

The Sixth Circuit also evaluated the substantive challenges *Oakland* presented against the regulation. In evaluating *Chevron* deference, the Court concluded that Subsection 170(h)(2)(C) was ambiguous as to post-donation improvements and to whom their value should accrue upon

---

unless the interest (1) includes a restriction that preserves the *entire exterior of the building (including the front, sides, rear, and height of the building)* and (2) prohibits any change in the exterior of the building that is inconsistent with the historical character of the exterior (italics added).

[24.4]"We thus conclude that the Commissioner's interpretation of § 1.170A-14(g)(6)(ii), *to disallow the subtraction of the value of post-donation improvements to the easement property in the extinguishment proceeds allocated to the donee,* is arbitrary and capricious and therefore invalid under the APA's procedural requirements." *Hewitt v. Comm'r of IRS*, 21 F.4th 1336, 1353 (11th Cir. 2021) (emphasis added). See also "Treasury failed to respond to the relevant and significant comment from NYLC *as to the post-donation improvements issue.*" *Hewitt v. Comm'r of IRS*, 21 F.4th 1336, 1351 (11th Cir. 2021) (emphasis added).

judicial extinguishments. The Court also found the regulation reasonable in light of the ambiguity (and thus valid).

On the "protected in perpetuity" requirement, the Court in *Pickens*, T.C. Memo 2022-22, declined to grant the motion under § 170(h)(5)(A) because "the question whether the exercise of a right to which consent is deemed given would impair any conservation purpose presents factual questions ill-suited to summary adjudication."[24.5] However, the Court granted the motion for summary judgment under § 6751(b)(1). In ruling on the penalty approval standard, the Court considered (1) whether there was supervisory approval before the date the IRS issued the FPAA; and if there was approval, (2) whether there was a formal communication of the penalty before the approval. The Court concluded that the FPAA was approved by the correct supervisory revenue agent and that his approval came before there was a formal communication to the taxpayer of the penalty. In so holding, the Court reaffirmed that: (1) approval only requires the supervisor's signature on the civil penalty approval form—there is no required showing of comprehensiveness of the supervisor's review; and (2) a formal communication requires a communication of unequivocal intent to assert penalties against the specific taxpayer—an announcement to the public does not suffice.

p. 1213. *Add the following to the end of footnote 25:*
Reconsideration denied, T.C. Memo 2013-172.

p. 1214. *Add the following to the end of footnote 30:*
However, the subordination requirement was not violated in a case where the donee organization was required to reimburse to government agencies, in the event of a condemnation of the property and extinguishment of the easements, funds they had provided to the donee organization to acquire the restricted property in a bargain purchase, because in such case the donor had no claims to the proceeds. *Irby v. Commissioner,* 139 T.C. 371 (2012). Issues regarding how extinguishment proceeds were determined were also addressed in more recent cases. In *PBBM-Rose Hill, Ltd., PBBM Corporation, Tax Matters Partner v. Commissioner,* Tax Court Docket No. 26096-14 (Bench Opinion Sept. 9, 2016), the easement failed the extinguishment requirement because it did not assure that the donee organization would receive the minimum amount required under the regulations in the event the easement is extinguished by a judicial proceeding. In *Carroll v. Commissioner,* 146 T.C. 196 (2016), the court denied a charitable deduction carryover because the easement terms failed to guarantee that the donee would receive a proportionate share of proceeds upon an extinguishment of the easement by a judicial proceeding. In *Palmolive* the court denied a § 170 deduction for a contribution of a façade easement because the easement deed provided that the mortgage holders had prior claims to that of the donee organization with respect to proceeds received from condemnation or insurance. The court rejected the donor's argument that the subordination requirement merely requires that the mortgage holder subordinate its rights to foreclosure, and refused to find that the defect was cured by a so-called savings clause that purported to retroactively amend the easement, because it required the mortgage holders' consent and thus was not satisfied at the time the contribution was made. *Palmolive Building Investors,* LLC v. Commissioner, 149 T.C. No. 18 (October 10, 2017).

A number of recent court cases have addressed the proceeds clause and perpetuity requirement. Some of these cases have involved reductions in the donee's proceeds by amounts attributable to post-gift improvements made by the donor or other claims, while others have involved a fixed proceeds value based on the value of the easement at the time of the gift. The Tax Court has repeatedly found that these proceeds clauses violate the perpetuity requirement.

[24.5]*Pickens*, at *5.

In *Oakbrook Land Holdings,* the United States Tax Court upheld the validity of the proceeds clause provisions of the Treasury Regulations against a challenge under the Administrative Procedures Act (*Oakbrook Land Holdings, LLC v. Commissioner,* 154 T.C. No. 10 (2020)). In a Tax Court memorandum decision involving the same taxpayer, the court held that the deed's proceeds clause violated the regulation because it failed to apply the fraction contained in the regulations against the ultimate proceeds, but instead provided that the grantee would receive as proceeds the difference between the fair market value of the unburdened property as a whole at the time of the gift and the fair market value of the property burdened by the easement on the date of the gift, less the value of improvements made by the donor after the contribution was made (*Oakbrook Land Holdings, LLC v. Commissioner,* T.C. Memo 2020-54) (strict compliance with the perpetuity requirement is required; substantial compliance is not sufficient). A similar result obtained in *TOT Property Holdings, LLC v. Commissioner,* United States Tax Court Docket No. 5600-17 (Bench Opinion issued December 13, 2019) (the extinguishment clause violated the perpetuity requirement because it reduced the donee's proceeds by the value of improvements made after the gift, despite the existence of a savings clause intended to retroactively amend the provision to comport with the regulations that the court regarded as unlikely to be enforced).

Other cases involving reductions in proceeds for post-gift improvements include *Coal Property Holdings, LLC v. Commissioner,* 153 T.C. 126 (2019) (the regulation requires the grantee's proportionate share upon extinguishment of a conservation easement to be a percentage determined by a fraction, the numerator of which is the fair market value of the easement on the date of the gift and the denominator of which is the fair market value of the property as a whole on the date of the gift; the deed violated the proceeds clause because it provided that the grantee would receive a proportion of the fair market value at the time of extinguishment sale reduced by the value attributable to post-donation improvements and other claims); *Plateau Holdings, LLC v. Commissioner,* T.C. Memo 2020-93 (the proceeds clause is essentially identical to that in *Coal Property Holdings* found to violate the perpetuities requirement); Lumpkin HC, LLC v. Commissioner, T.C. Memo 2020-95 (conservation purpose is not protected in perpetuity because the deed reduces the donee's share of proceeds by reducing the fair market value by any increase in value attributable to post-easement improvements; it upheld validity of the proceeds clause regulation); and *Lumpkin One Fifty Six, LLC v. Commissioner,* T.C. Memo 2020-94 (the extinguishment clause reducing the donee's proceeds by the amount of post-gift improvements violated perpetuity requirement; the regulation's perpetuity provision is valid). In Corning Place (*Corning Place Ohio, LLC v. Commissioner of Internal Revenue,* T.C. Memo 2022-12), the Court reviewed three issues: (1) whether an easement deed complied with the "proportionate share" rule related to the "protected in perpetuity" requirement, (2) whether special rules related to historic façade easements were complied with, and (3) whether filing fees were timely paid. The Court denied the IRS's Motion for Partial Summary Judgment on all three grounds.

First, the Court concluded that the deed specified: (1) the donee's percentage interest was to be determined by the fair market value of the easement divided by the fair market value of the property as a whole; (2) that those values were fixed on the recording date; and (3) that value was to remain constant, all of which satisfy the requirements of § 170(h).

Second, the Court reviewed whether the petitioner substantially complied with the special rules for historic preservation façade easements that require the taxpayer to: (1) include with its return a "qualified appraisal" as defined in § 170(f)(11)(E); and (2) include photographs of the building's exterior. The Court concluded that whether Corning Place substantially complied, or whether any shortfall was due to reasonable cause and not willful negligence, were issues that would benefit from further elaboration at trial.

Finally, the Court reviewed whether the deduction must be denied because Corning Place omitted a $500 filing fee when filing its original return in 2016. Because there were questions of whether the petitioner submitted the fee together with (or in advance of) a filing fee and whether a taxpayer could substantially comply with the filing fee requirement, the Court concluded that the issues would benefit from further elaboration at trial.

The United States Tax Court reached the same conclusion in three other cases involving proceeds clauses in which the donee's right to proceeds was constant and fixed as the value of the easement at the time of the contribution and did not entitle it to post-contribution appreciation. See *Railroad Holdings, LLC v. Commissioner,* T.C. Memo 2020-22; *Rock Creek Property Holdings, LLC v. Commissioner,* United States Tax Court Docket No. 5599-17 (order dated February 7, 2020); and *Woodland Property Holdings, LLC v. Commissioner,* T.C. Memo 2020-55 (the extinguishment clause in each case violated the perpetuity clause because the donee's right to proceeds was limited to a constant amount equal to the value of the easement on the date of the contribution and did not provide the donee with the proportionate share of potential appreciation).

Other cases in which the courts have found that the proceeds clause violated the perpetuity requirement because of reductions for improvements include *Sells v. Commissioner,* T.C. Memo 2021-12 (a deed's extinguishment proceeds clause included a reduction for post-donation improvements that violated the proportionate share provisions of the regulations); *Soddy Creek Preserve, LLC v. Commissioner,* T.C. Order February 9 (a reduction for post-easement improvements violated the proceeds extinguishment clause); *Glade 2021 Creek*

Partners, LLC v. Commissioner, T.C. Memo 2020-148 (a reduction in proceeds for post-easement improvements does not protect conservation purposes in perpetuity as required by § 170(h)(5)); Smith Lake, LLC v. Commissioner, T.C. Memo 2020-107 (a deed's proceeds clause violated the perpetuity requirement because it provided for a reduction in the donee's share for post-easement improvements); and *Hewitt v. Commissioner,* T.C. Memo 2020-89 (a deed's proceeds clause violated the perpetuity requirement because it provided for a reduction in the donee's share for post-grant improvements). The United States Tax Court addressed four other cases, all involving the same facts and issues pertaining to a reduction in proceeds for improvements that violated the proportionate share of proceeds rule, and granted the government's motion for summary judgment on multiple grounds: *Village at Effingham, LLC v. Commissioner,* T.C. Memo 2020-102; *Riverside Place, LLC v. Commissioner,* T.C. Memo 2020-103; *Maple Landing, LLC v. Commissioner,* T.C. Memo 2020-104; and *Englewood Place, LLC v. Commissioner,* T.C. Memo 2020-105. In *TOT Property Holdings, LLC v. Commissioner,* No. 20-11050 filed June 23, 2021 (11th Cir. 2021), the Eleventh Circuit upheld the Tax Court determination that the easement deed violated the perpetuities requirement due to the extinguishment proceeds provision and that it was not saved by an unenforceable condition-subsequent savings clause. In *Little Horse Creek Property, LLC v. Commissioner,* T.C. Order March 2, 2021, the court denied the government's motion for summary judgment on this issue, however, and allowed the taxpayer to argue that any reduction to the donee's share of proceeds due to improvements is de minimis and would not alter the proceeds payout.

Three of these cases—*Sells, Smith Lake,* and *Hewitt*—and a fourth, *Montgomery-Alabama River,* also addressed whether Alabama's state law satisfied the "state law exception" to the proportionate share proceeds requirement of the regulations, which applies if state law provides that the donor is entitled to the full proceeds from the conversion without regard to the terms of the prior perpetual conservation restriction. In each of these cases, the United States Tax Court held that the deed's violation of the proportionate share of proceeds rule was not saved by the regulations' "state law exception," and thus the deed violated the perpetuity requirements. *See Montgomery-Alabama River, LLC v. Commissioner,* T.C. Memo 2021-62 (the state law exception to Treasury Regulation's § 1.170A-14(g)(6)(ii) proportionate share of proceeds rule did not apply because Alabama law would entitle the donee to receive compensation in the event of judicial extinguishment; easement is defined as a nonpossessory interest of a holder in real property so a donor would not be entitled to full proceeds upon extinguishment; the Court declined to certify the question to the Alabama Supreme Court); *Sells v. Commissioner,* T.C. Memo 2021-12 (donated conservation easement is not a contract right but an interest in property whose holder must be compensated for its condemnation or destruction or other conversion; the deed's extinguishment proceeds clause included a reduction for post-donation improvements that violated the proportionate share provisions of the regulations; Alabama law did not rectify this because it treats a conservation easement as a property right to which holder is to be compensated in the event of condemnation); *Smith Lake, LLC v. Commissioner,* T.C. Memo 2020-107 (the deed's proceeds clause violated the perpetuity requirement because it provided for a reduction in the donee's share for improvements; the state law exception to the proportionate share of proceeds rule did not apply because Alabama law entitled the donee to a share of the proceeds as a holder of an interest in property); *Hewitt v. Commissioner,* T.C. Memo 2020-89 (the deed's proceeds clause violated the perpetuity requirement because it provided for a reduction in the donee's share for improvements; the state law exception to the proportionate share of proceeds rule did not apply because Alabama law entitled the donee to a share of proceeds as a holder of an interest in property). The "state law exception" issue was also raised in *Little Horse Creek Property LLC v. Commissioner,* T.C. Order March 2, 2021, involving Georgia state law. In that case, the court rejected the taxpayer's argument that Georgia state law satisfies the "state law exception" to the proportionate share of proceeds rule because the donee of a conservation easement would be entitled to post-extinguishment proceeds under Georgia law.

The United States Tax Court has also addressed additional cases involving a reduction in a donee's share of proceeds upon extinguishment for prior claims. In 901 *South Broadway Limited Partnership v. Commissioner,* T.C. Order April 27, 2021, the court denied the taxpayer's motion for summary judgment, finding that the proceeds clause permitting a reduction for prior claims violated the perpetuities requirement. In four cases with identical relevant facts and issues regarding the proceeds extinguishment clause (in addition to a reduction for improvements), the court found that the provision's reduction of the donee's share of proceeds for prior claims violated the perpetuities requirement. See *Village at Effingham, LLC v. Commissioner,* T.C. Memo 2020-102; *Riverside Place, LLC v. Commissioner,* T.C. Memo 2020-103; *Maple Landing, LLC v. Commissioner,* T.C. Memo 2020-104; and *Englewood Place, LLC v. Commissioner,* T.C. Memo 2020-105. In *Little Horse Creek Property LLC v. Commissioner,* T.C. Order March 2, 2021, however, the court denied the government's motion for summary judgment on the issue involving a reduction in proceeds for prior claims, determining there existed uncertain questions of fact and questions of contract interpretation and state law.

The United States Tax Court has continued to uphold the validity of the proportionate share provision of the regulations against taxpayer challenges. See *901 South Broadway Limited Partnership v. Commissioner,* T.C. Order April 27, 2021; *Little Horse Creek Property LLC v. Commissioner,* T.C. Order March 2, 2021; *Soddy Creek Preserve, LLC v. Commissioner,* T.C. Order February 9, 2021; *Smith Lake, LLC v. Commissioner,* T.C. Memo 2020-107; *Villages at Effingham, LLC v. Commissioner,* T.C. Memo 2020-102; *Riverside Place, LLC v. Commissioner,* T.C. Memo 2020-103; *Maple Landing, LLC v. Commissioner,* T.C. Memo 2020-104; and *Englewood Place, LLC v. Commissioner,* T.C. Memo 2020-105.

In *Little Horse Creek Property LLC v. Commissioner,* T.C. Order March 2, 2021, the United States Tax Court determined that absent a judicial determination of different fair market values, it is appropriate to use the fair market values claimed by a taxpayer for purposes of the proportionate share calculation to determine the distribution of proceeds upon extinguishment of the easement. The court observed that doing so assures that the grantee will get at least the full proportionate share as the taxpayer is very unlikely to have understated the claimed fair market value of the easement used as the numerator.

p. 1214. *Add the following after the first paragraph on this page (and before Note):*

The IRS's position in the latter case (*Mitchell*) was upheld on appeal, with the court concluding that the Commissioner is entitled to demand strict compliance with the mortgage subordination provision, irrespective of the likelihood of foreclosure in any particular case. The court also rejected the taxpayer's contention that subordinating the mortgage subsequent to the contribution of the easement satisfied the in perpetuity requirement, because a conservation easement subject to a prior mortgage obligation is at risk of extinguishment upon foreclosure, and thus requiring subordination at the time of the donation is consistent with the Code's requirement that the conservation purpose be protected in perpetuity.[31.1]

The conservation easement deed will not satisfy the in perpetuity requirement if it permits the substitution of other properties or modifies the boundaries of the restricted property.[31.2] Further, the grant of a conservation

---

[31.1]*Mitchell v. Commissioner,* 775 F.3d 1243 (10th Cir. 2015). The same result obtained in *Minnick v. Commissioner,* T.C. Memo 2012-345, *aff'd,* 796 F.3d 1156 (9th Cir. 2015), holding that, in order for the donation of a conservation easement to be protected "in perpetuity," any prior mortgage on the land must be subordinated at the time of the gift. *See also RP Golf LLC v. Commissioner,* T.C. Memo 2016-80 (the easement was not granted in perpetuity because the property was subject to preexisting unsubordinated mortgages at the time of the grant; consents to subordinate were not executed until after the contribution).

[31.2]*Bosque Canyon Ranch, L.P., BC Ranch, Inc., Tax Matters Partner v. Commissioner,* T.C. Memo 2015-130 (deeds permitting modification to boundaries between home sites and restricted property violated "in perpetuity" requirement); see also *Balsam Mountain Investments, LLC v. Commissioner,* T.C. Memo 2015-43 (substitution of 5 percent of the land initially subject to the easement violated the requirement); *Belk v. Commissioner,* 140 T.C. 1 (2013), *aff'd,* 774 F.3d 221 (4th Cir. 2014) (substitution of contiguous land for all or a portion of the initially restricted land violated the requirement). *Carter v. Commissioner,* T.C. Memo 2020-21 (the donor's reserved right to build residential homes on 11 areas within the restricted property not determined at the time of the contribution violated the perpetuity requirement and caused the easement not to constitute a qualified real property interest). *Pine Mountain Preserve, LLLP v. Commissioner,* 151 T.C. No. 14 (2018) (the court disallowed the deduction for the 2005 easement contribution because it allowed the donor and donee by mutual agreement to, among other things, modify the boundaries of specified sites on which residences could be built within the restricted property, and the deduction for the 2006 easement contribution because it allowed the donor, with the donee's consent, to identify specified areas on which six residential home sites could be constructed without limitation as to their

---

easement by a long-term lessee did not satisfy the in perpetuity requirement because a lessee does not possess perpetual property rights and thus could not grant a perpetual conservation restriction.[31.3]

p. 1214. *Add the following to the end of the Note:*

Consideration must also be given to any local law provisions that limit the duration of the easement.[31.4]

p. 1214. *Add the following at the end of this subsection:*

Numerous court decisions and pending cases in litigation involve the validity of amendments clauses in conservation easement deeds. In March 2020, the Internal Revenue Service Office of Chief Counsel released a memorandum, TAM 2020-001 (dated March 17, 2020), which concluded that the fact that a conservation easement includes an amendment clause does not necessarily cause the easement to fail to satisfy the requirements of section 170(h). After stating that an amendment clause must be considered in the context of the deed as a whole and the surrounding facts and circumstances, the memorandum provided: "With the caveat that the inquiry is based on the deed as a whole and the surrounding facts and circumstances, the following provision is compliant with the perpetuity requirements of section 170(h): Grantee and Grantor may amend this Easement to enhance the Property's conservation values or add real property subject to the restrictions set forth in this deed to the restricted property by an amended deed of easement, provided that no amendment shall (i) affect this Easement's perpetual duration, (ii) permit development, improvements, or uses prohibited

---

location on the restricted property; such rights violated the perpetuity requirement and caused the easements to fail the qualified real property interest definition). However, the Eleventh Circuit Court of Appeals reversed in part and remanded the Tax Court decision in *Pine Mountain Preserve*, finding that the reserved rights with respect to the 2005 and 2006 easements satisfied the § 170(h)(2)(C) prong of the definition of qualified real property interest because it constituted a restriction on the use, granted in perpetuity, that may be made of the real property. The Eleventh Circuit Court emphasized that the reserved rights to modify the boundaries or identify specified areas on which home sites could be built required that the home sites nonetheless be located within the easements' boundaries, and, unlike the situation in *Belk v. Commissioner*, 140 T.C. 1 (2013), *aff'd*, 774 F.3d 221 (4th Cir. 2014), did not permit an exchange of out-of-easement sites for in-easement sites. *Pine Mountain Preserve, LLLP v. Commissioner*, 978 F.3d 1200 (11th Cir. 2020). The Eleventh Circuit Court also noted that the movement of the home sites within the easement boundaries would not make appraisal infeasible because the changes would not return any value to the easement donor. The Court further noted that it was not addressing the separate perpetuity requirement of § 170(h)(5)(A) that requires the conservation purpose to be protected in perpetuity, and that the Court observed is a more rigorous inquiry than the § 170(h)(2)(C) requirement.

[31.3]*Harbor Lofts Assoc. v. Commissioner*, 151 T.C. No. 3 (2018). The *Harbor Lofts* court also held that the long-term lease was not a qualified real property interest, as required by § 170(h), because under Massachusetts law a commercial lease is a contract rather than a conveyance of real property and thus the lessee held contractual rather than real property rights.

[31.4]For example, North Dakota law limits the duration of a conservation easement to 99 years. In Wachter, the court found the 99-year limit violated the "in perpetuity" requirement, thus precluding the possibility of satisfying the § 170(h) requirements for conservation easement donations made in that state. *Wachter v. Commissioner*, 142 T.C. 140 (2014).

by this Easement on its effective date, (iii) conflict with or be contrary to or inconsistent with the conservation purposes of this Easement, (iv) reduce the protection of the conservation values, (v) affect the qualification of this Easement as a "qualified conservation contribution" or "interest in land," (vi) affect the status of Grantee as a "qualified organization" or "eligible donee," or (vii) create an impermissible private benefit or private inurement in violation of federal tax law. No amendment shall be effective unless documented in a notarized writing executed by Grantee and Grantor and recorded in the Clerk's Office of the Circuit Court of [County, State]."

In *Pine Mountain Preserve, LLLP v. Commissioner*, 151 T.C. No. 14 (2018), the court held that an amendment clause with respect to a 2007 conservation easement permitting the donor and donee to agree to amend the easement, provided the amendments are not inconsistent with the conservation purposes, did not violate the perpetuity requirement. In *Hoffman Properties II, L.P. v. Commissioner of Internal Revenue*, No. 19-1831 (6th Cir. 2020), the court held that a façade easement clause providing the donor the right to propose changes to the façade or airspace, after which the donee organization had a 45-day period in which to prevent these changes, violated the perpetuity requirement.

In *Pine Mountain Preserve, LLLP v. Commissioner*, 978 F.3d 1200 (11th Cir. 2020), the Eleventh Circuit Court of Appeals upheld the Tax Court's holding regarding the 2007 conservation easement's amendment clause (i.e., that it did not violate the § 170(h)(5)(A) requirement that the conservation purpose be protected in perpetuity), but did so on the basis that an easement is a bilateral contract (rather than a property interest) that always may be amended by the agreement of the contracting parties. The Eleventh Circuit Court stated that this is consistent with traditional servitude law, which has long allowed for amendment of easements, and the Uniform Conservation Easement Act, which provides for the possibility of bilateral amendments. The Court observed that the notion that an amendment clause alone renders a conservation easement neither granted-in-perpetuity nor protected-in-perpetuity on the grounds that the parties will agree to amendments that undermine the conservation purpose of the entire grant is a risk that is "so remote as to be negligible" as the easement holder would be "quite unlikely" to agree to amendments that would clearly violate the easement's conservation purposes. In *Rajagopalan v. Commissioner*, T.C. Memo 2020-159, the United States Tax Court held that the deed's amendment clause did not violate the perpetuity requirement of § 170(h)(2)(C), where the deed permitted amendments by the parties that were not inconsistent with the deed's conservation purposes, and provided that the donee shall have no power to agree to any amendments that would result in the easement failing to qualify as a conservation easement under state law or as a valid qualified conservation contribution under § 170(h).

(c) Qualified Farmers and Ranchers

p. 1214. *Add the following footnote at the end of the third sentence:*

31.5 In *Rutkoske v. Commissioner,* 149 T.C. No. 6 (August 7, 2017), the Tax Court held that income from the sale of farming property, including development rights, was not gross income from the trade or business of farming. The court concluded that disposition of the property and development rights was not an activity described in § 2032AE(5), the standard applicable to determining the meaning of a qualified farmer or rancher.

p. 1214. *Add this paragraph following the first paragraph of this subsection:*

Individuals who made qualified conservation contributions under § 170(h) between January 1, 2006, and December 31, 2009, were eligible for an enhanced deduction for the contribution, which was enacted by the Pension Protection Act of 2006 (PPA of 2006). See Pub. L. No. 109-280, § 1206(a)(1), 120 Stat. 780 (2006). Section 170(b)(1)(E), which was added to the Internal Revenue Code by the PPA of 2006, permits individuals to use a higher, 50 percent contribution base for purposes of deducting qualified conservation contributions (as opposed to the 30 percent limitation generally applicable to contributions of capital gain property under § 170(b)(1)(C)), as well as a 15-year carryforward period (rather than the usual five years permitted by § 170(d)(1)) for deducting amounts that exceed the 50 percent limitation. Individuals who are "qualified farmers and ranchers," as defined in new § 170(b)(1)(E)(v), are entitled to an enhanced, 100 percent contribution base for certain qualified conservation contributions made after December 31, 2005, and before January 1, 2010. Section 15302(b), PL 110-246, June 18, 2008; § 4(b), PL 110-246, June 18, 2008. These provisions were extended by the American Taxpayer Relief Act of 2012 and the Tax Increase Prevention Act of 2014 and made permanent by the Protecting Americans from Tax Hikes Act of 2015.

(d) Valuation Issues

p. 1214. *Add the following to the end of footnote 32:*

In *Wendell Falls Development,* the court determined the value of the donated conservation easement to be zero on the basis that the highest and best use of the property did not differ from its required use under the easement (i.e., as a park within a planned community), which was supported by the fact that the purchaser of the property did not reduce the purchase price of the encumbered property below the appraised value of the property unencumbered by the easement. *Wendell Falls Development, LLC v. Commissioner,* T.C. Memo 2018-45. In *Pine Mountain Preserve, LLLP v. Commissioner,* T.C. Memo 2018-214, the court addressed numerous valuation issues and ultimately gave equal weight to the donor's appraisal and the IRS's appraisal, finding that errors by each expert had effects of "roughly the same magnitude." In that case, the court concluded that the donor's expert should not have used the "before and after" general rule approach to valuation because it would result in overvaluing the value of the easement placed on highly developable property (saying the reduction in value of the underlying land caused by restricting the land does not necessarily translate into market value) and the IRS's appraiser provided evidence regarding comparable sales of easements. In *Pine Mountain Preserve, LLLP v. Commissioner,* 978 F.3d 1200 (11th Cir. 2020), the Eleventh Circuit Court of Appeals rejected what it called the Tax Court's "split the baby" approach as to valuation, and remanded the case back to the Tax Court. The Eleventh Circuit Court stated that the Tax Court applied an improper method of valuation and must apply a "discernible methodology that is appropriately tied to the standard set out in the governing regulations." In *Rajagopalan v. Commissioner,* T.C. Memo 2020-159, the Court upheld the taxpayer's claimed conservation easement deduction of approximately $4.9 million, finding that the easement's value was at least that amount, despite the fact that the property had been acquired less than three years earlier for approximately $3 million. The Court observed that the taxpayer donated the easement during a market bubble at a time when property values had substantially increased, as substantiated by applicable purchase-sale and borrowing transactions pertaining to the parcels. In *Kissling v. Commissioner,* T.C. Memo 2020-153, the Court addressed the valuation of a façade easement donation, determined that the easement imposed material restrictions that lowered the property's value when the city's enforcement of its preservation code was largely ineffective, and reduced the claimed deduction by approximately 15 percent after reviewing the experts' valuation methodologies. In *Johnson v. Commissioner,* T.C. Memo 2020-79, the United States Tax Court addressed the fair market value of a conservation easement donation for which the taxpayer claimed a deduction of $610,000, the taxpayer's appraiser valued the easement at $585,000, and the government's appraiser valued the easement at $275,000. In applying the before and after method, the Court rejected the government expert's before value and made adjustments to the taxpayer expert's before value. In determining the after value, the Court stated that both experts lacked suitable comparables and rejected them as to value, but accepted them to determine a proper diminution in value of the property as a result of the easement. The Court determined the after value of the property on the basis of comparables used by the two experts to apply a 36.5 percent diminution in value percentage to the property as a result of the easement, resulting in a value of the easement of $372,919.

(i) Valuation, Substantiation, and Appraisals.   p. 1216. *Add the following to the end of footnote 34:*

Ultimately, the gross undervaluation penalty in Whitehouse was vacated on the basis that the taxpayer demonstrated good-faith investigation as to value. 755 F.3d 236 (5th Cir. 2014).

p. 1216. *Add the following to the end of footnote 35:*

For a comprehensive article on conservation easement valuation difficulties, see *Conservation Easements and the Valuation Conundrum,* Nancy A. McLaughlin, 19 *Florida Tax Review* 225 (2016).

p. 1217. *Add the following to the end of footnote 36:*

For cases generally upholding the taxpayer's appraisal and valuation, *see Palmer Ranch Holdings, Ltd. v. Commissioner,* T.C. Memo 2014-79 (court valued easement at $19.955 million; IRS had asserted value of $6.978 million, and taxpayer had claimed value of $23.943 million) (pending appeal); and *SWF Realty v. Commissioner,* T.C. Memo 2015-63 (court determined easement value to be $7,350,000; IRS claimed value was $4,040,000, and taxpayer's two separate appraisals valued easement at $7,350,000 and $7,398,333, respectively).

For cases generally upholding the IRS's appraisal and valuation, see *Mountanos v. Commissioner,* T.C. Memo 2013-138, *reconsideration denied,* T.C. Memo 2014-38 (court valued easement at zero because taxpayer failed to show that the before and after highest and best uses differed; taxpayer claimed easement value of $4,691,500, asserting highest and best use changed from vineyard or development to recreation following the placement of the easement); *Mountanos v. Commissioner,* 651 Fed. Appx. 592 (9th Cir. 2016) affirmed the Tax Court decision's denial of the conservation easement deduction and upheld the accuracy-related overvaluation penalty; *Chandler v. Commissioner,* 142 T.C. 279 (2014) (court valued easement at zero, as IRS asserted; taxpayer had claimed values of $191,400 and $371,250, respectively, for two separate easements); *Scheidelman v. Commissioner,* 755 F.3d 148 (2nd Cir. 2014) (court valued easement at zero, agreeing with IRS and Tax Court; taxpayer claimed easement value of $115,000); *Seventeen Seventy Sherman Street L.L.C.,* T.C. Memo 2014-124 (court upheld IRS determination of contribution value to be zero in quid pro quo exchange because taxpayer failed to prove that the easement had any value beyond the value of development rights it received in the arrangement; taxpayer had claimed easement value of $5,125,000).

For cases generally disregarding the appraisals of both the taxpayer and the IRS, see *Gorra v. Commissioner,* T.C. Memo 2013-254 (court valued easement at $104,000; IRS had asserted zero value, and taxpayer claimed value of $605,000); *Schmidt v. Commissioner,* T.C. Memo 2014-159 (court determined easement value to be $1.152 million; IRS and taxpayer had asserted values of $195,000 and $1.6 million, respectively); and *Zarlengo v. Commissioner,* T.C. Memo 2014-161 (court determined easement value to be $157,500; IRS had claimed zero value, and the taxpayer had claimed $660,000).

p. 1218. *Add the following to the end of footnote 38:*

On motion for reconsideration, based on the appellate court's decision in *Scheidelman II,* 682 F.3d 189 (2nd Cir. 2012) (finding that the regulation requires only that the appraiser identify the valuation method used, not that the method be reliable), the Tax Court determined that the appraisal in Friedberg was a qualified appraisal, but stated that the reliability and accuracy of the appraisal were left to be decided at trial. *Friedberg v. Commissioner,* T.C. Memo 2013-224 (intervening change in controlling law warranted reconsideration; although on reconsideration the appraisal constituted a qualified appraisal, the reliability of the appraisal was still an issue). Failure to provide sufficient specified information regarding a description of the property can cause the appraisal to fail the qualified appraisal requirements. See, for example, *Belk v. Commissioner,* 140 T.C. 1 (2013), *aff'd,* 774 F.3d 221 (4th Cir. 2014); *Costello v. Commissioner,* T.C. Memo 2015-87.

p. 1220. *Add the following to the end of footnote 41:*

The doctrine of substantial compliance continues to be asserted by taxpayers in many cases. In *Costello v. Commissioner,* T.C. Memo 2015-87 (appraisal failed to substantially comply because it valued the fee simple interest rather than the easement and therefore did not contain an accurate description of the property), the Tax Court reiterated that the doctrine is not a substitute for missing entire categories of content in an appraisal, but rather is at most a means of accepting a nearly complete effort that has simply fallen short in regard to minor procedural errors or relatively unimportant clerical oversights. The court in *Costello* further stated that it has declined to apply the substantial compliance doctrine where the taxpayer's reporting fails to meet substantive requirements set forth in the regulations or omits entire categories of required information. These cases often involve defects in the appraisal or appraisal summary. *(Bosque Canyon Ranch, L.P., BC Ranch, Inc., Tax Matters Partner v. Commissioner,* T.C. Memo 2015-130 (the court rejected and found meritless the taxpayer's substantial compliance contention when the baseline documentation failed to establish the condition of the property, contrary to the requirements of Treasury Regulation § 1.170A-14(g)(5) in instances where the donor reserves right to the property); *Rothman v. Commissioner,* T.C. Memo 2012-218, slip op. at 10 (the taxpayer did not "substantially comply" where the appraisal valued "a property right different from the one petitioners contributed"); *Lord v. Commissioner,* T.C. Memo 2010-96 (the taxpayer did not substantially comply where the appraisal omitted the contribution date, the appraisal performance date, and the fair market value as of the contribution date); *Friedman v. Commissioner,* T.C. Memo 2010-45 (the taxpayer did not "substantially comply" where the appraisal omitted, inter alia, an adequate description of the donated property); *Zarlengo v. Commissioner,* T.C. Memo 2014-161 (finding that taxpayers substantially complied by disclosing contribution date on appraisal summary).) Importantly, in *Averyt (Averyt v. Commissioner,* T.C. Memo 2012-198), the court held that the doctrine of substantial compliance does not apply to excuse compliance with the strict substantiation requirements of § 170(f)(8)(B). In *PBBM-Rose Hill, Ltd., PBBM Corporation, Tax Matters Partner v. Commissioner,* Tax Court Docket No. 26096-14 (Bench Opinion Sept. 9, 2016), the court addressed a Form 8283 reporting issue and determined that the taxpayer substantially complied with the reporting requirements even though its Form 8283 failed to include a summary of the physical condition of the property, the date the property was acquired, how the property was acquired, the donor's cost, and the amount claimed as a deduction. In that case, the court concluded that the taxpayer substantially complied with the Form 8283 reporting requirement because the information was contained elsewhere on the taxpayer's Form 1065 return and attachments. In *RERI Holdings I, LLC v. Commissioner,* 149 T.C. No. 1 (July 3, 2017), a case involving the contribution of a remainder interest, the court disallowed a $33 million claimed deduction because the donor failed to report its $2.95 million cost or other basis on IRS Form 8283, and determined that the omission could not be excused on the grounds of substantial compliance because disclosure would have alerted the IRS to potential overvaluation of the property due to the large disparity between cost and the contribution value over a 17-month period. The Tax Court decision was affirmed in *Jeff Blau, Tax Matters Partner of RERI Holdings I, LLC v. Commissioner,* No. 17-1266 (D.C. Cir. 2019). In *Belair Woods, LLC v. Commissioner,* T.C. Memo 2018-159, the court held that the taxpayer did not comply with the requirement that cost or adjusted basis be reported on Form 8283, where it omitted the amount but attached a statement to the form stating that the basis information was omitted because basis is not relevant to the calculation of the deduction. In *Oakhill Woods, LLC v. Commissioner,* T.C. Memo 2020-24, the court granted in part the IRS's motion for summary judgment, finding that the taxpayer failed to attach a complete Form 8283 because it failed to report its cost or adjusted basis, but finding that a material fact existed as to whether the taxpayer had reasonable cause for its failure where the taxpayer stated it had relied upon the donee and a certified public accountant). In *Emanouil v. Commissioner,* T.C. Memo 2020-120, involving a contribution of a fee simple interest in property, the Court addressed whether the taxpayer's appraisal satisfied the qualified appraisal requirements. In that case, the appraisal did not include the actual or expected contribution date or explicitly state that it was for income tax purposes. The Court concluded that neither omission was fatal.

The Court determined that inclusion of the contribution date on the Form 8283 was sufficient, where the appraisal stated that it measured "current" market value and was within 30 days of the date of contribution, and that the appraisal substantially complied with the qualified appraisal requirements where the appraiser valued the correct asset according to the correct standard (fair market value), the appraisal was prepared within 30 days of the contribution and used a commonly accepted approach to estimate the fair market value of the contribution, which gave the IRS sufficient information to evaluate the reported contribution.

In *Little Horse Creek Property LLC v. Commissioner,* T.C. Order March 2, 2021, the United States Tax Court addressed an IRS Form 8283 reporting issue, and determined that a taxpayer may disclose when and how it acquired the donated property in an attachment rather than on the Form 8283 itself. In other cases, however, the Tax Court determined that the taxpayer failed to substantially comply with Form 8283 reporting when it declined to provide basis information on the form and instead stated that basis of the property is not taken into consideration when computing the amount of the deduction. *See Village at Effingham, LLC v. Commissioner,* T.C. Memo 2020-102; *Riverside Place, LLC v. Commissioner,* T.C. Memo 2020-103; *Maple Landing, LLC v. Commissioner,* T.C. Memo 2020-104; and *Englewood Place, LLC v. Commissioner,* T.C. Memo 2020-105 (all finding that the taxpayer did not substantially comply because its failure to supply cost basis violated the essence of the statute by depriving the IRS of an essential tool Congress intended it to have in order to efficiently identify overvalued property; appraisal summary reporting regulation is valid).

p. 1220. *Add the following after the first paragraph on this page (before the Note):*

Zarlengo v. Commissioner, T.C. Memo 2014-161.

p. 1220. *Add the following after the first paragraph on this page (before the Note):*

The Second Circuit's decision in *Scheidelman II*[42.1] was found by the Tax Court to constitute an intervening change in law that resulted in reconsideration of numerous qualified appraisal cases involving conservation easement donations that had been litigated in the Tax Court. In *Scheidelman I,* the Tax Court had held that the mechanical application of a percentage diminution in the market value before donation of a façade easement does not constitute a method of valuation as contemplated under the qualified appraisal regulations. In *Scheidelman II,* the appellate court stated that the regulation requires only that the appraiser identify the valuation method used and not that the method adopted be reliable. Based on *Scheidelman II,* the Tax Court subsequently reconsidered numerous prior decisions that had addressed the qualified appraisal issue. One example is *Friedberg v. Commissioner,* where the court determined on reconsideration that the appraisal constituted a qualified appraisal, but that the reliability of the appraisal was still an issue to be determined at trial.[42.2]

In addition, the separate "contemporaneous written acknowledgment" requirement of § 170(f)(8)(B) has been the subject of recent litigation. In *Schrimscher,*[42.3] the court stated that the acknowledgment need not take any particular form, but found the requirement was not satisfied where the

---

[42.1]*Scheidelman v. Commissioner,* 682 F.3d 189 (2nd Cir. 2012).

[42.2]*Friedberg v. Commissioner,* T.C. Memo 2013-224 (intervening change in controlling law warranted reconsideration; although on reconsideration the appraisal constituted a qualified appraisal, the reliability of the appraisal was still an issue to be determined at trial).

[42.3]*Schrimscher v. Commissioner,* T.C. Memo 2011-71.

only statement in the agreement considering consideration was the statement that the donee provided consideration of $10 plus other good and valuable consideration. The court found that this did not clearly state that no consideration was provided or, in the alternative, the amount of any consideration provided, so the acknowledgment was defective. A similar result was obtained in *Bruce*, where the court found that the requirements were not satisfied because there was no statement regarding whether any goods or services were provided in consideration for the contribution, and the acknowledgment was not received by the time the taxpayer filed his tax return.[42.4] On the other hand, in *Irby*[42.5] the court found that the contemporaneous written acknowledgment requirements were satisfied even though there was no statement in the acknowledgment that no goods or services were provided, on the basis that in this case involving a bargain sale, the overall documentation clearly demonstrated that consideration in the form of cash was provided to the donor for the sale component of the transaction.

In some cases the conservation deed may serve as the contemporaneous written acknowledgment, but if it does not contain an express statement regarding whether any goods or services were provided in consideration for the contribution, then the deed taken as a whole must prove compliance with the requirement.[42.6] However, in *French*[42.7] the court held that the conservation deed did not satisfy the acknowledgment requirements where it failed to state that no goods or services were provided in consideration for the contribution, and the deed did not contain a provision stating it was the only agreement of the parties such that the IRS could conclude no other consideration was provided in exchange. Importantly,

---

[42.4]*Bruce v. Commissioner*, T.C. Memo 2011-153. In *15 West 17th Street LLC v. Commissioner*, 147 T.C. 19 (2016), a $64.5 million conservation easement deduction was disallowed for failing to satisfy the § 170(f)(8(a) contemporaneous written acknowledgment requirement; the court held that the donor could not cure the defect by the donee organization filing an amended Form 990 return that included a statement by the donee that no goods or services were provided in consideration for the contribution.
[42.5]*Irby v. Commissioner*, 139 T.C. 71 (2012).
[42.6]For this purpose, factors to be taken into account that support compliance include that the deed recites no consideration other than the preservation of the property and that the deed contains a provision stating that the deed is the entire agreement of the parties. See, for example, *Averyt v. Commissioner*, T.C. Memo 2012-198 and *RP Golf LLC v. Commissioner*, T.C. Memo 2012-282. In *Big River Development* the court concluded that the easement deed constituted a contemporaneous written acknowledgment because it contained no reference to valuable goods or services being furnished to the donor, recited no receipt by the donee of any consideration for providing goods or services, and contained a term providing that the deed reflected the entire agreement of the parties and that any previous agreements were null and void. Although the court rejected the taxpayer's argument that the donee organization's amended Forms 990 stating no goods or services were provided were a contemporaneous written acknowledgment and acknowledged that the donee's contribution letter to the donor was untimely, it found that the deed of easement satisfied the requirements of § 170(f)(8). *Big River Development LP et al v. Commissioner*, T.C. Memo 2017-166.
[42.7]*French v. Commissioner*, T.C. Memo 2016-53.

in *Averyt*[42.8] the court held that the doctrine of substantial compliance does not apply to excuse compliance with the strict substantiation requirements of § 170(f)(8)(B).

(ii) Penalties and Burden of Proof.   p. 1222. *Add the following to the end of this subsection:*

Numerous cases have addressed the revisions to § 6662 made by the Pension Protection Act of 2006, including their application to carryovers of charitable deductions relating to conservation easement contributions made before the revisions were enacted. Sections 6662(a) and (b) generally impose a 20 percent accuracy-related penalty with regard to negligence, substantial understatement of income tax, and a substantial valuation misstatement. Section 6662(h) provides that the penalty is increased to 40 percent on the portion of an underpayment of tax that is attributable to a gross valuation misstatement. For returns filed on or before August 17, 2006, a gross valuation misstatement is a misstatement of the value of property by 400 percent or more of the property's value. For returns filed after August 17, 2006, the penalty applies to misstatements of the value of property by 200 percent. Treasury Regulation § 1.6662-5(g) provides that when the actual value of the property is zero and the value claimed is greater than zero, the gross valuation misstatement penalty applies. Effective for returns filed after August 17, 2006, § 6664(c)(3) provides that taxpayers may not claim a reasonable cause defense for gross valuation misstatements relating to charitable contribution deductions. Treasury Regulation § 1.6662-2(c) provides that the maximum accuracy-related penalty that may be imposed on any portion of an underpayment that is attributable both to negligence and a gross valuation misstatement is 40 percent of such portion.[49.1]

[42.8] *Averyt v. Commissioner*, T.C. Memo 2012-198, slip op. at 10.

[49.1] Cases addressing the generally applicable 20 percent accuracy-related penalty include *Scheidelman v. Commissioner*, T.C. Memo 2010-151 (court found reasonable cause even though it determined that the easement had zero value; no § 6662(a) accuracy-related penalties for 2004 and 2005 claimed deductions; taxpayer reasonably relied on tax return preparer and qualified appraiser); *Seventeen Seventy Sherman Street L.L.C.*, T.C. Memo 2014-124 (court upheld negligence penalty for underpayment relating to 2003 contribution); and *Schmidt v. Commissioner*, T.C. Memo 2014-159 (taxpayer found to have reasonable cause for understatement of income relating to 2003 contribution). Cases addressing the gross valuation misstatement penalty include *Gorra v. Commissioner*, T.C. Memo 2013-254 (penalty applied to 2006 and 2007 claimed deductions); *Chandler v. Commissioner*, 142 T.C. 279 (2014) (found reasonable cause for 2004 and 2005, but held that no reasonable cause defense was available for a 2006 underpayment attributable to a carryover of a 2004 claimed charitable deduction); *Seventeen Seventy Sherman Street L.L.C.*, T.C. Memo 2014-124 (court did not impose gross valuation misstatement penalty for underpayment relating to 2003 contribution); *Reisner v. Commissioner*, T.C. Memo 2014-230 (holding that the taxpayer was precluded from using a reasonable cause defense for its 2006 tax return involving the carryover of a charitable contribution deduction claimed for a contribution made in 2004; the court distinguished *Pollard v. Commissioner*, T.C. Memo 2013-38, because in that case the IRS stated in its brief that it would concede the gross valuation misstatement penalties for 2006 and 2007 if the taxpayer established reasonable cause for earlier years); *Bosque Canyon Ranch v. Commissioner*,

T.C. Memo 2015-130 (reasonable cause defense not available for 2007 return); *Kaufman v. Commissioner*, 784 F.3d 56 (1st Cir. 2015) (taxpayers did not rely on appraisal in good faith, so reasonable cause defense did not apply, when separately from the appraisal the taxpayers obtained information that the value of restricted property would not decrease as a result of the easement, but they failed to undertake further investigation as to the easement's impact on value; the court upheld the gross valuation misstatement penalty for the 2003 and 2004 tax years); and *Gemperle v. Commissioner*, T.C. Memo 2016-1 (taxpayers liable for penalty for 2007 and 2008 tax year underpayments relating to 2007 charitable contribution). In *PBBM-Rose Hill, Ltd., PBBM Corporation, Tax Matters Partner v. Commissioner*, Tax Court Docket No. 26096-14 (Bench Opinion Sept. 9, 2016), the taxpayer was found liable for the 40 percent penalty on the amount that the claimed $15.16 million deduction exceeded the court-determined value of $100,000, but was not liable for a penalty on the $100,000 court-determined value amount. In *Carroll v. Commissioner*, 146 T.C. 196 (2016), the court upheld the accuracy-related penalties under § 6662(a) because the taxpayers failed to demonstrate they acted with reasonable cause and good faith in not seeking competent tax advice regarding the easement. The court in that case failed to consider gross valuation misstatement penalties because the IRS did not assert them in the statutory notice of deficiency or in initial pleadings, but only attempted to assert them later in the proceedings. In *Wendell Falls Development* the court found the value of the conservation easement contribution to be zero, but failed to uphold the 20 percent penalty for negligence or substantial understatement because the taxpayer's failure to anticipate the substantial benefit it received as a result of the contribution did not show it did not make sufficient effort to assure proper tax treatment, and both the taxpayer and government appraisers failed to properly account for the enhancement conferred on the donor in their appraised values of the property. *Wendell Falls Development, LLC v. Commissioner*, T.C. Memo 2018-45. In *Triumph Mixed Use Investments III, LLC et al v. Commissioner*, T.C. Memo 2018-65, the court upheld the §§ 6662(a) and (b) negligence penalty where the taxpayer failed to report or establish the value of the benefit received in exchange for the property donation as part of a quid pro quo, finding that the taxpayer did not make a reasonable attempt to ascertain the correctness of the charitable deduction because it did not adjust the deduction for the consideration received. In *Oakbrook Land Holdings, LLC v. Commissioner*, T.C. Memo 2020-54, the court found that the taxpayer was not liable for § 6662(b) negligence and substantial understatement penalties on the basis that it had reasonable cause for its position that its proceeds clause satisfied the perpetuity requirements because it was consistent with a private letter ruling issued to another taxpayer and the validity of the regulations in dispute had not previously been challenged and upheld. In *Plateau Holdings, LLC v. Commissioner*, T.C. Memo 2020-93, the court upheld the imposition of the 40 percent gross valuation misstatement penalty with respect to two separate conservation easement donations, finding that the claimed easement values were 852 percent and 1031 percent, respectively, of the correct values.

Several recent cases have involved taxpayers challenging the assessment of penalties on the basis that the penalty was not properly approved in advance in accordance with Internal Revenue Code section 6751(b), which requires that the initial determination of a penalty be approved in writing by the immediate supervisor of the individual making the initial determination, and that it must be approved before the first formal communication to the taxpayer of the initial determination to assess penalties. See *TOT Property Holdings, LLC v. Commissioner*, United States Tax Court Docket No. 5600-17 (Bench Opinion Dec. 13, 2019) (penalty was properly approved in advance because the Letter 1807 transmitting the agent's summary report detailing the penalties was signed by the supervisor; section 6751(b) does not require written supervisory approval to be given on any particular document; see *PBBM-Rose Hill, Ltd. v. Commissioner*, 900 F. 3d 193, 213 (5th Cir. 2018) (supervisor's signature on a cover letter to a summary report proposing penalties was sufficient; *Palmolive Building Investors, LLC v. Commissioner*, 152 T.C. 75, 85-86 (2019) (supervisor's signature on a Form 5401-c containing proposed penalties and directing the FPAA be issued was sufficient)); *Belair Woods, LLC v. Commissioner*, 154 T.C. No. 1 (2020) (holding that the issuance of a Letter 1807 and summary report setting forth tentative proposed adjustments did not constitute the initial determination of a penalty assessment; the court found that § 6751(b) was satisfied for three § 6662 penalties, but not a fourth because the IRS did not show timely supervisory approval of that penalty); *Carter v. Commissioner*, T.C. Memo 2020-21 (taxpayers were not subject to gross valuation misstatement penalty because supervisory approval came 11 days after the agent sent revenue agent reports (RARs) and accompanying Letters 5153 to the taxpayers). The Tax Court's holding in *TOT Property Holdings* was affirmed by the Eleventh Circuit Court of Appeals. *TOT Property Holdings, LLC v. Commissioner*, No. 20-11050, filed June 23, 2021 (11th Cir. 2021). In *Soddy Creek Preserve, LLC v. Commissioner*, T.C. Order February 9, 2021, the Court determined that the issue as to

p. 1223. *Add the following new subsections (f) and (g) following subsection (e):*

(f)   IRS Conservation Easement Audit Guidelines (Rev. Nov. 4, 2016)

On November 4, 2016, the IRS revised its "Conservation Easement Audit Techniques Guide."[52.1] The purpose of the 89-page guide is to provide guidance for the IRS examination of charitable contributions of conservation easements. The guide includes examination techniques, an overview of the valuation of conservation easements, and a discussion of penalties that may be applicable to taxpayers and others involved in a conservation easement transaction. Topics covered by the guide include an overview of conservation easements, § 170 statutory requirements, substantiation, qualified appraisals, valuation considerations, state tax credits, and penalties. The guide also contains sections regarding preplanning, conducting, and concluding the examination.

(g)   IRS Notice 2017-10 Regarding Syndicated Conservation Easements (Revised)

In IRS Notice 2017-10,[52.2] the IRS expressed concern that promoters are syndicating conservation easements that purport to give investors charitable deductions significantly greater than amounts invested. The notice identifies certain syndicated conservation easement arrangements as

---

whether the § 6662 penalty was properly approved under § 6751(b) required more factual development and denied the taxpayer's motion for summary judgment with respect to that issue.

In *Hewitt v. Commissioner*, T.C. Memo 2020-89, the Court concluded that the § 6662(a) and 6662(b) accuracy-related penalties, including the penalty for substantial valuation misstatement, did not apply because the taxpayer acted with reasonable cause and had good faith with respect to its reliance on its tax lawyer, appraiser and conservation expert. The Court further concluded that the omission of basis information on the IRS Form 8283 did not preclude a reasonable cause defense to the § 6662(a) penalties. In *Glade Creek Partners, LLC v. Commissioner*, T.C. Memo 2020-148, the Court upheld the imposition of the §§ 6662(a) and 6662(b)(3) 20 percent accuracy-related penalty for a substantial valuation misstatement, because the taxpayer's managing member knew the easement was substantially overvalued and the valuation was not a good-faith valuation of the easement.

Plateau Holdings (*Plateau Holdings, LLC v. Commissioner of Internal Revenue*, T.C. Memo 2021-133) claimed a $25,449,000 deduction for the donation of easements. In the previous case, *Plateau I*, it was determined that the correct easement value was only $2,691,200—an overvaluation of more than $22 million. See T.C. Memo 2020-93. The IRS sought to impose a 20% penalty for negligence or substantial understatement of tax under code sections 6662(a), (b)(1), and (b)(2). In rejecting the penalty, the Court concluded that Plateau had reasonable cause and acted in good faith based on its reasonable belief, based on the Conservancy's attorney's experience in drafting easements, that the easement was drafted in a manner intended to comply with the regulations. The Court also noted that when Plateau filed its return, the validity of judicial extinguishment clauses had not been litigated. The Court was also persuaded by the existence of a contemporaneous private letter ruling, suggesting that it would not necessarily prevent the allowance of a charitable contribution deduction, which provided some objective support for the reasonableness of Plateau's position.

[52.1]https://www.irs.gov/pub/irs-utl/conservation_easement.pdf.

[52.2]IRS Notice 2017-10, I.R.B. 2017-4 (Jan. 23, 2017) (https://www.irs.gov/irb/2017-04_IRB/ar12.html).

tax-avoidance transactions and further designates them as listed transactions for purposes of Treasury Regulations §§ 1.6011-4(b)(2), 6111, and 6112. The notice imposes disclosure obligations on participants in such transactions, as well as on promoters of such transactions. The notice indicates that the IRS is particularly concerned with the use of appraisals that overstate the value of the easement based on unreasonable conclusions about the development potential of the property.

The notice treats as a listed transaction a conservation easement arrangement involving the following: (1) a partnership or other pass-through entity is used as an investment vehicle to own or acquire real property that will be subject to a conservation easement; (2) a promoter syndicates ownership interests in the pass-through entity, using promotional materials suggesting an investor may be entitled to a share of a charitable deduction that equals or exceeds 2.5 times the investor's investment; (3) the investor purchases, directly or indirectly, an interest in the pass-through entity that holds real property; (4) the pass-through entity donates a conservation easement on the property to a § 501(c)(3) organization that is then allocated to the investors; and (5) following the contribution of the easement, an investor claims a § 170 charitable deduction with respect to the conservation easement.

Participants in transactions that are described within the notice are subject to IRS Form 8886 reportable transaction reporting requirements and "failure to disclose" penalties under IRC § 6707A. They also may be subject to increased accuracy-related penalties applicable to listed transactions under IRC § 6662A.

Material advisors involved in a listed transaction described in Notice 2017-10 must file IRS Form 8918 detailing the specifics of the conservation easement syndication. In addition, the material advisor must maintain an information list similar to that set forth in IRS Form 13976, which must be made available to the IRS and Treasury Department upon written request. Failure to satisfy these requirements may result in "failure to disclose" penalties under IRC § 6707 and failing to provide the requested information list under IRC § 6708.

The notice generally applies to conservation easement transactions that are the same as, or substantially similar to, transactions described in the notice that are entered into after January 1, 2010. Participants and material advisors must consider statute of limitations provisions to determine the reporting obligations with respect to a particular tax year.

Syndicated conservation easements remain in the crosshairs of federal enforcement action. On September 10, 2018, the Large Business and International Division (LB&I) of the Internal Revenue Service announced a new compliance campaign involving syndicated conservation easements that it has identified as an area having a high risk of compliance issues. The campaign is designed to enhance IRS enforcement of the listed transaction disclosure requirements implemented by Notice 2017-10 and the structuring and valuation requirements of the purported donations. On December 18, 2018, the U.S. Department of Justice filed a complaint seeking an order stopping certain persons from organizing, promoting, or selling an allegedly abusive conservation easement syndication tax scheme. The Department of Justice complaint alleged that the transactions in question are shams that lacked economic substance, did not qualify as qualified conservation contributions, and involved grossly overvalued charitable deduction amounts.[52.3] On March 27, 2019, the Senate Finance Committee opened an investigation into the abuse of syndicated conservation easement transactions and sent 14 letters to persons appearing to be involved in the promotion of such transactions. The letters request extensive information and documentation pertaining to specific transactions and the persons' role in structuring and selling the arrangements.[52.4]

In June 2019, Senators Charles Grassley, Chairman of the Senate Finance Committee, and its ranking member, Ron Wyden, released copies of three letters to attorneys representing sponsors of controversial land conservation transactions. The substance of the letters follows 14 earlier ones sent by the senators to individuals in late March 2019. Lawmakers have requested detailed information, including names of investors and promotional materials that have been given to the investors. On a separate note, the IRS has announced that it is preparing to bring several cases involving syndicated conservation easements to trial. In December 2018, the Department

---

[52.3]*United States v. Nancy Zak, Claud Clark III, EcoVest Capital, Inc., Alan N. Solon, Robert M. McCullough, Ralph R. Teal Jr.,* filed in the United States District Court for the Northern District of Georgia Atlanta Division (Case 1:18-cv-05774-AT). The Department of Justice press release announcing the action is available at https://www.justice.gov/opa/pr/justice-department-sues-shut-down-promoters-conservation-easement-tax-scheme-operating-out (last searched June 1, 2019). The United States brought five counts against Zak (a conservation manager, consultant, and project manager who assisted in the planning and execution of conservation easement donations and conservation easement syndicates) and Clark (an appraiser) for involvement in 96 conservation easement syndications involving real property in Alabama, Georgia, Indiana, Kentucky, North Carolina, South Carolina, Tennessee, and Texas. The five counts were (1) § 6700, abusive tax shelters; (2) § 6695A(a), penalty on appraisers; (3) § 6694, penalty on tax return preparers for understating tax liability; (4) § 7402, injunctive order preventing Zak and Clark from participation in future conservation easement syndications; and (5) § 7402, disgorgement. Zak and Clark moved to dismiss certain of these counts. *In United States v. Zak,* Slip Opinion, 2019 WL 7476435, 124 A.F.T.R.2d 2019-6993 (Dec. 10, 2019), in the United States District Court, N.D. Georgia, Atlanta Division, the Court dismissed the second count against Zak and no counts against Clark. The Court dismissed the second count against Zak on the grounds that § 6695A applies to appraisers but not to those who assist appraisers. On November 9, 2020, the United States filed an amended complaint in *United States v. Nancy Zak, Claud Clark III, EcoVest Capital, Inc,, Alan N. Solon, Robert M. McCullough, Ralph R. Teal Jr.* filed in the United States District Court for the Northern District of Georgia Atlanta Division (Case 1:18-cv-05774-AT).

[52.4]Copies of the letters and the Committee's press release are available at https://www.finance.senate.gov/chairmans-news/grassley-wyden-launch-probe-of-conservation-tax-benefit-abuse (last searched June 1, 2019).

of Justice sued promotors of a Georgia land conservation transaction that involved more than $2 billion in alleged inflated tax deductions.

The IRS has continued its enforcement efforts in the syndicated conservation easement area. In IR-2020-196 (August 31, 2020), the IRS announced completion of the first settlement of a syndicated conservation easement case under the settlement initiative announced in June 2020. The announcement involved the partnership and its partners involved in *Coal Property Holdings, LLC v. Commissioner*, 153 T.C. 126 (2019) (granting the government's motion for partial summary judgment), who agreed to a disallowance of the entire $155 million claimed charitable deduction. In Notice CC-2020-008 (September 8, 2020), the IRS Office of Chief Counsel issued guidance on syndicated conservation easement third-party disclosures. Entitled "Examples Relating to Disclosure of Third Party Tax Information in Syndicated Conservation Easement Matters," the guidance provides examples in Q&A format regarding when the disclosure of third-party information is permitted, including (1) taxpayer return information is permitted to be disclosed to an appraiser in a § 6695A penalty examination of the appraiser; (2) promoter-partners' return information is permitted to be disclosed in a Tax Court proceeding involving assertion of partnership civil tax fraud; (3) disclosure of third-party returns or return information is permitted to be disclosed to the IRS Office of Professional Responsibility as part of a referral or investigation of a return preparer or appraiser; (4) disclosure of third-party returns or return information is permitted to be disclosed to the IRS Office of Fraud Enforcement and IRS Promoter Investigation Coordinator as part of an examination or investigation of another person, such as a partnership, promoter, tax return preparer, or appraiser; and (5) promoter-partners' tax information pertaining to a criminal investigation and civil investigation under §§ 6700 and 6701 is permitted to be disclosed to a partnership as part of conducting an examination of the partnership. In Notice 2021-001 (October 1, 2020), the IRS Office of Chief Counsel provided guidance regarding the settlement option offered in Notice 2017-10 transactions in certain cases pending before the United States Tax Court. The Notice's topics include the settlement generally, settlement terms (eligibility and election, financial and other), and finalizing the settlement. In Chief Counsel Memorandum 202044010 (October 30, 2020), the IRS Office of Chief Counsel addressed how to determine the §6663(a) fraud penalty in TEFRA syndicated conservation easement cases.

The United States Attorney's Office, Western District of North Carolina, and the IRS announced on December 21, 2020, that two Atlanta-based tax professionals (S. Agee and C. Agee) pleaded guilty for their roles in abusive tax schemes to defraud the IRS in syndicated conservation easement deals between 2013 and 2019, including soliciting investors after the tax year ended and advising them to backdate payments and documents, and preparation of false tax returns (https://www.irs.gov/compliance/criminal-investigation/atlanta-tax-professionals-plead-guilty-to-promoting-syndicated-conservation-easement-tax-scheme-involving-more-than-1-2-billion-in-fraudulent-charitable-deductions; https://www.justice.gov/usao-wdnc/pr/atlanta-tax-professionals-plead-guilty-promoting-syndicated-conservation-easement-tax). On June 9, 2021, the United States Department of Justice and the IRS announced the first federal indictment in cases involving syndicated conservation easements, with a federal grand jury sitting in Atlanta, Georgia, charging an Atlanta certified public accountant with conspiracy to defraud the United States, wire fraud, aiding or assisting in the preparation of false federal tax returns, and filing false federal tax returns. According to the indictment, H. Lewis conspired with others to market, promote, and sell fraudulent tax shelter transactions in the form of syndicated conservation easements, including allowing clients to purchase investments after the end of the tax year and advising clients to backdate checks and subscription agreements, and filing false income tax returns (https://www.irs.gov/compliance/criminal-investigation/georgia-cpa-indicted-for-promoting-syndicated-conservation-easement-tax-scheme-involving-fraudulent-charitable-deductions; https://www.justice.gov/opa/pr/georgia-cpa-indicted-promoting-syndicated-conservation-easement-tax-scheme-involving).

On August 25, 2020, the United States Senate Committee on Finance chairman and ranking member released their report on syndicated conservation easements. The report, entitled "Syndicated Conservation-Easement Transactions, Bipartisan Investigative Report as Submitted By Chairman Grassley and Ranking Member Wyden, Committee on Finance United States Senate," August 2020, S. Prt. 116-44, 116th Congress, 2nd Session, addressed transactions involving 6 of the 14 individuals the Committee sought information from as part of the investigation. The information was obtained by subpoena after the 6 individuals refused to voluntarily comply with the information request. The report's conclusion (p. 91) found that the transactions discussed in the report involve land valuations that appear so inflated above their original purchase prices that they cannot reasonably be characterized as anything other than abusive tax shelters, and that documentation showed that both the promoters and the taxpayers understood them to be tax shelters. Based on the investigation, the chairman and ranking member concluded that the IRS has strong reason for taking enforcement actions against syndicated conservation easement transactions, and recommended that Congress, the IRS, and the Department of Treasury take further action to preserve the integrity of the conservation easement tax deduction (p. 4).

> **CAVEAT**
>
> In addition, a bipartisan bill (S170) has recently been introduced by Senators Danes and Stabenow that would prevent partnerships from profiting from a donation of a conservation easement when a charitable deduction claim is more than two and half times the original amount invested. An identical bill (H.R. 1992) has been introduced in the House by Representatives Thompson and Kelly. The Senate bill was reintroduced as the Charitable Conservation Easement Program Integrity Act of 2020 in December 2020, and the House bill was reintroduced as the Charitable Conservation Easement Program Integrity Act of 2021 in June 2021.

On November 12, 2019, the IRS issued a press release, IR-2019-182 (November 12, 2019), announcing a significant increase in enforcement actions for syndicated conservation transactions, a priority compliance area for the agency. The press release stated that coordinated examinations and criminal investigations being conducted by the agency cover billions of dollars of potentially inflated deductions as well as hundreds of partnerships and thousands of investors. In response to a request from the United States Congress Senate Committee on Finance, on February 12, 2020, the IRS provided certain taxpayer disclosure information pertaining to Notice 2017-10 and syndicated conservation easement participation reported on IRS Forms 8886 for various tax years. In the letter, the IRS reported that the disclosures reported syndicated conservation easement transactions involving approximately $6 billion of claimed deductions for 2016 and nearly $7 billion of claimed deductions for the 2017 tax year (available at https://www.finance.senate.gov/imo/media/doc/2020-02-12%20 IRS%20to%20Grassley,%20Wyden%20(Syndicated%20Conservation%20 Easement%20Transactions).pdf).

On June 25, 2020, with the release of IRS News Release IR-2020-130, the IRS Office of Chief Counsel announced a time-limited settlement offer to certain taxpayers with pending docketed United States Tax Court cases involving syndicated conservation easement transactions. The release stated that taxpayers eligible for this offer will be notified by letter with the applicable terms, and that the settlement requires a concession of the income tax benefits claimed by the taxpayer and imposes penalties. The release further stated that as part of the IRS's strategy, it was creating two new offices to investigate these transactions: the Promoter Investigation Coordinator and the Office of Fraud Enforcement. Key terms of the settlement offer included the following: (1) the deduction for the contributed easement is disallowed in full; (2) all partners in the partnership must agree to settle, and the partnership must pay the full amount of tax, penalties, and interest before settlement; (3) "investor" partners can deduct their cost of acquiring their partnership interests and pay a reduced penalty of

10 to 20 percent, depending on the ratio of the deduction claimed to partnership investment; and (4) partners who provided services in connection with any syndicated conservation easement transaction must pay the maximum penalty asserted by the IRS (typically 40 percent) with no deduction for costs. The release stated that taxpayers should not expect to settle their docketed Tax Court cases on better terms, and that the IRS will continue to pursue litigation of the cases that are not resolved administratively.

Since 1980, high-income taxpayers have been able to shelter income from taxation through overvalued charitable deductions. Overvaluation has increased dramatically in the past 20 years: a 2016 study of all easement decisions since 1980 reported that while overvaluation had averaged by a factor of two before 1994, it averaged by a factor of ten for decisions between 1994 and 2016. IRS Statistics of Income (SOI) data disclose that aggregate easement contributions deducted on Schedule A grew from $2.26 billion in 2015 to $6.5 billion in 2018 (the most recent year available).

Most of the concern has been with "syndicated conservation easements." The same traits that produce overvalued syndicated conservation easements—allowing charitable deductions based on "fair market" value, which sanctions deducting unrealized appreciation without taxing the corresponding gain, combined with the unavoidable need to value contributed easements through as manipulable a process as appraisal—have facilitated abusive overvaluation of nonsyndicated easements. This can leave an easement contributor better off than if they had done anything else with the land, including selling it for its (true) fair market value. The only effective solution to easement overvaluation is to restrict the deductibility of easement contributions attributable to unrealized gain.

CAVEAT

Some commenters have proposed limiting charitable contributions of easements granted with respect to acquired property initially to cost, much as Congress has previously done with other contributions of appreciated property that are vulnerable to abuse, while allowing that limitation to evolve with real estate values over time. In addition, an upfront excise on unrealized appreciation in contributed easements, to increase the salience to prospective contributors of the risks of overvaluation, has been suggested.[52.5]

[52.5] Alan Feld, Theodore S. Sims, and Jacob Nielsen, "Green, or Greed? A Fresh Perspective on the Valuation of Conservation Easements" (April 5, 2022), Boston University School of Law Research Paper No. 2207. Available at SSRN: https://ssrn.com/abstract=4075225 or http://dx.doi.org/10.2139/ssrn.4075225.

§ 16.7 EMERGING ISSUES

(d) Developments at the State Level

p. 1233. *Add the following to the end of footnote 69:*
Aff'd, 744 F.3d 648 (10th Cir. 2014).

p. 1233. *Add the following new subsection (e):*

(e) Partnership and Disguised Sale Issues

The increase in structured conservation easement transactions involving the use of limited liability companies and other entities treated as partnerships for federal tax purposes has resulted in litigation involving both substantive § 170(h) requirements as well as tax abuse concerns. In some of these cases, the IRS has challenged the partnership status of the involved entity, or asserted that the structured arrangement was a disguised sale of the underlying property, to attack the transactions. In *SWF Real Estate LLC* and *Route 231 LLC*, the courts found that the arrangements constituted disguised sales of Virginia conservation tax credits requiring the partnerships to recognize income on the amounts received on the sale.[69.1] In *Bosque Canyon Ranch*, the court held that the arrangement constituted a disguised sale of real estate parcels requiring the partnership to recognize income on the amounts received on the sale.[69.2]

[69.1]*SWF Real Estate LLC v. Commissioner*, T.C. Memo 2015-63; *Route 231, LLC v. Commissioner*, T.C. Memo 2014-30. See § 3.9(d)(ii) regarding disguised sales partnership rules under § 707(a)(2).

[69.2]*Bosque Canyon Ranch, L.P., BC Ranch, Inc., Tax Matters Partner*, T.C. Memo 2015-130. These cases follow the principles analyzed in earlier tax credit cases, including *Virginia Historic Tax Credit Fund 2001 LP*, 639 F.3d 129 (4th Cir. 2011) (court found disguised sale of Virginia historic rehabilitation tax credits) and *Historic Boardwalk Hall LLC*, 694 F.3d 425 (3rd Cir. 2012) (court found the participants were not bona fide partners because they did not have meaningful risk or upside). On appeal, the Fifth Circuit Court of Appeals vacated and remanded the Tax Court's decision in *Bosque Canyon Ranch* on various grounds, including the Tax Court's determination that the entirety of the limited partners' contributions were disguised sales; with respect to this issue, the court remanded for the Tax Court to determine the correct amount of any taxable income that results from the disguised sales. *BC Ranch II, L.P., also known as Bosque Canyon Ranch II, L.P. v Commissioner*, Docket Numbers 16-60068 and 16-60069, United States Court of Appeals, Fifth Circuit (Aug. 11, 2017) (vacating and remanding to the Tax Court).

CHAPTER 17

International Joint Ventures

§ 17.5 GENERAL GRANTMAKING RULES

p. 1262. *Insert the following new subsection (c) following subsection (b):*

(c) Final Foreign Grantmaking Regulations

In September 2015, Treasury published final regulations for private foundations that participate in foreign grantmaking, which continue to permit a private foundation to make a good-faith determination that a prospective foreign grantee is the equivalent of a qualifying charitable organization. The final regulations redefine the IRS-favored approach to making such a determination.

The regulations state that a determination based solely on a "grantee" affidavit is no longer ordinarily considered a good-faith determination. Under the final regulations, a determination will be considered a good-faith determination only if it is based on an opinion from a qualified tax practitioner. Qualified tax practitioners include attorneys, certified public accountants, and enrolled agents, who are subject to the requirements of Circular 230. The change has been made to ensure that equivalency determinations will be based on opinions of persons likely to have a sufficient understanding of the U.S. tax law on charities.

CAVEAT

The opinion must be in the form of written advice that is "current," which means that, as of the date of the grant payment, the relevant law upon which the advice is based has not changed and the factual information on which the advice is based is from the grantee's

---

(Continued)

> current or prior year. Written advice that a grantee meets the public support test for purposes of § 170(b)(1)(A)(iv) will be treated as current for the two years following the end of the five-year test period.[116.1]

Accordingly, a foundation can no longer rely on a grantee's affidavit or on an opinion of counsel unless that counsel also happens to be a qualified tax practitioner. Grantee affidavits and opinions from foreign counsel, however, can be used as a resource in gathering information to be used in making a good-faith determination.[116.2]

CAVEAT

Foundations may continue to rely on determinations made under the 2012 proposed regulations for grants paid pursuant to a written commitment that was made on or before September 25, 2015. Such committed amounts must be paid out by September 25, 2020, to fall under this transition rule.

The IRS released Rev. Proc. 2017-53, which addresses many of the open issues regarding the foreign equivalency determination and expands on the regulations issued in 2015 referenced above.

Rev. Proc. 2017-53 sets forth the components of a "preferred written advice," a safe harbor in which private foundation may rely upon in making a reasonable judgment and good-faith determination that a grant meets § 501(c)(3) and the public charity requirement.[116.3] Preferred written advice (which must be in English) should attach the grantee's organizing document (translated to English if needed). It should also attach as support schedules (and foreign law translated).[116.4]

Preferred written advice should verify that the grantee has not been designated a terrorist organization by the U.S. government.

[116.1]A private foundation may rely only on advice received directly from a qualified tax practitioner, and not from another foundation, so that it can appropriately evaluate the reliability of the opinion.

[116.2]Until further guidance is issued, sponsoring organizations of DAFs may use these regulations to make equivalency determinations for purposes of distributions from DAFs to foreign organizations.

[116.3]This subsection is based on a paper submitted by David Kolokolo in his graduate tax class at Georgetown University Law Center, Special Topics in Exempt Organizations (Spring 2021).

[116.4]If the grantee has been in existence for more than five years and is publicly supported within the meaning of § 170(b)(1)(A)(vi) or 509(a)(2), preferred written advice should attach support schedules. The grantor and qualified tax practitioner may rely on translations of and public information concerning foreign laws.

> **CAVEAT**
>
> While not required for preferred written advice, the private foundation should also confirm that the grantee and certain related individuals are not foreign persons whose property and interests are blocked pursuant to Executive Order or OFAC regulations.

Rev. Proc. 2017-53 confirms that a hospital grantee need not comply with § 501(r), extensive requirements on domestic hospitals imposed in 2010. However, preferred written advice regarding a school grantee must confirm that the grantee does not discriminate on the basis of race, color, or national or ethnic origin, both by policy and in practice. The grantee may fulfill the first party of this requirement via a policy in its governing documents or adopted by its governing body.[116.5]

> **CAVEAT**
>
> A foreign grantee in its first five years of existence may be treated as publicly supported if the preferred written advice determines that, as of the time of the determination, the grantee can reasonably be expected to meet the applicable public support test.

The revenue procedure confirms that a foreign grantee's public support includes contributions and grants from charities described in § 509(a)(1), whether domestic or foreign. Grants from a domestic or foreign government, or international organization designated as such under 22 U.S.C. 288, also constitute public support. Finally, Rev. Proc. 2017-53 confirms that where a grantee has previously supplied an affidavit, an updated affidavit describing only material changes (along with the previously supplied affidavit) may be relied upon.

§ 17.11   APPLICATION OF FOREIGN TAX TREATIES

(c)   Joint Ventures with Canadian Nonprofits: The Legal Challenges

(i) In General.   p. 1282. *Insert the following paragraph after the first Caveat on this page:*

A joint venture structure that relies upon donations by Canadian residents to an American charity allows most Canadian donors to claim a

---

[116.5]While the procedures of Rev. Proc. 75-50 need not be followed, this remains an avenue by which a grantee may demonstrate that it actually operates in a racially nondiscriminatory manner.

donation tax credit or deduction against the donor's U.S.-sourced income when filing Canadian income tax returns. Those Canadian donors would normally rely upon the provisions of Article XXI(7) of the Canada-U.S. Tax Convention. However, residents of the Province of Quebec cannot do so under the Quebec Tax Act. Despite § 488 of the Quebec Tax Act allowing Quebec residents to exclude from their income amounts that are exempt as a result of a tax treaty, the Cour du Quebec held in *Emballages Starflex Inc. v. Agence du Revenu du Québec*[215.1] that the *Tax Act* section did not apply because Article XXI(7) references only "relief from taxation" rather than "exemption from taxation" (or more precisely, "*exonéré de l'impôt sur le revenu*") as set out in § 488. The appeal taken from this decision to the Quebec Court of Appeal[215.2] did not include this issue, but only whether the donations could be treated as expenses (which in that case was denied).

p. 1283. *Delete the first full paragraph on this page and replace with the following:*

The 2015 Canadian Federal Budget introduced a change in the treatment of limited partnership investments by a charity. Until then it had been the Canada Revenue Agency's view that investment in a limited partnership will always transform what might have been a nonbusiness investment into a business. The new view is that a registered charity can, in specific circumstances, invest as a limited partner provided it and all its non-arm's-length charities together hold less than 20 percent of the total partnership interests and it deals with the general partner at arm's length.[219]

(iii) Structure of Canadian Registered Charity and U.S. Tax-Exempt Organization. p. 1283. *Add the following to the end of the first paragraph of this subsection:*

Although this is usually thought of as a concern when the Canadian charity or joint venture is carrying on activities outside Canada, the requirement equally applies to ventures carried out solely within Canada.

p. 1284. *Add the following new paragraph after the first paragraph on this page:*

It is critical to note that compliance with the IRS's requirements for an American organization to exercise "direction and control" is not identical to the "direction and control" requirements discussed in Canada Revenue Agency Guidances (G-002 and G-004).

[215.1]2015 QCCQ 7455 (CanLII).
[215.2]215.2 2016 QCCA 1856 (CanLII).
[219]Canadian Federal Budget 2015, April 21, 2015, and Tax Guide 15-122, January 1, 2016.

p. 1285. *Add the following new paragraph following the last paragraph of this subsection:*

It is clear that failure to actually carry out (or rather prove) activities indicative of direction and control, particularly if there are documented agreements between the joint ventures, can lead to revocation, and that simply structuring through appropriate documentation is not sufficient.[224.1]

[224.1] *Public Television Association of Quebec v. Canada (National Revenue)*, 2015 F.C.A. 170 (CanLII).

CHAPTER 19

Debt Restructuring and Asset Protection Issues

§ 19.1 INTRODUCTION

p. 1336. *In footnote 1, delete 2013 and replace it with* 2018.

p. 1336. *In footnote 2, delete* (ALI-ABA, 4th ed. 1996) *and replace with* (ALI-ABA, 7th ed. 2011).

§ 19.2 OVERVIEW OF BANKRUPTCY

(a) Chapter 7 Bankruptcy

p. 1345. *In footnote 18, delete* faxed moment *and replace with* fixed moment.

(b) Chapter 11 Bankruptcy

(i) Generally. p. 1348. *In footnote 28, delete the last sentence and insert the following at the beginning of the footnote:*
See *In re E. End Dev., LLC*, 491 B.R. 633, 640 (Bankr. E.D.N.Y. 2013) (finding the debtor's managing member was authorized to file the Chapter 11 petition "[b]ased on the language of the Operating Agreement, and the clear intent to give the Managing Member broad authority to act on behalf of the Debtor and to bind third parties with respect to the Debtor");

(ii) Commencement of Chapter 11 Bankruptcy. *p. 1350. In footnote 31, add n. 15 after B.R. 43, 49 . . .*

p. 1350. Delete language in footnote 32 in its entirety and replace it with the following:
> *In re Market Center East Retail Property, Inc.*, 433 B.R. 335 (Bankr. New Mexico 2010); *UBS Commercial Mtge. Trust 2007-FL1 v. Garrison Special Opportunities Fund L.P.*, 938 N.Y.S.2d 230 (N.Y. Sup. Ct. Mar. 8, 2011).

p. 1353. Add footnote 48.1 after . . . if the debtor abandons the property) found on line 13 of the last paragraph on this page:
> [48.1] 11 U.S.C § 362(c)(1).

(iv) Plan/Sale. *p. 1356. Add the following to the end of footnote 59:*
> See also *In re Pursuit Capital Mgmt.*, LLC, No. BR 14-10610-LSS, 2016 WL 5402735, at *5 (D. Del. Sept. 26, 2016) (holding the Trustee requested approval of Purchasers' bid from the outset of the sale hearing, consistent with his business judgment, and the Bankruptcy Court's exercise of its discretion not to reopen the auction was consistent with the well-recognized policy concerns of finality and integrity in the auction process), appeal dismissed, 874 F.3d 124 (3d Cir. 2017); *In re Signature Apparel Grp., LLC,* 577 B.R. 54, 100 (Bankr. S.D.N.Y. 2017) ("[C]ourts have generally applied the business judgment rule to protect debtors in connection with their decisions to dispose of property of the estate when affirmatively seeking court approval for those transactions, such as to assume or reject an executory contract or to enter into a transaction outside of the ordinary course of business.")

p. 1356. Add on Bankruptcy *after* Collier *in footnote 60.*

p. 1357. Insert the following after the first sentence in footnote 61:
> *See In re HHH Choices Health Plan, LLC,* 554 B.R. 697, 702 (Bankr. S.D.N.Y. 2016) (querying "[w]hat relative weight am I to give to the interests of creditors and to the mission of the not-for-profit corporation where those considerations, at least potentially, are in conflict?");

§ 19.3 THE ESTATE AND THE AUTOMATIC STAY

p. 1360. In footnote 69, change Chapter 22 *to* Chapter 11.

(a) Automatic Stay: Generally

p. 1362. In footnote 70, delete the language after Citizens Bank v. Strumpf, *and replace with the following:*
> 516 U.S. 16 (1995) (holding that placing an administrative hold on the debtor's bank account did not violate the automatic stay provisions of § 362(a)(7) because bank did not refuse to pay its debt permanently and absolutely; rather, it only refused to pay its debt while seeking relief from the automatic stay).

(d)   Acts Done in Violation of the Stay

p. 1365. In the beginning of the first paragraph, delete The majority *and replace with* A general.

p. 1365. *Delete language in footnote 83 in its entirety and replace it with the following:*

See, for example, *In re Gruntz,* 202 F.3d 1074, 1082 (9th Cir. 2000); *Ellis v. Consolidated Diesel Electric Corp.,* 894 F.2d 371 (10th Cir. 1990); *Far Out Productions, Inc. v. Oskar,* 247 F.3d 986 (9th Cir. 2001); *In re Webb,* 472 B.R. 665 (B.A.P. 6th Cir. 2012).

(f)   Relief from the Automatic Stay

p. 1367. *Insert the following after* **See, e.g.,** *in footnote 89:*

In re Votaw, No. 10-63744, 2011 WL 5357719, at *3 (Bankr. N.D. Ohio Nov. 4, 2011);

p. 1367. *Insert the following at the end of footnote 90:*

In re A. Hirsch Realty, LLC, 583 B.R. 583,602 (Bank. D. Mass. 2018) (concluding a court-approved waiver of the protection of the automatic stay pursuant to a prior consensual reorganization plan "constitutes 'cause' under 11 U.S.C. § 362(d)(1) for relief from the automatic stay and that the Debtor has not satisfied that burden of demonstrating that Blue Hill is adequately protected or otherwise not entitled to rely upon the waiver").

(g)   Application of the Automatic Stay to Third Parties

p. 1369. *Add the following at the end of footnote 101:*

See also *Agrawal v. Ogden,* 753 Fed. Appx. 644 (10th Cir. 2018).

p. 1370. *Delete the language in footnote 103 and replace with the following:*

McHugh v. Otlowski, Bankruptcy No. 05-60442 (DHS), Adv. No. 10-02348-DHS, 2011 WL 1833370, at *4 (Bankr. D.N.J. May 11, 2011) (acknowledging cases in which the bankruptcy court granted injunctions blocking "actions against the debtor's principals, officers, directors, or guarantors").

p. 1370. *Insert the following after the first cite in footnote 104:*

In re Midway Games, Inc., 428 B.R. 327, 33 (Bankr. D. Del 2010), opinion clarified No. ADV. 09-5228 (KG), 2010 WL 2076955 (Bankr. D. Del May 20, 2010);

(h)   Application of Automatic Stay to IRS Revocation of Tax-Exempt Status

p. 1371. *Footnote 108 should read* 26 U.S.C. § 7421(a).

p. 1371. *Delete language in footnote 109 in its entirety and replace it with the following:*

Bob Jones University v. Simon, 416 U.S. 725 (1974), *overruled on other grounds*; see also Supreme Court's Construction and Application of Anti-Injunction Act (26 USC § 7421(a)) Prohibiting Suits to Restrain Assessment or Collection of Federal Taxes, 46 L. Ed. 2d 956.

§ 19.4   CASE ADMINISTRATION

(b)   Use of Cash: HUD Context

p. 1373. *Delete language in footnote 121 in its entirety and replace it with the following:*

In re EES Lambert Associates, 62 B.R. 328, 336 (Bankr. N.D. Ill. 1986).

p. 1374. *Delete language in footnote 122 in its entirety and replace it with the following:*

Indian Motorcycle Associates III Ltd. Partnership v. Massachusetts Housing Finance Agency, 66 F.3d 1246, 1250 (1st Cir. 1995).

(c) Postpetition Financing

p. 1374. *Insert the following at the beginning of footnote 124:*

See In re 211 Waukegan, LLC, 479 B.R. 711, 779 (Bankr. N.D. Ill. 2012) ("Some courts have adopted a two-prong test to determine whether a transaction is in the ordinary course of business. The two-part test has a 'vertical' and a 'horizontal' dimension. Applying this test, courts consider whether the transaction is consistent with the debtor's prepetition transactions and, second, with transactions in the industry in which the debtor is engaged.");

p. 1375. *The first citation in footnote 126 should read* **11 U.S.C. § 364(b)-(d).**

(d) Sale of Property/Rejection, Assumption or Assignment of Contracts

p. 1376. *Under footnote 132, the first and second conditions are reversed.*

§ 19.5 CHAPTER 11 PLAN

p. 1378. *Insert* the exclusive *before* period within *in the third sentence of the first full paragraph on this page.*

(a) Basic Contents of Plan

p. 1379. *Delete the language in item 7 and replace with the following:*

The plan must give impaired creditors who do not accept the plan at least as much as they would get in a Chapter 7 liquidation (also known as the "best interests of creditors" test).[147]

(b) Acceptance Requirements

p. 1381. *Under footnote 158, 2. a., delete the language and replace with the following:*

cures, any such default that occurred before or after the commencement of the case under this title, other than a default of the kind specified in § 365(b)(2) of this title or of a kind that § 365(b)(2) expressly does not require to be cured;

(d) Cramdown

(ii) Fair and Equitable Requirement: Secured Claims. **p. 1384.** *Delete language in footnote 167 following U.S.C. cite and replace with the following:*

see also RadLAX Gateway Hotel, LLC v. Amalgamated Bank, 566 U.S. 639, where debtors proposed to sell their property free and clear of the bank's liens and repay the bank with the sale proceeds, as contemplated

---

[147]11 U.S.C. § 1129(a)(7).

by clause 1129(b)(2)(A)(ii). The debtors claimed that their plan could instead satisfy clause (iii) by providing the bank with the "indubitable equivalent" of its secured claim, in the form of cash generated by the auction. However, the court stated that because the debtors' auction procedures did not permit the bank to credit-bid, the proposed sale could not satisfy the requirements of clause (ii) when property is sold free and clear of lien.

p. 1384. *Insert the following at the end of footnote 168:*

See also *In re Sugarleaf Timber, LLC,* 529 B.R. 317, 328 (M.D. Fla. 2015) (citations omitted) (holding that "in order to qualify as the 'indubitable equivalent' of its claim, 'the treatment must be completely compensatory,'" i.e., "no reasonable doubt exists that the creditor will be paid in full").

(iii) Fair and Equitable Requirement: Unsecured Claims—Absolute Priority (Whether and When It Applies) and New Value.   p. 1386. *Delete language in footnote 173 in its entirety and replace it with the following:*

See, for example, *Farms v. Gen. Teamster (In re General Teamsters),* 265 F.3d 869,874 (9th Cir. 2001); *In re Havre Aerie No. 166 Eagles,* No. 12-60679-11, 2013 WL 1164422 (Bankr. D. Mont. Mar. 20, 2013) ("The absolute priority rule of 11 U.S.C. § 1129(b)(2)(B)(ii) does not apply to a nonprofit entity such as the Debtor. . . .")

p. 1387. *Delete language in footnote 176 in its entirety and replace it with the following:*

Bank of America v. 203 North LaSalle Street Partnership, supra; Case v. Los Angeles Lumber Products Co., 308 U.S. 106 (1939) (holding that debtor's prebankruptcy equity holders could not, over objections of senior class of impaired creditors, contribute new capital and receive ownership interests in reorganized entity without allowing others to compete for that equity or propose a competing reorganization plan).

(e)   Effect of Plan Confirmation on HUD Regulatory Agreement

p. 1389. *At the end of footnote 183, it should read* cases cited in n. 120.

§ 19.6   DISCHARGE

p. 1393. *Insert the following at the end of footnote 200:*

In re Millennium Lab Holdings II, LLC, 575 B.R. 252, 272 (Bankr. D. Del. 2017).

§ 19.7   SPECIAL ISSUES: CONSEQUENCES OF DEBT REDUCTION

p. 1393. *Change footnote 201 to read as follows:*

26 U.S.C. § 61(a)(11).

Index

Note: References are to book section numbers (§), complete chapters (Ch.), appendices (App.), and/or exhibits (Exh.). A zero section reference (e.g., §1.0) indicates unnumbered introductory material at the beginning of a chapter.